ARTIFICIAL INTELLIGENCE AND INNOVATIONS 2007: FROM THEORY TO APPLICATIONS

IFIP – The International Federation for Information Processing

IFIP was founded in 1960 under the auspices of UNESCO, following the First World Computer Congress held in Paris the previous year. An umbrella organization for societies working in information processing, IFIP's aim is two-fold: to support information processing within its member countries and to encourage technology transfer to developing nations. As its mission statement clearly states,

> IFIP's mission is to be the leading, truly international, apolitical organization which encourages and assists in the development, exploitation and application of information technology for the benefit of all people.

IFIP is a non-profitmaking organization, run almost solely by 2500 volunteers. It operates through a number of technical committees, which organize events and publications. IFIP's events range from an international congress to local seminars, but the most important are:

• The IFIP World Computer Congress, held every second year;
• Open conferences;
• Working conferences.

The flagship event is the IFIP World Computer Congress, at which both invited and contributed papers are presented. Contributed papers are rigorously refereed and the rejection rate is high.

As with the Congress, participation in the open conferences is open to all and papers may be invited or submitted. Again, submitted papers are stringently refereed.

The working conferences are structured differently. They are usually run by a working group and attendance is small and by invitation only. Their purpose is to create an atmosphere conducive to innovation and development. Refereeing is less rigorous and papers are subjected to extensive group discussion.

Publications arising from IFIP events vary. The papers presented at the IFIP World Computer Congress and at open conferences are published as conference proceedings, while the results of the working conferences are often published as collections of selected and edited papers.

Any national society whose primary activity is in information may apply to become a full member of IFIP, although full membership is restricted to one society per country. Full members are entitled to vote at the annual General Assembly, National societies preferring a less committed involvement may apply for associate or corresponding membership. Associate members enjoy the same benefits as full members, but without voting rights. Corresponding members are not represented in IFIP bodies. Affiliated membership is open to non-national societies, and individual and honorary membership schemes are also offered.

ARTIFICIAL INTELLIGENCE AND INNOVATIONS 2007: FROM THEORY TO APPLICATIONS

Proceedings of the 4th IFIP International Conference on Artificial Intelligence Applications and Innovations (AIAI 2007)

Edited by

Christos Boukis
Athens Information Technology, Greece

Aristodemos Pnevmatikakis
Athens Information Technology, Greece

Lazaros Polymenakos
Athens Information Technology, Greece

Library of Congress Control Number: 2007932609

Artificial Intelligence Applications and Innovations 2007: From Theory to Applications

Edited by C. Boukis, A. Pnevmatikakis, and L. Polymenakos

p. cm. (IFIP International Federation for Information Processing, a Springer Series in Computer Science)

ISSN: 1571-5736 / 1861-2288 (Internet)
ISBN: 13: 978-0-387-74160-4
eISBN: 13: 978-0-387-74161-1
Printed on acid-free paper

9 8 7 6 5 4 3 2 1
springer.com

Contents

viii

Intelligent Processing of Audiovisual Content **297**

Foreword

It is our pleasure to present to you the Proceedings of AIAI 2007, the 4th IFIP Conference on Artificial Intelligence Applications & Innovations being held from 19th till 21st of September, in Peania, Athens, GREECE.

Relying on a solid theoretical background and exploiting the outcomes of exhaustive research efforts, artificial intelligence technology has been widely applied to various areas aiming at the development of intelligent systems that resemble to an extent human thinking and decision-making. These efforts are supported by the ever-expanding abundance of information and computing power. Typical applications of AI include the personalized access and interactivity to multimodal information based on user preferences and semantic concepts and human-machine interface systems utilizing information on the affective state of the user. Also, advancements in AI gave rise to the science of machine learning whose concern is the development of algorithms and techniques that allow computers to learn.

The purpose of the 4th IFIP Conference on Artificial Intelligence Applications and Innovations (AIAI) is to bring together researchers, engineers and practitioners interested in the technical advances, business and industrial applications of intelligent systems. AIAI 2007 is focused on providing insights on how AI can be implemented in real world applications.

The response to the 'Call for Papers' has been warm, attracting submissions from ten countries. The task of the Technical Program Committee was very challenging putting together a Program containing 42 high quality contributions. The collection of papers included in the proceedings offers stimulating insights into emerging applications of AI and describes advanced prototypes, systems, tools and techniques. AIAI Proceedings will interest not only academics and researchers, but IT professionals and consultants by examining technologies and applications of demonstrable value.

One session in theoretical advances and six more sessions dedicated to specific AI applications are affiliated within the AIAI 2007 conference:

- Theoretical Advances in AI
- Intelligent Internet Systems: Emerging Technologies and Applications
- Intelligent Systems in Electronic Healthcare
- AI in Business and Finance

- Applications of AI in Industry and Daily Round
- Applications of AI in Communications and Networks
- Intelligent Processing of Audiovisual Content

Two plenary talks are also scheduled:

- Building Relationships and Negotiating Agreements in a Network of Agents
  John Debenham, Faculty of Information Technology, University of Technology, Sydney Australia
- The AI singularity: Will machines take over the world?
  George Zarkadakis, Director of Science Communication, Euroscience (Greece)

The wide range of topics and the outstanding quality of the contributions guarantee a very successful conference.

Finally, we would like to express our sincere gratitude to all who have contributed to the organization of this conference: firstly to the authors and the plenary speakers, and then to the special session organizers, the reviewers and the members of the Program and Organization Committees.

September, 2007   AIAI 2007 Conference Chairs:

Aristodemos Pnevmatikakis, Athens Information Technology, Greece

Ilias Maglogiannis, University of Aegean, Greece

Lazaros Polymenakos, Athens Information Technology, Greece

Max Bramer, University of Portsmouth, UK

Acknowledgments

The AIAI 2007 conference is organized by Athens Information Technology (AIT) and is actively supported by the Department of Information and Communications Systems Engineering of the University of Aegean. AIAI is the official conference of WG12.5 "Artificial Intelligence Applications" working group of IFIP TC12 the International Federation for Information Processing Technical Committee on Artificial Intelligence (AI).

Conference General Chairs

Aristodemos Pnevmatikakis, Athens Information Technology, Greece
Ilias Maglogiannis, University of Aegean, Greece
Lazaros Polymenakos, Athens Information Technology, Greece
Max Bramer, University of Portsmouth, UK

Organizing Committee Chairs

John Soldatos, Athens Information Technology, Greece
Christos Boukis, Athens Information Technology, Greece

Publicity Chair

Fotios Talantzis, Athens Information Technology, Greece

Technical Program Committee

Program Committee Chairs

Ilias Maglogiannis, University of Aegean, Greece
Lazaros Polymenakos, Athens Information Technology, Greece

Special Sessions' and Workshops' Chair

Kostas Karpouzis, National Technical University of Athens, Greece

Program Committee Members

Christos Anagnostopoulos, University of Aegean, Greece
Ioannis Anagnostopoulos, University of Aegean, Greece
Andreas Andreou, University of Cyprus
Zdzislaw Bubnicki, Institute of Control and Systems Engineering, Wroclaw
University of Technology, Poland
Luigia Carlucci Aiello, University di Roma La Sapienza, Italy
Weiqin Chen, Dept. of Information Science and Media Studies, University of
Bergen, Norway
John Debenham, University of Technology, Sydney, Australia
Yves Demazeau, CNRS/IMAG Institute, France
Nikos Dimakis, Athens Information Technology
Christos Douligeris, University of Piraeus, Greece
Sofoklis Efremidis, Athens Information Technology
Ana Garcia-Serrano, Technical University of Madrid (UPM), Facultad de
Informatica, Spain
Timo Honkela, Helsinki University of Technology, Finland
Achilles Kameas, Hellenic Open University, Greece
Vangelis Karkaletsis, NCSR Demokritos, Greece
Kostas Karpouzis, National Technical University of Athens, Greece
Dimitris Kosmopoulos, NCSR Demokritos, Greece
Efthyvoulos Kyriacou, University of Cyprus
John W.T. Lee, Hong Kong Polytechnic University, Hong Kong
Daoliang Li, China Agricultural University, Laboratory of Precision Agriculture
System Integration, China
Filia Makedon, Department of Computer Science, Dartmouth College, USA
Yannis Manolopoulos, Aristotle University Thessaloniki, Greece

Eunika Mercier-Laurent, KIM, France
Daniel O'Leary, University of Southern California, USA
George Papakonstantinou, National Technical Universtiy of Athens, Greece
Constantinos Pattichis, University of Cyprus
Symeon Retalis, University of Pireus, Greece
Angelos Rouskas, University of Aegean, Greece
Kostas Siassiakos, University of Piraeus, Greece
Harry Skiannis, NCSR Demokritos, Greece
Costas Spyropoulos, NCSR Demokritos, Greece
Vagan Terziyan, MIT Depatment, University of Jyvaskyla, Finland
Sofia Tsekeridou, Athens Information Technology
Dimitris Vergados, University of Aegean, Greece
Demosthenes Vouyioukas, University of Aegean, Greece
Manolis Wallace, University of Indianapolis, Athens Campus, Greece
Michalis Xenos, Hellenic Open University, Greece

Section 1

Theoretical Advances in AI

An Evolving Oblique Decision Tree Ensemble Architecture for Continuous Learning Applications

Ioannis T. Christou , and Sofoklis Efremidis
1 Athens Information Technology
19 Markopoulou Ave P.O. Box 68 Paiania 19002 GREECE
{itc,sefr}@ait.edu.gr,
WWW home page: http://www.ait.edu.gr/faculty/I_Christou.asp

Abstract. We present a system architecture for evolving classifier ensembles of oblique decision trees for continuous or online learning applications. In continuous learning, the classification system classifies new instances for which after a short while the true class label becomes known and the system then receives this feedback control to improve its future predictions. We propose oblique decision trees as base classifiers using Support Vector Machines in order to compute the optimal separating hyper-plane for branching tests using subsets of the numerical attributes of the problem. The resulting decision trees maintain their diversity through the inherent instability of the decision tree induction process. We then describe an evolutionary process by which the population of base classifiers evolves during run-time to adapt to the newly seen instances. A latent set of base-classifiers is maintained as a secondary classifier pool, and an instance from the latent set replaces the currently active classifier whenever certain criteria are met. We discuss motivation behind this architecture, algorithmic details and future directions for this research.

1 Introduction

Classifier ensembles were first proposed a long time ago, but recently they have received a lot of attention in the machine learning community [1] because of their potential to overcome difficulties associated with any single algorithm's capabilities for a learning task. Classifier ensembles can be considered as meta-classifiers in that after the base classifiers reach their decisions, a final decision combining the various classifiers' results must be made. For this reason, the theoretical analysis of the power of classifier ensembles has been in general more difficult than that of individual learning algorithms. Nevertheless, classifier ensembles have been

Please use the following format when citing this chapter:

Christou, I. T., Efremidis, S., 2007, in IFIP International Federation for Information Processing, Volume 247, Artificial Intelligence and Innovations 2007: From Theory to Applications, eds. Boukis, C., Pnevmatikakis, L., Polymenakos, L., (Boston: Springer), pp. 3-11.

successfully applied in many diverse areas ranging from multimedia and musical Information Retrieval [2] to Intrusion Detection [3] to recommender systems [4], etc.

One of the most important design decisions to be made in combining pattern classifiers is the choice of the base-classifier. In order to benefit the most from the combination of multiple classifiers, the ensemble should have sufficient diversity [1], for otherwise the decisions reached by the individual classifiers will be highly correlated and the probability that the performance of the overall system will be better than that of a single classifier will be slim. For this reason, unstable classifiers such as neural net-works and decision trees are often preferred as the base classification algorithms of a classifier ensemble.

In this paper we propose a classifier ensemble architecture suitable for online learning tasks in mixed-attribute domains where some attributes in the feature space are nominal whereas others are continuous-valued. We propose a modification of the classical C4.5 system architecture resulting in an oblique decision tree that branches on tests involving more than one continuous attribute using Support Vector Machines [5], and we present the details of the hybrid algorithm called SVM-ODT. We then propose new adaptive ensemble architecture for online learning applications using two evolving and alternating populations of SVM-ODT classifiers.

2 Building Oblique Decision Trees via Support Vector Machines

2.1 Decision Trees Overview

Tree classifiers work by constructing a decision tree for distinguishing data points between a finite set of classes. Starting from the root, decision tree construction proceeds by selecting an attribute from the feature space of the problem and splitting the data among two or more data sets depending on the values the selected attribute may take (Fig. 1).

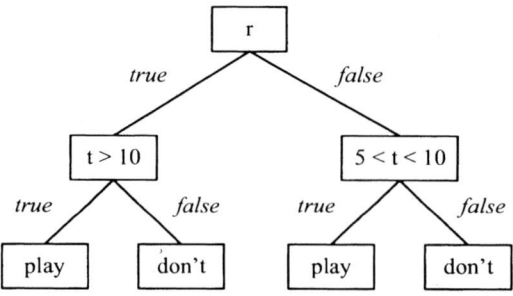

Fig. 1. A Decision Tree

Each "split" subset of the data set becomes a new node in the tree, under the current node. A node is considered a leaf node of the tree, and no further splitting occurs from this node on if the data set of this node is sufficiently "pure", for example all data points in this data set belong to the same class. Selecting the attribute to split on can be done in many different ways reflecting different objective criteria that the method is supposed to optimize. The entropy-based measure of impurity dictates that the at-tribute to split on is the one providing maximum information gain: it is the attribute on which, if we split, the resulting children nodes maximize their "purity"; the split is locally optimal in dichotomizing the data set. The ID3 system, in particular [6], which is designed to work with nominal attributes only, works by producing splits on a node that completely use up the attribute selected. For example if an attribute can take on four different values in the data set, splitting on this attribute will result in four different children, one for each different value the attribute can take on. Since ID3 cannot work with continuous attributes, such attributes need to be discretized first. This discretization process can easily lead to low-performing classifiers. C4.5 extends the ID3 algorithm by allowing continuous variables to be split without completely consuming the attribute, and in most cases this results in serious performance gains.

Because decision trees have the ability to classify all data points in the training set with zero classification error, they belong to the category of "unstable" classifiers, meaning that small perturbations in the data set may lead to drastically different decision trees produced. This phenomenon is closely related to the generalization ability of a classifier to correctly classify previously unseen instances. Decision trees that obtain zero classification errors on the training set are more liable to overtraining, meaning the classifier has essentially "memorized" the training set instead of having "learned" concepts underlying the classification problem at hand. To improve the generalization capabilities of the classifier, pruning methods attempt to prune the decision tree after its initial construction so as to maintain small classification errors on the training set, but with expected enhanced accuracy of classification in new unseen instances. On the other hand, this inherent instability of decision trees makes them perfect candidates for the base classifiers of an ensemble classification scheme.

2.2   Oblique Decision Trees via Support Vector Machine

It is clear from the discussion above that in C4.5 and all standard decision tree classi-fiers the split of the feature space at each branching node occurs along axis-parallel hyper-planes, since every branching test involves only a single attribute (Fig. 2)

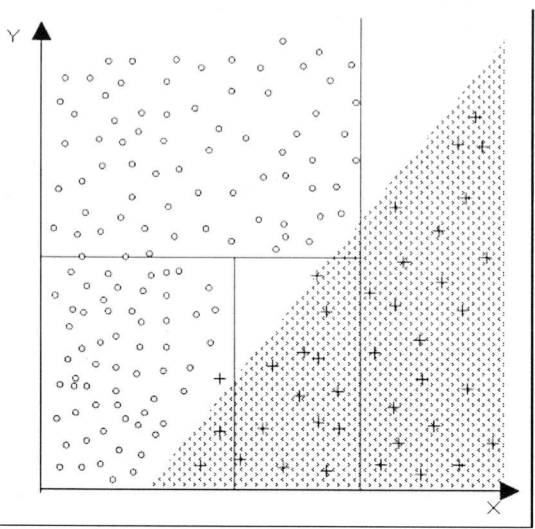

Fig. 2. Decision Trees split the data set of each node along axis-parallel hyper-planes

Quinlan [7] argues that for many application domains this restriction on the directions the splitting hyper-planes may take is not a problem, as evidenced by performance tests on a number of test-domains. Nevertheless, there are many application domains (especially ones where many of the domain attributes are continuous-valued) where decision trees are outperformed by more robust optimization methods such as Support Vector Machines (SVM).

SVM-based classifiers use rigorous mathematical programming theory to formulate the classification problem as an optimization problem in a vector space: the problem becomes that of finding the optimal separating hyper-plane that best separates the training set instances among the problem classes. SVM classifiers obviously work with data points belonging to $\mathbf{R}^n$. Problems involving attributes that are not continuous-valued must then be mapped somehow into a vector space and back. A popular technique for converting such problem sets into formats suitable for SVM optimization requires that each nominal attribute *attr* taking, say, m distinct values, be mapped into a set of m new $\{0,1\}$ variables $e1...e_m$. A data point in the original space having for the nominal attribute *attr* the i-th discrete value, will be transformed into a point in an expanded vector space where the e_i variable for this point will take the value 1, and all the other $e_j, j \neq i$ variables for this attribute will be 0. There is a problem though with this technique. The data set corresponding to the problem for which the decision tree in Fig. 1 has been constructed is transformed in the vector space shown in Fig. 2. As can be seen, there is no single hyper-plane that will optimally decide which class a data point belongs to.

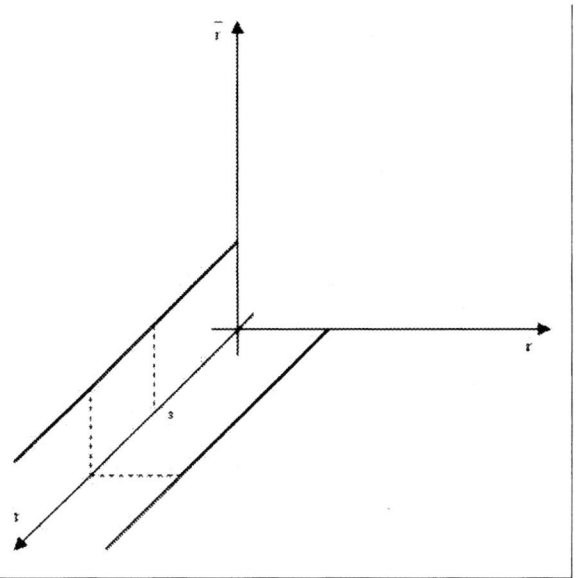

Fig. 3. Embedding a mixed-attribute space (t,r) into a higher (3) dimensional vector space

In general, trying to tweak a problem to fit into a domain that does not naturally fit in, is a practice that should be done with extreme care and only if there are no other tools available that can work directly with the problem domain.

Oblique Decision Trees are trees that branch using tests involving more than one at-tribute at any node. Many techniques for constructing oblique trees have been proposed in the past (see [8] for an approach building oblique trees using a random search procedure to combine attributes in each branching node). We propose to combine the strength of SVM in the continuous domain with that of decision trees in the discrete domain in an easy fusion.

In the following we discuss the 2-class classification problem, but it is easy to generalize the algorithm to deal with multiple classes. In particular, we propose an algorithm that is identical to ID3 except that its branching strategy is as follows: At every node, all the free continuous attributes of the problem are used to build a new problem set in the sub-space spanning all the continuous problem attributes. An SVM classifier is then built on the reduced continuous subspace, and an optimal hyper-plane separating the points of the current node's subset is constructed. The Information Gain of this split is then computed, along with the gains of the splits produced by the branching on each of the remaining non-continuous attributes. In the usual decision tree greedy manner, the split resulting in the highest gain is then selected and forms the test of the current node. The procedure is shown in detail in Fig. 4.

```
Algorithm ODT-SVM
  Input:  a labeled training set
  Output: an Oblique Decision Tree for Classifying New
          Instances
     1.   Begin with the root node t, having X(t) = X
     2.   For each new node t do
   2.1.     For each non-continuous feature xₖ k=1,…,l do
 2.1.1.       For each value aₖₙ of the feature xₖ do
2.1.1.1.        Generate X(t)ᵧₑₛ and X(t)ₙₒ according to the
                answer in the question: is xₖ(i)=aₖₙ,
                i=1,2,…,Nₜ
2.1.1.2.        Compute the Impurity decrease
 2.1.2.       End-for
 2.1.3.       Choose the aₖₙ' leading to the maximum
              decrease with respect to xₖ
   2.2.     End-for
   2.3.     Compute the optimal SVM separating the points
            in X(t) into two sets X(t)₁ and X(t)₂
            projected to the subspace spanned by all the
            free (i.e. not currently constrained)
            continuous features xₖ, k=l+1,…,m
   2.4.     Compute the impurity decrease associated with
            the split of X(t) into X(t)₁ and X(t)₂
   2.5.     Choose as test for node t, the test among 2.1
            - 2.4 leading to the highest impurity
            decrease
   2.6.     If stop-splitting rule is met declare node t
            as leaf and designate it with a class label;
            else generate 2 descendant nodes t1 and t2
            according to the test chosen in step 2.5
     3.   End-for
     4.   End
```

Fig. 4. ODT-SVM algorithm

In fact, the algorithm is a template, defining a family of algorithms, in that different choices for measuring the impurity of a set or different stopping-splitting rules will lead to different algorithms. Moreover, step 2.3 can easily be modified so that instead of computing the optimal hyper-plane separating the data X(t) in node t projected in the subspace spanned by all the continuous features of the problem (thus likely consuming all continuous attributes in one test node) the test may select a subset of the set of continuous features –randomly or not– and compute the optimal SVM that separates the points of the node in that reduced subspace.

3   Evolving ODT-SVM Ensembles

Recently, classifier ensembles using pairs of classifiers trained of randomly chosen complementary sub-sets of the training set have been proposed in the literature as a means to improve both the stability as well as the diversity of the ensemble [9]. This approach leads to a pair of ensembles operating statically on the problem domain in that the population does not evolve after it has been trained on the training set. Similarly, evolving classifiers using Genetic Algorithms ideas has been proposed in [10] but the approach is not intended for online learning tasks.

For applications in online or continuous learning, we propose to use evolutionary methodology to evolve pairs of ODT-SVM ensembles, in the following way. A set S = $\{(c_1, c_1'), (c_2, c_2') \dots (c_L, c_L')\}$ of L classifier pairs is first trained on the initially available training set T as follows: the first classifier of each pair i is trained on a randomly chosen subset of the training set $T_i \subseteq T$ and the second classifier of the pair is trained using the points $x_j \in T_i$ that were misclassified by the first classifier (the hard instances for the first classifier of the pair). The classifiers in each pair swap positions if the performance of the second classifier in the initial testing set is better than the performance of the first on the testing set.

During the online operation of the system (the continuous learning mode) new instances are given to the ensemble for classification. The system uses only the votes of the first classifier in each pair to reach a decision using any fusion or consensus strategy 1. However, all $2L$ classifiers classify the new instance, and when the true label for that instance becomes known (since the application is an online application) the classification accuracy of each classifier is updated to take into account the performance in the last received instance. When the performance of any of the top classifiers on a given number of the last arrived instances drops below the performance of its pair or some other criterion is met, the second and dormant classifier in the pair becomes the first active classifier and the original first is discarded. A new classifier is then trained on the instances the previously dormant classifier had missed and assumes the role of the dormant classifier of the pair.

The process is an evolving process with new classifiers being created and replacing old ones when those old classifiers' performance degrades. The system essentially remains static for as long as the ensemble's "knowledge" is adequate for the instances continuously arriving, but starts adapting itself to the new environment by modifying its population as soon as performance deteriorates enough. The process is depicted in Fig. 5. The decision maker could implement the Hedge(β) algorithm [1], as has been done successfully in [4]

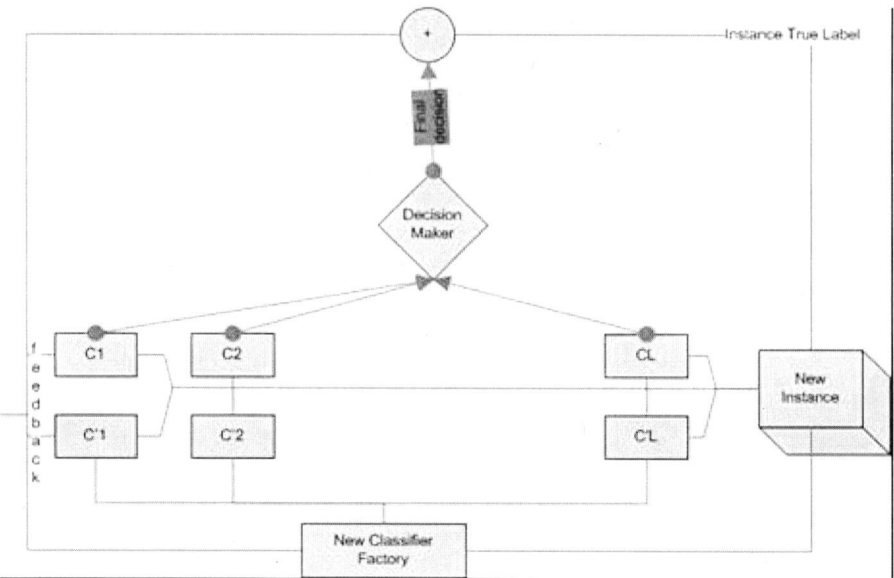

Fig. 5. Ensemble of ODT-SVM classifier pairs for online learning

4   Conclusions and Future Directions

We have presented an adaptive ensemble architecture for online learning tasks in changing environments. The architecture is based on Oblique Decision Trees using a modified C4.5 algorithm that treats the continuous attributes of a problem using Support Vector Machine technology while allowing for the discrete attributes of the same problem to be treated in the more natural decision tree philosophy. The Decision Tree philosophy of the base classifiers allows for more variety in the ensemble due to its inherent instability, variety which also comes from the fact that each base classifier in the ensemble is trained on a randomly selected subset of the training set.

For applications such as monitoring user profiles in the context of TV-program watching or movie-going recommendations, etc., the architecture has great promise in that it can follow the user's changing habits and adapt to them quickly enough so as to be very accurate most of the time. We plan to apply the system to the task of Anomaly Detection in surveillance systems using CCTV or other multi-media sources to reduce the number of false alarms while maintaining high accuracy rates.

References

1. Kuncheva, L. I. "Combining Pattern Classifiers – Methods and Algorithms", Wiley, Hoboken, NJ, 2004.
2. McKay C., et al: "ACE: A General Purpose Ensemble Classification Framework". Proceedings of the ICMC 05, 2005.

3. Koutsoutos S., Christou I.T. and Efremidis S.: "A Classifier Ensemble Approach to Intrusion Detection for Network-Initiated Attacks" - *invited contributed chapter in Emerging Artificial Intelligence Applications in Computer Engineering,* eds. John Soldatos et al, IOS Press, 2007.
4. Chistou I.T., Gkekas G., and Kyrikou, A.: "A Machine Learning Approach to the TV-Viewer Profile Adaptation Problem", submitted for publication, Dec. 2006.
5. Theodoridis, S. and Koutroumbas, K.: "Pattern Recognition", 3rd ed. Academic Press, San Diego, CA, 2006.
6. Quinlan, R.: "Induction on decision trees". Machine Learning, 1:1, 1986.
7. Quinlan, R.: "C4.5 Programs for Machine Learning". Morgan Kaufmann Publishers, San Francisco, CA, 1993.
8. Heath, D., Kasif, S., and Salzberg, S.: "Induction of Oblique Trees", IJCAI, 1993.
9. Kuncheva, L.I. and Rodriguez, J.J.: "Classifier Ensembles with a Random Linear Oracle", IEEE Transactions on Knowledge and Data Engineering, 19:4, 2007.
10. Ko, A. H.-R., Sabourin, R., and de Souza Britto, A. Jr.: "Evolving Ensemble of Classifiers in Random Subspace", Proc. Genetic and Evolutionary Computation Conf., GECCO 06, Seattle, WA, 2006.

Clustering Improves the Exploration of Graph Mining Results

Edgar H. de Graaf, Joost N. Kok, and Walter A. Kosters

Leiden Institute of Advanced Computer Science,
Leiden University, The Netherlands
edegraaf@liacs.nl

Abstract. Mining frequent subgraphs is an area of research where we have a given set of graphs, and where we search for (connected) subgraphs contained in many of these graphs. Each graph can be seen as a transaction, or as a molecule — as the techniques applied in this paper are used in (bio)chemical analysis.

In this work we will discuss an application that enables the user to further explore the results from a frequent subgraph mining algorithm. Such an algorithm gives the frequent subgraphs, also referred to as fragments, in the graphs in the dataset. Next to frequent subgraphs the algorithm also provides a lattice that models sub- and supergraph relations among the fragments, which can be explored with our application. The lattice can also be used to group fragments by means of clustering algorithms, and the user can easily browse from group to group. The application can also display only a selection of groups that occur in almost the same set of molecules, or on the contrary in different molecules. This allows one to see which patterns cover different or similar parts of the dataset.

1 Introduction

Mining frequent patterns is an important area of data mining where we discover substructures that occur often in (semi-)structured data. The research in this work will be in the area of frequent subgraph mining. These *frequent subgraphs* are connected vertex- and edge-labeled graphs that are subgraphs of a given set of graphs, traditionally also referred to as *transactions*, at least *minsupp* (a user-defined threshold) times. If a subgraph occurs at different positions in a graph, it is counted only once. The example of Figure 1 shows a graph and two of its subgraphs.

In this paper we will use results from frequent subgraph mining and we will present methods for improved exploration by means of clustering, where co-occurrences in the same transactions are used in the distance measure. Grouping patterns with clustering makes it possible to browse from one pattern and its corresponding group to another group close by. Or, depending on the preference of the user, to groups occurring in a separate part of the dataset.

Please use the following format when citing this chapter:

De Graaf, E. H., Kok, J. K., Kosters, W. A., 2007, in IFIP International Federation for Information Processing, Volume 247, Artificial Intelligence and Innovations 2007: From Theory to Applications, eds. Boukis, C., Pnevmatikakis, L., Polymenakos, L., (Boston: Springer), pp. 13-20.

Before explaining what is meant by lattice information we first need to discuss *child-parent* relations in frequent subgraphs, also known as patterns. Patterns are generated by extending smaller patterns with one extra edge. The smaller pattern can be called a *parent* of the bigger pattern that it is extended to. If we would draw all these relations, the drawing would be shaped like a lattice, hence we call this data *lattice information*.

We further analyze frequent subgraphs and their corresponding lattice information with different techniques in our framework LATTICE2SAR for mining and analyzing frequent subgraph data. One of the techniques in this framework is the analysis of graphs in which frequent subgraphs occur, via competitive neural networks as presented in [1]. Another important functionality is the browsing of lattice information from parent to child and from one group of fragments to another as presented here.

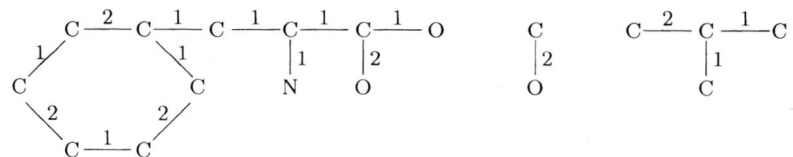

Fig. 1. An example of a possible graph (the amino acid Phenylalanine) in the molecule dataset and two of its many (connected) subgraphs, also called patterns or fragments.

Our application area is the analysis of fragments (patterns) in molecule data. The framework was originally made to handle (bio)chemical data. Obviously molecules are stored in the form of graphs, the molecules can be viewed as transactions (see Figure 1 for an example). However, the techniques presented here are not particular to molecule data (we will also not discuss any chemical or biological issues). For example one can extract user behavior from access logs of a website. This behavior can be stored in the form of graphs and can as such be analyzed with the techniques presented here.

The distance between patterns can be measured by calculating in how many graphs (or molecules) only one of the two patterns occurs. If this never happens then these patterns are very close to each other. If this is always the case, their distance is very large. In both cases the user is interested to know the reason. In our application the chemist might want to know which different patterns seem to occur in the same subgroup of effective medicines or on the other hand which patterns occur in different subgroups of effective medicines. In this paper we will present an approach to solve this problem that uses clustering. Furthermore all occurrences for the frequent subgraphs will be discovered by a graph mining algorithm and this occurrence information will be highly compressed before storage. Because of this, requesting these occurrences will be costly.

We will define our techniques for browsing the lattice of fragments. To this end, this paper makes the following contributions:

— An **application** will be introduced that **integrates techniques that facilitate browsing** of the lattice as provided by the frequent subgraph miner

(Section 2).

— We will use a **distance measure based on the co-occurrence of fragments to browse** from one fragment group to another (Section 3 and Section 4).

— We will give an **algorithm for grouping** very similar subgraphs using hierarchical cluster methods and lattice information (Section 4).

— Finally through experiments we will take a **closer look at runtime performance** of the grouping algorithm and discuss it (Section 5).

The algorithm for grouping was also used in [1], both papers discuss a component of the same framework. However in this work groups are used differently, for fragment suggestion during browsing.

This research is related to research on clustering, in particular of molecules. Also our work is related to frequent subgraph mining and frequent pattern mining when lattices are discussed. In [8] Zaki et al. discuss different ways for searching through the lattice and they propose the ECLAT algorithm.

Clustering in the area of biology is important because of the improved overview it provides the user with. E.g., [4] Samsonova et al. discuss the use of Self-Organizing Maps (SOMs) for clustering protein data. SOMs have been used in a biological context many times, for example in [2, 3]. There is also a relation with work done on hierarchical clustering in the biological context, e.g., as presented in [5]. In some cases molecules are clustered via numeric data describing each molecule; in [6] clustering such data is investigated.

Our package of mining techniques for molecules makes use of a graph miner called GSPAN, introduced in [7] by Yan and Han. This implementation generates the patterns organized as a lattice and a separate compressed file of occurrences of the patterns in the graph set (molecules).

2 Exploring the Lattice

We propose a *fragment exploration tool* to explore fragments in a dataset of molecules, the whole process is visualized in Figure 2. The application requires both fragment and lattice information from the frequent subgraph miner. This information is already extracted from the dataset when the application starts. All this data is first read and an in-memory lattice structure is built, where each node is a fragment. Occurrences are kept in a compressed format since the user wants to view this data when required. Also this data is needed by our distance measure which will be explained in Section 3; to make a distance matrix for all fragments will probably cost too much memory. First we make groups using information from the lattice only. Then we fill a matrix storing the distances between groups, which is possible if we assume to have far less groups of similar fragments.

After this process it is possible for the user to browse from fragment to fragment by adding or removing possible edges, where an edge is possible if it leads to a child or parent fragment. Figure 3 shows the current fragment in the

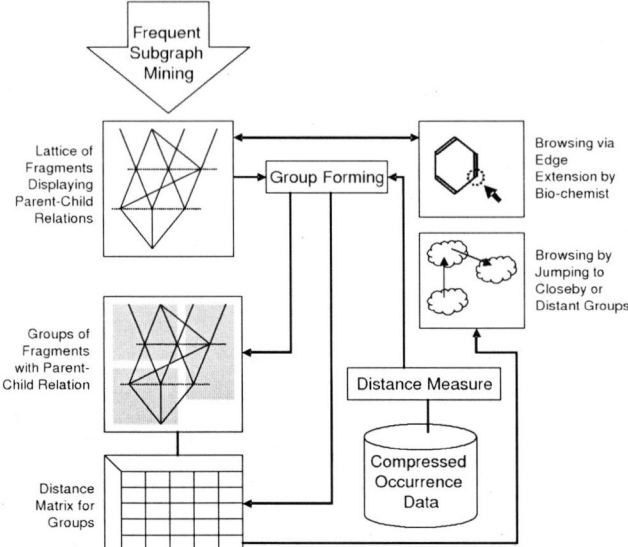

Fig. 2. The process of exploring the fragment lattice.

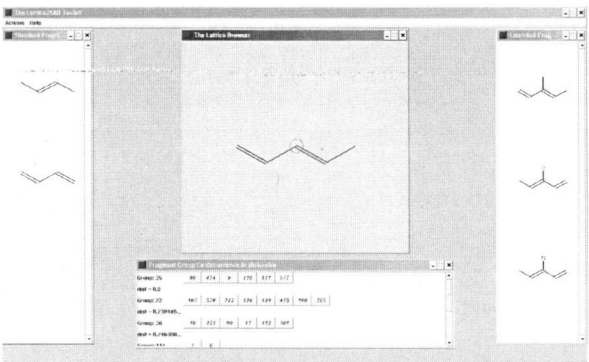

Fig. 3. Fragment exploration with the possible ways of shrinking and extending.

center window. The user must select a molecule to which an edge should be added. After an edge is selected one can select a possible extension, leading to a child, from the right window. It is also possible to shrink the current fragment towards a parent fragment, the possibilities are always shown in the left window.

The user can also jump to a fragment in a group that occurs either often in the same molecules or almost never, so fragments in close by or distant groups. Each molecule has a group and in Figure 4 it shows its group, and the other fragments in that group, first. Then it lists all close by groups and their corresponding fragments (here close by is defined as *group_dist* ≤ 0.3, see also Section 4). For every group it shows the distance, indicated with "dist", to the group of the current fragment.

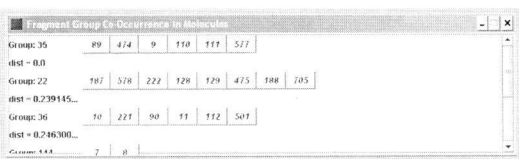

Fig. 4. Co-occurrence view for groups, showing all groups close by (*group_dist* ≤ 0.3).

3 Distance Measure

The distance measure will compute how often frequent subgraphs occur in the same graphs of the dataset. In the case of our working example it will show if different fragments (frequent subgraphs) exist in the same molecules. Formally we will define the distance measure in the following way (for graphs g_1 and g_2):

$$dist(g_1, g_2) = \tag{1}$$
$$\frac{sup(g_1) + sup(g_2) - 2 \cdot sup(g_1 \wedge g_2)}{sup(g_1 \vee g_2)} = \frac{sup(g_1) + sup(g_2) - 2 \cdot sup(g_1 \wedge g_2)}{sup(g_1) + sup(g_2) - sup(g_1 \wedge g_2)}$$

Here $sup(g)$ is the number of times a (sub)graph g occurs in the set of graphs; $sup(g_1 \wedge g_2)$ gives the number of graphs (or transactions) with both subgraphs and $sup(g_1 \vee g_2)$ gives the number of graphs with at least one of these subgraphs. The numerator of the *dist* measure computes the number of times the two graphs do not occur together in one graph of the dataset. We divide by $sup(g_1 \vee g_2)$ to make the distance independent from the total occurrence, thereby normalizing it. By reformulating we remove $sup(g_1 \vee g_2)$, saving us access time for the compressed dataset.

The distance measure satisfies the usual requirements, such as the triangular inequality. Note that $0 \leq dist(g_1, g_2) \leq 1$ and $dist(g_1, g_2) = 1 \Leftrightarrow sup(g_1 \wedge g_2) = 0$, so g_1 and g_2 have no common transactions in this case. If $dist(g_1, g_2) = 0$, both subgraphs occur in the same transactions, but are not necessarily equal.

While computing the support for the graphs not all frequent subgraphs are known and not all distances can be computed while running GSPAN.

4 Grouping Fragments

We will have to store the distance for all frequent subgraph combinations in order to decide fragments at an interesting distance. If we have n frequent subgraphs then storing the support for all $n(n-1)/2$ combinations might be too much. However many frequent subgraphs often are very similar in both structure and support and often there exists a parent-child relation.

Now we will propose a step where we group close subgraphs to reduce both the number of distances to store and the exploration time by grouping redundant graphs. We first define a distance $grdist$ (C_1, C_2) between groups (clusters) C_1 and C_2 as the maximal $dist$ between parent and child graphs in the two groups. This can be calculated fast by traversing the lattice.

This distance has a special value -1 if there is no pair (g_1, g_2) with $g_1 \in C_1$ and $g_2 \in C_2$, such that they have a parent-child relation, otherwise the maximum $dist$ between such elements is used.

All information used to compute these distances can be retrieved from the lattice information provided by the graph mining algorithm, when we focus on the subgraph-supergraph pairs. This information is already there to discover the frequent subgraphs, the only extra calculation is done when searching for $dist$ in this information.

Now we propose the GROUPFRAGMENTS algorithm that will organize close subgraphs/supergraphs into groups. The groups will be organized in a set $\mathcal{P}$. The outline of our algorithm based on hierarchical clustering is the following:

---

initialize $\mathcal{P}$ with sets of subgraphs of size 1 from the lattice
while $\mathcal{P}$ was changed or was initialized
    Select C_1 and C_2 from $\mathcal{P}$ with minimal $grdist$ $(C_1, C_2) \geq 0$
    if $grdist(C_1, C_2) \leq maxdist$ **then**
        $\mathcal{P} = \mathcal{P} \cup \{C_1 \cup C_2\}$
        Remove C_1 and C_2 from $\mathcal{P}$

GROUPFRAGMENTS

The parameter $maxdist$ is a user-defined threshold giving the largest distance allowed for two clusters to be joined.

Once the clusering has been done, we redefine the distance between groups as the distance between a smallest graph of each of the two groups, representing the most essential substructure of the group ($size$ gives the number of vertices): for $g_1 \in C_1$ and $g_2 \in C_2$ with $size(g_1) = min(\{size(g) \mid g \in C_1\})$ and $size(g_2) = min(\{size(g) \mid g \in C_2\})$, we let $group\_dist(C_1, C_2) = dist(g_1, g_2)$. So even if $grdist$ (C_1, C_2) would give the special value -1, $group\_dist(C_1, C_2)$ will provide a reasonable distance.

Now we allow the user to define which groups are interesting. These are mostly extremes: close by or far away groups. So the set $\mathcal{P}'$ of interesting groups with a relation to group C_w will be: $\mathcal{P}' = \{C_v | group\_dist(C_w, C_v) \leq interest\_min \lor group\_dist(C_w, C_v) \geq interest\_max\}$, where $interest\_max$ defines the largest distance of interest and $interest\_min$ the smallest. The user can now browse fragments in these interesting groups.

5 Experimental Results

The experiments were done for three main reasons. First of all we want to show the development of *runtime performance as maxdist decreases*. Secondly we want to show *the effect of fragment size* on the grouping algorithm with the distance measure. Finally the *effect of using a distance matrix* for storing distances between groups will be measured.

We make use of a molecule dataset, containing 4,069 molecules; from this we extracted a lattice with the 1,229 most frequent subgraphs. All experiments were performed on an Intel Pentium 4 64-bits 3.2 GHz machine with 3 GB memory. As operating system Debian Linux 64-bits was used with kernel 2.6.8-12-em64t-p4.

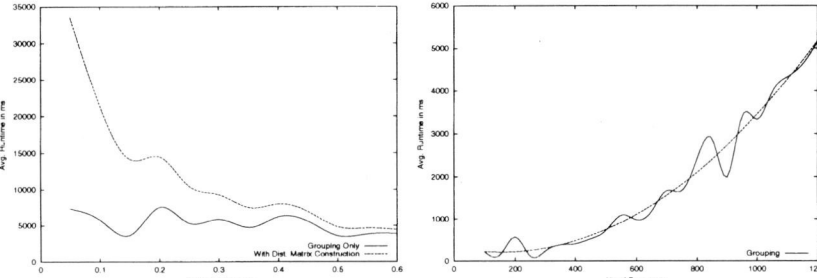

Fig. 5. Runtime in ms for different *maxdist* settings and the influence of distance matrix construction.

Fig. 6. Runtime in ms for different fragment set sizes (*maxdist* = 0.3), with quadratic regression

Figure 5 shows how runtime drops if we increase the *maxdist* threshold. This is mainly caused by the decrease of groups and so the size of the distance matrix. However the use of a distance matrix will provide the necessary speedup during exploration. Furthermore we also see that a low *maxdist* gives a large runtime due to a large distance matrix. This seems to show that making groups enables the application to store a distance matrix in memory and this allows the application to faster find close by groups (so faster browsing). Note that in practice we should store the distance matrix, for each dataset, on the disk and construct it only once.

In Figure 6 we see the runtime for the grouping algorithm as the number of fragments to be grouped increases. This runtime depends on the distance measure and the grouping algorithm, and runtime seems to increase polynomially.

6 Conclusions and Future Work

The application discussed in this work facilitates the exploration of fragments extracted from a dataset of molecules. With fragments we mean frequent subgraphs occurring in a dataset of graphs, the molecules.

We introduced two methods of browsing fragments. Firstly one can browse between parent and child by adding or removing edges from the fragments (only if it leads to another existing fragment). Our second method of browsing required us to first group fragments into groups of very similar fragments. We consider a fragment to be similar to another one if they have a parent-child relation and they occur in (almost) the same molecules. This allows the (bio)chemist to quickly jump to fragments that are biologically more interesting or cover a different subgroup of molecules.

Finally we discussed the runtime performance of our fragment grouping algorithm with different settings. Results showed that the construction of a distance matrix, needed for fast browsing, takes the most time. Furthermore results suggested that grouping improves the runtime, since less (redundant) distances are stored.

In the future we hope to include other innovative ways of browsing and analyzing the lattice of fragments, and we want to improve scalability where possible.

Acknowledgments: This research is carried out within the Netherlands Organization for Scientific Research (NWO) MISTA Project (grant no. 612.066.304). We thank Jeroen Kazius and Siegfried Nijssen for their help.

References

1. Graaf, E.H. de, Kok, J.N. and Kosters, W.A.: *Visualization and Grouping of Graph Patterns in Molecular Databases*, Submitted.
2. Hanke, J., Beckmann, G., Bork, P. and Reich, J.G.: *Self-Organizing Hierarchic Networks for Pattern Recognition in Protein Sequences*, Protein Science Journal 5 (1996), pp. 72–82.
3. Mahony, S., Hendrix, D., Smith, T.J. and Golden, A.: *Self-Organizing Maps of Position Weight Matrices for Motif Discovery in Biological Sequences*, Artificial Intelligence Review Journal 24 (2005), pp. 397–413.
4. Samsonova, E.V., Bäck, T., Kok, J.N. and IJzerman, A.P.: *Reliable Hierarchical Clustering with the Self-Organizing Map*, in Proc. 6th International Symposium on Intelligent Data Analysis (IDA 2005), LNCS 2810, pp. 385–396.
5. Uchiyama, I.: *Hierarchical Clustering Algorithm for Comprehensive Orthologous-Domain Classification in Multiple Genomes*, Nucleic Acids Research Vol. 34, No. 2 (2006), pp. 647–658.
6. Xu, J., Zhang, Q. and Shih, C.K.: *V-Cluster Algorithm: A New Algorithm for Clustering Molecules Based Upon Numeric Data*, Molecular Diversity 10 (2006), pp. 463–478.
7. Yan, X. and Han, J.: *gSpan: Graph-Based Substructure Pattern Mining*. In Proc. 2002 IEEE International Conference on Data Mining (ICDM 2002), pp. 721–724.
8. Zaki, M., Parthasarathy, S., Ogihara, M. and Li, W.: *New Algorithms for Fast Discovery of Association Rules*, in Proc. 3rd International Conference on Knowledge Discovery and Data Mining (KDD 1997), pp. 283–296.

Robustness of learning techniques in handling class noise in imbalanced datasets

D. Anyfantis, M. Karagiannopoulos, S. Kotsiantis and P. Pintelas
Educational Software Development Laboratory
Department of Mathematics, University of Patras, Greece
{dany,mariosk,sotos,pintelas}@math.upatras.gr,
WWW home page: http://www.math.upatras.gr/~esdlab

Abstract. Many real world datasets exhibit skewed class distributions in which almost all instances are allotted to a class and far fewer instances to a smaller, but more interesting class. A classifier induced from an imbalanced dataset has a low error rate for the majority class and an undesirable error rate for the minority class. Many research efforts have been made to deal with class noise but none of them was designed for imbalanced datasets. This paper provides a study on the various methodologies that have tried to handle the imbalanced datasets and examines their robustness in class noise.

1   Introduction

In many applications classifiers are faced with imbalanced data sets, which can cause the classifier to be biased towards one class. This bias is the result of one class being seriously under represented in the training data compared to the other classes. It can be qualified to the way in which classifiers are designed. Inductive classifiers are normally designed to minimize errors over the training examples. Learning algorithms, because of the fact that the cost of performing well on the over-represented class outweighs the cost of poor accuracy on the smaller class, can ignore classes containing few examples [16]. For a number of application domains, a massive disproportion in the number of cases belonging to each class is common. For example, in detection of fraud in telephone calls [9] and credit card transactions the number of legitimate transactions is much higher than the number of fraudulent transactions. Moreover, in direct marketing [19], it is frequent to have a small response rate (about 1%) for most marketing campaigns. Other examples of domains with intrinsic imbalance can be found in the literature such as rare medical diagnoses [22] and oil spills in satellite images [18].

The machine learning community has mostly addressed the issue of class imbalance in two ways. One is to give distinct costs to training instances [8]. The

---

Please use the following format when citing this chapter:

Anyfantis, D., Karagiannopoulos, M., Kotsiantis, S., Pintelas, P., 2007, in IFIP International Federation for Information Processing, Volume 247, Artificial Intelligence and Innovations 2007: From Theory to Applications, eds. Boukis, C., Pnevmatikakis, L., Polymenakos, L., (Boston: Springer), pp. 21-28.

other is to re-sample the original dataset, either by oversampling the minority class and/or under-sampling the majority class [17], [12]. Thus, existing research endeavors have made significant progress in exploring techniques for handling imbalanced datasets with assumptions that the input data are noise-free or noise in the data sets is not significant. However, real-world data are rarely perfect and can often suffer from corruptions that may impact interpretations of the data, models created from the data, and decisions made on the data.

Many research efforts have been made to deal with class noise [14], [23], [4], [11], [24], and have suggested that in many situations, eliminating instances that contain class noise will improve the classification accuracy. Although, many research efforts have focused on noise identification and data cleansing, none of them was originally designed for imbalanced datasets. In this study, the effectiveness of techniques for handling imbalanced datasets in class noise is evaluated over 7 imbalanced datasets using the C4.5 [20], Naive Bayes [6] and 5NN [1] as classifiers and the geometric mean of accuracies as performance measure [17].

Section 2 reviews the attempts for handling imbalanced datasets, while section 3 presents experimental results of the techniques for handling imbalanced datasets in class noise. Finally, section 4 discusses the results and suggests directions.

2   Review of existing techniques for handling imbalanced datasets

A simple method that can be used to imbalanced data sets is to reweigh training examples according to the total cost assigned to each class [6]. The idea is to change the class distributions in the training set towards the most costly class. The effect of imbalance in a dataset is also discussed in [12]. Japkowicz mainly evaluated two strategies: under-sampling and resampling. She noted that both the sampling approaches were helpful. In [17] the researchers selectively under-sampled the majority class while keeping the original population of the minority class with satisfied results. Batista et al. [2] used a more sophisticated under-sampling technique in order to reduce the amount of potentially useful data. Another approach is that of [19]. They combined over-sampling of the minority class with under-sampling of the majority class. However, the over-sampling and under-sampling combination did not provide significant improvement. In [5] they recommend an over-sampling approach in which the minority class is over-sampled by creating "synthetic" instances rather than by over-sampling with replacement with better results.

Changing the class distribution is not the only technique to improve classifier performance when learning from imbalanced data sets. A different approach to incorporating costs in decision-making is to define fixed and unequal misclassification costs between classes. Cost model takes the form of a cost matrix, where the cost of classifying a sample from a true class j to class i corresponds to the matrix entry λ_{ij}. This matrix is usually expressed in terms of average misclassification costs for the problem. The diagonal elements are usually set to zero, meaning correct classification has no cost. We define conditional risk for making a decision α_i as: $R(a_i \mid x) = \sum_i \lambda_{ij} P(v_j \mid x)$. The equation states that the risk of choosing class i is defined by fixed misclassification costs and the uncertainty of our knowledge about the true class of x expressed by the posterior probabilities. The goal in cost-sensitive classification is to minimize the cost of misclassification, which can be realized by choosing the class (v_j) with the minimum conditional risk.

An alternative to balancing the classes is to develop a learning algorithm that is intrinsically insensitive to class distribution in the training set. An example of this kind of algorithm is the SHRINK algorithm [17] that finds only rules that best summarize the positive instances (of the small class), but makes use of the information from the negative instances. MetaCost [6] is another method for making a classifier cost-sensitive. The procedure begins to learn an internal cost-sensitive model by applying a cost-sensitive procedure, which employs a base learning algorithm. Then, MetaCost procedure estimates class probabilities using bagging and then re-labels the training instances with their minimum expected cost classes, and finally relearns a model using the modified training set.

3   Experiments

For the aim of our study the most well-known decision tree algorithm - C4.5 [20] – was used. One of the latest researches that compare decision trees and other learning algorithms is made in [21] and shows that the mean error rates of most algorithms are similar and that their differences are statistically insignificant. But, unlike error rates, there are huge differences between the training times of the algorithms. C4.5 has one of the best combinations of error rate and speed. Decision tree classifiers, regularly, employ post-pruning techniques that evaluate the performance of decision trees as they are pruned using a validation set. Any node can be removed and assigned the most common class of the training examples that are sorted to the node in question. As a result, if a class is rare, decision tree algorithms often prune the tree down to a single node that classifies all instances as members of the common class leading to poor accuracy on the examples of minority class. The extreme skewness in class distribution is problematic for Naïve Bayes [7]. The prior probability of the majority class overshadows the differences in the attribute conditional probability terms. Instance-based learning algorithms belong to the category of lazy-learning algorithms, as they delay the induction until classification is performed. One of the most straightforward instance-based learning algorithms is the nearest neighbour algorithm [1]. In our study, we made use of the commonly used 5-NN algorithm. In imbalanced data sets as the number of the instances of the majority class grows, so does the likelihood that the nearest neighbour of any instance will belong to the majority class. This leads to the problem that many instances of the minority class will be misclassified.

In Table 1, there is a brief description of the data sets that we used for our experiments. Except for the "eap" data set, all were drawn from the UC Irvine Repository [3]. Eap data is from Hellenic Open University and was used in order to determine whether a student is about to drop-out or not [15].

Table 1. Description of the data sets

Data sets	Instances	Categorical Features	Numerical Features	Instances of minority class	Classes
breast-cancer	286	9	0	85	2
credit-g	1000	13	7	300	2
Diabetes	768	0	8	268	2
Haberman	306	0	3	81	2
Hepatitis	155	13	6	32	2
Ionosphere	351	34	0	126	2
Eap	344	11	0	122	2

For most of the datasets we used, they don't actually contain noise, so we use manual mechanisms to add class noise. For class noise, we adopt a pairwise scheme [24]: given a pair of classes (X, Y) and a noise level x, an instance with its label X has an x*100% chance to be corrupted and mislabeled as Y, so does an instance of class Y. Meanwhile, we only report the value x of class noise (which is not the actual class noise level in the dataset) in all tables below.

When comparing the performance of different classifiers in imbalanced data sets, accuracy as a measure is not enough. A classifier's performance of two class problems can be separately calculated for its performance over the positive instances (denoted as α^+) and over the negative instances (denoted as α^-). The true positive rate (α^+) or sensitivity is the fraction of positive instances predicted correctly by the model. Similarly, the true negative rate (α^-) or specificity is the fraction of negative instances predicted correctly by the classifier. In [17] they propose the geometric mean of the accuracies: $g = \sqrt{a^+ \times a^-}$ for imbalanced data sets. The basic idea behind this measure is to maximize the accuracy on both classes. Classification ability of the learning methods in our experiments was measured with geometric mean of the accuracies. For the examined models, the relationship between false negative and false positive costs was chosen to be the inverse of the assumed prior to compensate for the imbalanced priors.

In Table 2, one can see the comparisons with class noise of the attempts that have tried to obtain the best performance of a given imbalance data set using Naive Bayes (NB) as base classifier. Three well-known algorithms were used for the comparison: Reweighing and Cost Sensitive method [6] and Metacost algorithm [8]. We also present the accuracy of the simple Bayes algorithm as borderline. It must be mentioned that we used the free available source code for these methods [22] for our experiments. In Table 2 and Table 3 except for geometric mean we also present the true-positive rate, and true-negative rate. It must be mentioned that positive class is the majority class for our experiments. In the last row of Table 2, the average value of the geometric means is also calculated in all data sets. It must be mentioned that for Naïve Bayes classifier, modifying the decision boundary (Cost Sensitive method) is equivalent to reweighing training instances so as the relationship between false negative and false positive costs to be the inverse of the imbalanced priors. All the tested techniques give better results than the single Naive Bayes in class noise. The Reweighing and Cost Sensitive method gave better results with little class noise; however Metacost can handle better more class noise.

Table 2. Accuracy on majority class ($\alpha+$), accuracy on minority class ($\alpha-$) and geometric mean (g) with NB as base classifier

Datasets		ReWNB or CostNB Without Noise	ReWNB or CostNB With 10% Noise	ReWNB or CostNB With 20% Noise	Meta-cost NB Without Noise	Meta-cost NB With 10% Noise	Meta-cost NB With 20% Noise	NB Without Noise	NB With 10% Noise	NB With 20% Noise
breast-	g	0.66	0.65	0.54	0.65	0.67	0.63	0.6	0.62	0.61
cancer	$\alpha+$	0.74	0.65	0.43	0.79	0.72	0.59	0.85	0.84	0.8
	$\alpha-$	0.58	0.66	0.69	0.54	0.62	0.67	0.43	0.46	0.46
credit	g	0.72	0.72	0.7	0.66	0.69	0.7	0.65	0.68	0.68
-g	$\alpha+$	0.75	0.68	0.59	0.77	0.73	0.65	0.86	0.85	0.84
	$\alpha-$	0.69	0.77	0.82	0.57	0.65	0.75	0.49	0.54	0.55
diabetes	g	0.73	0.74	0.71	0.70	0.71	0.7	0.71	0.72	0.72
	$\alpha+$	0.78	0.76	0.68	0.75	0.72	0.66	0.84	0.84	0.85
	$\alpha-$	0.68	0.72	0.75	0.66	0.71	0.74	0.6	0.62	0.61
Haber-	g	0.56	0.58	0.46	0.57	0.59	0.5	0.44	0.45	0.39
man	$\alpha+$	0.89	0.83	0.26	0.87	0.84	0.3	0.94	0.94	0.95
	$\alpha-$	0.35	0.4	0.83	0.38	0.42	0.82	0.21	0.22	0.16
Hcapa-	g	0.8	0.79	0.78	0.81	0.8	0.8	0.78	0.79	0.8
titis	$\alpha+$	0.83	0.81	0.67	0.79	0.76	0.73	0.87	0.83	0.82
	$\alpha-$	0.78	0.78	0.91	0.84	0.84	0.88	0.7	0.75	0.78
Iono-	g	0.82	0.83	0.81	0.77	0.77	0.76	0.83	0.82	0.81
sphere	$\alpha+$	0.78	0.8	0.81	0.68	0.68	0.69	0.8	0.83	0.84
	$\alpha-$	0.87	0.86	0.81	0.88	0.88	0.84	0.86	0.81	0.79
cap	g	0.85	0.82	0.78	0.85	0.84	0.8	0.84	0.82	0.82
	$\alpha+$	0.87	0.79	0.68	0.88	0.85	0.72	0.9	0.88	0.87
	$\alpha-$	0.83	0.85	0.89	0.83	0.83	0.88	0.78	0.76	0.78
Average	g	0.73	0.73	0.68	0.72	0.72	0.7	0.7	0.7	0.69

In Table 3, one can see the comparisons with class noise of the attempts that have tried to obtain the best performance of a given imbalance data set using C4.5 as base classifier. The same three well-known techniques for handling imbalanced data sets were also used for this comparison. In general, all the tested techniques give better results than the single C4.5 in class noise. The Reweighing method gave better results with little class noise, however Metacost can handle better more class noise.

In Table 4, one can see the comparisons of the proposed technique with other attempts that have tried to obtain the best performance of a given imbalance data sets using 5NN as base classifier. The same three well-known techniques for handling imbalanced data sets were also used for this comparison. It must be mentioned that for 5NN classifier, modifying the decision boundary (Cost Sensitive method) is equivalent to reweighing training instances so as the relationship between false negative and false positive costs to be the inverse of the imbalanced priors. In general, all the tested techniques give similar better results than the single 5NN in class noise and there was no difference between them.

Table 3. Accuracy on majority class (α+), accuracy on minority class (α-) and geometric mean (g) with C4.5 as base classifier

Data-sets		ReW-C4.5 Without Noise	ReW-C4.5 With 10% Noise	ReW-C4.5 With 20% Noise	Cost-C4.5 Without Noise	Cost-C4.5 With 10% Noise	Cost-C4.5 With 20% Noise	Meta-cost C4.5 Without Noise	Meta-cost C4.5 With 10% Noise	Meta-cost C4.5 With 20% Noise	C4.5 Without Noise	C4.5 With 10% Noise	C4.5 With 20% Noise
breast-cancer	g	0.57	0.58	0.47	0.5	0.52	0.44	0.55	0.61	0.53	0.5	0.46	0.46
	α+	0.72	0.56	0.29	0.85	0.84	0.73	0.84	0.78	0.39	0.95	0.9	0.85
	α-	0.45	0.6	0.77	0.3	0.32	0.27	0.36	0.48	0.72	0.26	0.24	0.25
credit-g	g	0.66	0.63	0.6	0.61	0.63	0.64	0.64	0.65	0.66	0.58	0.6	0.61
	α+	0.67	0.57	0.47	0.82	0.76	0.68	0.76	0.71	0.65	0.85	0.83	0.79
	α-	0.65	0.69	0.76	0.46	0.52	0.6	0.54	0.6	0.68	0.4	0.44	0.47
Diabetes	g	0.72	0.69	0.63	0.72	0.66	0.65	0.73	0.7	0.65	0.7	0.67	0.65
	α+	0.72	0.66	0.47	0.78	0.79	0.63	0.78	0.73	0.59	0.82	0.8	0.87
	α-	0.73	0.72	0.84	0.67	0.56	0.68	0.67	0.68	0.71	0.6	0.56	0.49
Haberman	g	0.63	0.59	0.42	0.58	0.58	0.4	0.62	0.59	0.38	0.52	0.56	0.43
	α+	0.68	0.56	0.19	0.66	0.81	0.19	0.76	0.61	0.16	0.85	0.83	0.9
	α-	0.58	0.62	0.95	0.51	0.41	0.83	0.52	0.58	0.91	0.32	0.38	0.21
Hepatitis	g	0.73	0.72	0.59	0.64	0.54	0.51	0.68	0.67	0.71	0.58	0.52	0.51
	α+	0.62	0.69	0.55	0.86	0.77	0.47	0.83	0.76	0.63	0.9	0.87	0.84
	α-	0.85	0.75	0.63	0.48	0.38	0.56	0.56	0.59	0.81	0.37	0.31	0.31
Ionosphere	g	0.89	0.83	0.8	0.88	0.82	0.77	0.9	0.85	0.78	0.88	0.82	0.77
	α+	0.94	0.88	0.91	0.94	0.94	0.92	0.98	0.92	0.86	0.94	0.94	0.92
	α-	0.85	0.79	0.7	0.82	0.71	0.64	0.82	0.78	0.71	0.82	0.71	0.64
eap	g	0.81	0.78	0.71	0.83	0.8	0.79	0.82	0.79	0.76	0.83	0.83	0.86
	α+	0.86	0.76	0.57	0.94	0.84	0.75	0.89	0.78	0.69	0.94	0.94	0.92
	α-	0.77	0.8	0.89	0.74	0.76	0.84	0.76	0.8	0.84	0.74	0.74	0.8
Average	g	0.72	0.69	0.6	0.68	0.65	0.6	0.71	0.69	0.64	0.66	0.64	0.61

As a general conclusion, the Reweighing method is a more appropriate technique in the presence of little class noise, however Metacost can handle better more class noise.

4 Conclusion

Existing research endeavors have made significant progress in exploring techniques for handling imbalanced datasets with assumptions that the input data are noise-free or noise in the data sets is not significant. However, real-world data are rarely perfect and can often suffer from corruptions that may impact interpretations of the data, models created from the data, and decisions made on the data. In this study, the effectiveness of techniques for handling imbalanced datasets in class noise is evaluated over 7 imbalanced datasets. Metacost seems to be more robust as the class noise increased. In a following study, we will examine multi-class imbalanced datasets and will propose a more robust technique in the class noise.

Table 4. Accuracy on majority class (α+), accuracy on minority class (α-) and geometric mean (g) with 5NN as base classifier

Data sets		ReW5NN Or Cost5NN Without Noise	ReW5NN Or Cost5NN With 10% Noise	ReW5NN Or Cost5NN With 20% Noise	Metacost 5NN Without Noise	Metacost 5NN With 10% Noise	Metacost 5NN With 20% Noise	5NN Without Noise	5NN With 10% Noise	5NN With 20% Noise
breast-cancer	g	0.62	0.6	0.59	0.51	0.59	0.58	0.45	0.44	0.47
	α+	0.73	0.6	0.47	0.86	0.67	0.51	0.96	0.95	0.92
	α-	0.52	0.61	0.73	0.3	0.52	0.67	0.21	0.2	0.24
credit-g	g	0.66	0.63	0.58	0.63	0.66	0.59	0.57	0.58	0.59
	α+	0.69	0.58	0.44	0.73	0.64	0.45	0.89	0.85	0.76
	α-	0.63	0.69	0.77	0.55	0.67	0.78	0.37	0.39	0.46
diabetes	g	0.71	0.67	0.62	0.71	0.69	0.64	0.68	0.65	0.59
	α+	0.69	0.61	0.51	0.75	0.69	0.58	0.83	0.84	0.78
	α-	0.74	0.74	0.75	0.68	0.7	0.71	0.56	0.5	0.45
haberman	g	0.57	0.54	0.5	0.59	0.53	0.49	0.39	0.41	0.44
	α+	0.68	0.55	0.41	0.66	0.53	0.62	0.9	0.84	0.76
	α-	0.47	0.53	0.61	0.52	0.53	0.39	0.17	0.2	0.25
hepatitis	g	0.69	0.68	0.6	0.8	0.7	0.6	0.66	0.6	0.64
	α+	0.79	0.73	0.55	0.84	0.62	0.41	0.94	0.93	0.83
	α-	0.6	0.63	0.66	0.76	0.78	0.88	0.46	0.41	0.5
ionosphere	g	0.83	0.83	0.76	0.79	0.78	0.75	0.78	0.76	0.73
	α+	0.97	0.88	0.7	0.98	0.94	0.85	0.98	0.95	0.9
	α-	0.71	0.78	0.83	0.63	0.64	0.67	0.62	0.61	0.6
eap	g	0.8	0.75	0.62	0.77	0.75	0.59	0.78	0.76	0.73
	α+	0.84	0.64	0.44	0.87	0.7	0.4	0.9	0.89	0.88
	α-	0.76	0.87	0.88	0.69	0.8	0.88	0.68	0.65	0.61
Average	g	0.7	0.67	0.61	0.69	0.67	0.61	0.62	0.6	0.6

References

1. Aha, D. (1997). Lazy Learning. Dordrecht: Kluwer Academic Publishers.
2. Batista G., Carvalho A., Monard M. C. (2000), Applying One-sided Selection to Unbalanced Datasets. In O. Cairo, L. E. Sucar, and F. J. Cantu, editors, Proceedings of the Mexican International Conference on Artificial Intelligence – MICAI 2000, pages 315–325. Springer-Verlag.
3. Blake, C., Keogh, E. & Merz, C.J. (1998). UCI Repository of machine learning databases [http:// www.ics.uci.edu/~mlearn/MLRepository.html]. Irvine, CA: University of California.
4. Brodley, C. E. & Friedl, M. A. (1999). Identifying Mislabeled Training Data. Journal of Artificial Intelligence Research 11: 131–167.

5. Chawla N., Bowyer K., Hall L., Kegelmeyer W. (2002), SMOTE: Synthetic Minority Over-sampling Technique, Journal of Artificial Intelligence Research 16, 321 - 357.
6. Domingos P. (1998), How to get a free lunch: A simple cost model for machine learning applications. Proc. AAAI-98/ICML98, Workshop on the Methodology of Applying Machine Learning, pp1-7.
7. Domingos P. & Pazzani M. (1997). On the optimality of the simple Bayesian classifier under zero-one loss. Machine Learning, 29, 103-130.
8. Domingos, P. (1999). MetaCost: A General Method for Making Classifiers Cost-Sensitive. Proceedings of the Fifth International Conference on Knowledge Discovery and Data Mining, 155-164. ACM Press.
9. Fawcett T. and Provost F. (1997), Adaptive Fraud Detection. Data Mining and Knowledge Discovery, 1(3):291–316.
10. Friedman J. H. (1997), On bias, variance, 0/1-loss and curse-of-dimensionality. Data Mining and Knowledge Discovery, 1: 55-77.
11. Gamberger, D., Lavrac, N. & Dzeroski, S. (2000). Noise Detection and Elimination in Data Preprocessing: experiments in medical domains. Applied Artificial Intelligence 14, 205-223.
12. Japkowicz N. (2000), The class imbalance problem: Significance and strategies. In Proceedings of the International Conference on Artificial Intelligence, Las Vegas.
13. Japkowicz N. and Stephen, S. (2002), The Class Imbalance Problem: A Systematic Study Intelligent Data Analysis, Volume 6, Number 5.
14. John, G. H. (1995). Robust Decision Trees: Removing Outliers from Databases. Proc. of the First International Conference on Knowledge Discovery and Data Mining. AAAI Press, pp. 174–179.
15. Kotsiantis, S., Pierrakeas, C., Pintelas, P., Preventing student dropout in distance learning systems using machine learning techniques, Lecture Notes in Artificial Intelligence, KES 2003, Springer-Verlag Vol 2774, pp 267-274, 2003.
16. Kotsiantis S., Kanellopoulos, D. Pintelas, P. (2006), Handling imbalanced datasets: A review, GESTS International Transactions on Computer Science and Engineering, Vol.30 (1), pp. 25-36.
17. Kubat, M. and Matwin, S. (1997), 'Addressing the Curse of Imbalanced Data Sets: One Sided Sampling', in the Proceedings of the Fourteenth International Conference on Machine Learning, pp. 179-186.
18. Kubat, M., Holte, R. and Matwin, S. (1998), 'Machine Learning for the Detection of Oil Spills in Radar Images', Machine Learning, 30:195-215.
19. Ling, C., & Li, C. (1998). Data Mining for Direct Marketing Problems and Solutions. In Proceedings of the Fourth International Conference on Knowledge Discovery and Data Mining (KDD-98) New York, NY. AAAI Press.
20. Quinlan J.R. (1993), C4.5: Programs for machine learning. Morgan Kaufmann, San Francisco.
21. Tjen-Sien Lim, Wei-Yin Loh, Yu-Shan Shih (2000), A Comparison of Prediction Accuracy, Complexity, and Training Time of Thirty-Three Old and New Classification Algorithms. Machine Learning, 40, 203–228, 2000, Kluwer Academic Publishers.
22. Witten Ian H. and Frank Eibe (2005) "Data Mining: Practical machine learning tools and techniques", 2nd Edition, Morgan Kaufmann, San Francisco, 2005.
23. Zhao, Q. & Nishida, T. (1995). Using Qualitative Hypotheses to Identify Inaccurate Data. Journal of Artificial Intelligence Research 3, pp.119–145.
24. Zhu, X., Wu, X. & Yang, Y. (2004). Error Detection and Impact-sensitive Instance Ranking in Noisy Datasets. In Proceedings of 19th National conference on Artificial Intelligence (AAAI-2004), San Jose, CA.

A Wrapper for Reweighting Training Instances for Handling Imbalanced Data Sets

M. Karagiannopoulos, D. Anyfantis, S. Kotsiantis and P. Pintelas
Educational Software Development Laboratory
Department of Mathematics, University of Patras, Greece
{ mariosk,dany,sotos,pintelas}@math.upatras.gr,
WWW home page: http://www.math.upatras.gr/~esdlab

Abstract. A classifier induced from an imbalanced data set has a low error rate for the majority class and an undesirable error rate for the minority class. This paper firstly provides a systematic study on the various methodologies that have tried to handle this problem. Finally, it presents an experimental study of these methodologies with a proposed wrapper for reweighting training instances and it concludes that such a framework can be a more valuable solution to the problem.

1 Introduction

Classifiers are often faced with imbalanced data sets for various reasons; the latest can cause the classifier to be biased towards one class. This bias is the outcome of one class being seriously under represented in the training data in favor of other classes. It can be qualified to the way in which classifiers are designed. Inductive classifiers are normally designed to minimize errors over the training examples. Learning algorithms on the other hand ignore classes containing few examples [11]. For a number of application domains, a massive disproportion in the number of cases belonging to each class is common. For example, in detection of fraud in telephone calls and credit card transactions. Moreover, in direct marketing, it is frequent to have a small response rate (about 1%) for most marketing campaigns.

The machine learning community has mostly addressed the issue of class imbalance in two ways. One is to give distinct costs to training instances [6] while the other is to re-sample the original dataset, either by oversampling the minority class and/or under-sampling the majority class [12], [9]. Although many methods for coping with imbalanced data sets have been proposed, there are still several open questions. One open question is whether simply changing the distribution skew can improve predictive performance steadily. To handle the problem, we developed a

Please use the following format when citing this chapter:

Karagiannopoulos, M., Anyfantis, D., Kotsiantis, S., Pintelas, P., 2007, in IFIP International Federation for Information Processing, Volume 247, Artificial Intelligence and Innovations 2007: From Theory to Applications, eds. Boukis, C., Pnevmatikakis, L., Polymenakos, L., (Boston: Springer), pp. 29-36.

wrapper for reweighting training instances. The effectiveness of our approach is evaluated over eight imbalanced datasets using the C4.5 [15], Naive Bayes [5] and 5NN [1] as classifiers and the geometric mean of accuracies as performance measure [12].

In the following section we review the attempts for handling imbalanced data sets, while section 3 presents the details of our approach. Section 4 presents experimental results comparing our approach to other approaches. Finally, section 5 discusses the results and suggests directions for future work.

2 Review of existing techniques for handling imbalanced data sets

A simple method that can be used to imbalanced data sets is to reweigh training examples according to the total cost assigned to each class [4]. The idea is to change the class distributions in the training set towards the most costly class. In [8] the effect of imbalance in a dataset is discussed. Two main strategies are evaluated: Under-sampling and Resampling. Both the two sampling approaches were helpful, and is observed that sophisticated sampling techniques does not give any clear advantage in the domain considered.

Another approach is presented in [13]. They combined over-sampling of the minority class with under-sampling of the majority class. However, the over-sampling and under-sampling combination did not provide significant improvement. In [3] an over-sampling approach is presented according to which the minority class is over-sampled by creating "synthetic" instances rather than by over-sampling with replacement with better results.

Changing the class distribution is not the only technique to improve classifier performance when learning from imbalanced data sets. A different approach to incorporating costs in decision-making is to define fixed and unequal misclassification costs between classes [8].

An alternative to balancing the classes is to develop a learning algorithm that is intrinsically insensitive to class distribution in the training set. An example of this kind of algorithm is the SHRINK algorithm [12] that finds only rules that best summarize the positive instances (of the small class), but makes use of the information from the negative instances. MetaCost [6] is another method for making a classifier cost-sensitive. The procedure begins to learn an internal cost-sensitive model by applying a cost-sensitive procedure, which employs a base learning algorithm. Then, MetaCost procedure estimates class probabilities using bagging and then re-labels the training instances with their minimum expected cost classes, and finally relearns a model using the modified training set.

In [16] different weights for false positives and false negatives are used to apply AdaBoost than bagging in text-filtering. AdaBoost uses a base classifier to induce multiple individual classifiers in sequential trials, and a weight is assigned to each training instance. At the end of each trial, the vector of weights is adjusted to reflect the importance of each training instance for the next induction trial. This adjustment effectively increases the weights of misclassified examples and decreases the weights of the correctly classified examples. A similar technique is proposed in [7].

3   Proposed Technique

The problem of determining which proportion of positive/negative examples is the best for learning is an open problem of learning from imbalanced data sets. The proposed technique is based on the previous referred reweighting technique; however, we do not apply a single cost matrix for reweighting training instances. We did not only examine the relationship between false negative and false positive costs to be the inverse of the assumed prior to compensate for the imbalanced priors. We examine all the cost matrixes:

$$\begin{bmatrix} 0 & 1 \\ x & 0 \end{bmatrix}$$

Where x takes the values from [(Number of Instances of the Majority Class)/ (Number of Instances of the Majority Class)-1] to [(Number of Instances of the Majority Class)/ (Number of Instances of the Majority Class)+1], with step 0.1. The cost-matrix with the best performance using 10-fold cross validation is then applied for the classification of new instances. The proposed technique (WRTI) is presented in Fig. 1. A key feature of our method is that it does not require any modification of the underlying learning algorithm.

In the following section, we empirically evaluate the performance of our approach with the other well known techniques using a decision tree, an instance base learner and a Bayesian model as base classifiers.

```
RatioA =ClassWithMoreInstances)/ClassWithLessInstances);
for (s = RatioA - 1.0; s < RatioA + 1.0; s = s + 0.1)
         {
               CostMatrix cm;
for (int i=0; i<2; i++)
         {
               for (int j=0; j<2; j++)
               {
                   if (i == j)
                       cm.setCell(i, j, 0);
                   if (i == 0 && j == 1)
                       cm.setCell(i, j, 1);
                   if (i == 1 && j == 0)
                       cm.setCell(i, j, s);
               }
         }
           CostSensitiveClassifier csc = new
CostSensitiveClassifier();
           csc.setCostMatrix(cm);
           csc.setClassifier(UsedClassifier);
           eval.crossValidateModel(csc, data, 10);
           result =
eval.truePositiveRate(ClassIndexWithLessInstances) *
```

```
eval.truePositiveRate(ClassIndexWithMoreInstances);
                if (result > BestResult)
                {   BestResult = result;
                    BestCM = cm;
                }
    }
```

Fig. 1. A wrapper for reweighting training instances

4   Experiments

In Table 1, there is a brief description of the data sets that we used for our experiments. Except for the "eap" data set, all were drawn from the UC Irvine Repository [2]. Eap data is from Hellenic Open University and was used in order to determine whether a student is about to drop-out or not [10].

Table 1. Description of the data sets

Data sets	Instances	Categorical features	Numerical features	Instances of minority class	Classes
breast-cancer	286	9	0	85	2
credit-g	1000	13	7	300	2
Diabetes	768	0	8	268	2
Haberman	306	0	3	81	2
Hepatitis	155	13	6	32	2
Ionosphere	351	34	0	126	2
Eap	344	11	0	122	2
Sick	3772	22	7	231	2

A classifier's performance of two class problems can be separately calculated for its performance over the positive instances (denoted as α^+) and over the negative instances (denoted as α^-). The true positive rate (α^+) or sensitivity is the fraction of positive instances predicted correctly by the model. Similarly, the true negative rate (α^-) or specificity is the fraction of negative instances predicted correctly by the classifier. In [12] the authors propose the geometric mean of the accuracies: $g = \sqrt{a' \times a^-}$ for imbalanced data sets. Moreover, ROC curves (Receiving Operator Characteristic) provide a visual representation of the trade off between true positives (α^+) and false positives (α^-). These are plots of the percentage of correctly classified positive instances α^+ with respect to the percentage of incorrectly classified negative instances α^- [14]. The method for plotting a ROC curve is closely related to a method for making algorithms cost-sensitive, that we call Threshold method [17]. This method uses a threshold so as to maximize the given performance measure in the curve. Classification ability of the learning methods in our experiments was measured with geometric mean of the accuracies. For the examined cost models, the relationship between false negative and false positive costs was chosen to be the inverse of the assumed prior to compensate for the imbalanced priors. In the following Tables, win (v) indicates that the proposed method along with the learning algorithm performed statistically better than the other classifier according to t-test with p<0.05. Loss (*) indicates that the proposed method along with the learning algorithm performed statistically worse than the other classifier according to t-test with p<0.05. In all the other cases, there is no significant statistical difference between the results.

In Table 2, one can see the comparisons of the proposed technique with other attempts that have tried to obtain the best performance of a given imbalance data set using Naive Bayes (NB) as base classifier. Five well-known algorithms were used for the comparison: Threshold method [17], Reweighting and Cost Sensitive method [4], Adaboost cost sensitive method [16], and Metacost algorithm [6]. We also present the accuracy of the simple Bayes algorithm as borderline. It must be mentioned that we used the free available source code for these methods [17] for our experiments. In the Table 2 except for geometric mean we also present the true-positive rate, and true-negative rate. The positive class for our experiments is the majority class. In the last row of the Table 2, the average value of the geometric means is also calculated in all data sets.

Table 2. Accuracy on majority class ($\alpha+$), accuracy on minority class ($\alpha-$) and geometric mean (g) with NB as base classifier

Data sets		WRTINB	RcWNB	ThresNB	CostNB	AdabcosNB	MetacostNB	NB
breast-cancer	g	0.67	0.66	0.63*	0.66	0.63*	0.65	0.6*
	α+	0.66	0.74 v	0.62 *	0.74 v	0.72 v	0.79 v	0.85v
	α-	0.68	0.58 *	0.65 *	0.58 *	0.56 *	0.54 *	0.43*
credit-g	g	0.73	0.72	0.71	0.72	0.71	0.66 *	0.65*
	α+	0.71	0.75 v	0.69	0.75 v	0.75 v	0.77 v	0.86v
	α-	0.75	0.69 *	0.74	0.69 *	0.67 *	0.57 *	0.49*
diabetes	g	0.74	0.73	0.72	0.73	0.73	0.70 *	0.71*
	α+	0.75	0.78 v	0.65 *	0.78 v	0.77	0.75	0.84v
	α-	0.73	0.68 *	0.8 v	0.68 *	0.69 *	0.66 *	0.6 *
haberman	g	0.6	0.56 *	0.59	0.56*	0.56*	0.57*	0.44*
	α+	0.88	0.89	0.64 *	0.89	0.88	0.87	0.94v
	α-	0.41	0.35 *	0.55 v	0.35 *	0.36 *	0.38 *	0.21*
hepatitis	g	0.8	0.8	0.76 *	0.8	0.78	0.81	0.78
	α+	0.86	0.83 *	0.87	0.83 *	0.86	0.79 *	0.87*
	α-	0.75	0.78 v	0.67 *	0.78 v	0.71 *	0.84 v	0.7*
ionosphere	g	0.84	0.82	0.88 v	0.82	0.91 v	0.77*	0.83
	α+	0.87	0.78 *	0.93 v	0.78 *	0.93 v	0.68 *	0.8*
	α-	0.81	0.87	0.81	0.87 v	0.9 v	0.88 v	0.86v
eap	g	0.85	0.85	0.83	0.85	0.83	0.85	0.84
	α+	0.87	0.87	0.86	0.87	0.85	0.88	0.9 v
	α-	0.83	0.83	0.81	0.83	0.82	0.83	0.78*
sick	g	0.86	0.86	0.76*	0.86	0.87	0.8*	0.86
	α+	0.82	0.82	0.98 v	0.82	0.88 v	0.73 *	0.94v
	α-	0.9	0.9	0.59 *	0.9	0.86 *	0.87 *	0.78*
Average	g	0.76	0.75	0.74	0.75	0.75	0.73	0.71

In general, all the tested techniques give better results than the single Naive Bayes. The most remarkable improvement is from our technique, even though the

Threshold method gives, on average, the best accuracy in the minority class. The Metacost cannot improve the results of the NB as his author suspects. It must be noted that for NB classifier, modifying the decision boundary (Cost Sensitive method) is equivalent to reweighting training instances so as the relationship between false negative and false positive costs to be the inverse of the imbalanced priors. Moreover, Adaboost cost sensitive method cannot give better results than Cost Sensitive, even though it is a more time consuming technique.

In Table 3, one can see the comparisons of the proposed technique with other attempts that have tried to obtain the best performance of a given imbalance data sets using C4.5 as base classifier.

Table 3. Accuracy on majority class (α+), accuracy on minority class (α-) and geometric mean (g) with NB as base classifier

Data sets		WRTIC4.5	ReWC4.5	ThresC4.5	CostC4.5	Adabcos C4.5	Metacost C4.5	C4.5
breast-cancer	g	0.59	0.57	0.45*	0.5 *	0.56 *	0.55 *	0.5 *
	α+	0.66	0.72 v	0.8 v	0.85 v	0.77 v	0.84 v	0.95 v
	α-	0.52	0.45 *	0.25 *	0.3 *	0.41 *	0.36 *	0.26 *
credit-g	g	0.67	0.66	0.64*	0.61*	0.62*	0.64*	0.58 *
	α+	0.75	0.67 *	0.7*	0.82 v	0.81 v	0.76	0.85 v
	α-	0.6	0.65 v	0.58	0.46 *	0.47 *	0.54	0.4 *
diabetes	g	0.73	0.72	0.7*	0.72	0.67*	0.73	0.7*
	α+	0.71	0.72	0.69	0.78 v	0.79 v	0.78 v	0.82 v
	α-	0.75	0.73	0.71 *	0.67 *	0.57 *	0.67 *	0.6 *
haberman	g	0.65	0.63	0.56 *	0.58 *	0.57 *	0.62 *	0.52 *
	α+	0.65	0.68 v	0.61 *	0.66	0.76 v	0.76 v	0.85 v
	α-	0.65	0.58 *	0.51 *	0.51 *	0.43 *	0.52 *	0.32 *
hepatitis	g	0.72	0.73	0.62 *	0.64 *	0.7	0.68 *	0.58 *
	α+	0.83	0.62 *	0.78 *	0.86 v	0.9 v	0.83	0.9 v
	α-	0.63	0.85 v	0.49 *	0.48 *	0.55 *	0.56 *	0.37 *
ionosphere	g	0.91	0.89	0.88 *	0.88 *	0.9	0.9	0.88 *
	α+	0.96	0.94	0.95	0.94	0.94	0.98	0.94
	α-	0.87	0.85	0.81*	0.82 *	0.86	0.82 *	0.82 *
eap	g	0.84	0.81 *	0.69 *	0.83	0.79 *	0.82	0.83
	α+	0.95	0.86 *	0.91 *	0.94	0.85 *	0.89 *	0.94
	α-	0.74	0.77 v	0.53 *	0.74	0.74	0.76	0.74
sick	g	0.97	0.97	0.92 *	0.96	0.95	0.96	0.93 *
	α+	0.99	0.99	0.99	0.99	1 v	0.98	0.99
	α-	0.95	0.95	0.85 *	0.92 *	0.9 *	0.95	0.87 *
Average	g	0.76	0.75	0.68	0.72	0.72	0.74	0.69

The same five well-known techniques for handling imbalanced data sets were also used for this comparison. Likewise with the previous experiment, our method has better performance than the other techniques. However, Metacost has really better performance with C4.5 than NB. It must also be mentioned that Threshold method gives worst performance than single C4.5. Adaboost cost sensitive method, as in the previous experiment, cannot give better results than reweighting method even though it uses more time for training.

In Table 4, one can see the comparisons of the proposed technique with other attempts that have tried to obtain the best performance of a given imbalance data sets using 5NN as base classifier. The same five well-known techniques for handling imbalanced data sets were also used for this comparison. Likewise with the previous experiment, our method has better performance than the other techniques. It must be mentioned that Adaboost cost sensitive method and Metacost algorithm are extremely time consuming techniques if they are combined with lazy algorithm 5NN without offering spectacular improvement in the performance. Threshold method gives, on average, the least improvement in the performance of 5NN.

Table 4. Accuracy on majority class (α+), accuracy on minority class (α-) and geometric mean (g) with 5NN as base classifier

Data sets		WRTI5NN	ReW5NN	Thres5NN	Cost5NN	Adabcos 5NN	Metacost 5NN	5NN
breast-cancer	g	0.64	0.62	0.6 *	0.61*	0.61*	0.51 *	0.45*
	α+	0.73	0.73	0.57 *	0.72	0.7 *	0.86 v	0.96v
	α-	0.56	0.52 *	0.63 v	0.52 *	0.53*	0.3 *	0.21*
credit-g	g	0.66	0.66	0.59 *	0.66	0.63 *	0.63 *	0.57 *
	α+	0.68	0.69	0.84 v	0.69	0.7	0.73 v	0.89 v
	α-	0.64	0.63	0.42 *	0.63	0.56 *	0.55 *	0.37 *
diabetes	g	0.70	0.71	0.69	0.71	0.66 *	0.71	0.68
	α+	0.76	0.69 *	0.79 v	0.69 *	0.71 *	0.75	0.83v
	α-	0.71	0.74 v	0.61 *	0.74 v	0.62 *	0.68 *	0.56*
haberman	g	0.57	0.57	0.58	0.57	0.53	0.59	0.39*
	α+	0.61	0.68 v	0.52 *	0.68 v	0.68 v	0.66 v	0.9v
	α-	0.48	0.47	0.65 v	0.47	0.41 *	0.52 v	0.17*
hepatitis	g	0.74	0.69 *	0.68 *	0.73	0.58 *	0.8 v	0.66 *
	α+	0.77	0.79	0.91 v	0.85 v	0.8 v	0.84 v	0.94 v
	α-	0.7	0.6 *	0.51 *	0.62 *	0.42 *	0.76 v	0.46 *
ionosphere	g	0.83	0.83	0.82	0.83	0.83	0.79 *	0.78*
	α+	0.97	0.97	0.97	0.97	0.95	0.98	0.98
	α-	0.71	0.71	0.7	0.71	0.72	0.63 *	0.62 *
eap	g	0.81	0.8	0.79	0.8	0.78 *	0.77 *	0.78 *
	α+	0.81	0.84 v	0.83	0.84 v	0.79	0.87 v	0.9 v
	α-	0.82	0.76 *	0.75 *	0.76 *	0.77 *	0.69 *	0.68 *
sick	g	0.89	0.84 *	0.62 *	0.84 *	0.87	0.79 *	0.61 *
	α+	0.93	0.89 *	0.99 v	0.89 *	0.98 v	0.9 *	0.99 v
	α-	0.85	0.79 *	0.39 *	0.79 *	0.77 *	0.7 *	0.37*
Average	g	0.73	0.72	0.67	0.72	0.69	0.7	0.62

5   Conclusion

The problem of imbalanced data sets arises frequently. In this work, we survey some methods proposed by the ML community to solve the problem, we discuss some limitations of these methods and we propose a wrapper for weighting training instances technique as a more effective solution to problem. Our method allows improved identification of difficult small classes in predictive analysis, while keeping the classification ability of the other classes in an acceptable level. In a following study, we will examine the proposed technique in multi-class datasets.

References

1. Aha, D. (1997). Lazy Learning. Dordrecht: Kluwer Academic Publishers.
2. Blake, C., Keogh, E. & Merz, C.J. (1998). UCI Repository of machine learning databases [http:// www.ics.uci.edu/~mlearn/MLRepository.html]. Irvine, CA: University of California.
3. Chawla N., Bowyer K., Hall L., Kegelmeyer W. (2002), SMOTE: Synthetic Minority Over-sampling Technique, Journal of Artificial Intelligence Research 16, 321 - 357.
4. Domingos P. (1998), How to get a free lunch: A simple cost model for machine learning applications. Proc. AAAI-98/ICML98, Workshop on the Methodology of Applying Machine Learning, pp1-7.
5. Domingos P. & Pazzani M. (1997). On the optimality of the simple Bayesian classifier under zero-one loss. Machine Learning, 29, 103-130.
6. Domingos, P. (1999). MetaCost: A General Method for Making Classifiers Cost-Sensitive. Proceedings of the 5th International Conference on Knowledge Discovery and Data Mining, 155-164. ACM Press.
7. Fan, W., Stolfo, S.J., Zhang, J. & Chan, P.K. (1999). AdaCost: Misclassification costsensitive boosting. Proceedings of the Sixteenth International Conference on Machine Learning, 97-105. San Francisco: Morgan Kaufmann.
8. Japkowicz N. (2000), The class imbalance problem: Significance and strategies. In Proceedings of the International Conference on Artificial Intelligence, Las Vegas.
9. Japkowicz N. and Stephen, S. (2002), The Class Imbalance Problem: A Systematic Study Intelligent Data Analysis, Volume 6, Number 5.
10. Kotsiantis, S., Pierrakeas, C., and Pintelas, P., Preventing student dropout in distance learning systems using machine learning techniques, LNAI, Vol 2774, pp 267-274, 2003
11. Kotsiantis S., Kanellopoulos, D. Pintelas, P. (2006), Handling imbalanced datasets: A review, GESTS International Transactions on Computer Science and Engineering, Vol.30 (1), pp. 25-36.
12. Kubat, M., Holte, R. and Matwin, S. (1998), 'Machine Learning for the Detection of Oil Spills in Radar Images', Machine Learning, 30:195-215.
13. Ling, C., & Li, C. (1998). Data Mining for Direct Marketing Problems and Solutions. In Proceedings of the Fourth International Conference on Knowledge Discovery and Data Mining (KDD-98) New York, NY. AAAI Press.
14. Provost, F. and Fawcett, T. (2001). Robust Classification for Imprecise Environments", Machine Learning, 42, 203–231.
15. Quinlan J.R. (1993), C4.5: Programs for machine learning. Morgan Kaufmann, San Francisco.
16. Schapire R., Singer Y. and Singhal A. (1998). Boosting and Rochhio applied to text filtering. In SIGIR'98.
17. Witten Ian H. and Frank Eibe (2005) "Data Mining: Practical machine learning tools and techniques", 2nd Edition, Morgan Kaufmann, San Francisco, 2005.

Solving Traveling Salesman Problem Using Combinational Evolutionary Algorithm

Mohammad Reza Bonyadi[1], S.Mostafa Rahimi Azghadi[1] and Hamed Shah Hosseini[2]

1 Department of Electrical & Computer Engineering, Shahid Beheshti University, Tehran, Iran
{m_bonyadi, m_rahimi} @std.sbu.ac.ir
2 Department of Electrical & Computer Engineering, Shahid Beheshti University, Tehran, Iran
h_shahhosseini@sbu.ac.ir

Abstract. In this paper, we proposed a new method to solve TSP (Traveling Salesman Problem) based on evolutionary algorithms. This method can be used for related problems and we found out the new method can works properly in problems based on permutation. We compare our results by the previous algorithms and show that our algorithm needs less time in comparison with known algorithms and so efficient for such problems.

1 Introduction

It is natural to wonder whether all problems can be solved in polynomial time. The answer is no. For example, there are problems, such as Turing's famous "Halting Problem," that cannot be solved by any computer, no matter how much time is provided. There are also problems that can be solved, but not in time O(   ) for any constant k. Generally, we think of problems that are solvable by polynomial-time algorithms as being tractable, or easy, and problems that require super-polynomial time as being intractable, or hard.

There is an interesting class of problems, called the "NP-complete" problems, whose status is unknown. No polynomial-time algorithm has yet been discovered for an NP-complete problem, nor has anyone yet been able to prove that no polynomial-time algorithm can exist for any one of them. This so-called $P \neq NP$ question has been one of the deepest, most perplexing open research problems in theoretical computer science since it was first posed in 1971[1]. TSP is the problem in this class.

Please use the following format when citing this chapter:

Bonyadi, R. M., Azghadi, S. M. R., Hosseini, H., S., 2007, in IFIP International Federation for Information Processing, Volume 247, Artificial Intelligence and Innovations 2007: From Theory to Applications, eds. Boukis, C., Pnevmatikakis, L., Polymenakos, L., (Boston: Springer), pp. 37-44.

In other hand, in recent years, AI (artificial intelligent) and its searching algorithms becomes attracted. As an example, one approach that has been used in searching problems is Genetic Algorithm to search the space of problems and finding solutions. Nevertheless, these solutions have no guarantee to be the best [6].

Therefore, in this paper we attempt to use a combinational evolutionary algorithm to find the solutions of the TSP and show our algorithm can be used for finding better minimum cycles in the graph, in comparison to preceding algorithms.

2   Background Material

2.1   Traveling Salesman Problem (TSP)

Traveling sales man, is a famous problem that in this problem a person wants to visit all the cities exactly once in his region and back to the first city that ha started his traveling from, assumes that, he wants to minimize his tour value. This problem is a combinational minimization problem and has so many utilizations. The problem been analyzed using many algorithms like branch-and-bound, greedy searching algorithms etc. In recent years, the genetic algorithms been used for analyzing this problem widely [1].

We can assume this problem as an undirected graph problem. In this problem, we are searching for minimum path where visits all the nodes exactly once and finishes at the node start from that. Fig1 indicates an example with its optimal solution. A, B, C... are the cities and the numbers on the edges are the cost of links [1].

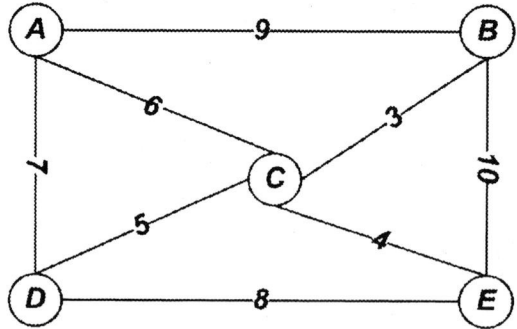

Fig 1 :The tour with A=>B =>C =>E =>D => (A) optimal tour

One way to indicate the solution of the problem is the sequence of the city names. We have to remove the last city from the sequence because it must be same as the first one. Note that for calculating the path value, we do not forget the last city. With indicating the solutions as the permutation of the cities, every city will come exactly once in the sequence. However, some permutations might not be the solution because the graph might not be the complete graph. We can solve this problem by assuming two nodes that not connected to each other, are connected by the edge that its value is infinite.

We can use a scale function to reach that. As an example consider the whole path value to be S, so we can use the simple function f(S) =S for minimization problem. We can use so many functions like f(S) =1/S or f(S) =1/(S^2) as the functions for maximization [2].

In the condition that our solutions are the permutation of integers, the simple crossover might cause the creating of invalid solutions, too. For example, the one point crossover in 4th place of two follows solutions:

ADEBC, AECDB

Can lead to create these two invalid solutions:

ADEDB, AECBC

We have to use the crossover that always leads to a permutation for solving this problem.

2.2 Partially Matched Crossover

We can use the modified crossover that always leads to a permutation of genes. This modified crossover called partially matched (PMX) crossover. All the problems that their solutions must be the permutations can use this crossover method. We introduce this operation in the following example:

Let

ADEBC, AECDB

be two solutions of the problem and we use the two point crossover in 3rd and 4th indices in the sequence. We call the substrings between crossover points as matching sections. The crossover operation have to change the substrings in the sequences (In this example (EB) from the first sequence and (CD) from second one). Symbol (E, C) shows Replacing E from the first sequence by C. Therefore, the symbol (B, D) shows replacing of fourth index from the first sequence with fourth of the second sequence. The next step of the PMX operation is replacing the elements of these pairs in each sequence. In this example, we have to change the place of E with C and B with D in each sequence. The result of (E, C) in first sequence is ADCBE and the result of (B, D) is ABCDE and the second sequence changes from AECDB to ABCDE and then to ACEBD. As it seems, the results are permutations and have no repetition. Fig 2 can help to understanding the PMX crossover.

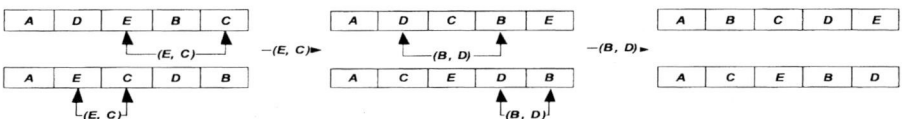

Fig 2: The PMX Crossover

The other GA operations don't need to change and can be used as the standard GA. Using the GA in combination with the local search algorithms can work better than standard algorithms.

2.3   Introduction to Swap Sequence

We show the swap operator as SO (i1, i2) and define it as follow:
In solution S, we change the place of i1 & i2 and we write as:

$$S'=S+SO (i1, i2)$$

As an example, consider S is a solution of a problem and:

$$S= (1, 3, 5, 2, 4)$$

So:

$$S'=S+SO(1,2)=(1,3,5,2,4)+SO(1,2)=(3,1,5,2,4)$$

2.4   Swap Sequence

The swap sequence is consisting of one or more swap operators.

$$SS = (SO1, SO2, SO3… SOn)$$

By applying SS to the solution, SO1 will works first, SO2 will work second and so on.

The different swap sequences might have the same effect on different solutions. We know these sequences as set of equivalent swap sequences. In this set, the basic swap operator is the element that has the minimum swap operators [5].

2.5   Creation of the basic Swap Sequences

Consider we have two solutions named A, B and we want to change B to A using some swap sequences:

$$SS=A-B -> A=B+SS$$

Consider:

$$A= (1, 2, 3, 4, 5), B = (2, 3, 1, 5, 4)$$

The first swap operator is:

$$SO1 (1, 3) -> B1 =B+SO1 = (1, 3, 2, 5, 4)$$

The next one is:

$$SO2 (2, 3) -> B2 =B1+SO2 = (1, 2, 3, 4, 5)$$

And the last one is SO (4, 5) and we reach A.
We can define the Move function as follow: with finding difference between two points A, B, we apply some swap operators of swap sequence on B randomly to reach the new solution [5].

3   Proposed algorithm

The proposed algorithm is an evolutionary algorithm where combined from GA idea and Shuffled Frog Leaping (SFL), Civilization and Society algorithms [4].
In each loop, like GA, the elements of production group perform the mutation or crossover in random order. Then for every element of the group, we call a local searching algorithm. Fig 3 indicates its pseudo code [1, 3].

The local search algorithm is the combinational algorithm from SFL and Civilization and Society algorithm. In this phase (Local search), first of all we create the population consisting of P elements. All P elements are same as each other. This is one of the main differences between the proposed algorithm and the SFL algorithm. In SFL, the elements that we perform searching on them are same as the reference set but in proposed algorithm, a population will consist of the same elements and after several loops, the element that has the best fitness, will be replaced by the main element and back to the reference population [4]. Fig.3 shows the local search pseudo code.

```
Pseudo code for a GA procedure
Begin;
 Generate  random  population  of  P  solutions
(chromosomes);
 For each individual i∈P: calculate fitness (i);
  For i=1 to number of generations;
   Randomly select an operation
   (crossover or mutation);
  If crossover
   Select two parents at random ia and ib;
   Generate an offspring ic=crossover(ia and ib);
  Else If mutation;
   Select one chromosome I at random;
   Generate an offspring ic=mutate(i);
  End if;
  Local Search(ic);
  Calculate the fitness of the offspring ic;
  If ic is better than the worst chromosome then
   replace the worst chromosome by ic;
  Next i;
 Check if termination = true;
End;
```

Fig 3: Genetic Algorithm pseudo code

Here we will have a glance look at the meaning of memeplexes. According to memetic theory, a **meme** (a unit of cultural information, cultural evolution or diffusion) propagates from one mind to another analogously to the way in which a gene propagates from one organism to another as a unit of genetic information and of biological evolution. Multiple memes may propagate as cooperative groups called *memeplexes* (meme complexes). For more information, see [7].

```
Pseudo code for local Search procedure
local Search(solution S)
Begin;
 Generate a population of P solutions equal to S;
 For each individual i∈P
  Assign a random swap sequence to i;
```

```
calculate fitness (i);
Divide P into m memeplexes at random;
For k=1 to number of iterations
  For each memeplexes, set best solution as leader
of memeplexes;
  Set best solution of community as community
leader;
  For each individual i€P
  if i is not a leader
    Move i → its group leader
  if i is a group leader
    Move i → the community leader
  End;
  Next k;
End;
```

Fig 4: Local search pseudo code

As an another difference between the proposed algorithm and SFL, we can say that in each loop in SFL, only the worst element in each group will be moved to its group leader. Therefore, if the solution, which implemented by that element, gave better result, the changes will be applied, and in other case, the solution will be moved to the best global solution. If the solution did not change or became worst, we apply a random solution. Nevertheless, in Civilization and Society Algorithm, in each loop, all the elements in similar groups, will move to their group leaders and the leaders will move to the population leader. We use the latter in our proposed approach.

Because the elements, which have been selected by local search, are same as each other, the convergence of population elements differs from the SFL and Civilization and society algorithms. Note that in Traveling Salesman Problem, it is not possible to choose a point as the solution on the line between two known solutions. Because it is not guaranteed that, the new solutions will have any link and relation to their parents. For simulation of moving the solutions close to each other, we use the swap sequence idea.

```
Pseudo code for a SFL procedure
Begin;
  Generate    random    population    of    P
solutions(frogs);
  For each individual i€P: calculate fitness (i);
  Sort the population P in descending order of their
fitness;
  Divide P into m memeplexes;
  For each memeplexes;
    Determine the best and worst frogs;
    Improve the worst frog position to its best
element;
```

```
    Repeat for a specific number of iterations;
End;
Combine the evolved memeplexes;
Sort the population P in descending order of their
fitness;
    Check if termination = true;
End;
```

Fig 5: SFL Algorithm pseudo code

```
Pseudo  code  for  Civilization  and  Society
Algorithm
Begin;
    Generate N individuals representing civilization
    Compute fitness;
    Create m clusters based on Euclidean distance
    Identify leader for each cluster
    For each cluster
        For each member I in cluster
            Move I → its leader
        Move leader of cluster → global leader
    End;
End;
```

Fig 6: CS Algorithm pseudo code

4 Experimental Results

The algorithms have tested on three inputs with 30, 89, and 929 points for 50 times. For the first case input, all the algorithms found the optimum solution and we perform our experiments on these algorithms in limited time (60 sec.). As we can see in Table1, in the TSP solved using standard GA with 30 cities, the average time for the implementations was 36 seconds and in 35 times the algorithm found the optimum path. We use our proposed combinational algorithm for solving the problem and the average time for the implementations was 2 seconds. Moreover, in 85% of solving the problems, our algorithm found the optimum path.

Table 1 : The results of 30 point graph for TSP

Algorithm	Time(Sec)	Success percentage
GA	36	70%
GA using SFL method	2	60%
GA using Proposed approach	2	85%

We authorized the algorithm to function in 10 min, then the inputs were 89 points for the first time and 929 points for the second time applied to algorithms and the results are listed in Table 2.

According to the explained algorithms, it seems that each of them have their advantages and disadvantages. Our proposed approach converges faster than the two other algorithms but it seems the local search in complex spaces may not be very efficient and its effects must be reduced proportional to time elapsing.

Table 1

Algorithm	Average path value for 80 point input(million)	Average path value for second input(million)
GA	26	19
GA using SFL method	19	20
GA using Proposed approach	14	18
Exact solution	10	13

References

1. Thomas H. Cormen Charles E. Leiserson Ronald L. Rivest ,"Introduction to Algorithms, " Second Edition Clifford Stein The MIT Press Cambridge , Massachusetts London, England McGraw-Hill Book Company
2. Mitchell Melanie , "An Introduction to Genetic Algorithms, " A Bradford Book The MIT Press, Cambridge, Massachusetts • London, England, fifth printing 1999
3. J.H. Holland, "Adaption in Natural and Artificial Systems, " University of Michigan Press, Ann Arbor (USA), 1975
4. Eusuff, M.M. and Lansey, K.E.,(2003). "Optimization of Water Distribution Network Design Using the Shuffled Frog Leaping Algorithm." Journal of Water Resources Planning and Management, ASCE, Vol. 129, No. 3, pp. 210-225
5. D.E.Knuth, "The Art of Computer Programming," Vol.3:sorting and Serching. Addison-Wesley, reading, MA, Second Edition, 1998, pp. 222-223
6. Stuart J. Russell and Peter Norvig, "Artificial Intelligence A Modern Approach, " 1995 by Prentice-Hall, Inc.
7. Richard Dawkins, "The Selfish Gene, " 1989 Oxford: Oxford University Press, ISBN 0-19-217773-7 page 192

Graph Based Workflow Validation

Anastasios Giouris and Manolis Wallace
Department of Computer Science,
University of Indianapolis Athens,
Ipitou 9, Syntagma, 10557, GREECE
http://cs.uindy.gr
cs@uindy.gr

Abstract. Content Management Systems in the field of content production and publishing need to monitor the progress of large numbers of simultaneously evolving workflows. In order to make such systems adaptive to the varying needs of their organizations, the utilization of a graphical editor for workflows has been proposed, thus generating the hazard of the specification of erroneous and invalid workflows. In this paper we provide a formal modeling for workflows and then, based on it, we explain how the validity of a simple workflow can be evaluated through the examination of the transitive closure of its graph. Continuing to the more general case, we develop a problem transformation methodology that allows for all workflows to be validated using a transitive closure examination approach. The Python implementation of our methodology is provided as is freely to all interested parties.

1 Introduction

Living in the information age, we are constantly faced with the need to be able to handle large amounts of content. Especially with the constant expansion of Web 2.0 type websites which are becoming increasingly popular along with which the content handled by such websites grows also.

In this direction, content management systems (CMSs) have been developed that undertake the burden of online monitoring of the managing process for large numbers of elements. Of course, in order for this managment to take place, detailed production workflows need to be defined in a formal and machine understandable way [1].

Please use the following format when citing this chapter:

Giouris, A., Wallace, M., 2007, in IFIP International Federation for Information Processing, Volume 247, Artificial Intelligence and Innovations 2007: From Theory to Applications, eds. Boukis, C., Pnevmatikakis, L., Polymenakos, L., (Boston: Springer), pp. 45-53.

Manually editing a workflow can become a cumbersome task and often the source of operational errors; it is not always easy for a human user to detect all possible deficiencies associated with a complex graphical workflow description and, consequently, problems in the specification of the workflow will reflect in the operation of the overall system. Therefore, what is needed is an automated tool that is able to inspect the manually provided workflow specifications and assess their validity [2,3].

In this paper, utilizing a graph-based model for workflows, we propose a transitivity based methodology for the validation of workflows. The structure of the paper is as follows: In section "Workflow graph model" we discuss workflows and present our graph based workflow model. In section "Workflow Validation" we present our methodology for automated validation of workflows and in section "Experimental results" we provide results from the experimental application of our approach. Finally, section "Conclusions" lists our concluding remarks.

2   Workflow graph model

A workflow can best be described as an outline of the path that needs to be followed in order for a task to be successfully completed. The specific path that is followed often determines not just the quality of the results, but also whether the task is ever completed or not [4,5].

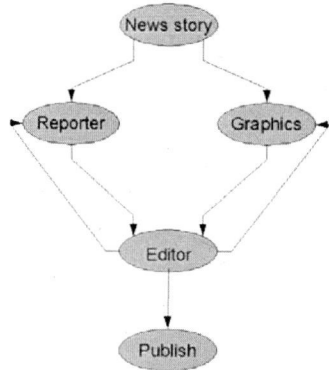

Fig. 1. An example of a workflow

Visually, a workflow can be thought of as a flowchart. From a mathematical point of view, it can be thought of as a Finite State Machine. But neither of these two views can exactly represent the complicated conditions a workflow requires, such as handling different and multiple inputs and outputs. Also, where in programming we consider the termination problem unsolvable, we wish to have an automated methodology that is able to determine whether a workflow specification will lead to successful completion of the task which it describes. Therefore, an alternative model is required for the representation of the workflow.

The following is a simplified real world graphical example of a workflow: in a moderated news portal environment that publishes edited versions of articles provided by users, each article submitted needs to be tracked though the process displayed in Fig 1. The article is first forwarded for both text proofs and graphics touch up. Either of these two sub-processes could develop into a longer sequence of edit-review iterations, until the desired quality has been reached. Finally, when the editor has approved both the textual and graphical part of the article, it can be published. Clearly, the real life version of this workflow is even more complex, also describing the editor's ability to totally reject the article, re-assign it to different proofreaders or graphics artists, merging it with other articles, associating it with a specific section of the portal, requesting changes to its length and so on.

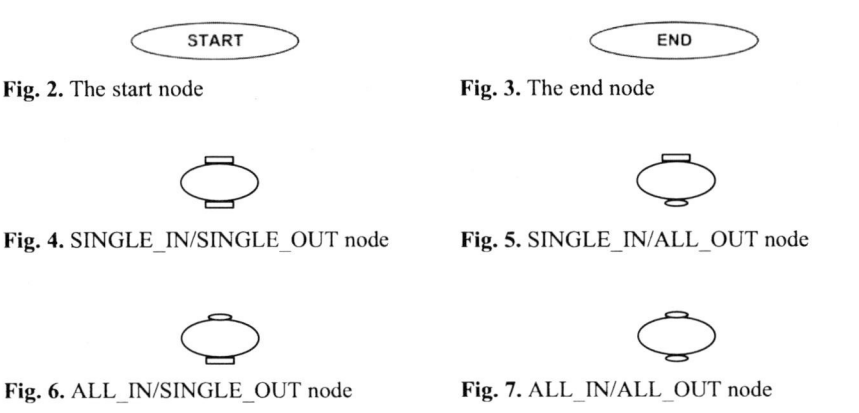

Fig. 2. The start node   **Fig. 3.** The end node

Fig. 4. SINGLE_IN/SINGLE_OUT node   **Fig. 5.** SINGLE_IN/ALL_OUT node

Fig. 6. ALL_IN/SINGLE_OUT node   **Fig. 7.** ALL_IN/ALL_OUT node

In order to construct a formal model for the workflow presented above we will extend on the notion of a graph by providing definitions for six different types of graph vertices, as explained in the following:

- The start of the process is a special node in the graph, as all paths originate there. We depict the start using the type of node presented in Fig. 2.
- The end of the process is also important as it automatically signifies the end of the task. This is depicted with the type of node presented in Fig. 3.
- Proof readers, right after the article has been assigned to them, as well as when the editor returns the article for further proofing, need to work on the document. Therefore we have a node with multiple inputs either of which may activate the node. This is called a SINGLE_IN node and is depicted with a rectangle in the input area, as shown in Fig. 4 and Fig 5.
- The editor, when receiving proofs from the proof readers, has the option to either accept the proofed article or return it for further proofing. Therefore we have a node with multiple outputs only one of which is activated in each case. This is called a SINGLE_OUT node and is depicted with a rectangle in the output area, as shown in Fig. 4 and Fig. 6.

- In order for the overall article to be accepted, both the text and the graphics need to be approved by the editor. This operation corresponds to a multiple input node for which all of the inputs are required for activation. This is called an ALL_IN node and is depicted with an oval in the input area, as shown in Fig. 6 and Fig. 7.
- When an article has been received it needs to be forwarded to both proof readers and graphics artists. This corresponds to a multiple output node that activates all of its outputs concurrently. This is called an ALL_OUT node and is depicted with an oval in the output area, as shown in Fig. 5 and Fig. 7.

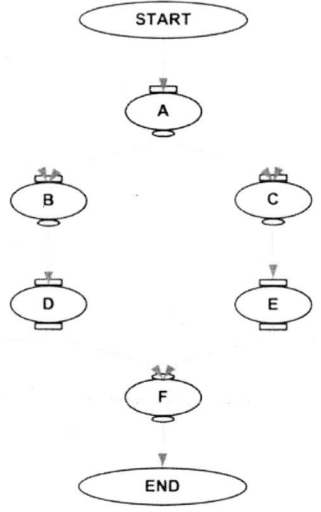

Fig. 8. The graph for the workflow of the example

Using the above, the workflow of the example is modeled as shown in Fig. 8. Of course, in cases where only one input or only one output is connected to a node, there is more than one type of node that can be utilized. For reasons that will become obvious in the following section where the workflow validation methodology will be presented, SINGLE_IN and ALL_OUT are preferred options for the nodes and are always preferred when it does not make any difference.

3   Workflow validation

When a user is allowed to specify workflows in a graphical manner, by providing graphs such as the one depicted in Fig. 8 (or much more complex) using a graphical editing tool, there is always the possibility of a logical error. Therefore, a methodology needs to be developed for the identification of such erroneous cases. In the following we explain how the inspection of the transitive closure of workflow graphs can be utilized to automate the process.

2.1 SINGLE_IN/ALL_OUT case

Having a workflow consisting of nodes of which any input can activate a node and nodes that activate all of their outputs, a simple connectivity test can assure that the workflow is correct. Since the mathematical counterpart of network connectivity is transitivity of relations, we will utilize the operation of transitive closure in order to evaluate the validity of workflows.

In order to best demonstrate this we present the example workflows of Fig 9. In Table 1 we present the matrix representations of the graphs of Fig. 9. The transitive closure of these matrices is presented in Table 2. The connectivity checks that need to be made are:

- do all states lead to successful completion of the task?
- are all states meaningful?

In order to assess whether a state leads to the completion of the task we need to assess whether it leads to the end state. Therefore, we require that all nodes lead to the end node, i.e. that the last column in the transitive closure matrix is filled with ones except for the last row For example, we can see in the transitive closure of the first graph that node C does not lead to completion.

In order to assess whether a state is meaningful we need to assess whether it can be reached. Therefore, we require that all nodes are subsquent to the start node, i.e. that the first row in the transitive closure matrix is filled with ones (first position excluded). For example, we can see in the transitive closure of the second graph that node C is not reachable.

Table 1. Matrix representations of Fig 9. graphs

	START	A	B	C	END			START	A	B	C	END
START	0	1	0	0	0	START	0	1	0	0	0
A	0	0	1	1	0	A	0	0	1	0	0
B	0	0	0	0	1	B	0	0	0	0	1
C	0	0	0	0	0	C	0	0	0	0	1
END	0	0	0	0	0	END	0	0	0	0	0

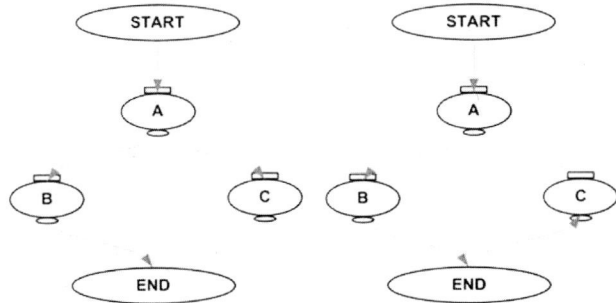

Fig. 9. SINGLE_IN/ALL_OUT checks

Table 2. Transitive closure of the two matrices

	START	A	B	C	END		START	A	B	C	END
START	0	1	1	1	1	START	0	1	1	0	1
A	0	0	1	1	1	A	0	0	1	0	1
B	0	0	0	0	1	B	0	0	0	0	1
C	0	0	0	0	0	C	0	0	0	0	1
END	0	0	0	0	0	END	0	0	0	0	0

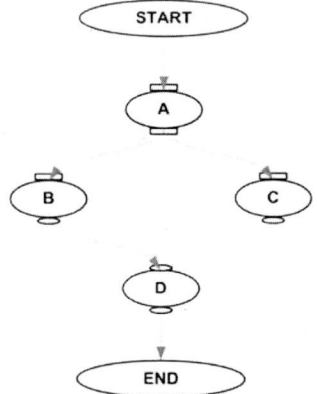

Fig. 10. An example including SINGLE_OUT and ALL_IN graphs

2.2 SINGLE_OUT and ALL_IN cases

When not all nodes in the workflow are of the SINGLE_IN/ALL_OUT type a simple transitive closure is not enough to ensure validity. See for example the workflow graph of Fig. 10. Although a transitivity check would indicate that there is nothing wrong with this workflow, a more careful examination reveals that this workflow will never lead to a successful completion of its task. Due to the fact that both nodes B and C are required for the activation of node D but only one of them may be activated by node A.

Since the transitive closure methodology can only handle correctly the case of SINGLE_IN/ALL_OUT nodes, we need to transform the workflow graphs of the more general cases to graphs comprising only SINGLE_IN/ALL_OUT nodes, so that the methodology can be applied.

As far as the SINGLE_OUT nodes are concerned, these are handled by creating multiple copies of the graph; one for each activated output. In order for the workflow to be validated, each node needs to be found to be meaningful on at least one graph and leading to the end on at least one graph; there is no need for these to happen on the same graph.

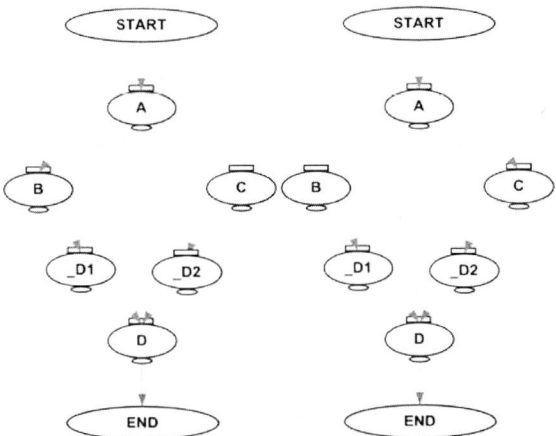

Fig. 11. The transformed multiple graph problem

When it comes to ALL_IN nodes, we need to have a means of making sure that all possible inputs are activated at the same time. In order to avoid confusions in the case of multiple output and multiple input nodes that are linked together in more than one ways, we utilize the following approach: Extra "dummy" nodes are added to the graph, one for each required input of an ALL_IN node. The node is found to be meaningful only if all of the dummy nodes associated with it are activated at the same time, i.e. in the same transitive closure graph.

The validation of the workflow presented in Fig. 10 is transformed into the multiple graph validation problem presented in Fig 11. In the transitive closure of the two graphs (Table 3) we can see that although all nodes are found to be reasonable and terminating in at least one of the two matrices, the two dummy nodes are not activated simultaneously on either of the two examined instances of the problem. Therefore, we correctly conclude that there is a problem with the activation of node D, and thus the workflow of our example is not validated.

4   Experimental results

The methodology presented in this paper has been coded using the Python programming language.Input, in the current stage of the implementation, is provided in the form of text files, such as the one presented bellow:

```
name=S;connections=A;intype=none;outype=ALL_OUT;
name=A;connections=B,C;intype=SINGLE_IN;outype=SINGLE_OUT;
name=B;connections=D;intype=SINGLE_IN;outype=ALL_OUT;
name=C;connections=D;intype=SINGLE_IN;outype=ALL_OUT;
name=D;connections=nE;intype=ALL_IN;outype=ALL_OUT;
name=E;connections=none;intype=SINGLE_IN;outype=null;
```

Table 3. Transitive closures for the multiple graph problem

	START	A	B	C	D1	D2	D	END
START	0	1	1	0	1	0	1	1
A	0	0	1	0	1	0	1	1
B	0	0	0	0	1	0	1	1
C	0	0	0	0	0	1	1	1
_D1	0	0	0	0	0	0	1	1
_D2	0	0	0	0	0	0	1	1
D	0	0	0	0	0	0	0	1
END	0	0	0	0	0	0	0	0

	START	A	B	C	D1	D2	D	END
START	0	1	0	1	0	1	1	1
A	0	0	0	1	0	1	1	1
B	0	0	0	0	1	0	1	1
C	0	0	0	0	0	1	1	1
_D1	0	0	0	0	0	0	1	1
_D2	0	0	0	0	0	0	1	1
D	0	0	0	0	0	0	0	1
END	0	0	0	0	0	0	0	0

The workflow described in this example is actually the workflow presented in Fig. 10. The output of the module for this example is provided bellow.

```
@!ERROR: ALL_IN check failed for D
@!The Workflow is not Valid
```

Using another sample workflow with the following properties our validator produces correct results

```
name=S;connections=A;intype=none;outype=ALL_OUT;
name=A;connections=B,C;intype=SINGLE_IN;outype=ALL_OUT;
name=B;connections=D,E;intype=SINGLE_IN;outype=SINGLE_OUT;
name=C;connections=F;intype=SINGLE_IN;outype=ALL_OUT;
name=D;connections=H;intype=SINGLE_IN;outype=ALL_OUT;
name=H;connections=G;intype=SINGLE_IN;outype=SINGLE_OUT;
name=F;connections=G,E;intype=ALL_IN;outype=SINGLE_OUT;
name=G;connections=E;intype=ALL_IN;outype=SINGLE_OUT;
name=E;connections=none;intype=SINGLE_IN;outype=ALL_OUT;
```

Producing the following output

```
@!ERROR: ALL_IN check failed for G Possible Workflow #0
@! Workflow is not valid
```

By changing the output type of nodes F and B to ALL_OUT, eliminating the problem of G not being activated in the previous cases, the validator produces the following result guarantying us a valid workflow.

@! Workflow is valid

5   Conclusions

In this paper we have focused on the problem of automatic workflow validation. As we have explained, the validation of workflows can be a tricky task, due to the fact that different types of nodes can be associated with a workflow, some of which are quite difficult to handle.

After providing a formal model for workflows and following a transitive closure based approach, we have provided a methodology for the automated validation of workflows comprising SINGLE_IN/ALL_OUT nodes. Then, through problem transformation, we explained how the same methodology can be utilized to also treat the more general cases. The proposed methodology has been tested theoretically, but also practically through implementation into a working stand-alone module.

What remains to be done is the integration of the developed module and methodology with the graphical workflow editor. This will also open the way for real life application and testing under heavier loads. One point that is expected to be of augmented interest is that of the operation of transitive closure, as the complexity of the conventional approach is too high to consider for real time operation under heavy load. In this direction, novel transitive closure approaches can be applied [6,7], taking advantage the sparse nature of the workflow graphs.

References

1.   A. P. Barros, A. H. M. ter Hofstede, Towards the construction of workflow-suitable conceptual modelling techniques, Information Systems Journal 8 (4), 313–337, 1998.
2.   W. M. P. van der Aalst, A. H. M. ter Hofstede, B. Kiepuszewski and A. P. Barros, Workflow Patterns, Distributed and Parallel Databases 14(1), pp. 5-51, 2004.
3.   W. M. P. van der Aalst, M. Weske, G. Wirtz, Advanced topics in workflow management: issues, requirements, and solutions, Journal of Integrated Design and Process Science 7(3), 2003.
4.   M. M. Compton, S. Wolfe, Intelligent validation and routing of electronic forms in adistributed workflow environment, Proceedings of the Tenth Conference on Artificial Intelligence for Applications, 1994.
5.   S. Sadiq, M. Orlowska, W. Sadiq, C. Foulger, Data flow and validation in workflow modeling, Proceedings of the 15th Australasian database conference, 2004.
6.   M. Wallace, S. Kollias, Two Algorithms For Fast Incremental Transitive Closure Of Sparse Fuzzy Binary Relations, International Journal of Computational Methods, in press.
7.   M. Wallace, Y. Avrithis, S. Kollias, Computationally efficient sup-t transitive closure for sparse fuzzy binary relations, Fuzzy Sets and Systems 157(3), pp. 341-372, 2006.

Section 2

Intelligent Internet Systems: Emerging Technologies and Applications

Resource sharing in multi-agent systems through multi-stage negotiation

Panos Alexopoulos

IMC Research,
Fokidos 47, Athens, 11527,Greece
palexopoulos@imc.com.gr

Abstract. In this paper we try to solve the Temporal Resource Reallocation Problem (TRR-P) in multi-agent systems by having the agents negotiate periods of time during which they can have use of resources. Our work is based on and extends a previous work in which a multi-stage negotiation framework that defines the way agents negotiate over resources and time is defined. The approach in this framework suggests that the negotiating agents use a sequence of stages, each characterized by an increased chance of success and amount of exchanged information. In the same work two negotiation stages are defined each of which solves a specific range of TRR-P instances. In this paper we propose a third negotiation stage which is more sophisticated than the first two and is able to solve a larger range of TRR-P instances.

1 Introduction

Temporal Resource Reallocation Problem (TRR-P) is a problem which arises when agents own resources for specific periods of time and have activities that need to carry out within other specific time periods which might or might not coincide with the first ones. In the latter case, agents have to exchange resources in order to achieve a resource distribution which will allow them to perform their activities within their specified time-windows. For example, an agent x might own a resource r from time 1 to 10 but need it from time 12 to 15. If another agent y owns r at this interval and does not need it, then y can give r to x. If y, on the other hand, needs r from time 12 to 15, then it cannot give r to x unless it manages to reschedule its activity.

In this paper we attempt to solve TRR-P through a multi-stage negotiation process that is described in [1]. In that paper, two negotiation stages are defined each of which consists of a protocol and a policy according to which agents engage themselves into dialogues. The higher a stage is, the higher is the amount of the exchanged information and the likelihood that a dialogue will be successful. In this paper we extend the negotiating framework of [1] by proposing a third negotiation stage which is more complicated compared to the existing stages but manages to solve a larger range of TRR-P instances. The structure of the rest paper is as follows: The next section describes the negotiation framework as suggested in [1] focusing on the agent representation schema and the

Please use the following format when citing this chapter:

Alexopoulos, P., 2007, in IFIP International Federation for Information Processing, Volume 247, Artificial Intelligence and Innovations 2007: From Theory to Applications, eds. Boukis, C., Pnevmatikakis, L., Polymenakos, L., (Boston: Springer), pp. 57-64.

negotiation language. In section three we describe the two existing stages of the multi-stage negotiation process defined in [1] and we indicate their merits and limitations in solving the TRR-P problem. Finally, in section four we present our proposed third stage and we define the range of problems it can solve. It should be noted that due to space limitations the exact semantics of the stages' policies are omitted.

2 Negotiation Framework

2.1 Agent Representation

According to [1] the knowledge of an agent is represented as a tuple $< B, R, I, D, G >$ where B is the set of the agent's beliefs (domain-dependent beliefs such as information about itself and the other agents as well as domain-independent beliefs such as dialogue policies), R contains the resources the agent owns before the dialogue starts, I is the agent's current intention (i.e. the plan which will enable the agent to achieve its goal, the agent's available resources and the resources which he needs in order to execute the plan), D contains the current dialogue store (i.e. past dialogue performatives) and G is the agent's goal.

Agent intentions are sets of activities. Each activity is represented as a tuple $< a, R_a, D_a, Ts_a, Te_a >$. This representation denotes that an activity a requires a resource R_a, has duration D_a, its earliest start time is Ts_a and its latest end time is Te_a. Furthermore, the agent's knowledge includes a (possibly empty) concrete schedule $\widehat{I}$ for activities represented as $< a, t_s, t_e >$ where $t_e - t_s = D_a$, $t_s \geq Ts_a$ and $t_e \leq Te_a$.

The concrete schedule practically indicates the time interval during which the agent has decided to carry out its activity and it is vital for the agent's request generation mechanism. The reason is that it helps the agent determine what resources to ask from the other agents and for how long. The activity schedule, on the other hand, determines the range of the concrete schedules that the agent can adopt. That is useful when the agent reasons about how to react to another agent's request. For example, in the first stage defined in [1] the agent is willing to change its concrete schedule in order to be able to accept an incoming request. Whether this is possible depends on its activity schedule.

2.2 Negotiation Language

The negotiation language of the framework in [1] defines the *primitives (performatives)* that all negotiating agents use. These dialogue performatives are of the form $tell(X, Y, Move, D, T)$ where X and Y are the sending and receiving agents respectively, T is the time of the performative utterance and *Move* is a *dialogue move*. Allowed dialogue moves are:

- $tell(x, y, request(give(r, (T_s, T_e))), D, T)$: Agent x requests a resource r from agent y for the time interval (T_s, T_e).
- $tell(x, y, accept(request(give(r, (T_s, T_e)))), D, T)$: Agent x accepts y's request.
- $tell(x, y, refuse(request(give(r, (T_s, T_e)))), D, T)$: Agent x denies y's request.
- $tell(x, y, promise(r, (T'_s, T'_e), (T_s, T_e))), D, T)$: Agent x promises to agent y that he shall give him r for the interval (T_s, T_e) if he gives him r for the interval (T'_s, T'_e)".
- $tell(x, y, accept(promise(r, (T'_s, T'_e), (T_s, T_e))), D, T))$: Agent x accepts the exchange proposed by y.
- $tell(x, y, change(promise(r, (T'_s, T'_e), (T_s, T_e))), D, T))$: Agent x asks from agent y to propose a deal different that the one already proposed.

Finally, D is the dialogue in which the dialogue move belongs. Each time a dialogue performative is uttered, it is recorded on a blackboard *(dialogue store)* which is shared amongst the agents. This store grows monotonically as a dialogue takes place and it is reset when the dialogue ends.

3 Existing Negotiation Stages

A negotiation stage consists of a **protocol**, namely a set of rules to which the negotiating agents conform and a **policy**, namely a set of rules that the agents use for generating dialogue locutions. It is also characterized by the amount of information that the agents need to exchange in order to reach an agreement. The approach in [1] suggests that the negotiating agents use a sequence of stages, each characterized by an increased chance of success and an increased amount of exchanged information. If a stage fails to produce an agreement, then the agents adopt the next stage in the sequence.

The first negotiation stage defined in [1] conforms to the protocol depicted in figure 1. In this stage, an agent accepts a request for a resource r either if it doesn't intend to use r during the requested interval or if it can change its activity schedule so that it doesn't need r in that interval.

The dialogues that can be generated by conforming to the protocol of figure 1 have a fixed number of steps which means that they always terminate. The range of allocation problems that can be solved by the second stage is defined as follows: if there exists a time window in which an agent x needs a resource r and another agent y has this resource available in that window then the stage's policy can generate a dialogue which solves x's reallocation problem about r.

A case in which Stage 1 fails to solve the reallocation problem is when the initial resource assignment is the following: $I_y = \{< a, r, 5, 10, 20 >\}$, $I_x = \{< b, r, 5, 10, 15 >\}$, $R_y = \{have(r, 10, 15))\}$, $R_x = \{have(r, 15, 20))\}$. It is obvious that y cannot give r to x since it won't be able to carry out activity a.

With such cases deals the second negotiation stage which tries to solve a greater range of problems than the first one by allowing a more elaborate interaction between the agents. This stage's protocol is depicted in figure 2. This stage is different from stage 1 in that the agent that receives a request can

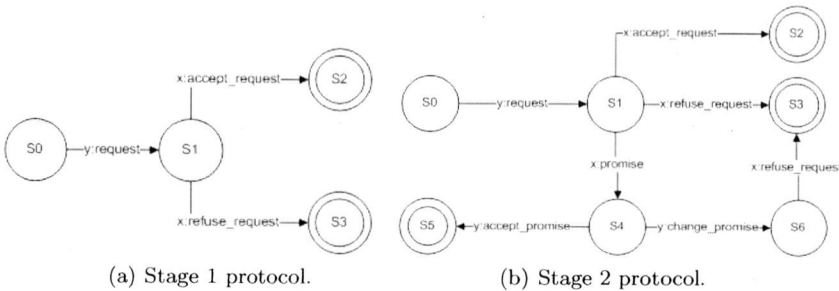

(a) Stage 1 protocol.   (b) Stage 2 protocol.

accept it or deny it or, additionally, propose a deal. The requester can either accept the deal or reject it.

Considering the example that stage 1 could not solve, stage 2 solves it through the following dialogue:

– $tell(x, y, request(give(r, (10, 15))), d(2), 1)$
– $tell(y, x, promise(r, (15, 20), (10, 15))), d(2), 2)$
– $tell(y, x, accept(promise(r, (15, 20), (10, 15)))), d(2), 3)$

As it can be inferred by the protocol of stage 2, dialogues might never terminate. Termination is ensured by making the dialogue terminate after a certain time T_{max} and by not allowing repetition of dialogue moves. The range of problems that are solved by stage 2 is defined by the following theorem:

Theorem: If a system consists of two agents x,y, each having an initial resource assignment, then for all system resources r, all activities a and b , all times τ and all intervals $[T_s, T_e]$ such that $K_{x,\tau} \vdash miss(r, (T_s, T_e), a) \wedge K_{y,\tau} \vdash need(r, (T_s, T_e), b) \wedge \exists [T'_s, T'_e]$ such that $K_{y,\tau} \cup \{give\_away(r, (T_s, T_e)), obtain(r, (T'_s, T'_e))\} \vdash feasible(b, (T''_s, T''_e))$ for some $[T''_s, T''_e]$, there exists a dialogue d, induced by the policy of Stage 2, starting at time τ and ending at time τ' such that $K_{x,\tau'} \vdash need(r, (T_s, T_e), a, \tau') \wedge K_{y,\tau'} \vdash indiff(r, (T_s, T_e))$.

The symbol $K_{x,\tau'}$ denotes the agent x's knowledge at time τ. The predicate **miss** denotes the agent's lack of a required resource in a given interval, **need** that the agent cannot give away a resource for a given interval and **feasible** his ability to perform an activity during a given interval.

The above theorem practically says that if agent x can propose y an alternative time interval during which y can carry out his activity (by x giving y resource r), then y will change its schedule and will give resource r to x. Thus the allocation problem is solved by this exchange of resource r.

However, stage 2 doesn't cover the case in which more than one exchange is required. For example, if the resource and activity assignment is as follows: $I_y = \{< a, r, 2, 10, 15 >, < c, r, 2, 15, 20 >\}, I_x = \{< b, r, 5, 10, 20 >\}, R_y =$

$\{have(r, 13, 17))\}$, $R_x = \{have(r, 10, 13)), have(r, 17, 20))\}$ then x will try to get r from y either for the period $[13,15]$ or period $[15,17]$. In the first case y will answer by asking r either for the period $[10,12]$ or $[11,13]$ neither of which makes x's activity b feasible. The same happens if x asks r for period $[15,17]$ so there is no dialogue that can lead to a solution.

4 Stage 3

4.1 General description

Stage 2 cannot solve problems where more than one exchange is required and the reason is that in a dialogue, only one of the agents makes the promises while the other merely accepts or rejects them. For tackling that we propose stage 3 in which we allow the agents to respond to promises with complementary promises that extend previous promises. For example, in the dialogue

- $tell(x, y, request(give(r, (13, 15))), d(3), 1)$
- $tell(y, x, promise(r, (10, 12), (13, 15)), d(3), 2)$
- $tell(x, y, promise(r, (15, 17), (10, 12)), d(3), 3)$

agent x responds to y's promise with another promise which practically says: "I will give you the resource r for the interval (10,12) if you give me r for the interval (15,17) and of course for the interval (13,15) as you have already promised".

Hence each new promise extends the previous one and allows to reach agreements in which more than one exchange of a resource is required. For example, the problem that stage 2 could not solve $I_y = \{< a, r, 2, 10, 15 > , < c, r, 2, 15, 20 >\}$, $I_x = \{< b, r, 5, 10, 20 >\}$, $R_y = \{have(r, 13, 17))\}$, $R_x = \{have(r, 10, 13)), have(r, 17, 20))\}$ can be solved by stage 3 through the following dialogue:

- $tell(x, y, request(give(r, (13, 15))), d(3), 1)$
- $tell(y, x, promise(r, (10, 12), (13, 15)), d(3), 2)$
- $tell(x, y, promise(r, (15, 17), (10, 12)), d(3), 3)$
- $tell(y, x, promise(r, (18, 20), (15, 17)), d(3), 4)$
- $tell(x, y, accept(promise(r, (18, 20), (15, 17)), d(3), 5))$

The result of this dialogue is that agent x obtains r for the intervals (13,15) and (15,17) and agent y for the intervals (10,12) and (18,20). After these exchanges both agents can carry out their activities, x in the interval (13,17) and y in the intervals (10,12) and (18,20).

A sequence of promises stops when an agent accepts the last promise or when it cannot make another promise. In the latter case, this agent asks the other agent to change its latest promise. If the other agent cannot make another promise then it asks the first agent to change its previous promise. Thus, the request for change propagates backwards until the initial promise is reached.

4.2 Stage Policy

The agent policy can be represented by 15 move generation rules. The first rule suggests that if an agent receives a request for a resource, has the resource during the requested interval and can give it away (either because he doesn't need it or because he can change his schedule) then he accepts the request. The second rule suggests that if the agent doesn't have at all the requested resource then he refuses the request. The third rule is applicable when the agent has the resource, needs it and there is an exchange that that he could suggest in order to carry out his activity in during another time interval. In such a case he makes a promise to the other agent. Rule 4 is for the exact opposite situation, namely when the agent cannot find a valid deal to suggest and consequently refuses the request.

Rules 5 to 7 are applicable when an agent receives a promise in a dialogue that has been initiated by a request made by itself. In order to evaluate this promise, the agent recalls all the previous promises related to this promise and checks whether the resource exchange that they suggest makes its activity feasible. If that's the case then it accepts the promise otherwise it tries to find a new time interval to use for a new promise. If it cannot find such an interval then it asks from the other agent to change its promise.

Rules 8 to 10 are applicable when an agent receives a promise in a dialogue that has been initiated by a request made by the other agent. In order to evaluate this promise, the agent recalls all the previous promises related to this promise and checks whether the resource exchange that they suggest makes any of its activities not feasible. If that's not the case then it accepts the promise otherwise it tries to find a new time interval to use for a new promise. If it cannot find such an interval then it asks from the other agent to change its promise.

Rules 11 to 12 are applicable when an agent receives a change_promise message in a dialogue that has been initiated by a request made by itself. The agent recalls all the previous promises related to this promise and tries to find a new time interval to use for a new promise. If it cannot find such an interval then it asks from the other agent to change its promise.

Finally, rules 13 to 15 are applicable when an agent receives a change_promise message in a dialogue that has been initiated by a request made by the other agent. The agent recalls all the previous promises related to this promise and tries to find a new time interval to use for a new promise. If it cannot find such an interval then it asks from the other agent to change its promise. If there is no such promise then it refuses the other agent's request.

4.3 Stage Properties

The dialogues that can be generated by stage 3 conform to the protocol of figure 3. As in stage 2 termination is ensured by making the dialogue terminate after a certain time T_{max} and by not allowing repetition of dialogue moves. The range

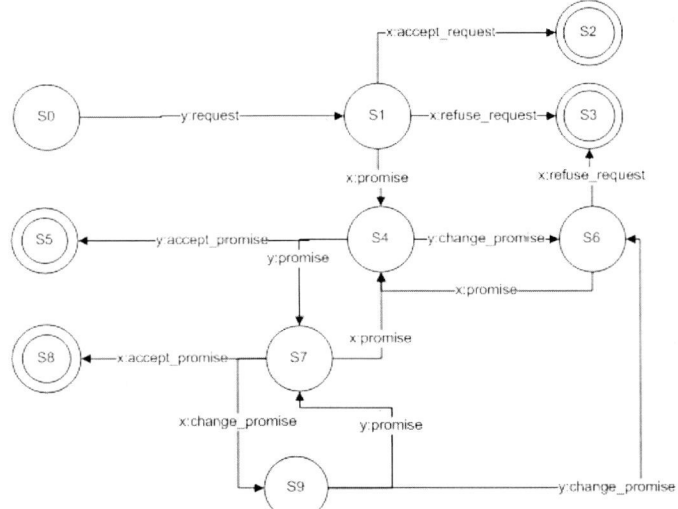

Fig. 1. Stage 3 protocol.

of allocation problems that can be solved by the third stage is defined by the following theorem:

Theorem: If a system consists of two agents x,y then for all system resources r, all activities a assigned to x, all times τ and all intervals $[T_s, T_e]$ such that

$$K_{x,\tau} \vdash miss(r, (T_s, T_e), a) \wedge K_{y,\tau} \vdash need(r, (T_s, T_e), b) \wedge ($$
$$\exists [T_{s1}, T_{e1}, T_{s2}, T_{e2}, ..., T_{s(2k+1)}, T_{e(2k+1)}], [a_1, a_2, ..., a_k], \ k \in N, \ |$$
$$need(r, (T_{s2}, T_{e2}), a_1) \wedge \ need(r, (T_{s4}, T_{e4}), a_2) \wedge, ..., \wedge need(r, (T_{s2k}, T_{e2k}), a_k) \wedge$$
$$K_{y,T} \ \cup \ \{give\_away(r, (T_s, T_e)), obtain(r, (T_{s1}, T_{e1})), \{give\_away(r, (T_{s2}, T_{e2})),$$
$$obtain(r, (T_{s3}, T_{e3})), ..., give\_away(r, (T_{s2k}, T_{e2k})), obtain(r, (T_{s(2k+1)}, T_{e(2k+1)}))\}$$
$$\vdash \qquad feasible(b, (T_{s'}, T_{e'})) \qquad \wedge \qquad feasible(a_1, (T_{s1'}, T_{e1'})) \qquad \wedge$$
$$feasible(a_2, (T_{s2'}, T_{e2'})) \wedge, ..., \wedge feasible(a_k, (T_{sk'}, T_{ek'})) \vee$$
$$\exists [T_{s1}, T_{e1}, T_{s2}, T_{e2}, ..., T_{s(2k)}, T_{e(2k)}], [a_1, a_2, ..., a_{k-1}], \ k \in N, \ |$$
$$need(r, (T_{s2}, T_{e2}), a_1) \wedge need(r, (T_{s4}, T_{e4}), a_2) \wedge, ..., \wedge$$
$$need(r, (T_{s(2k-2)}, T_{e(2k-2)}), a_{k-1}) \qquad \wedge \qquad K_{y,T} \qquad \cup$$
$$\{give\_away(r, (T_s, T_e)), obtain(r, (T_{s1}, T_{e1})), \{give\_away(r, (T_{s2}, T_{e2})),$$
$$obtain(r, (T_{s3}, T_{e3})), ..., give\_away(r, (T_{s2k}, T_{e2k}))\}$$
$$\vdash \qquad feasible(b, (T_{s'}, T_{e'})) \qquad \wedge \qquad feasible(a_1, (T_{s1'}, T_{e1'})) \qquad \wedge$$
$$feasible(a_2, (T_{s2'}, T_{e2'})) \wedge, ..., \wedge$$
$$feasible(a_{k-1}, (T_{s(k-1)'}, T_{e(k-1)'})))$$

for   some $(T_{s'}, T_{e'}, T_{s1'}, T_{e1'}, ...,$ $T_{sk'}, T_{ek'})$ or
$(T_{s'}, T_{e'}, T_{s1'}, T_{e1'}, ..., T_{s(k-1)'}, T_{e(k-1)'})$, there exists a dialogue d induced
by the policy of stage 3, starting at time τ and ending at time τ' such that
$K_{x,\tau'} \vdash need(r, (T_s, T_e), a, \tau') \wedge K_{y,\tau'} \vdash indiff(r, (T_s, T_e))$.

The intuitive meaning of this theorem is that if an agent x misses a resource
r for an activity a and another agent y needs r for some activity b and there is a
set of time intervals whose sequential exchange between x and y makes feasible
x's activity a, y's activity b and all y's activities whose feasibility might be
disturbed by some step of the exchange sequence, then there exists a dialogue
d induced by the policy of stage 3 that generates this exchange sequence and
results in x acquiring the missing resource with y not needing it anymore.

5 Conclusions

In this paper we presented an approach in solving the Temporal Resource Reallocation Problem (TRR-P) in multi-agent systems through multi-stage negotiation. Our work extended the negotiation framework defined in [1] by proposing
a third negotiation stage that overcomes the limitations of the two existing
ones and solves a larger variety of TRR-P instances. The key enabler of this
advanced effectiveness was our allowing the agents to exchange sequences of
complementary promises and to achieve thus more complex resource exchange
deals.

Our third stage comprised a protocol to which the dialogues generated by
the stage conform and a policy the agents should follow in order to implement
this protocol.The semantic representation of the policy was omitted due to space
limitations.

Our current work focuses in the development on a variation of the multi-
stage negotiation framework in which agents negotiate not only over resources
but also over tasks. Another dimension we also examine is negotiation over
divisible resources.

References

1. Fariba Sadri, Francesca Toni, Paolo Torroni: Minimally intrusive negotiating
   agents for resource sharing. IJCAI 2003: 796-804
2. Sadri, F.,Toni, F. & Torroni, A multi-stage negotiation architecture for sharing resources amongst logic-based agents. Department of Electronics, Computer
   Science, an Systems, University of Bologna, Italy. DEIS Technical Report DEIS-
   LIA-02-008, Universita di Bologna, LIA Series No 61, November 2002 (21 pages).

Increasing interactivity in IPTV using MPEG-21 descriptors

Christos-Nikolaos Anagnostopoulos[1], George Tsekouras[1] , Damianos Gavalas[1], Daphne Economou[1] and Ioannis Psoroulas[2]

1 University of the Aegean, Cultural Technology and Communication Dpt., 5 Sapfous Str., Mytilene, Greece, 81100,
{canag,gtsek,dgavalas.d.economou}@ct.aegean.gr
2 National Technical University of Athens, Electrical and Computer Engineering Dpt., NTUA Campus, Athens, Greece
psoroulas@telecom.ntua.gr

Abstract. This paper introduces a novel approach for authoring a diversity of multimedia resources (audio, video, text, images, etc). An authoring tool (Developer21) supporting a metadata model according MPEG-21 XML schema files is described. The main scope of Developer21 is to increase interactivity resulting from the use of metadata in several broadcast scenarios in interactive or IP television. In addition to basic functionalities (editing and enrichment of audiovisual contents), innovative content management functionalities of the Developer21 are briefly presented. As the focus of this paper was to provide a brief description of a novel authoring tool for metadata and descriptor management, only core functionalities are presented.

1 Introduction

The number of available digital contents is increasing over Internet and broadcast networks. Such a quantity of documents requires new ways to handle them. Besides, new services need tools to describe and organize these documents in an efficient and extensible way. These issues make metadata an interesting subject of research. Metadata are "information about data" and can include characteristics about the data such as the content, accuracy, reliability and the source. Metadata provide the mechanism to describe data in a consistent form which allows users to gain a uniform understanding of the content and fitness for purpose of datasets. Metadata have many applications and they can be used to:

Please use the following format when citing this chapter:

Anagnostopoulos, C.-N., Tsekouras, G., Gavalas, D., Economou, D., Psoroulas, I., 2007, in IFIP International Federation for Information Processing, Volume 247, Artificial Intelligence and Innovations 2007: From Theory to Applications, eds. Boukis, C., Pnevmatikakis, L., Polymenakos, L., (Boston: Springer), pp. 65-72.

- concisely describe datasets and other resources using elements such as the name of the dataset, the quality, how to access the data, what is the purpose of data and other related information
- enable effective management of resources
- enable accurate searching and resource discovery
- provide an online interface to a dataset and link to other information about it
- accompany a dataset when it is transferred to another computer so that the dataset can be fully understood, and put to proper use.

The majority of metadata specifications use the eXtensible Markup Language (XML) [1]. The XML language permits to build hierarchical structures suitable for most types of documents and therefore facilitates advanced search. XML is often used with XML schemas [2]. An XML schema is an XML language expressing rules to create XML documents. Most metadata standards for multimedia content are built on this language, among them MPEG-7 [3], MPEG-21 [4]. The primary goal of metadata is to manage the huge number of digital sources, thus facilitating the search. However, metadata is employed for many other functions. Metadata is useful to give information about multimedia resources. For instance, information can be displayed on the client screen in interactive TV while playing the audiovisual content. This also can be applied in all applications of IPTV.

Therefore, metadata are quite useful for building interactive interfaces. Such devices collect multiple mixed multimedia contents inside the same structure. Metadata defines the spatial and temporal layout as well as hyperlinks. Examples of such interactive interfaces lie in DVD movies where images, texts, audio tracks, audiovisual sequences are combined. Another example of such interactivity could be when a character appears in a movie, a textual description of this character is displayed and a hyperlink is proposed to see a biography of this actor. Metadata is also used for content protection which restricts content usage to a particular user or group of users; it is particularly useful for service providers in a pay-per-view scenario. Finally, adaptation can be performed by using metadata; In this case metadata describes terminal capabilities, network characteristics and the way data has to be modified.

In this paper an authoring tool under the name Developer21, which supports the MPEG-21 standard is described. Section 2 shows similar works and gives the background of MPEG-21, which is the standard implemented in this tool. The main characteristics and the scopes of Developer21 are described in Section 4. Finally, the last section concludes this paper.

2 Literature-market review

Surprisingly, very few authoring tool based on the MPEG-21 standard are present in the market as well as in the literature. In contrast, several metadata authoring tools based on the MPEG-7 standard have been exhaustively described and presented in the market [5-8].

Enikos [9] designed a MPEG-21 authoring tool, called DIEditor, allowing users to link multiple resources inside a MPEG-21 structure. In addition, in the framework of ENTHRONE project [10], the M-Tool was created combining and unifying TV-Anytime and the MPEG-21 standard. In the latter work, MPEG-21 provided content protection, network adaptation, client terminal adaptation and a structure to link several multimedia contents while TVAnytime provided content-descriptive metadata and temporal segmentation.

MPEG-21 [4] aims at defining an open framework for the delivery and consumption of multimedia contents in heterogeneous conditions. In other words, the goal of MPEG-21 is to define a metadata model to support users to exchange, access, consume and manipulate Digital Items in an efficient, transparent and interoperable way. MPEG-21 is based on two essentials concepts: the definition of a fundamental unit of distribution and transaction (called the Digital Item or DI) and the concept of users interacting with Digital Items.

The MPEG-21 specification is flexible and enables higher level functionality and interoperability by allowing the connection of the several parts of MPEG-21, the inclusion of other description schemes, etc. The DID [11] represents a complete separation of metadata from its associated media resource. The DID specifications encompass the following features:

- the Digital Item Declaration Model ,
- the Digital Item Declaration Representation in XML and
- XML schemas comprising grammars for the Digital Item Declaration representation in XML

The Digital Item Identification (DII) schema (MPEG-21, part 3) [12] uniquely identifies Digital Items and parts thereof, relationship between Digital Items (and parts thereof) and relevant description schemes. The 4th part of MPEG-21 [13] defines an interoperable framework for Intellectual Property Management and Protection (IPMP). The framework includes standardized ways of retrieving IPMP tools from remote locations, exchanging messages between IPMP tools and between these tools and the terminal.

MPEG-21 Intellectual Property Management and Protection (IPMP) manages rights and intellectual property of a specific resource. It also addresses authentication of IPMP tools, and has provisions for integrating Rights Expressions according to the Rights Expression Language REL [14] and the Rights Data Dictionary (RDD) [15], which are MPEG-21 parts 5 and 6 respectively.

MPEG-21 Right Expression Language (REL) specifies whether a given group of people can perform a given right upon a given resource under a given condition. Finally, MPEG-21 Digital Item Adaptation (DIA) [16] has recently been finalized as part of the MPEG-21 Multimedia Framework. DIA specifies metadata for assisting the adaptation of Digital Items according to constraints on the storage, transmission and consumption, thereby enabling various types of quality of service management.

3   The MPEG-21 Authoring tool (Developer21)

3.1 Problem Description

Developer21 for MPEG-21 serves as a multimedia authoring tool adding or extracting MPEG-21 descriptors and metadata in various multimedia assets as shown in Figure 1. Once created, these descriptors (in XML schema files) are locally stored and its list is displayed to the user. The user is then allowed to select one or more descriptor schema which can be further processed and visualized using the respective graphical user interface (GUI). Users have the possibility to create a new MPEG-21 Digital Items, edit, delete, convert or send this metadata document to a specific (local or external) metadata database.

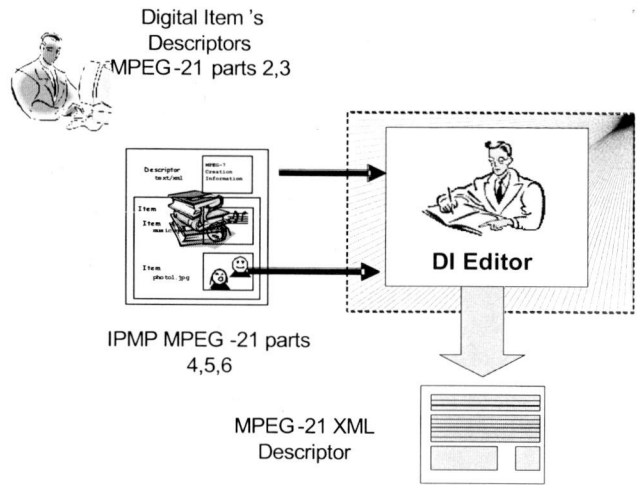

Fig. 1. The operation of Developer21 for authoring XML descriptors.

MPEG-21 enables the hierarchical representation of multimedia contents which is useful to create advanced and interactive multimedia contents. Every resource is described using the MPEG-21 standard and more specifically through the relevant XML schema which is provided by MPEG-21 standard. Developer21 is designed to support 6 different XML schemas, each one dedicated to the respective MPEG-21 part. The MPEG-21 descriptors that are provided by Developer21 are the following:
- Digital Item Declaration
- Digital Item Identification
- Intellectual Property Management and Protection
- Rights Expression Language
- Rights Data Dictionary
- Digital Item Adaptation

DID was almost totally covered in Developer21 as it is the core definition part of the MPEG-21standard, including all the necessary architecture for the creation, the exchange and the manipulation of the DIs. However, special emphasis was given to the protection of the Intellectual Property Rights and therefore important parts of MPEG-21's IPMP, REL and RDD schemas are supported.

Developer21 is a prototype that provides all the necessary operations to create or manage metadata or descriptors relevant to multimedia assets. The main scope is to provide the end-user and content provider with a reference tool that enable annotating, browsing, maintaining, monitoring and querying multimedia descriptors.

According to MPEG-21, a user is anyone that interacts with Digital Items. Hence, a User can be an individual, an organization, corporation, any community, consortium or even a government. Moreover, Users act in various roles including creators, consumers, rights holders, content providers, distributors, etc. Therefore, it is designed to help them in annotating and authoring multimedia resources. In other words, this application allows users to create objects' relationships to each other in order to enrich multimedia resources with metadata both formatted and stored in XML or in a relational database. This type of service is useful for applications that present a mixture of textual, graphical, and audio data.

3.2   Modules of Developer21

Developer21 is composed of two modules, namely the Digital Item editor (DI editor) and Digital Item Manager (DI manager). It is a Digital Item Declaration model editor, Digital Item generator and Digital Item Browser. A DI is edited or generated by inserting, deleting or modifying metadata on account of the DID, DII, IPMP, RDD, REL and DIA specifications.

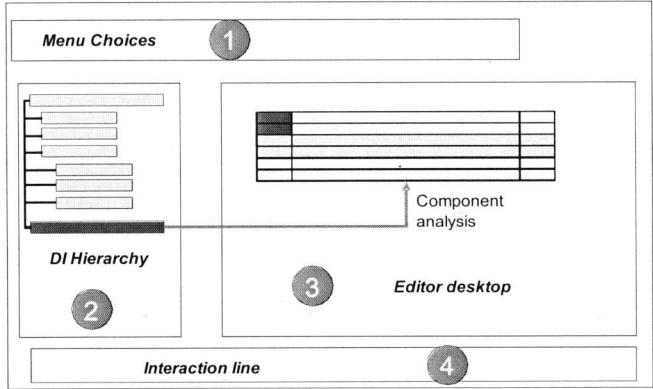

Fig. 2. The architecture of Developer21's editor panel.

When a user requests to create a new Digital Item, DI editor is invoked to create the MPEG-21 structure according the respective part of this standard. For example, if the user intends to create a very simple DI, only MPEG-21 part 2 and the relevant XML is sufficient. However, if Intellectual Property Rights need to be specified, the user should use the respective protection model which is defined in MPEG-21 part 4. In any case, the DID generation is achieved through a graphical representation of the MPEG-21 structure in explorer-like panel as shown in Figure 2. New elements are simply added by performing a drag and drop from the desktop to the MPEG-21 structure. These elements consist of MPEG-21 structure elements (Container, Item and Component) and Descriptor elements (REL, RDD and DIA metadata).

The MPEG-21 DI editor is composed of four areas as represented in Figure 2, the Menu choices (1), the relevant hierarchy and tree visualization (2), the editor desktop where the manipulation of elements takes place (3) and the user-tool interaction line where messages generated from the software appear (4). Similarly to the creation of a new MPEG-21 document, updates to the current document are achieved by dragging and dropping different icons from area 3 to area 2. The tree view in area 2 gives the XML structuring components while area 3 gives the details of each selected component. Selecting fields in the top tree displays its full content in the bottom tree.

Basic information about descriptors is provided by the graphical representation: the type of descriptor (DID,DII, IPMP, RDD, REL, DIA), the type of program information (general information or only audio and video attributes). The schema file can be selected from a pull-down menu in the menu bar. Selecting a particular MPEG21 part triggers the appropriate XML schema for edition and visualization.

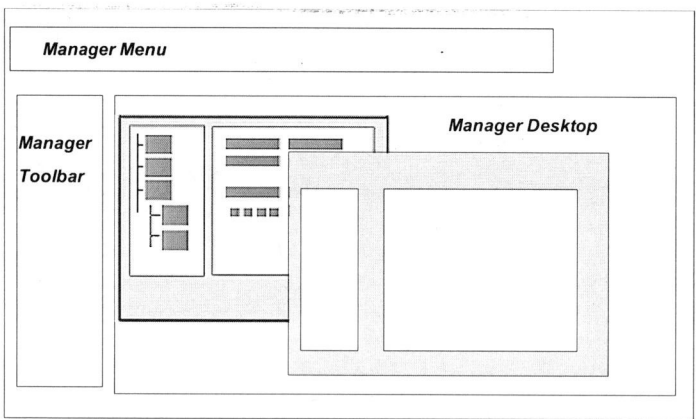

Fig. 3. The architecture of Developer21's manager panel.

3.3 Increasing interactivity in IPTV with Developer21

In parallel with the editing and browsing capabilities of theDeveloper21 tool, metadata management is also supported. Binding of metadata and XML descriptors with the actual multimedia content is performed in order to create the integrated Digital Item that contains the actual content and the descriptive information. The manager is able for controlling, refreshing and synchronizing metadata files in conformance with their content including detection and elimination of XML metadata (sub-)item (or component) duplicates, and checking freshness and consistency of both metadata associated to distributed digital resources.

When a Digital Item is processed with DI Manager (see Figure 3), it is in the appropriate form to interact with an Expert System that is currently implemented for increasing the interactivity in IPTV or iTV. The expert system will be able to assign a TV viewer to a specific social category and then match the appropriate audiovisual content according the respective MPEG-21 descriptors. The whole architecture is depicted in Figure 4.

In general, personalization allows users to browse programs much more efficiently according to their preferences. On the other hand, personalization also enables to build social networks that can improve the performance of current IPTV systems considerably by increasing content availability, trust and the realization of proper incentives to exchange content.

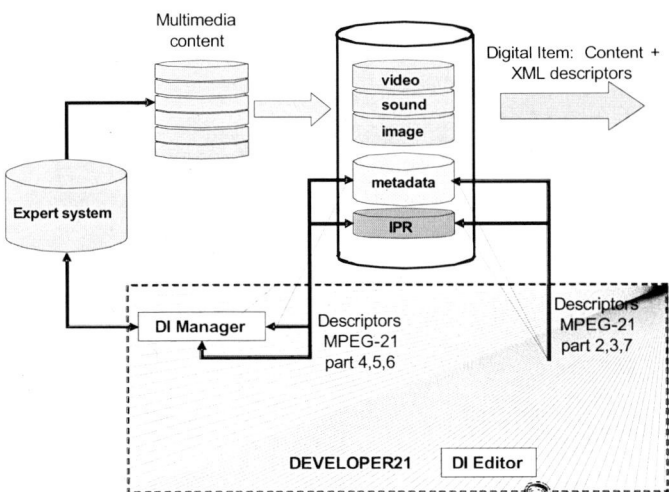

Fig. 4. The operation of Developer21 for authoring XML descriptors joined with an expert system for content personalization.

4   Conclusions

In this paper we have proposed an novel authoring tool implementing MPEG-21 XML schemas for modeling and managing content descriptive metadata associated to audiovisual resources. The functionalities of the authoring tool have been presented and associated with content personalization and improvement of interactivity in IPTV. The novelties introduced by this work is also highlighted as to our knowledge Developer21 is the only MPEG-21 authoring tool capable to produce and manage DI that support IPMP, REL and RDD schemas.

Acknowledgements: This work is supported by the General Secretariat of Research and Technology (Project "Software Application in Interactive Kids TV-MPEG-21", project framework "Image, Sound, and Language Processing", project number : EHΓ-16). The participants are the University of the Aegean, the Hellenic Public Radio and Television (ERT) and the Time Lapse Picture Hellas.

References

1. eXtensible Markup Language (XML), http://www.w3.org/XML
2. XML Schema, http://www.w3.org/XML/Schema
3. ISO MPEG-7, part 8: Information technology -- Multimedia content description interface -- Part 8: Extraction and use of MPEG-7 descriptions, ISO/IEC TR 15938-8:2002.
4. ISO MPEG-21, part1: Information technology — Multimedia framework (MPEG-21) — Vision, Technologies and Strategy, ISO/IEC TR 21000-1:2004.
5. J.M. Martinez, "Standards - MPEG-7 overview of MPEG-7 description tools", part 2, IEEE Multimedia, Volume 9, Issue 3, July-Sept. 2002 Page(s):83 - 93
6. Jae-Ho Lee, Gwang-Gook Lee, Whoi-Yul Kim, "Automatic video summarizing tool using MPEG-7 descriptors for personal video recorder" IEEE Transactions on Consumer Electronics, Volume 49, Issue 3, Aug. 2003 Page(s):742 – 749
7. D. Bulgarelli, R. Cucchiara, C. Grana, R. Vezzani, "A Semi-Automatic Video Annotation tool with MPEG-7 Content Collections", Multimedia, 2006. ISM'06. Eighth IEEE International Symposium on Dec. 2006 Page(s):742 – 745
8. J.A. Lay, Ling Guan, "SOLO: an MPEG-7 optimum search tool", IEEE International Conference on Multimedia and Expo, vol. 2, 30 July-2 Aug. 2000 pp. 777 – 780.
9. Enikos DI Creator, http://www.enikos.com. Last accessed on the 1th of April 2007.
10. Boris Rousseau, Wilfried Jouve, Laure Berti-Équille, "Enriching Multimedia Content Description for Broadcast Environments: From a Unified Metadata Model to a New Generation of Authoring Tool", Proc. of the 7th IEEE International Symposium on Multimedia (ISM'05), 2005, pp.8-15.
11. ISO MPEG-21, part 2: Information technology - Multimedia framework (MPEG-21) — Digital Item Declaration, ISO/IEC TR 21000-2, 2nd Edition, 2005.
12. ISO MPEG-21, part 3: Information technology - Multimedia framework (MPEG-21) — Digital Item Identification, ISO/IEC TR 21000-3, 1st, 2003.
13. ISO MPEG-21, part 4: Information technology - Multimedia framework (MPEG-21) — Intellectual Property Management and Protection Components, ISO/IEC TR 21000-4, 1st Edition, 2006.
14. ISO MPEG-21, part 5: Information technology - Multimedia framework (MPEG-21) — Part 5: Rights Expression Language, ISO/IEC TR 21000-5, 1st Edition, 2004.
15. ISO MPEG-21, part 6: Information technology - Multimedia framework (MPEG-21) — Part 6: Rights Data Dictionary, ISO/IEC TR 21000-6, 1st Edition, 2004.
16. ISO MPEG-21, part 7: Information technology - Multimedia framework (MPEG-21) — Part 7: Digital Item Adaptation, ISO/IEC TR 21000-7, 1st Edition, 2004.

Dynamic Reliability Assessment of Multiple Choice Tests in distributed E-Leaning Environments: A Case Study

Ioanna Likourentzou, George Mpardis ,Vassilis Nikolopoulos and Vassili Loumos

National Technical University of Athens
School of Electrical and Computer Engineering,
Iroon Politechniou 7, Zografou, Athens, GR 15773
{ioanna,gmpardis,vnikolop}@medialab.ntua.gr, loumos@cs.ntua.gr

Abstract. The development of high-quality e-learning products is one of the most demanding areas in the field of educational research. Reliability of the students' grading mechanisms especially in the case of virtual classrooms, which lack in physical student-instructor interaction, is extremely important. In this paper, based on real data, we utilize two reliability estimation methods to calculate several multiple choice tests' reliability. Moreover, since multiple choice tests are an imperfect measure of students' knowledge, we also estimate the students' true ability of scoring using the tests' standard error of measurement. Concluding this study embeds reliability assessment methods in the e-learning process and then carefully analyzes the produced data to provide the strengths and weaknesses of the analyzed course's multiple choice tests.

1 Introduction

An issue that nowadays concerns both the educational industry and the research community is the subject of e-learning evaluation. As e-learning includes more technological than human factors, compared to conventional education, its proper evaluation is vital. In an e-learning environment the trainer does not have direct contact with the trainees and this may result in a difficulty of proper student grading. The only student evaluation means is via assigned open-answer projects and multiple choice tests that the students deliver. Subsequently it is obvious that e-learning courses aiming to provide trainees with high quality education should consist of highly reliable projects and multiple choice tests which will accurate measure the students' level of knowledge. Especially in the case of multiple choice tests, which

Please use the following format when citing this chapter:

Likourentzou, I., Mpardis, G., Nikolopoulos, V., Loumos, V., 2007, in IFIP International Federation for Information Processing, Volume 247, Artificial Intelligence and Innovations 2007: From Theory to Applications, eds. Boukis, C., Pnevmatikakis, L., Polymenakos, L., (Boston: Springer), pp. 73-80.

are not subjectively corrected by a human trainer, the reliability issue is even more significant.

In this paper we estimate the reliability of several e-learning multiple choice tests, the error of measurement they present, compare them and then discuss the results.

2   Educational Framework

The learning object of this e-lesson is an introductory course to computer network communication. The course runs in the open source platform Moodle. The existing analyzed data were derived from three classes corresponding to three semesters (Fall 05, Spring 06 and Spring 07) of approximately ten weeks each. Every class took four twenty-question multiple choice tests, each test corresponding to four learning weeks in the duration of the e-learning course. The students could choose to repeat the test in order to achieve better results, therefore providing our study with the necessary data to use with the test-retest method. This is considered a rare opportunity not only in the e-learning field but generally in education, because usually students do not take the same test more than once.

3   Methods of calculation and Standard Error of Measurement

3.1   Multiple choice test reliability

A multiple choice test reliability is the extend to which this test produces consistent, stable, trustworthy and repeatable results when administered by the same group of students twice [1]. For a particular set of test/retest scores one can plot the scores on a scatter-gram to obtain a general idea of the reliability that this test presents. The more the sets of scores deviate from the x=y line the more unreliable they are.

3.2   Methods of calculation

There are two methods to estimate a multiple choice test's reliability based on the number of times this test was administered by the same group of students:

a. Multiple-administration methods require two or more assessments of the same test. The most appropriate multiple-administration technique for multiple choice tests is the test/retest evaluation method [2], which lies in having the same group of students take the same test two times. If the test is reliable most of the examinees will tend to get the same or very similar scores on both administrations. The evaluator can use a coefficient to calculate the test's reliability. The most widely used one the Pearson product-moment correlation coefficient (PMCC) between two administrations of the same measure.

Assuming that X and Y are the two sets of student scores, then the test's reliability based on PMCC is defined as following:

$$r_{tr} = \frac{\sum XY - \frac{\sum X \sum Y}{N}}{\sqrt{\left(\sum X^2 - \frac{(\sum X)^2}{N}\right)\left(\sum Y^2 - \frac{(\sum Y)^2}{N}\right)}}$$

b. Single-administration methods are used in cases when a test can be assessed only once [3]. A typical single-administration method is the split-half reliability technique in which the evaluator divides the test into two halves and treats them as alternate administrations of the same test. The reliability correlation of these two halves is then calculated. Since this correlation is based only on half the test length, it cannot be fully indicative of the tests' reliability. To fix this inaccuracy we used the Spearman-Brown prediction formula which predicts the full-test reliability based on the half-test reliability correlation. The Spearman-Brown split-half reliability is defined as following:

$$r_{SB} = \frac{m^\star r_{XY}}{1 + (m-1)^\star r_{XY}}$$

where

r_{SB} is the Spearman-Brown split-half reliability
r_{XY} is the Pearson correlation between forms X and Y
m is the total sample size divided by sample size per form (m is usually 2)

As with other split-halves measures, the Spearman-Brown reliability coefficient is highly influenced by alternative methods of sorting items into the two forms. We used a random assignment of items to the two forms as this is considered to be amongst the most effective means to assure equality of variances between the forms. The above methods of reliability estimation should not be expected to be equal since they are prone to different sources of error.

Due to the type of our available data (some of the examinees had the opportunity to take the multiple choice tests twice in order to optimize their scores while others took the tests only once), in this study we will be able to use both multiple and single administration methods .

3.3 Standard error of measurement

Multiple choice tests are an imperfect measure of a student's knowledge level since they may be influenced by extraneous factors such as chance error, differential testing conditions, imperfect reliability and other errors of measurement. A way to estimate a band or interval within which a person's true score (true ability of the student) would fall is the standard error of measurement (SEM). SEM is calculated using the standard deviation and the reliability of test scores and represents the amount of variance in a score resulting from factors other than achievement. [4]:
The SEM is calculated using the formula:

$$\text{SEM} = \sigma_x \sqrt{(1-r)}$$

where σ_x is the test's standard deviation and r is the test's reliability estimate.

3.4   Reliability coefficient interpretations

Table 1 indicates the evaluation of a reliability test/retest correlation coefficient r_{tr}. Note that as the coefficient's values decrease so the proportion of the incorrectly awarded examinees increases [5]:

Table 1 Reliability Interpretation

Reliability (r_{tr})	Coefficient Evaluation
0.90 – 1.00	High reliability - Appropriate for the assessment of a student on the basis of a single test score.
0.80 – 0.89	Acceptable reliability. Appropriate for the evaluation of an individual student if averaged with a few other scores of similar reliability.
0.60 – 0.79	Low to moderate reliability. Appropriate for the evaluation of a student only if averaged with numerous other scores of similar reliability.
0.40 – 0.59	Uncertain reliability. Should be used with great watchfulness when evaluating individual students. May be suitable for the calculation of average score variations between groups

Values of 0.80 and higher, are generally considered to be satisfying. However, one should not be based on a single test score to make significant decisions about individual examinees when the corresponding reliability coefficient is less than 0.80.

4   Results - Discussion

4.1   Comparison of the scores on the same test on different semesters

The mean of the grades that the students accomplished in all three semesters, as depicted in figure 1, seem to be consistent. This means that all three classes received approximately the same scoring results. If the trainer is based only on this observation, the tests all seem to be appropriate for student evaluation. However, following it is analyzed that based on their reliability the tests do not prove to be equally appropriate for an accurate and fair student evaluation.

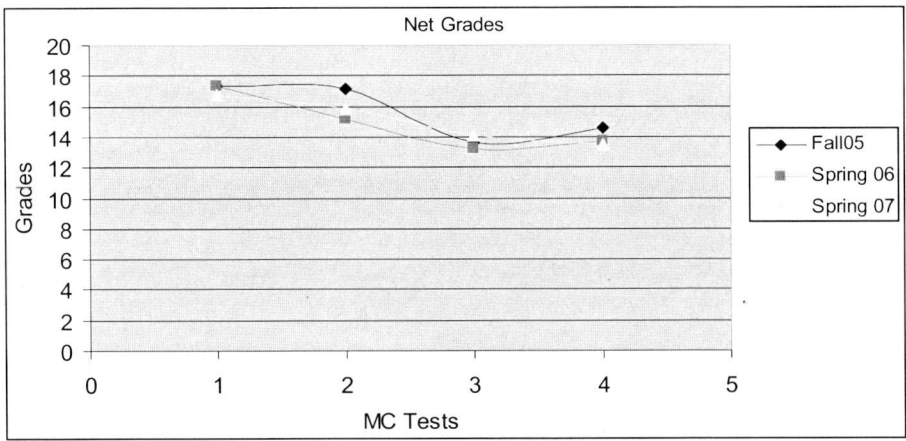

Fig. 1. Multiple Choice Test Grades

4.2   Tables with calculations of reliability for each lesson/semester

4.2.1 Spearman-Brown Reliability Results

The Spearman-Brown method indicates (figure 2) that the first two multiple choice tests resulted in the most reliability inconsistencies. MC1 yields from near-zero (0, 11) to low (0, 62) reliability and MC2 yields from uncertain (0, 46) to acceptable (0, 85) reliability. These reliability results indicate that MC1 and MC2 tests (and especially MC1 that did not achieve acceptable reliability in neither of the three course classes) need to be ameliorated in order to be solely trusted for student evaluation. At this point MC1 should only be utilized to assess students' comprehension only if supported by other assessment sources such as written projects, forum participation and correctness of answers in teachers' on-line questions. The above are also applied to MC2 with the exception of class spring '06 for which the test scores yielded acceptable reliability. Nevertheless, our suggestion regarding this test is to be treated with carefulness since the high reliability value of class Spring 06 may be due to the test scores' splitting. Tests MC3 and MC4 produce moderate (0, 71) to high reliability (~0, 9) and are thus considered appropriate for student assessment. Consequently, alternative assessment sources like the ones mentioned above are auxiliary but not necessary for the evaluation of the students of these learning weeks.

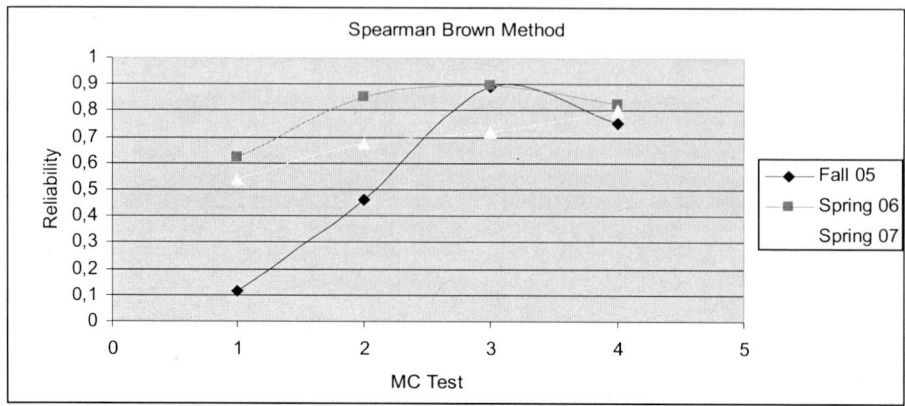

Fig. 2. The multiple choice test reliabilities calculated according to the Spearman-Brown prophecy formula.

4.2.2 Test – Retest Reliability Results The test retest method is generally expected to produce lower reliability results that the spearman brown prophecy formula. This is explained mainly due to the memory effect that influences the students in their scoring. The above means that, since the students were allowed to retake the test in the same learning week they tend to remember some of the questions and thus score better. In most cases their scoring increases compared to the first test-taking, thus lowering reliability. This is mostly expected to occur in the latter multiple choice tests and not in the first one mainly due to the fact that the students need some time to be accustomed to the e-learning environment and take advantage of the memory effect on retaking the test. According to the test retest method, the first two multiple choice tests yield the most reliability inconsistencies. MC1 yields acceptable reliability for classes Spring 06 and Spring 07 while it yields an uncertain reliability for class Fall 05. The second multiple choice test MC2 generally yields very low reliability for classes Fall 05 and Spring 07 with the exception of class Spring 06 where it yields acceptable reliability. On the other hand multiple choice tests MC3 and MC4 although they yield low to moderate reliability they tend to produce these results consistently. Due to the memory effect and also the fact that less students participate in the test re-taking, the test-retest method is less indicative of the true tests' reliability.

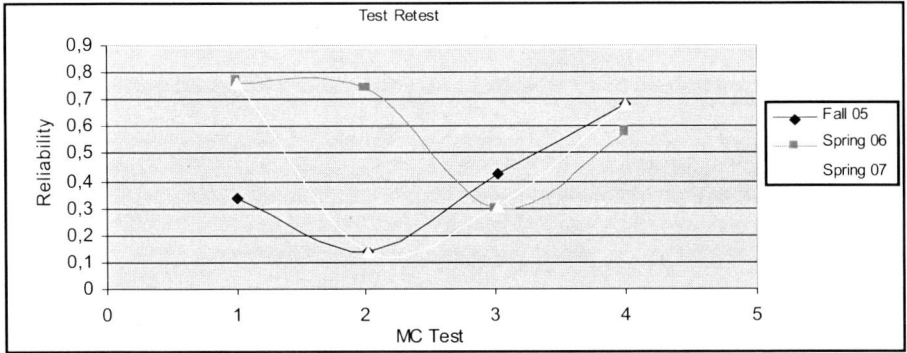

Fig. 3. The multiple choice test reliabilities calculated according to the test-retest method.

4.3 Student standard error of measurement As mentioned above, the tests are not perfectly reliable and thus, a student's observed score and true score will differ. The standard errors of measurement that yield the range of values that would most likely contain the student's true scores are depicted in Table 2. The more unreliable the test scores are the more standard error of measurement these tests yield.

Table 2 Student scores' standard error of measurement

	Fall 05		Spring 06		Spring 07	
	Reliability	SEM	Reliability	SEM	Reliability	SEM
MC1	0,11	2,02	0,62	1,31	0,54	1,60
MC2	0,46	0,91	0,85	1,62	0,67	1,79
MC3	0,89	1,26	0,90	1,30	0,72	1,89
MC4	0,75	1,40	0,83	1,70	0,80	1,60

Following we provide an example of the evaluation process that the instructor could perform based on the previous results. The example utilizes a randomly selected student and can be applied to any course student. Figure 4, depicts the standard error of measurement on the grades of a student that belongs to the class Fall 05. MC1 yields the highest error of measurement, followed by MC4, MC3 and MC2. Moreover, MC1 produced a very low reliability and this fact along with the high SEM it produces, should make the instructor very careful on utilizing this item in the student evaluation process. MC3 yields both low SEM and high reliability and is thus the most indicative of the students' progress. MC2 and MC4 should also be taken into consideration in the evaluation process, but especially MC2, although it produces the lowest SEM should not be highly valued since its reliability is uncertain.

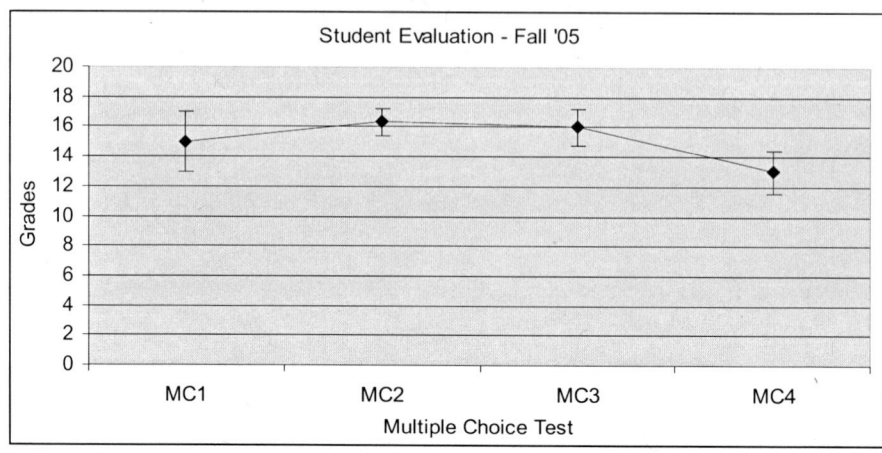

Fig. 4. Scores and SEM for a random student – Fall 05

5   Conclusion

This study focuses on e-learning reliability by estimating the reliability of several multiple choice tests of an introductory e-learning course. The tests' distinctive accuracy is precisely calculated using reliability methods (Spearman-Brown formula and the test-retest method) and the standard error of measurement (SEM), thus enabling trainers to improve their evaluating process. This methodology significantly contributes in delivering a better and more reliable e-learning course by making it strongly competitive and trustworthy.

References

1. Wallace R. Blischke, D. N. Prabhakar Murthy ,Reliability Modeling Prediction and Optimization , Wiley Series in Probability and statistics,2000, p.18,19
2. Renee Bradley, Reliability Issues And Evidence, U.S Department of Education, Office of Special Education Programs (OSEP), Toolkit on Teaching and Assessing students with Disabilities
3. Richard A. Zeller, Edward G. Carmines, Reliability and Validity Assessment, Sage Publications, 1979
4. Rudner, L. M., & Schafer, W. D,Reliability, (ERIC Digest). College Park, MD: ERIC Clearinghouse on Assessment and Evaluation. (ERIC Document Reproduction Service No. ED458213) ,2001
5. Leo M. Harvill, An NCME Instructional Module on. Standard Error of Measurement, Educational Measurement: Issues and Practice 10 (2), 33–41, 1991

Service Decomposition and Task Allocation in Distributed Computing Environments

Malamati Louta and Angelos Michalas
Department of Business Administration
Technological Educational Institute of Western Macedonia
Koila, Kozani, 50100, Greece, louta@kozani.teikoz.gr
Department of Information and Communication Technologies
Engineering
University of Western Macedonia
Department of Informatics and Computer Technology
Technological Educational Institute of Western Macedonia
Fourka, Kastoria, 52100, Greece, amichalas@kastoria.teikoz.gr

Abstract. Highly competitive and open environments should encompass mechanisms that will assist service providers in accounting for their interests, i.e., offering at a given period of time adequate quality services in a cost efficient manner. Assuming that a user wishes to access a specific service composed of a distinct set of service tasks, which can be served by various candidate service nodes, a problem that should be addressed is the allocation of service tasks to the most appropriate service nodes. This scenario accounts for both the user and the service provider. Specifically, service providers succeed in efficiently managing their resources, while users implicitly exploit in a seamless way the otherwise unutilized power and capabilities of the provider's network. In general, service task allocation is founded on general and service specific user preferences, service provider's specific service logic deployment and current system & network load conditions. The pertinent problem is concisely defined, mathematically formulated, optimally solved and evaluated through simulation experiments.

1   Introduction

The main role of all players in the liberalised, deregulated and competitive telecommunication market is to constantly monitor the user demand, and in response to create, promote and provide the desired services and service features. In

Please use the following format when citing this chapter:

Louta, M., Michalas, A., 2007, in IFIP International Federation for Information Processing, Volume 247, Artificial Intelligence and Innovations 2007: From Theory to Applications, eds. Boukis, C., Pnevmatikakis, L., Polymenakos, L., (Boston: Springer), pp. 81-91.

accordance with a business model applying to the telecommunications world, five main different entities can be identified, namely, user, service provider, (third party) application (content) provider, broker and network provider. The role of the (third party) application (content) provider is to develop and offer applications (content). The role of the service provider is to provide the means through which the users will be enabled to access the applications (content) of (third party) application (content) providers. The broker assists business level entities in finding other business entities. Finally, the role of a network provider is to offer the network connectivity needed for service provision.

Service provisioning in such open models is a quite complex process since it involves various diverse actors. The following are some key factors for success. First, the efficiency with which services will be developed. Second, the quality level, in relation with the corresponding cost, of new services. Third, the efficiency with which the services will be operated, controlled, maintained, administered, etc. The challenges outlined above have brought to the foreground several new important research areas. Some of them are the specification of service architectures (SAs) [1,2], the development of advanced service creation environments (SCEs) and grid computing architectures [3,4] and service characteristics (e.g., the personal mobility concept), and the exploitation of advanced software technologies, (e.g., distributed object computing [5] and intelligent mobile agents [6]). The aim of this paper is, in accordance with the cost-effective QoS provision and the efficient service operation objectives, to propose enhancements to the sophistication of the functionality that can be offered by service architectures in open competitive communications environments.

In accordance with the SA concept and exploiting advanced software paradigms, the service logic is realised by a set of autonomous co-operating components, which interact through middleware functionality that runs over Distributed Processing Environments (e.g., Common Object Request Broker Architecture - CORBA). Limited by techno-economic reasons or considering administrative, management and resilience/ redundancy purposes it is assumed that each service provider deploys service components realising service logic in different service nodes, residing in the same and/or different domains. Moreover, it can be envisaged that a service will in general comprise a set of distinct service tasks, which could be executed by different service nodes.

Highly competitive and open environments should encompass mechanisms that will assist service providers in accounting for their interests, i.e., offering at a given period of time adequate quality services in a cost efficient manner which is highly associated to efficiently managing and fulfilling current user requests. Thus, assuming that a user wishes to access a specific service composed of a distinct set of service tasks, which can be served by various candidate service nodes (CSNs), a problem that should be addressed is the allocation of service tasks to the most appropriate service nodes. In this paper, the pertinent problem is called service task allocation. The aim of this paper is to address the problem from one of the possible theoretical perspectives and to show the software architecture that supports its solution and how it can be incorporated in service architectures that run in the open environment.

In general, service task allocation is founded on general and service specific user preferences, service provider's specific service logic deployment and current system & network load conditions. A high level problem statement may be the following. Given the set of candidate service nodes and their layout, the set of service tasks constituting the required service, the resource requirement of each service task in terms of CPU utilization, memory and disk space, the cost of deploying each service node, the current load conditions of each service node and of the network links, find the minimum cost assignment of tasks to service nodes (in terms of the number of nodes that need to be deployed, the communication cost introduced during the execution of service tasks, and the management cost imposed by the arrangement) subject to a set of constraints, associated with the capabilities of the service nodes.

The approach in this paper is the following. The starting point (section 2) is the service task allocation architecture, presenting the software elements required for the realisation of the assignment process. Additionally, our assumptions regarding the model of service provisioning system are presented. Section 3 presents a concise definition, mathematical formulation and optimal solution of the service task allocation problem, while one possible formulation of the communication cost taken into account in our framework is provided. Section 4 gives a set of experimental results, indicative of the efficiency of the proposed service task assignment scheme. Finally, section 5 gives future plans and concluding remarks.

2   Service Task Allocation Architecture

Service task assignment process, as a first step, requires a computational component that will act on behalf of the user. Its role will be to capture the user preferences, requirements and constraints regarding the requested service and to deliver them in a suitable form to the appropriate service provider entity. As a second step, service task allocation requires an entity that will act on behalf of the service provider. Each role will be to intercept user requests, acquire and evaluate the corresponding service node and network load conditions, and ultimately, to select the most appropriate service nodes for the realisation of the service. Furthermore, a monitoring module is required. Monitoring module consists of a distributed set of agents, which run on each service node of the service provider. Each agent is responsible for monitoring the load conditions and available resources of the service node and delivering them to the service provider related entity. Additionally, a distributed set of network provider related entities will be responsible for providing the service provider entity with network load conditions and managing the network connections necessary for the service provision.

The following key extensions are made so as to cover the functionality that was identified above. First, the *Service Provider Agent* (SPA) is introduced and assigned with the role of selecting on behalf of the service provider the best service task assignment pattern. Second, the *User Agent* (UA) is assigned with the role of promoting the service request to the appropriate SPA. Third, the *Service Node Agent* (SNA) is introduced and assigned with the role of promoting the current load conditions of a CSN. Finally, the *Network Provider Agent* (NPA) is introduced and assigned with the task of providing current network load conditions (i.e., bandwidth availability) to the appropriate SPA. In essence, the distributed set of the SNAs and NPAs forms the monitoring module. In other words, the SPA interacts with the UA in order to acquire the user preferences, requirements and constraints, analyses the user request in order to identify the service tasks constituting the service and their respective requirements in terms of CPU, memory and disk space, identifies the set of CSNs and their respective capabilities, interacts with the SNAs of the candidate service nodes so as to obtain their current load conditions and with the NPAs so as to acquire the network load conditions, and ultimately selects the most appropriate service task assignment pattern for the provision of the desired service.

Regarding the system model, we consider a set of service nodes SN and a set of links L. Each service node $n_i \in SN$ corresponds to a server, while each link $l \in L$ corresponds to a physical link that interconnects two nodes $n_i, n_j \in SN$. Our system operates in a multi-tasking environment, i.e., several tasks may be executed on a single service node sharing its resources (e.g., CPU utilization, memory, disk space). Let D_i denote a set of nodes grouped to form a domain. A pattern for the physical distribution of the related components to the service task assignment scheme is given in Fig. 1. Each SPA controls the service nodes of a domain. Each SNA is associated with each node, while each NPA is associated with the network elements (e.g., switches or routers) necessary for supporting service node connectivity. The SNA, NPA role (in a sense) is to represent the service nodes or network elements, respectively, and to assist SPA by providing information on the availability of resources of the service node/network element. Domain state information (load conditions of the service nodes of the particular domain and link utilisation) is exchanged between the SPA and the SNAs/NPAs residing in the specific domain, while SPAs residing in different domains exchange their domain state info. This approach increases scalability as it reduces the requirements in terms of computation, communication and storage. At this point it should be noted that for simplicity reasons the network elements needed for the service node connectivity are not depicted in Fig. 1.

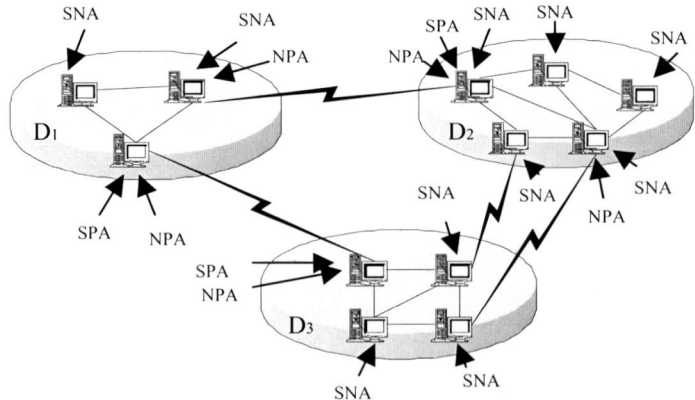

Fig. 1. System Model and physical distribution of the service task allocation related components

3   Problem Formulation & Optimal Solution

User u wishes to use a given service s. A fundamental assumption at this point is that service s may be decomposed in a set of distinct service tasks, which will be denoted as $ST(s)$. Among these service tasks, of interest to the user are those designated in the user profile and will be denoted as $ST(u,s)$ ($ST(u,s) \subseteq ST(s)$).

Let's assume the existence of multiple service nodes for the provision of service s, denoted by $SN(s) = \{n_1,...,n_{|s|}\}$. Each service node- n_j contains a collection of components, denoted as $A_{n_j}(i)$, which inter-work with other components that may reside in the same or in a different service node in order to accomplish each service task $i \in ST(s)$. Let A_{n_j} and C be the total set of components residing in the n_j service node and the various service nodes in total, respectively. Hence, the following relationship holds: $A_{n_j}(i) \subseteq A_{n_j} \subseteq C$. Each service task $i \in ST(s)$ may be executed on an associated set of possible candidate service nodes, represented by the set $SN(i)$, ($i \in ST(u,s)$). Thus, $SN(i) \subseteq SN(s)$. The service logic deployment pattern adopted by service providers determine each of these service node sets.

Task i, ($i \in ST(s)$) requires for its completion consumption of $r_{CPU}(i)$, $r_{mem}(i)$ and $r_{disk}(i)$ resources of service node(s) n_j, ($n_j \in SN(i)$). A realistic assumption is that SPA being in charge of assisting the service providers in the competitive telecommunication market, has a solid interest in as accurately as possible identifying the resources $r_a(i)$ (where $a \in \{CPU, mem, disk\}$) needed for the provisioning of service task i in terms of CPU utilization, memory and disk space. In this respect, the SPA can be the entity that configures these values based on the service task characteristics, user preferences and requirements, exploiting also previous experience.

Let c_D denote the cost of involving service node n_j, ($n_j \in SN(i)$), in the service provision. For notation simplicity it is assumed that the cost of involving a service node in the solution is the same for all service nodes. As an alternative this cost could be taken variant (depending on the cost of acquiring and/or maintaining the node etc.). Notation may readily be extended.

The objective of our problem is to find a service task assignment pattern, i.e., an allocation $A_{ST}(s)$ of service tasks i ($i \in ST(u,s)$) to service nodes n_j, ($n_j \in SN(i)$), that is optimal given the current load conditions and number of service tasks being served by each service node n_j, represented as $r_a^{pre}(n_j)$ and $k^{pre}(n_j)$, respectively. The assignment should minimise an objective function $f(s, A_{ST}(s))$ that models the overall cost introduced due to system/network resources consumption. Among the terms of this function there can be the overall cost due to the deployment of various service nodes to the service provisioning process, the communication cost introduced due to the interaction of the components A_{n_j} residing in n_j service node with the components A_{n_k} residing in service node n_k for the completion of each service task i, ($\forall i \in ST(s)$), as well as the management cost $c_M(i,i')$ introduced due to the assignment of $(i,i') \in ST^2(s)$ service tasks to different service nodes

$(n_j, n_{j'}) \in SN^2(s)$.

The constraints of our problem are the following. First, each service task i ($i \in ST(u,s)$) should be assigned to only one service node n_j, ($n_j \in SN(i)$). Second, the capacity constraints of each service node should be preserved. Lets assume that r_a^{max} and k^{max} represent the maximum load and the maximum number of service tasks that a service node may handle. For notation simplicity, these parameters are assumed to be the same for each service node n_j, ($n_j \in SN(s)$). Thus, the constraints are $r_a^{post}(n_j) \le r_a^{max}$ and $k^{post}(n_j) \le k^{max}$, ($\forall n_j \in SN(s)$), where $r_a^{post}(n_j)$ and $k^{post}(n_j)$ denote the potential load conditions of service node n_j, after the service task assignment process. Notation may readily be extended.

The general problem version presented is open to various solution methods. Its generality partly lies in the fact that the objective and the constraint functions are open to alternate implementations. Thus, the problem statement can be distinguished from the specific solution approach adopted hereafter. In order to describe the allocation $A_{ST}(s)$ of service tasks to service nodes we introduce the decision variables $x_{ST}(i,j)$ ($i \in ST(u,s)$, $n_j \in SN(i)$) that take the value 1(0) depending on whether service task i is (is not) executed by service node-n_j. The decision variables $y_{SN}(j)$ assume the value 1(0) depending on whether candidate service node n_j ($n_j \in SN(i)$) is (is not) deployed (involved in the solution). In addition, we define the set of variables $z_{ST}(i,i')$ ($\forall (i,i') \in ST(u,s)^2$) that take the value 1(0) depending on whether the service tasks i and i' are (are not) assigned to the same service node. The variables $z_{ST}(i,i')$ are related to variables $x_{ST}(i,j)$, $x_{ST}(i',j)$, through the relation

$z_{ST}(i,i') = \sum_{j=1}^{|SN(i)|} x_{ST}(i,j) \cdot x_{ST}(i',j)$, which may be turned into a set of linear constraints

through the technique of [7]. Allocation $A_{ST}(s)$ may be obtained by reduction to the following 0-1 linear programming problem.

Service Task Assignment Problem:
Minimise

$$f(s, A_{TN}(s)) = c_D \cdot \sum_{n_j \in SN(s)} y_{SN}(j) \cdot (1 + b \cdot \sum_{a \in \{CPU, memory, disk\}} w_a \cdot \frac{r_a^{pre}(n_j)}{r_a^{max}(n_j)})$$

$$+ \sum_{i \in ST(s)} \sum_{n_j \in SN(i)} C(i,n_j) \cdot x_{ST}(i,j) + \sum_{i \in ST(s)} \sum_{i' \in ST(s)} c_M(i,i') \cdot (1 - z_{ST}(i,i')) \qquad (1),$$

where $C(i,n_j)$ denotes the communication cost introduced in case n_j service node has undertaken the responsibility for the execution of service task i ($i \in ST(u,s)$),
subject to the constraints:

$$\sum_{n_j \in SN(i)} x_{ST}(i,j) = 1 \quad \forall i \in ST(s) \qquad (2),$$

$$r_a^{pre}(n_j) + \sum_{i \in ST(s)} r_a(i) \cdot x_{ST}(i,j) \le r_a^{max}(j) \cdot y_{SN}(j) \qquad \forall n_j \in SN(s) \qquad (3),$$

$$k^{pre}(n_j) + \sum_{i \in ST(s)} x_{ST}(i,j) \le k^{max}(j) \cdot y_{SN}(j) \qquad \forall n_j \in SN(s) \qquad (4)$$

Cost function (1) penalises the aspects identified previously (i.e., cost of the service node involved in the solution, communication cost introduced during the realisation of each service task, and management cost of service tasks that are assigned to different service nodes). In order for the service providers to better utilize their resources, the cost of each service node deployment introduced in cost function (1) takes also into account the node's current load conditions in order to obtain a load balancing solution. Parameters β, ($\beta < 1$), and w_a denote the relative significance of load balancing and of each resource type a to the service provider. Constraints (2), guarantee that each service task will be assigned to one service node. Constraints (3) and (4) guarantee that each service node will not have to cope with more load and service tasks than those dictated by its pertinent capacity constraint.

In the rest of the section, we present a model for the overall communication cost $C(i,n_j)$ introduced in case n_j service node has undertaken the responsibility for the execution of service task i ($i \in ST(u,s)$). In essence, the model covers the case in which the components of set $A_{n_j}(i)$ need to interact with the components of set $A_{n_k}(i)$ residing in service node n_k in order to provide service task i, ($i \in ST(s)$). It should be noted that service nodes n_j and n_k may reside even in different domains. At this point, a major assumption adopted in our study, is that part of A_{n_j} components are implemented as mobile agents, while the rest are supposed to be fixed service agent components. Let $A_{n_j}^M$ and $A_{n_j}^F$ be the subset of components of A_{n_j} that are implemented as mobile and fixed agents, respectively.

The volume of messages exchanged between each pair of components (e.g., dependent on the number of messages and size of each message) for the accomplishment of task i ($i \in ST(s)$) will be represented as $m_{wv}(i)$, $\forall (w,v) \in C^2$ and $\forall i \in ST(s)$. Let $cc(n_j,n_k)$ be the communication cost per unit message that is exchanged between service nodes n_j and n_k, $\forall (n_j,n_k) \in SN(s)^2$. This factor may be proportional to the distance (e.g., number of hops) between the two service nodes and the load conditions (e.g., bandwidth availability) of the communication link interconnecting the two nodes. Another factor that should be taken into account is the cost associated with the migration of a component (implemented as a mobile agent) from one service node to another. In this respect, let $mc(w,n_j,n_k)$ be the migration cost of component-w from service node n_j to service node n_k, $\forall w \in C$ and $\forall (n_j,n_k) \in SN(s)^2$.

The overall cost for the completion of task i ($i \in ST(s)$) can be calculated by the following formula.

$$C(i,n_j) = \sum_{\forall n_k \in SN(s)} [\sum_{w \in A_{n_j}^F} \sum_{v \in A_{n_k}} m_{wv}(i) \cdot cc(n_j,n_k) + \sum_{w \in A_{n_j}^F} \sum_{v \in A_{n_j}} m_{wv}(i) \cdot cc(n_j,n_j) +$$
$$\sum_{w \in A_{n_j}^M} mc(w,n_j,n_k) + \sum_{w \in A_{n_j}^M} \sum_{v \in A_{n_k}} m_{wv}(i) \cdot cc(n_k,n_k)] \qquad , \forall i \in ST(s) \text{ (5)}$$

In the previous formulation three main factors are identified. The first one is related to the communication cost deriving from the fixed components and is proportional to the messages (their number and size) that are exchanged between every pair of components (w,v) and the communication cost per unit message between different service nodes.

The second factor is associated with the migration cost of mobile agent components between two different service nodes. This factor is dependent on the path which the mobile agent will follow (i.e., number of hops) and the information encryption and code execution cost, as well as the load conditions of the communication links. The last factor is the communication cost within the same service node, which in practice may be negligible, and in the context of this study is taken equal to zero. It is noted that only the involved to the provisioning process components are taken into account.

Apparently, the designation of the components that will be included in sets $A_{n_j}^M$ and $A_{n_j}^F$ by the service providers may be based on factors such as the overall communication and migration costs as well as estimation of the respective component invocations. In our study, the service logic deployment pattern (i.e., service components/nodes) adopted by the service providers is known.

4   Experimental Results

In this section, indicative results are provided in order to assess the proposed framework, which allows for effective service provisioning. In order to test the performance of the service task allocation scheme, we assume a simple application executing on a single PC performing a configurable number of queries on a database (that is, the service considered is composed of one service task that involves execution of one service component which interacts with the database).

Concerning the implementation issues of our experiments, the overall Service Provisioning System (SPS) has been implemented in Java. The Voyager mobile agent platform [8] has been used for the realisation of the software components as well as for the inter-component communication. To be more specific, the system components (SPA and the monitoring module SNAs, NPAs) have been implemented as fixed agents and the service task constituting the service as intelligent mobile agent, which can migrate and execute to remote service nodes.

A copy of the database exists on each service node, thus, the communication cost in practice is negligible and is taken equal to zero. In this case, only the service node deployment cost factor is considered and the performance of the system is tested using as decision parameter the load conditions of the service nodes.

The network topology that has been adopted for the experiments consists of five service nodes residing in a single domain. Specifically, all service nodes reside on a 100Mbit/sec Ethernet LAN. The configuration of the service nodes is as follows: two service nodes with 2GHz CPU and 2 GB RAM and three service nodes with 1GHz CPU and 1 GB RAM. All service nodes are running the Linux Redhat OS.

The idle states of the CPUs of the service nodes are simulated to follow the Exponential distribution, with mean value 50,000 ms and maximum value 100,000 ms. In all cases, the duration in which the CPU load of the service nodes is above 50% is 20,000 ms.

The graphical user interface of the SPA module, which implements the service task assignment process, is given in Fig. 2.

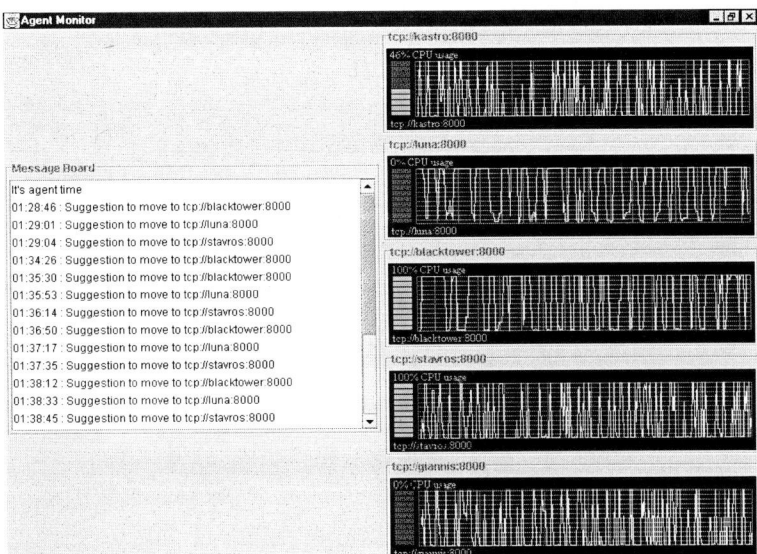

Fig. 2. User interface of the SPA module

We have performed 100 experiments with the mobile agent realising the service logic performing tasks varying from 100 to 1000 queries (with interval 100 queries). The same experiments have also been conducted without using our service task allocation scheme. In the latter case, service tasks are assigned randomly to service nodes.

The mean execution time when the service task assignment process is applied and when the service node is selected randomly are illustrated in Fig. 3. From the obtained results, we observe a decrease in the service completion time when the service task assignment system is used. At this point, it should be mentioned that the performance improvement introduced is tightly related to the number of queries the service task needs to perform at the remote service node and the time that the service node's CPU is idle. It may be observed that for small and large tasks (from 100 to 400 and from 800 to 1000 queries) the improvement in performance is bigger than in medium sized tasks (from 500 to 700 queries). It may also be derived that we have about 6% improvement for small tasks and about 9% for the large ones, while for medium sized tasks the improvement in performance is minor. This could be explained as follows. From Fig. 3, it could be extracted that the mean time required for initialisation of the mobile agent on a service node is approximately 35,000 ms. Also the execution of a task consisting of 100 queries when CPU is idle is 5,500 ms. Thus, small tasks can be performed during one slope of a CPU load (i.e., time during which CPU load is below 50%), while large tasks require for their completion one CPU slope, one CPU peak (i.e., time during which CPU load is above 50%) and finally another CPU slope. The completion of medium tasks usually requires one CPU slope and one CPU peak. Thus, the application of service task allocation process results in minor performance improvement.

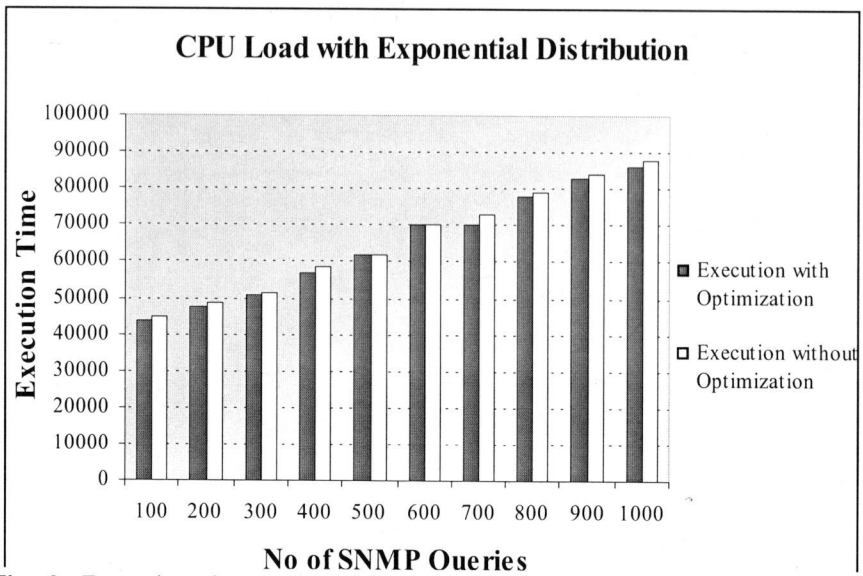

Fig. 3. Execution times with/without optimization for exponential CPU load distribution

5 Conclusions

The highly competitive communications markets should encompass mechanisms that will assist service providers in accounting for their interests, i.e., offering at a given period of time adequate quality services in a cost efficient manner which is highly associated to efficiently managing and fulfilling current user requests. This paper presented such mechanisms. Specifically, the contribution of this paper lies in the following areas. First, the definition and mathematical formulation of (one possible version) of the service task allocation problem, while a model for the communication cost between the service components involved during the provision of a service task was also provided. Through this work it is shown that the problem can be reduced to well-known optimisation problems, which can be solved by relevant standard algorithms. Second, the presentation of a software architecture, which is adopted for acquiring the best service task configuration pattern, i.e., assignment of service tasks to service nodes for efficient service provisioning.

Experimental results indicate that the proposed framework produces good results in relatively simple contexts (e.g., a service, which is composed of one service task that involves execution of one service component). Specifically, when the load conditions of the service nodes is the only factor considered for deciding on the most appropriate service node for the service provisioning, an overall improvement in service completion time of about 7% is introduced (especially, for the small and the large sized service tasks). What remains is to evaluate the performance of the proposed service task allocation scheme in complex contexts where communication cost factor is also involved.

Directions for future work include, but are not limited to the following. First, the realisation of further wide scale trials, so as to experiment with the applicability of the framework presented herewith. Second, the experimentation with alternate approaches (e.g., market-based techniques) for solving the service task allocation problem.

References

1. Trigila S., Raatikainen K., Wind B., Reynolds P., 1998. "Mobility in long-term service architectures and distributed platforms", IEEE Personal Communications, vol. 5, no. 4, pp. 44-55.
2. Magedanz, T., 1997. "TINA-Architectural basis for future telecommunications services", Computer Communications, vol. 20, no. 4, pp. 233-245.
3. Tag M., 1996. "Service creation environment engineering", Proc. Interworking'96 Conference, Japan.
4. Special Issue, 2003. "Special section on grid computing", ACM SIGMETRICS Performance Evaluation Review, vol. 30, no. 4, pp. 12-49.
5. Vinoski S., 1997. "CORBA: Integrating diverse applications within distributed heterogeneous environments", IEEE Commun. Mag., vol. 35, no. 2, pp. 46-55.
6. Morreale P., 1998. "Agents on the move", IEEE Spectrum, vol. 35, no. 4, pp. 34-41.
7. Papadimitriou C., Steiglitz K, 1982. Combinatorial optimization: Algorithms and complexity. Prentice Hall, Inc.
8. The Voyager Platform, Recursion Software Inc. http://www.recursionsw.com/

Classification of Web Documents using Fuzzy Logic Categorical Data Clustering

George E. Tsekouras, Christos Anagnostopoulos, Damianos Gavalas, and
Economou Dafni
University of the Aegean, Department of Cultural Techonoly and
Communication, Laboratory of Intelligent Multimedia, Sapfous 5,
Mytilene, Lesvos Island, 81100, Greece,
gtsek@ct.aegean.gr
WWW home page: http://www.aegean.gr/culturaltec

Abstract. We propose a categorical data fuzzy clustering algorithm to classify
web documents. We extract a number of words for each thematic area
(category) and then, we treat each word as a multidimensional categorical data
vector. For each category, we use the algorithm to partition the available
words into a number of clusters, where the center of each cluster corresponds
to a word. To calculate the dissimilarity measure between two words we use
the Hamming distance. Then, the classification of a new document is
accomplished in two steps. Firstly, we estimate the minimum distance between
this document and all the cluster centers of each category. Secondly, we select
the smallest of the above minimum distance and we classify the document in
the category that corresponds to this distance.

1 Introduction

The continuous growth in the size and use of the Internet creates difficulties in
searching information. One of the most important functions of the Internet is the
information retrieval [1]. The main problem involved in information retrieval is that
the web pages are diverse, with an enormous number of ill-structured and
uncoordinated data sources and a wide range of content, format and authorships [2].
New pages are being generated at such rate that no individual or organization is
capable of keeping track of all of them, organizing them or presenting adequate tools
for managing, manipulating and accessing the associated information.

In order to build efficient information retrieval systems, a solution is to perform
web document classification under certain similar characteristics [2]. The steps to
classify web documents involve the utilization of already classified documents in
combination with specially designed algorithms to extract words and phrases usually
called *items* [3]. These items and their synonyms form collections where indices are

Please use the following format when citing this chapter:

Tsekouras, G. E., Anagnostopoulos, C., Gavalas, D., Dafni, E., 2007, in IFIP International Federation for Information
Processing, Volume 247, Artificial Intelligence and Innovations 2007: From Theory to Applications, eds. Boukis, C.,
Pnevmatikakis, L., Polymenakos, L., (Boston: Springer), pp. 93-100.

used to indicate which item is related to a specific class. Moreover, the collections along with the respective indices carry information about how strong each item is associated with a specific class [4]. The task of assigning a new document to a class is accomplished thought the definition of appropriate similarity or dissimilarity measure.

One of the most efficient approaches to classify web documents is to use cluster analysis. Clustering is an unsupervised learning method that partitions a set of patterns into groups (clusters), where elements (patterns) that belong to the same group are as similar as possible, while elements belonging to different groups are as dissimilar as possible [5]. We distinguish two main categories of clustering algorithms. The first category is called hierarchical clustering and it produces nested partitions generated by sequential agglomerative of divisive algorithms, which are based on distance measures between clusters (such as single link, average link, complete link, etc) [6]. A major drawback of sequential algorithms is their strong dependence on the order in which the patterns are elaborated. The second category is referred to the so-called partitional clustering algorithms [7]. Their implementation is based on the alternating optimization of a certain objective function. Many clustering algorithms assume that the patterns are real vectors, called numerical patterns. However, in the web we usually consider non-numerical patterns. These patterns can be categorized into two types: (a) web documents presented in a specific document formats like HTML containing control strings and text [8], and (b) web server log files containing access sequences of web pages visited by specific users [9]. Relations between non-numerical patterns can be obtained by using the well-known Hamming distance or the Levenshtein distance [10].

In this paper we propose a systematic approach to cluster web documents. The basic idea is to define a number of web page categories and to download a number of pages each of which is related to a category. For each category we extract a number of words, which are treated as categorical data vectors. Then, we apply a novel algorithm to cluster these words into a number of clusters. The resulted cluster centers are words from the original data set. Finally, each web document is classified to a category based on the minimum Hamming distance.

2   Categorical Data Clustering

Categorical data clustering (CDC) is an important operation in data mining. A well-known categorical data clustering approach is the fuzzy c-modes [11]. Next, we describe the basic design steps of this algorithm.

Let $X = \{x_1, x_2, ..., x_n\}$ be a set of categorical objects. Each object is described by a set of attributes $A_1, A_2, ..., A_p$. The j-th attribute A_j $(1 \leq j \leq p)$ is defined on a domain of q_j categories. Thus, the k-th categorical object x_k $(1 \leq k \leq n)$ is described as: $x_k = [x_{k1}, x_{k2}, ..., x_{kp}]$.

Let $x_k = [x_{k1}, x_{k2}, ..., x_{kp}]$ and $x_l = [x_{l1}, x_{l2}, ..., x_{lp}]$ be two categorical objects. Then, the matching dissimilarity between them is defined as [11],

$$D(\boldsymbol{x}_k, \boldsymbol{x}_l) = \sum_{j=1}^{p} \delta(x_{kj}, x_{lj}) \quad (1 \le k \le n, 1 \le l \le n, \ k \ne l) \tag{1}$$

where

$$\delta(x_{kj}, x_{lj}) = \begin{cases} 0, & if \ \ x_{kj} = x_{lj} \\ 1, & otherwise \end{cases} \tag{2}$$

The fuzzy c-modes algorithm is based on minimizing the following objective function,

$$J = \sum_{k=1}^{n} \sum_{i=1}^{c} (u_{ik})^m \, D(\boldsymbol{x}_k, \boldsymbol{v}_i) \tag{3}$$

subject to the following equality constraint,

$$\sum_{i=1}^{c} u_{ik} = 1 \tag{4}$$

where n is the number of categorical objects, c is the number of clusters, $\boldsymbol{x}_k$ $(1 \le k \le n)$ is the k-th categorical object, $\boldsymbol{v}_i$ $(1 \le i \le c)$ is the i-th cluster center, u_{ik} is the membership degree of the k-th categorical object to the i-th cluster, and $m \in (1, \infty)$ is a fuzziness parameter to adjust the membership degree weighting effect.

The membership degrees that solve the above constrained optimization problem are given as [11],

$$u_{ik} = 1 \Bigg/ \left[\sum_{j=1}^{c} \left(\frac{D(\boldsymbol{x}_k, \boldsymbol{v}_i)}{D(\boldsymbol{x}_k, \boldsymbol{v}_j)} \right)^{1/(m-1)} \right] \quad (1 \le i \le c, 1 \le k \le n) \tag{5}$$

On the other hand, the locations of the cluster centers (modes) that minimize the objective function in (3) are determined as [11]:
$$\boldsymbol{v}_i = [v_{i1}, v_{i2}, ..., v_{ip}], \text{ where}$$

$$v_{ij} = a_j^r \in DOM(A_j) \text{ with, } \sum_{k, x_{kj} = a_j^r} (u_{ik})^m \ge \sum_{k, x_{kj} = a_j^t} (u_{ik})^m \quad (1 \le t \le q_j, r \ne t) \tag{6}$$

3 The Proposed Fuzzy Categorical Data Clustering Algorithm

The proposed fuzzy clustering algorithm utilizes a number of steps each of which is described within the next subsections.

3.1 Potential Based Clustering

The potential of the k-th categorical object is defined as follows,

$$P_k = \sum_{l=1}^{n} \exp\{-a \, D(\boldsymbol{x}_k, \boldsymbol{x}_l)\} \tag{7}$$

where $D(x_k, x_l)$ is given in (1) and $a \in (0,1)$. Observing that an object with a high potential value is a good nominee to be a cluster center, the potential-based clustering algorithm is given next:

Select values for the design parameter $a \in (0,1)$ and for the parameter $\beta \in (0,1)$. Initially, set the number of clusters equal to $c=0$.

Step 1)   Using eq. (7) determine the potential values for all data vectors
           x_k $(1 \le k \le n)$

Step 2)   Set $c=c+1$

Step 3)   Calculate the maximum potential value $P_{max} = \max_{k}\{P_k\}$ and select the
           object x_{max} that corresponds to P_{max} as the center element of the c-th
           cluster: $v_c = x_{max}$

Step 4)   Remove from the set X all the categorical objects having similarity with
           x_{max} greater than β and assign them to the c-th cluster

Step 5)   If X is empty stop; Else turn the algorithm to step 2.

3.2 Cluster Merging

In the first place we use (1) to calculate the matching dissimilarities between all pairs of cluster centers. Then, we compute the weighted matching dissimilarities between pairs of clusters according to the following formula,

$$D_w(v_i, v_j) = D(v_i, v_j) \sqrt{\sum_{k=1}^{n} u_{ik} \sum_{k=1}^{n} u_{jk} \Big/ \left(\sum_{k=1}^{n} u_{ik} + \sum_{k=1}^{n} u_{jk} \right)} \quad (1 \le i, j \le c; \ i \ne j) \quad (8)$$

where $\sum_{k=1}^{n} u_{ik}$ and $\sum_{k=1}^{n} u_{jk}$ are the fuzzy cardinalities of the i-th and j-th cluster. To decide which clusters are similar enough to be merged, we use the following similarity relation between two distinct clusters:

$$S_{ij} = \exp\{\theta D_w(v_i, v_j)\} \quad (1 \le i, j \le c, \ i \ne j) \text{ and } \theta \in (0,1) \quad (9)$$

3.3 Validity Index

Cluster validity concerns the determination of the optimal number of clusters. In this section we use the cluster validity index developed in [12]. This validity index is given by the following equation,

$$G = \frac{\sum_{i=1}^{c} \dfrac{\sum_{k=1}^{n} (u_{ik})^m D(v_k, v_i)}{n_i}}{\sum_{i=1}^{c} \sum_{\substack{j=1 \\ j \ne i}}^{c} (\mu_{ij})^m D(v_i, v_j)} \quad (10)$$

where

$$n_i = \sum_{k=1}^{n} u_{ik} \quad , \quad 1 \leq i \leq c$$

and

$$ì_{ij} = \frac{1}{\sum_{\substack{l=1 \\ l \neq j}}^{c} \left(\frac{D(v_j, v_i)}{D(v_j, v_l)} \right)^{1/(m-1)}} \quad (i \neq j)$$

is the membership degree between the i-th and the j-th cluster center taking into account the rest of the cluster centers. The basic idea is to select the partition that corresponds to the minimum value of the index G_{min}.

3.4 The Algorithm

Step 1)   Apply the potential-based clustering algorithm to obtain a number of cluster centers v_i $(1 \leq i \leq c)$

Step 2)   Using (5) calculate the u_{ik} $(1 \leq i \leq c, 1 \leq k \leq n)$ and determine the value of J in (3)

Step 3)   Set $J^{old} = J$

Step 4)   Using (6) update the cluster centers

Step 5)   Using (5) calculate the u_{ik} $(1 \leq i \leq c, 1 \leq k \leq n)$ and determine the value of J in (3).
If $\left| J_m(U,V) - J_m^{old}(U,V) \right| \leq \varepsilon$ go to step 6, else go to step 3

Step 6)   Calculate the value of the validity index G in (10)

Step 7)   Calculate all the similarities S_{ij} $(1 \leq i, j \leq c)$ in (9) and select the maximum: $S_{max} = \max_{i,j} \{ S_{ij} \}$. The clusters that correspond to S_{max} are denoted as: i_0 and j_0

Step 8)   If $S_{max} > \delta$ then
merge the clusters i_0 and j_0 into a new cluster l_0 as follows,
$$u_{l_0 k} = \left(u_{i_0} + u_{j_0} \right) / 2$$
and set $c = c - 1$.
Using (6) determine the new cluster centers v_i $(1 \leq i \leq c)$,
calculate the new value of J and go to step 3
Else
    Stop
EndIf

Step 9)   Select the partition that corresponds to the minimum valued of the validity index (G_{min})

4 Web Document Classification

To apply the algorithm we choose the following 10 web page categories: (1) process engineering, (2) organic chemistry, (3) inorganic chemistry, (4) material analysis and design, (5) electrical engineering, (6) hardware, (7) software, (8) mechanical engineering, (9) civil engineering, and (10) marine science. We searched the yahoo.com and collected 28678 pages for all of the categories. Then, we used the 20000 to train the algorithm and the rest 8678 to test its performance.

Table 1: Number of clusters obtained by the algorithm for each category.

Category	Number of Clusters
Process Engineering	28
Organic Chemistry	33
Inorganic Chemistry	24
Material Analysis and Design	28
Electrical Engineering	43
Hardware	29
Software	35
Mechanical Engineering	46
Civil Engineering	52
Marine Science	38

The web documents are described in HTML format and texts are marked by the HTML tags. For each website category we downloaded the documents using a web crawler and we removed all the HTML tags in order to extract the texts from the web pages. We used a dictionary to separate the nouns from other words, since there is stronger relation between nouns and the web page theme. In the next step, we applied the algorithm developed in [13] to filter out insignificant nouns and certain types of word endings, like "ing" and "ed". Then, we selected the 1000 most frequently reported words, using the inverse document frequency (IDF) for each word. The IDF is given by the following equation [14],

$$ fr_{IDF} = \frac{f_w}{f_{w\_max}} \log\left(\frac{P}{P_w}\right) $$

where f_w is the frequency of occurrence of the word in the category's document collection, f_{w_max} is the maximum frequency of occurrence of any word in the category's collection, P is the number of documents of the whole collection, and P_w is the number of documents that include this word.

From the set of the 10000 words we found the word with the maximum number of characters, which defines the dimensionality of the discrete space and is denoted as p. Then, we represented the rest of the words in a sequence of p characters inserting where it is necessary the blank character. Therefore for each category, the k-th word can be described as:

$$ x_k = [x_{k1}, x_{k2}, ..., x_{kp}] \qquad (1 \le k \le 1000) $$

To this end, all the words have been transformed into categorical data vectors and thus, we can use the clustering approach presented in the previous section to partition the available 1000 words into a number of clusters for each category. Table

1 presents the categories and the respective number of clusters (i.e. words) obtained by the algorithm. For example, for the category "process engineering" the cluster centers (keywords) in alphabetical order are:

absorption, balance, batch, column, component, conservation, distillation, dryer, energy, equilibrium, evaporation, exchanger, fluid, furnace, heat, kinetics, liquid, mass, pressure, pump, reactor, saturation, separation, steam, temperature, thermodynamic, valve, viscosity

Table 2: Classification results of the proposed algorithm.

Category	Fuzzy c-Modes	c-Modes
Process Engineering	65.78%	57.86%
Organic Chemistry	67.11%	68.01%
Inorganic Chemistry	61.56%	60.23%
Material Analysis and Design	67.63%	63.10%
Electrical Engineering	60.89%	59.12%
Hardware	62.03%	58.85%
Software	66.34%	52.71%
Mechanical Engineering	60.09%	66.58%
Civil Engineering	69.90%	62.08%
Marine Science	66.55%	59.32%

Keywords extracted from the proposed approach can be used to automatically classify unknown texts. For this purpose we used the 8678 pages mentioned previously. Each document consists of a sequence of words $(x_1, x_2, ..., x_r)$ and each word has a minimum distance to one of the cluster centers of each of the 10 categories. Thus, for each document we determine 10 minimum distances. Then, the document is assigned to the category that appears the smallest of the above 10 distances. The results of this simulation are presented in table 2. For comparison reasons, this table also reports the results obtained by the c-modes [15] when it is used in the place of the fuzzy c-modes. From this table, we clearly see that except the categories "organic chemistry" and "mechanical engineering" the fuzzy c-modes outperformed the c-modes. The qualitative reason is that there are common words in all of the engineering categories. This fact directly implies the presence of uncertainty in the data set and therefore the use of the fuzzy logic-based clustering appears to be more efficient since it is able to quantitatively model this uncertainty.

5   Conclusions

We have shown how categorical data fuzzy clustering can be implemented to classify web documents. The basic idea of the approach is to extract a set of words and then transform them into categorical data vectors. The dissimilarity between two distinct words is measured using the well-known Hamming distance. Then, we apply a sequence of steps aiming towards generating a number of clusters, each of which is described by a single word. The classification of web documents is accomplished by using the minimum Hamming distance. The simulation results verified the efficiency of the proposed method.

Acknowledgements: This work is supported by the General Secretariat of Research and Technology (Project "Software Application in Interactive Kids TV-MPEG-21", project framework "Image, Sound, and Language Processing", project number : EHΓ-16). The participants are the University of the Aegean, the Hellenic Public Radio and Television (ERT) and the Time Lapse Picture Hellas.

References

1. Smith, K.A, and Ng, A.: Web page clustering using a self-organizing map of user navigation patterns, Decision Support Systems 35 (2003) 245-256
2. Macskassy, S. A., Banerjee, A., Davison, B. D., and Hirsh, H.: Human performance on clustering web pages: a preliminary study, Proceedings of the 4th International Conference on Knowledge Discovery and Data Mining (1998)
3. Anagnostopoulos, I., Anagnostopoulos, C., Loumos, V., and Kayafas, E.: Classifying web pages employing a probabilistic neural network, IEE Proceedings on Software 151(3) (2004) 139-150
4. Qi, D., and Sun, B.: A genetic k-means approach for automated web page classification, Proceedings of the 2004 IEEE International Conference on Information Reuse and Integration (2004) 241-246
5. Jain, A.K., Murty, M.N., and Flynn, P.J.: Data clustering: a review, ACM Computing Survey 31(3) (199) 264-323
6. Runkler, T.A., and Bezdek, J.C.: Web mining with relational clustering, International Journal of Approximate Reasoning 32 (2003) 217-236
7. Bezdek, J.C., and Pal, K.: Fuzzy models for pattern recognition: methods that search for structures in data, IEEE Press (1992), New York, NY
8. Manning, C.D., and Schutze, H.: Foundations of statistical natural language processing, MIT Press (1999), Cambridge, MA
9. Punin, J.R., Krishnamoorthy, M.S, and Zaki, M.J.: Web usage mining-languages and algorithms, Technical Report, Rensselaer Polytechnic Institute, NY (2001)
10. Levenshtein, V.I.: Binary codes capable of correcting deletions, insertions and reversals, Sov. Phys. Dokl. 6 (1966) 705-710
11. Z. Huang, and M. K. Ng, A fuzzy k-modes algorithm for clustering categorical data, *IEEE Transactions on Fuzzy Systems*, Vol. 7, no 4, 1999, pp. 446-452
12. Tsekouras, G. E., Papageorgiou, D., Kotsiantis, S., Kalloniatis, C., and Pintelas, P.: Fuzzy Clustering of Categorical Attributes and its Use in Analyzing Cultural Data, International Journal of Computational Intelligence 1(2) (2004) 147-151
13. Chen, J., Miculcic, A., and Kraft, D.H.: An integrated approach to information retrieval with fuzzy clustering and inferencing, in *Knowledge Management in Fuzzy DataBases*, Pons, O., Vila, M.A., and Kacprzyk, J. (Eds), Physic Verlag, Vol. 163 (2000)
14. Jones, K.S.: A statistical interpretation of tem specificity and its application in retrieval, J. Domument 28(1) (1972) 11-20
15. Huang, Z.: Extensions of the k-means algorithm for clustering large data sets with categorical values, Data Mining and Knowledge Discovery 2 (1998) 283-304

Measuring Expert Impact on Learning how to Play a Board Game

Dimitris Kalles

Hellenic Open University, Sachtouri 23, 26222, Patras, Greece
kalles@eap.gr,
WWW home page: http://dimitris.kalles.googlepages.com

Abstract. We investigate systematically the impact of human intervention in the training of computer players in a strategy board game. In that game, computer players utilise reinforcement learning with neural networks for evolving their playing strategies and demonstrate a slow learning speed. Human intervention can significantly enhance learning performance, but carrying it out systematically seems to be more of a problem of an integrated game development environment as opposed to automatic evolutionary learning.

1 Introduction

Several machine learning concepts have been tested in game domains, since strategic games offer ample opportunities to automatically explore, develop and test winning strategies. The most widely publicised results occurred during the 1990s, when IBM made strenuous efforts to develop (first with Deep Thought, later with Deep Blue) a chess program comparable to the best human player.

As early as 1950, Shannon [14] studied how computers could play chess and proposed the idea of using a value function to compete with human players. Following that, Samuel [13] created a checkers program that tried to find "the highest point in multidimensional scoring space", only to have his research rediscovered by Sutton [15] who formulated the $TD(\lambda)$ method for temporal difference reinforcement learning (RL). Since then, more games such as Tetris, Blackjack, Othello [10], chess [19] and backgammon [17, 18] were analysed by applying $TD(\lambda)$ to improve their performance.

TD-Gammon [17, 18] was the most successful early application of $TD(\lambda)$ for the game of backgammon. Using RL techniques and after training with 1.5 million self-playing games, a performance comparable to that demonstrated by backgammon world champions was achieved.

As far as strategy games are concerned, the most important and critical point of them is to select and implement the computer's strategy during the game. The term

Please use the following format when citing this chapter:

Kalles, D., 2007, in IFIP International Federation for Information Processing, Volume 247, Artificial Intelligence and Innovations 2007: From Theory to Applications, eds. Boukis, C., Pnevmatikakis, L., Polymenakos, L., (Boston: Springer), pp. 101-113.

strategy stands for the selection of the computer's next move considering its current situation, the opponent's situation, consequences of that move and possible next moves of the opponent. RL helps solve this problem by formulating strategies in terms of policies. In theory, the advantage of RL to other learning methods is that the target system itself detects which actions to take via trial and error, with limited need for direct human involvement.

In our research, we use a new strategy game to gain insight into the question of how game playing capabilities can be efficiently and automatically evolved. The problem that we aim to highlight in this paper is that the usual arsenal of computational techniques does not readily suffice to develop a winning policy and that one must couple automation with careful experimental design. Our contribution is the development and experimental validation of simple quantitative indices, that measure performance improvement of automatic game playing, to better support our decisions about which training paths to follow. For this reason we have designed and carried out several experimental sessions comprising in total well over 400,000 computer-vs.-computer games and over 200 human-vs.-computer games.

The rest of this paper is organised in four sections. The next section presents the basic details of the game and its introductory analysis. The third section describes our experimentation on training. The fourth section discusses the impact and the limitations of human-assisted learning and states the recommended directions for future development. The concluding section summarises the work.

2   A brief background on a strategy game workbench

The game is played on a square board of size *n*, by two players. Two square bases of size *a* are located on opposite board corners. The lower left base belongs to the white player and the upper right base belongs to the black player. At game kick-off each player possesses β pawns. The goal is to move a pawn into the opponent's base.

The base is considered as a single square, therefore every pawn of the base can move at one step to any of the adjacent to the base free squares (see Fig. 1 for examples and counterexamples of moves). A pawn can move to an empty square that is vertically or horizontally adjacent, provided that the maximum distance from its base is not decreased (so, backward moves are not allowed). Note that the distance from the base is measured as the maximum of the horizontal and the vertical distance from the base (and not as a sum of these quantities). A pawn that cannot move is lost (more than one pawn may be lost in one round). If some player runs out of pawns he loses.

The leftmost board in Fig. 1 demonstrates a legal and an illegal move (for the pawn pointed to by the arrow). The rightmost boards demonstrate the loss of pawns (with arrows showing pawn casualties). Such (loss incurring) moves bring about the direct adjustment of the moving pawn with some pawn of the opponent. In such cases the "trapped" pawn automatically draws away from the game. As a by-product of this rule, when there is no free square next to the base, the rest of the pawns of the base are lost.

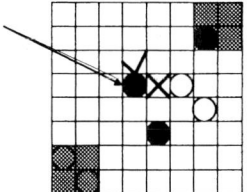 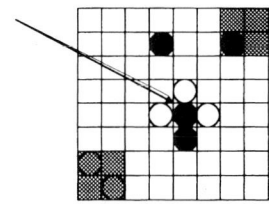 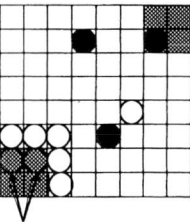

Fig. 1. A sample decision tree

2.1 The analysis context

Past research [7] initially demonstrated that, when trained with self-playing games, both players had nearly equal opportunities to win and neither player enjoyed a pole position advantage. Follow-up research [8] furnished preliminary results that suggested a computer playing against itself would achieve weaker performance when compared to a computer playing against a human player.

The game is a discrete Markov procedure, since there are finite states and moves. Each episode terminates and the game is thus amenable to analysis by reinforcement learning [16]. The *a priori* knowledge of the system consists of the rules only. The agent's goal is to learn a policy that will maximize the expected sum of rewards in a specific time; this is called an optimal policy. A policy determines which action should be taken next given the current state of the environment. As usual, at each move the agent balances between choosing an action that will straightforward maximize its reward or choosing an action that might prove to be better. A commonly used starting ε-greedy policy with $\varepsilon=0.9$ was adopted, i.e. the system chooses the best-valued action with a probability of 0.9 and a random action with a probability of 0.1.

At the beginning all states have the same value except for the final states. After each move the values are updated through TD(λ), where λ determines the reduction degree of assigning credit to some action and was set to $\lambda=0.5$.

Neural networks were used to interpolate between game board situations (one for each player, because each player has a unique state space). The input layer nodes are the board positions for the next possible move, totalling n^2-2a^2+10. The hidden layer consists of half as many hidden nodes, whereas the output node has only one node, which can be regarded as the probability of winning when one starts from a specific game-board configuration and then makes a specific move.

Note that, drawing on the above and the game description, we can conclude that we cannot effectively learn a deterministic optimal policy. Such a policy does exist for the game [11], however the use of an approximation (neural network) effectively rules out such learning. Of course, even if that was not the case, it does not follow that converging to such a policy is computationally tractable [2].

3 The experimental setup

To focus on how one could measurably detect improvement in automatic game playing, we devised a set of experiments with different options in the reward policies
while at the same time adopting a relatively narrow focus on the moves of the human
(training player).

Herein we report experiments with 8 game batches. Each game batch consists of
50,000 computer-vs.-computer (CC) games, carried out in 5 stages of 10,000 games
each. For batches that have involved human-vs.-computer (HC) games, each CC
stage is interleaved with a HC stage of 10 games. Thus, HC batches are 50,050
games long. In HC games, a human is always the white player.

We now show the alternatives for the human player in Table 1. Briefly describing them, we always move from the bottom-left base to the north and then move
right, attempting to enter the black base from its vertical edge (see Fig. 2). We explore a mix of learning scenarios, whereby at some experiments we explicitly wander
around with the human player, allowing the black player to discover a winning path
to the white base. Of course, if the human player wants to win, this is straightforward.

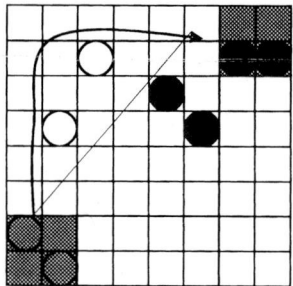

Fig. 2. The path of a human player

Table 1. Policies of white human player

	White player always starts from bottom-left
1	North, then Right, attempting to enter from vertical edge
2	Allows Black to win 5 games, then Policy #1
3	Allows Black to win 10 games

The alternatives for the rewards are shown in Table 2. Briefly describing them,
the first reward type assigns some credit to states that involve a pawn directly neighbouring the enemy base. It also rewards captured pawns by calculating the difference
of pawn counts and by scaling that difference to a number in [-1,1]. The other two
polices have been developed with a view towards simplification (by dropping the
base adjacency credit) and towards better value alignment.

Table 2. Reward types

	White player always starts from bottom-left
1	Win: 100, Loss: -100 Win-at-next-move: 2, Loss -at-next-move: -2 Pawn difference scaled in [-1,1]
2	Win: 100, Loss: -100 Pawn difference scaled in [-1,1]
3	Win: 100, Loss: -100 Pawn difference scaled in [-100,100]

3.1 Varying only the white player policy (HC)

The white player policy can be deliberately varied in HC games only, of course. We report below the results of three HC batches, where the reward type was set to 1. A short description of the batches is shown in Table 3, whereas the results are shown in Fig. 3, Fig. 4 and Fig. 5.

Table 3. Description of batches 1 - 3

	Game Type – Reward - Policy
1	HC, 1, 1
2	HC, 1, 2
3	HC, 1, 3

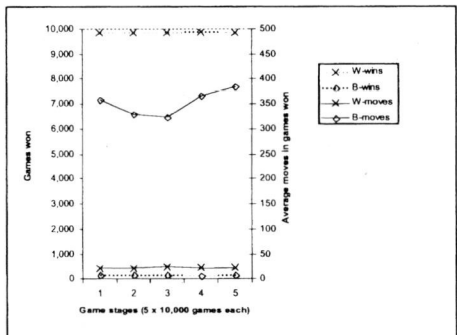

Fig. 3. 1st Experimental Session.

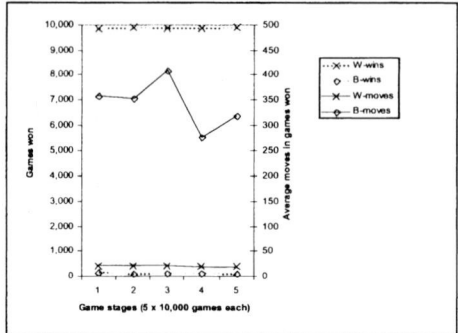

Fig. 4. 2nd Experimental Session.

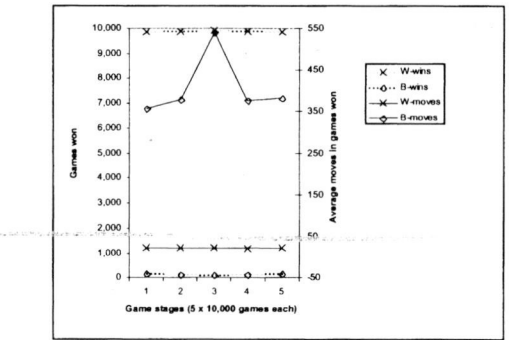

Fig. 5. 3rd Experimental Session.

First, we observe that the white player overwhelms the black one. The black player's performance can be seen to improve only in the third batch, where the white player aims not to win. Still, this improvement is indirect (note that the white player requires a larger average number of moves to win). This suggests that the number of CC games may be too few to allow the pole position advantage of the white player to diminish. In that respect, it also seems that when the white player wins, even in few of the games, the efficiency of the human-induced state-space exploration can be picked up and sustained by the subsequent exploitation of the CC stage.

3.2 Varying only the reward

In the next experimental round, we froze the policy type to 1. A short description of the batches is shown in Table 4. The results are shown in Fig. 3, Fig. 6 and Fig. 7.

Table 4. Description of batches 1, 4, 5

	Game Type – Reward - Policy
1	HC, 1, 1
4	HC, 2, 1
5	HC, 3, 1

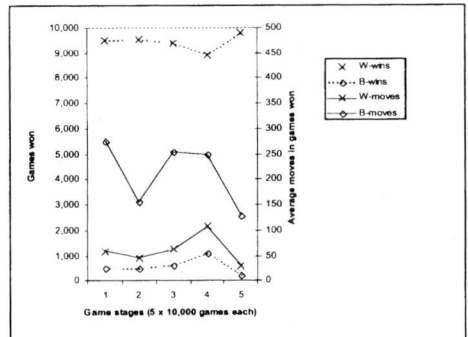

Fig. 6. 4th Experimental Session.

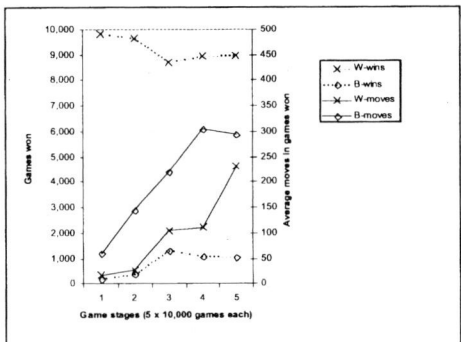

Fig. 7. 5th Experimental Session.

We now observe that the fifth experiment suggests a clear improvement for the black player, as the number of moves required by the white CC player consistently increases. In any case, we also observe again that as the while HC player wins, so does the white CC player seem able to sustain its own wins. Note also the highly irregular behaviour in the fourth batch, where the fourth stage witnesses a strong turn. It is interesting that this is associated with a superficially rewarded pawn advantage. These results are an indication that pawn advantage rewards should be commensurate with their expected impact in the game outcome; losing many pawns and not capturing any indicates that we are about to lose.

3.3 Interleaving CC and HC games

The above findings lead us to experiment with the following scenario: first conduct a CC batch, then use its evolved neural network to spawn experimentation in two separate batches, one CC and one HC. Note that, until now, all experiments were *tabula-rasa* in the sense that each experiment started with a "clean" neural network. In all these experiments, we used the reward type (3) that aligns pawn advantage with winning a game. A short description of the batches is shown in Table 5, whereas the results are shown in Fig. 8, Fig. 9 and Fig. 10.

Table 5. Description of batches 6 - 8

	Game Type – Reward - Policy
6	CC, 3, -
7	CC, 3, - (based on batch 6)
8	HC, 3, 1 (based on batch 6)

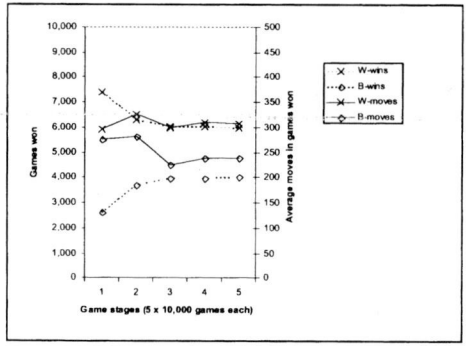

Fig. 8. 6th Experimental Session.

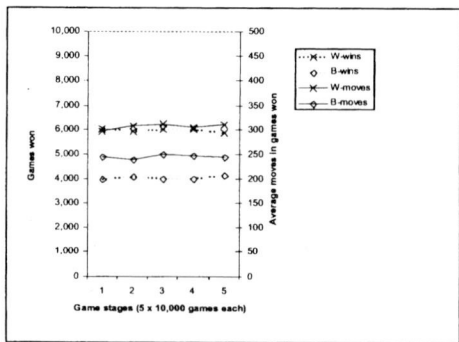

Fig. 9. 7th Experimental Session.

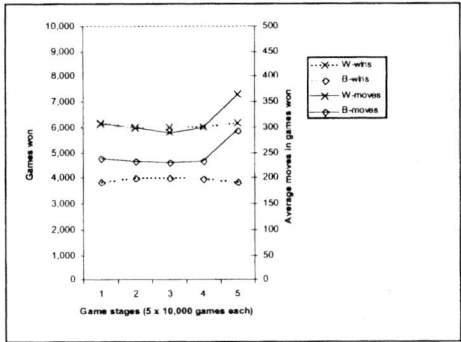

Fig. 10. 8th Experimental Session.

The succession of the two CC games is quite revealing: while the white player does enjoy a pole position advantage, this is subsequently eroded. This is surely obvious if one observes the number of games won. Note that the short distance between the lines showing the average number of moves is another testimony. This further supports our initial experimentation that suggested both players had equal chances to win; our experiments now show that this equality is progressively brought about by the convergent behaviour of the two players.

Quite as importantly, one can note that the introduction of human intelligence eventually allows the white CC player to immediately increase the performance gap.

It is most instructive to compare the fifth and eighth batches (Fig. 7 and Fig. 10 respectively) since their only difference is that the eighth batch is based on a previous CC batch. It seems that the CC batch has instilled some knowledge in the white player that stabilizes its behaviour relative to the black player. This very inefficient knowledge is not straightforward to "forget" in order to be replaced by human playing RL values. Perhaps, it would be more precise to call it knowledge inertia since, if left unattended to, the two computer players will most likely reach an uninteresting equilibrium (as Fig. 8 and Fig. 9 show).

4   Discussion

We definitely need more experiments if we are to train our computer players to a level comparable to that of a human player. The options can be numerous, but we can name a few obvious ones that are also clearly independent between them: experimentation with more exploration-exploitation trade-offs or alternative RL parameters, experimentation with the learning parameters or the input-output representation of the neural network, experimentation with alternative reward types or human playing policies. Last but not least, any combination of the above may be a plausible one to investigate. In fact, we cannot directly attribute which part of the learning inefficiencies spotted in the long experimental runs of the above section may be due to the parameters of the reinforcement learning algorithm, or the parameters of the neural network.

The results we have obtained to-date clearly suggest that it is very important to find an efficient and effective way to achieve learning. We must optimize the use of expensive resources (human player) so that they are intelligently placed at critical points of the learning process, which will mostly be done automatically. Note that even though the number of HC games is relatively very small to the number of CC games, the impact of HC games can be clearly detected. Accurately measuring this impact is not straightforward, however. Therefore, it is of less importance to discuss how much to increase human involvement as opposed to gauging how to best spread a given amount of such involvement.

The question, of course, is "which options to select for experimentation". In answering this question, there are two major directions to follow [4].

The first one is to devise an experimentation engine that will attempt to calculate the best parameters for effective and efficient learning. This option has conceptual simplicity, technical appeal and has delivered some interesting results [12]. However, we believe that it would be an expensive addition to an already expensive task, as, still more parameters must be specified (and experimented with). By deploying a meta-experimentation level, we practically shift the problem. Moreover, we would have to define the "supervision" level of the learning process and craft appropriate measures. Beyond the number of games won and the average number of moves in such games which seem to be good candidates for this task, we may also have to come up with measures of interestingness [5, 9].

The second one is to embed some ad-hoc knowledge into the learning process. This is not a new concept; a combination of RL and Explanation Based Learning was initially supposed to be able to benefit the game with faster learning and the ability to scale to large state spaces in a more structured manner [3]. Why, then, did it not materialize in published benefits? We believe that this is due to the inherent difficulty of attempting to merge numeric and symbolic representation and classification paradigms, and especially so in the context of large experimentations, where the coarse or fine resolution of the merging process might result in substantially different outcomes.

In retrospect, both directions seem to suggest that the numeric approach to automatic learning has some very pronounced practicality limitations. Simply put, some domains are too premature (in how we comprehend them) to lend themselves to general-purpose evolutionary improvement. It is for this reason, we believe, that our experiments demonstrate measurable improvements when subjected to human "tutoring". Though automatic playing has long been testified to deliver good results [18, 1] and still is a vibrant area, we emphasize human impact in a new game (simple, yet state-space consuming) because we are interested precisely in exploring *disturbance* during learning, not unlike the dice in back-gammon. Note that an interesting and probably useful extension would be to develop a mini-max (computer) player and then use that player as a teacher for the learning computer [11].

Interactive evolution might be promising, however. In such a course, one would ideally switch from focused human training to autonomous crawling between promising alternatives. But, as we have discovered, during the preparation of this work, the interactivity requirements of the process of improving the computer player is very tightly linked to the availability of a computer-automated environment that supports this development. Such an environment was not available and was missed.

As a matter of fact, the above experiments may have cost in total about one month of computing from a relatively high-end desktop. The visualization of the intermediate results, the data processing and visualization, as well as the selection of which extract of the results to choose may have cost about twice as much in human resources. (On top of that human resources cost, it would be difficult to quantify the context switching effort between several other occupations.)

This may be sustainable if we want to provide some incremental improvement to automatic game playing but it seems hardly sustainable if we aim to develop the level of automatic playing to that of the human player. In terms of the experiments described above, we have noticed several features of an experimentation system that we have deemed indispensable if one views the project from the point of system efficiency. Such features range from being able to easily design an experimentation batch, direct its results to a specially designed database (to also facilitate reproducibility), automatically process the game statistics and observe correlations, link experimentation batches in terms of succession, while at the same time being able to pre-design a whole series of linked experiments with varying parameters of duration and succession and then guide the human player to play a game according to that design.

As it seems, being able to provide a tool that captures the lifecycle of the development of an AI application is a strong contributor to the success of the take-up of that application. Perhaps, it is not surprising that when data mining (which, in principle, is close to what this research is about) started its applied steps, it was with the availability of workflow-like tools that researchers and practitioners alike managed to navigate efficiently through the data mining process. In that sense, we aim to pursue these directions towards the automatic discovery of knowledge in game playing as opposed to equipping the computer with more detailed domain modelling [6] or with standard game-tree search techniques.

5 Conclusion

This paper focused on the presentation of carefully designed experiments, at a large scale, to support the claim that human playing can *measurably* improve the performance of computer players in a board game.

After describing the experimental setup, we presented the results which are centred on two key statistics: number of games won and average number of moves in games won. Arguably, the high level of abstraction of these statistics should render them (as well as the proposed process) useful in the development process and evaluation of similar board games.

The computation of these statistics is a trivial task, but the key challenge is how to decide the succession of experiments, taking into account that each experiment is specified by some parameters, so as to efficiently and effectively guide the learning process. The importance of such guiding is underlined by the fact that we must thoughtfully exploit human contribution, which will undoubtedly be a scarcely available resource.

We have concluded that while most of the fundamental AI arsenal needed is already available significant applied research is required for the establishment of tools that will streamline the experimentation process. We believe that workflow-like tools will first beat the path of such streamlining before we effectively address the autonomous management of this process.

Acknowledgements: This paper has not been published elsewhere and has not been submitted for publication elsewhere. The paper shares some setting-the-context paragraphs with three referenced papers [3, 8, 9], with which it is neither identical nor similar.

No methodology, experiments or results are duplicated. All game data have been recorded for potential examination and reproducibility tests. These data, along with the game code, are available on demand for academic research purposes.

Mr. Christos Kalantzis designed and carried out, during the 2005-6 academic year, long series of experiments that generated heated discussions on the interpretation of their results and have influenced this work. Ms. Athanassia Vlasi toiled with web technologies attempting to port the game to the web, during the 2006-7 academic year.

References

1. K. Chellapilla, D.B. Fogel (1999). "Co-Evolving Checkers Playing Programs using only Win, Lose, or Draw," Symposium on Applications and Science of Computational Intelligence II, Vol. 3722, K. Priddy, S. Keller, D.B. Fogel, and J.C. Bezdek (eds.), SPIE, Bellingham, WA, pp. 303-312, 1999.
2. A. Condon (1992). "The Complexity of Stochastic Games", *Information and Computation* 96, pp. 203-224.
3. T. Dietterich, N. Flann (1997). "Explanation-Based Learning and Reinforcement Learning: A Unified View", Machine Learning, Vol. 28.
4. I. Ghory (2004). "Reinforcement Learning in Board Games", Technical report CSTR-04-004, Department of Computer Science, University of Bristol.
5. H.J. van den Herik, H.H.L.M. Donkers, P.H.M. Spronck (2005). "Opponent Modelling and Commercial Games", Proceedings of IEEE 2005 Symposium on Computational Intelligence and Games, Essex University, Colchester, UK. pp 15-25.
6. A. Junghanns, J. Schaeffer (2001). "Sokoban: Enhancing General Single-Agent Search Methods using Domain Knowledge", Artificial Intelligence, Vol. 129, pp. 219-251.
7. D. Kalles and P. Kanellopoulos (2001). "On Verifying Game Design and Playing Strategies using Reinforcement Learning", *ACM Symposium on Applied Computing, special track on Artificial Intelligence and Computation Logic*, Las Vegas.
8. D. Kalles, E. Ntoutsi (2002). "Interactive Verification of Game Design and Playing Strategies", IEEE International Conference on Tools with Artificial Intelligence, Washington D.C.
9. D. Kalles (2007). "Player co-modelling in a strategy board game: discovering how to play fast", accepted for publication at Cybernetics and Systems.
10. A. Leouski (1995). "Learning of Position Evaluation in the Game of Othello", M.Sc. Thesis, University of Massachusetts, Amherst.
11. M.L. Littman (1994). "Markov Games as a Framework for Multi-Agent Reinforcement Learning", *Proceedings of 11th International Conference on Machine Learning,* San Francisco, pp 157-163.

12. I. Partalis, G. Tsoumakas, I. Katakis and I. Vlahavas (2006). "Ensembe Pruning Using Reinforcement Learning", Proceedings of the 4th Panhellenic conference on Artificial Intelligence, Heraklion, Greece, Springer LNCS 3955, pp. 301-310.
13. A. Samuel (1959). "Some Studies in Machine Learning Using the Game of Checkers", IBM Journal of Research and Development, Vol. 3, pp. 210-229.
14. C. Shannon (1950). "Programming a computer for playing chess", Philosophical Magazine, Vol. 41(4), pp. 265-275.
15. R.S. Sutton (1988). "Learning to Predict by the Methods of Temporal Differences", Machine Learning, Vol. 3, pp. 9-44.
16. R. Sutton and A. Barto (1998). "Reinforcement Learning - An Introduction", MIT Press, Cambridge, Massachusetts.
17. G. Tesauro (1992). "Practical issues in temporal difference learning", Machine Learning, Vol. 8, Nos. 3-4.
18. G. Tesauro (1995). "Temporal Difference Learning and TD-Gammon", Communications of the ACM, Vol. 38, No 3.
19. S. Thrun (1995). "Learning to Play the Game of Chess". Advances in Neural Information Processing Systems, Vol. 7.

Section 3

Intelligent Systems in
Electronic Healthcare

A Web Based System Enabling Distributed Access and Intelligent Processing of Bioinformatics Data in Grid Environments

Ilias Maglogiannis[1], John Soldatos[2], Aristotelis Chatzioannou[1],
Vasilis Milonakis[2], Yiannis Kanaris[1]

[1]University of the Aegean, [2]Athens Information Technology,

e-mail: {imaglo@aegean.gr, achatzi@eie.gr, jsol@ait.edu.gr,
vmil@ait.edu.gr, icsdm05004@icsd.aegean.gr}

Abstract This paper presents a Web based portal, which enables intelligent processing of biological data in Grid environments. The deployed software aims at creation of tools for processing data from microarray experiments over the Hellenic Grid infrastructure. Emphasis is given on user interface and access issues, while the paper describes also the data parsing and parallelization of the microarray data processing. The description of the system is oriented to Grid developers and users, since it focuses on the customization and use of the microarray applications over the Grid. Apart from supporting the high performance and economical execution of microarray experiments, the proposed system endeavors to provide access to a distributed repository of experiments information and results.

1 Introduction

The completion of the Human Genome Project and the emergence of high-throughput technologies at the dawn of the new millennium, are rapidly changing the way biomedical research is performed. Microarray experiments permit a genome-scale evaluation of gene functions and are therefore among the most topical and prominent developments of biomedical research. A microarray

Please use the following format when citing this chapter:

Maglogiannis, I., Soldatos, J., Chatzioannou, A., Milonakis, V., Kanaris, Y., 2007, in IFIP International Federation for Information Processing, Volume 247, Artificial Intelligence and Innovations 2007: From Theory to Applications, eds. Boukis, C., Pnevmatikakis, L., Polymenakos, L., (Boston: Springer), pp. 117-126.

experiment may produce great amounts of biological digital data that require further processing towards their exploitation. To alleviate the high cost of computing equipment required to support microarray experiments, researchers can leverage the computing power and the quality of service provided by Grid computing infrastructures. The amount of power offered by Grid infrastructures has been already exploited in the scope of a significant number of e-science applications, in particular applications with stringent computational and storage requirements. Bioinformatics applications in general and microarray experiments in particular are perfectly tailored to Grid infrastructures due to the need for high computing power and storage capacity [1]. Motivated by this fact, the aim of this research is to 'Gridify' and put on the Grid a selected number of microarray analysis, normalization and processing applications for cDNA arrays. The target Grid infrastructure is the Hellenic portion of the pan-European Grid infrastructure developed for e-science in the scope of the EGEE (Enabling Grids for E-Science in Europe) project and its successors [2]. The proposed platform is called hereafter HECTOR or EKTORAS in Greek, since it is funded by the Greek Secretariat of Research and Technology under a project named EKTORAS [9].

Figure 1 provides an overview of the application components comprising the EKTORAS application environment. At a high level the microarray experiments are conducted, processed and analyzed based on the following steps:

– Selecting a particular experiment among the pool of available normalization and clustering methods for cDNA microarrays. This selection task is performed by end users.

– Providing the microarray input files, which are usually structured according to formats that are standard for the microarray bioinformatics community. Microarray input files are specified by the end user and can be either files provided by the researchers themselves or even files residing in microarray public databases (i.e. European Bioinformatics Institute Database http://www.ebi.ac.uk/).

– Pre-processing the input files as so to render them usable by the range of algorithms available. The results of this pre-processing will be directed to the Grid's storage elements (SE).

– Parallelizing the application and distributing the parallel chunks & jobs to various nodes-processors of the Grid. Accumulating, storing and post-processing the results. This step contributes to create a large-scale virtualized database of microarray experiments.

The architecture presented in Figure 1 supports the above steps through a variety of software elements that are placed either within the Grid infrastructure, or as part of the access portal supporting interaction with the end users as described in the remainder sections.

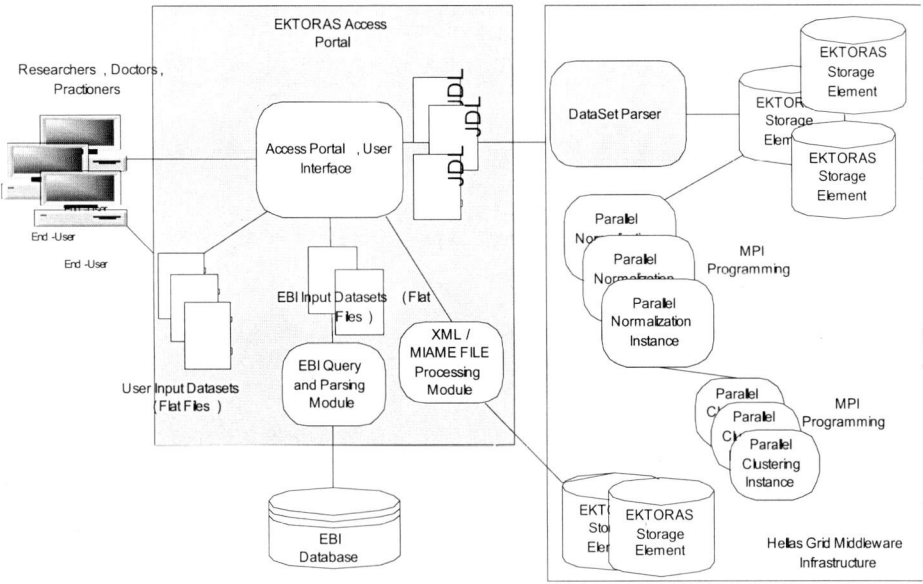

Fig.1. Overview of the HECTOR application architecture

2 User Interface - Access Portal

Users accessing the Web Interface through the implemented portal are given the ability to submit their experiments, retrieve their results and also compare them with formerly submitted experiments. Since the portal is set up on Hellas Grid User Interface (HG-UI), users have the ability to actually access the whole Grid infrastructure, consisting of many grid nodes. Access to services is enabled by parsing input files and accordingly activating the 'gridified' algorithms for processing the microarray experiments. Both data parsing operations and launching of experiments are specified as Grid jobs, using the Job Description Language (JDL). JDL is a high-level language, which is used to describe jobs and to aggregate jobs with arbitrary dependency relations. In the scope of the Grid, JDL is used to specify the desired job characteristics and constraints, which are used by the match-making process to select the best resource to execute the job. A job description is a file (called JDL file) consisting of lines having the format: attribute = expression; and terminated by a semicolon. Expressions can span several lines, but only the last one must be terminated by a semicolon.

Users of the EKTORAS portal are not required to be familiar with the procedure of creating the JDL files. They just have to set up a few parameters from the Web Portal that describes their experiment as shown in Figure 2, and to either upload their input files consisting of gene description, or even select them from a third party library-database of microarray files (e.g., the EBI Database). Accordingly the portal dynamically produces a JDL file specifying:

o   Commands for parsing the inputs files and producing output files enabling
    the execution of the experiments. The parsing process is illustrated in the
    following section 3.

o   Commands for activating the experiments over the Grid infrastructure. The
    later commands exploit the MPI capabilities of the Grid [3-4], while also
    leveraging appropriate data files produced after the parsing process.

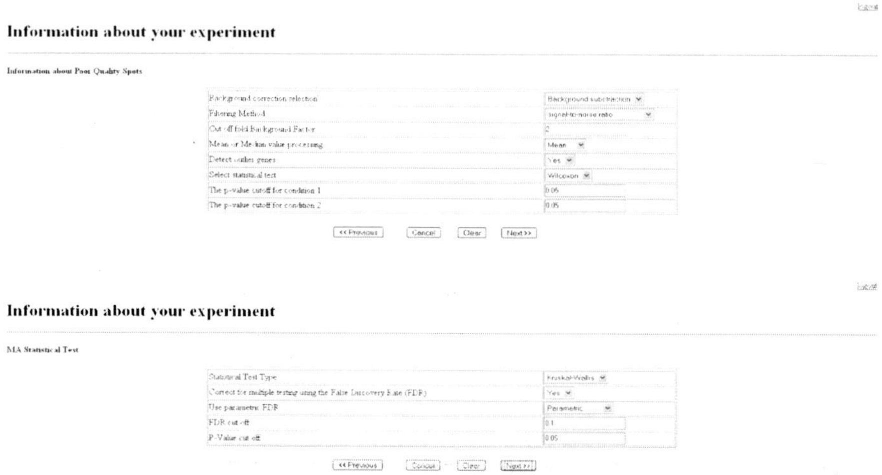

Fig. 2. Some steps from the input of parameters for the Experiment in the EKTORAS Portal

Following the dynamic production of the JDL file based on input files and
configuration parameters, the portal submits this file to the Workload Management
System (WMS) of the Grid for execution. The EKTORAS portal is accessible over
the World Wide Web, through the URL http://www.icsd.aegean.gr/ektoras/. From an
implementation perspective the portal is implemented using JSP (Java Server Pages)
technology over a Tomcat/Jakarta infrastructure. The Jakarta infrastructure is hosted
in a machine that is owned by the University of Aegean. Nevertheless, this machine
becomes part of the Grid, in the form of a Grid UI. Implementing the portal
within a Grid UI ensures that the access part of the EKTORAS application can
directly leverage middleware services (e.g., security, reliability, resource
management) of the underlying Grid infrastructure.

3 Input Data Parsing and Storage

Input data parsing constitutes an expedient pre-processing step to running
microarray experiments. As outlined in the previous section and depicted in Figure 3,
a data set parser module undertakes the transformation of input data files to other
data storage structures (e.g., Matlab/Octave project files) that can be executed in
conjunction with the gridified application. In order to maximize the impact and
utility of EKTORAS services, we have tried to support a broad range of input files

formats. The development of the EKTORAS data parsing functionality supports the most popular formats, starting with the Imagene format [5-6]. The ImaGene format is the format specified and used within the ImaGene microarray image analysis software; a popular software for quick, automated measurement and visualization of gene expression data from spotted arrays. The ImaGene software extracts and quantifies spotted data from any 16-bit TIFF image file, and exports processed data in either text or XML files. In addition to Imagene other popular software tools are supported including QuantArray, GenePix, TIGR Spotfinder and the generic tab-delimited format used by EBI for storing data. By supporting these entire different formats EKTORAS platform is compliant with the vast majority of experiment data produced. Parsers are implemented in Python scripts, and manage to convert any of these aforementioned formats to Octave ASCII workspace files, storing the data into certain structures needed by the Octave code to run.

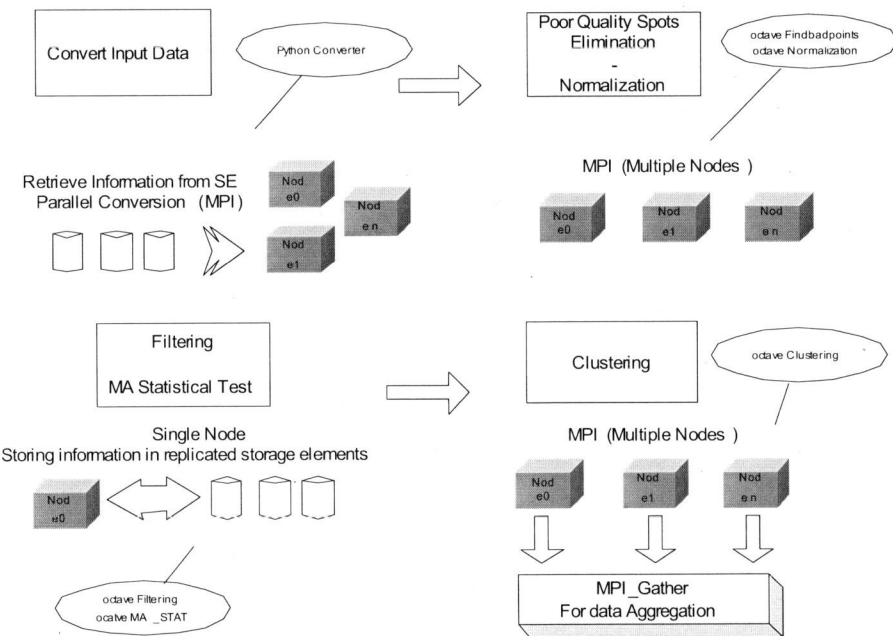

Fig. 3. Graphical representation of code parallelization

The parsing process produces a set of output files, which accordingly are stored within the Grid. Storage of output files is implemented using the Storage Elements (SEs) of the EGEE. SEs are services which allow a user or an application to store data for future retrieval. Currently, data storage within SEs is not subject to policies for space quota management. Moreover, all data in a SE are considered permanent and it is user responsibility to manage the available space in a SE (e.g., removing unnecessary data, moving files to mass storage systems etc.). As a result, the EKTORAS system stores outputs of the parsing process to one or more storage elements that are allocated to the project. These files are therefore available to the experiments code, which also manages these files based on commands of the LCG File Catalog (LFC) and using the following abstractions:

o   Logical File Name (LFN), which is an alias created by a user to refer to some item of data, e.g. "lfn:cms/20030203/run2/track1"

o   Globally Unique Identifier (GUID), which is a non-human-readable unique identifier for an item of data, e.g., "guid:f81d4fae-7dec-11d0-a765-00a0c91e6bf6"

o   Site URL (SURL) (or Physical File Name (PFN) or Site FN), which represents the location of an actual piece of data on a storage system, e.g., "srm://pcrd24.cern.ch/flatfiles/cms/output10_1"   (SRM)   and "sfn://lxshare0209.cern.ch/data/alice/ntuples.dat" (Classic SE)

o   Transport URL (TURL), which corresponds to the temporary locator of a replica along with its access protocol: understood by a SE, e.g., rfio://lxshare0209.cern.ch//data/alice/ntuples.dat.

4   Grid Enabling Applications

The EKTORAS microarray processing algorithms have been initially provided by NHRF (National Hellenic Research Foundation) as a set of MATLAB libraries. However, no nodes of the Hellenic Grid Infrastructure provide support for MATLAB execution. Furthermore MATLAB is a commercial product, which raises intricate licensing issues when it comes to installing it in the Grid and makes it unlikely to become available in the near future. Therefore, we have investigated possible alternatives, the most prominent being the use of Octave Forge, which is the GNU open-source alternative to MATLAB. As a result, the first Grid application development step involved the conversion of the MATLAB code to (results) equivalent Octave Forge code.

Accordingly, we dealt with the task of parallelizing the (Octave Forge) microarray application and accordingly making it appropriate for use over the Grid. Initially, emphasis was given in placing the existing system into the grid environment. This task can be generally achieved through "wrapping" the existing code. The wrapping process has to audit the existing applications for their appropriateness for the Grid based on their following characteristics [7]:

o   Their inter-process communications between jobs, without high speed switch connection (for example, MPI). In general, multi-threaded applications need to be checked for their need of inter-process communication.

o   Their level of job scheduling requirements depending on data provisioning by uncontrolled data producers

o   Unresolved obstacles to establish sufficient bandwidth on the network.

o   Strongly limiting system environment dependencies for the jobs.

o   Requirements for safe business transactions (commit and roll-back). At the moment, there are no standards for transaction processing on grids.

o   High interdependencies between the jobs, which expose complex job flow management to the grid server and cause high rates of inter-process communication.

o   Unsupported network protocols used by jobs, which may be prohibited to
    perform their tasks due to firewall rules.

Accordingly, we examined the application and job flows. Application flows is
the flow of work between the jobs that make up the grid application. The internal
flow of work within a job itself is called the job flow. During the grid enablement of
the microarray processing algorithms we classified application flows into the
following three basic types:

o   Parallel flow: If an application consists of several jobs that can all be executed in
    parallel, a grid may be very suitable for effective execution on dedicated nodes,
    especially in the case when there is no (or a very limited) exchange of data
    among the jobs. From an initial job, a number of jobs are launched to execute on
    pre-selected or dynamically assigned nodes within the grid. Each job may
    receive a discrete set of data, fulfill its computational task independently and
    deliver its output. The output is collected by a final job or stored in a defined
    data store. For a given problem or application, it would be necessary to break it
    down into independent units. To take advantage of parallel execution of the
    microarray application in a grid, it is important to analyze tasks within an
    application to determine whether they can be broken down into individual and
    atomic units of work that can be run as individual jobs. This parallel application
    flow type is well suited for deployment on the EGEE grid. Significantly, this
    type of flow can occur when there are separate data sets per job and none of the
    jobs need result from another job as input. Classical examples of parallel flows
    are mathematical calculations, where the commutative and associative laws can
    be exploited.

o   Serial flow: In contrast to the parallel flow is the serial application flow. In this
    case, there is a single thread of job execution where each of the subsequent jobs
    has to wait for its predecessor to end and deliver output data as input to the next
    job. This means that any job is a consumer of its predecessor, the data producer.
    In this case, the advantages of running in a grid environment are not based on
    access to multiple systems in parallel, but rather on the ability to use any of
    several appropriate and available resources. Note that each job does not
    necessarily have to run on the same resource, so if a particular job require
    specialized resources, this can be accommodated, while the other jobs may run
    on more standard and inexpensive resources. The ability for the jobs to run on
    any of a number of resources also increases the application's availability and
    reliability. In addition, it may make the application inherently scalable through
    the ability to utilize larger and faster resources at any particular point in time.
    Nevertheless, when encountering such a situation, it may be worthwhile to
    check whether the single jobs are really dependent on each other, or whether,
    due to their nature, they can be split into parallel executable units for submission
    on a grid. A prominent example of serial application flows are iterative
    scenarios (for example, convergent approximation calculations) where the
    output of one job is required as input to the next job of the same kind, a serial
    job flow is required to reach the desired result.

o   Networked flow: In this case certain jobs within the application are executable
    in parallel, but there are inter-dependencies between them. In the scope of
    application with a networked flow we will exploit loose coupling, which implies
    a need for a job flow management service to handle the synchronization of the

individual results. Loose coupling between the jobs avoids high inter-process communication and reduces overhead in the grid. In the case of such experiments we will analyze how to best split the application into individual jobs, with a view to maximizing parallelism.

During grid programming we also introduced a hierarchical system of sub-jobs. Specifically, it is likely that a job could utilize the services of the grid environment to launch one or more sub-jobs. For this kind of environment, an application can be partitioned and designed in such a way that the higher-level jobs could include the logic to obtain resources and launch sub-jobs. This can facilitate large applications to isolate and pass the control and management of certain tasks to the individual components. Since the microarray processing algorithms deal with multiple replicates of data and the main process is independent for each replicate, they are highly parallelizable. So the elimination of poor quality spots and the normalization process can be executed in parallel. This parallel flow makes them appropriate for execution over a grid environment, towards meeting the economic goals set in the introductory paragraph of this report. In implementing the parallelization and exploiting multiple processors within the Grid, we exploited the MPI programming model. The following table provides pseudo code illustrating the use of MPI to launch parallel Octave forge instances executing normalization-related functions for the microarray instances.

Table 1. Sample MPI Pseudo code

```
#include <mpi.h>
int main(int argc, char *argv[])
{
... //----initializing MPI
MPI_Init(&argc, &argv);
//----learn node number
MPI_Comm_rank(MPI_COMM_WORLD, &rank);
// load files          (in parallel for each file)
// Start Find Bad Points (in parallel for each experiment)
[exptab,TotalBadpoints]=FindBadpoints(datstruct,t,exprp,imgsw);
// Normalize Data     (in parallel for each experiment)
[DataCellNormLo]=NormalizationLO(exptab,exprp,t,gnID);
   Gather processed data  (On node 0)
for (i=1;i<NumOfExperiments;i++)
   MPI_Recv(rcvbuf,count,datatype,i,tag,MPI_INT, MPI_COMM_WORLD,
&status);
/* MPI shutdown MPI */
MPI_Finalize();
//Filter Replicates
[DataCellFiltered]=FilterReplicates2(DataCellNormLo);
//Statitical Test
[DataCellStat]=MA_StaTestExp_New_total(DataCellFiltered,DataCellNormLo)
;
//CLUSTERING
.....................  .  .
}
```

Table 1 refers to a simple parallelization of the microarray processing application, based on the number of input files/slides and their subsequent normalization processes. This is the most straightforward and simplistic parallelization approach for the available microarray applications. A thorough analysis and structuring based on the above-mentioned jobs-subjobs hierarchical approach can in a later stage boost the application to much better performance levels. Figure 3 shows a more detailed view of the steps executed by our code and how it is parallelized in more nodes.

The aggregation of the results as it is depicted in Figure 3 runs in single node since it requires information from all experiments and it is not heavy computationally. Finally the clustering of the results runs in parallel on many nodes since it can run independently for each experiment and has increased computation complexity. Following the initial interaction of the end user with the access portal, there are is virtually no essential on-going interaction between user and grid application. During the course of the application's execution users limit themselves to monitoring the status of their job submissions.

5 Distributed Elements for Experiments Storage and

Virtualization

Apart from supporting the high performance and economical execution of microarray experiments, the EKTORAS system endeavors to provide access to a repository of experiments information and results. Specifically, following the completion of an experiment over the EKTORAS application infrastructure, the experimental results are stored within appropriate SEs. These results are provided to the SE along with experiment meta-data specified according to MIAME (Minimum Information About a Microarray Experiment) XML format [8]. These metadata are requested by end-user through the access portal, prior to the execution of the experiment. Accordingly the portal structures a MIAME XML file. During implementation we tried to conform to microarray data standards, which are developed by the Microarray Gene Expression Data (MGED) Society (http://www.mged.org/). MIAME (www.mged.org/miame) is a prominent such standard, which outlines the minimum information that should be reported about a microarray experiment to enable its unambiguous interpretation and reproduction. Following the structuring of experiment meta-data as MIAME files, and their storage in SEs, we also developed a browsing mechanism that navigates across all the distributed SEs that contain experiments' information. This mechanism exports a browsing interface, along with a query/search interface to the access portal, in order to allow the end user query, search and access experiments' information and results. The distributed browsing mechanism is implemented as a C wrapper over the Grid data management functions and APIs. The latter APIs are exploited to deal with:

o   Heterogeneity, since experiments' data will be stored on different storage systems using different access technologies
o   Distribution, since experiments' data is likely to be stored in different locations, while also data needs to be moved between different locations.
o   Different Administrative Domains, since data is likely to be stored at places where different access policies are applied and hence the browsing

mechanism will have to deal with the relevant security and auditing implications.

The EKTORAS access portal allows end-users to retrieve experiment files from the EBI microarray library. To this end the access portal provides an adapter to the EBI database system, which allows EKTORAS user to view, browse and select EBI files.

6 Conclusions

In this paper we strived to underpin the importance of grid computing for DNA microarray experiments. Accordingly, we have described the main components comprising the proposed 'gridification' of EKTORAS microarray data processing applications, along with the key technologies that support the implementation and integration of these components. We have also elaborated on a set of structuring principles for building the EKTORAS Grid Portal. This work serves as a starting point for building a more complete and integrated Grid enabled microarray experimentation environment.

Acknowledgment: This Research work is funded by the Greek Secretariat of Research and Technology under the Grant "Distributed Biological Data Processing of existing Open Public Databases (EKTORAS)".

References

1. I. Foster, 'What is the Grid? A Three Point Checklist', GRIDToday (http://www.gridtoday.com), July 20, 2002.
2. I. Foster, C. Kesselman, S. Tuecke, 'The Anatomy of the Grid: Enabling Scalable Virtual Organizations', International Journal of Supercomputer Applications, Vol.15, No.3, 2001.
3. Yukiya Aoyama et. al. 'RS/6000 SP: Practical MPI Programming', IBM redbook, August 1999.
4. Hellas Grid Training Material, available at: http://grid-training.ekt.gr/
5. http://www.biodiscovery.com/index/imagene
6. M. Kapushesky, P. Kemmeren, A.C. Culhane, S. Durinck, J. Ihmels, C. Kr, M. Kull, A. Torrente, U. Sarkans, J. Vilo and A. Brazma, 'Expression Profiler: next generation-an online platform for analysis of microarray data', Nucleic Acids Research, July 2004, Volume: 32: 1362-4962.
7. Luis Ferreira et al. 'Introduction to Grid Computing with Globus', IBM redpaper, December 2002.
8. A Brazma et al, 'Minimum information about a microarray experiment (MIAME)-toward standards for microarray data', in the Proc. Nat Genet. 2001 Dec;29(4):365-71.
9. I. Maglogiannis et al., "An Application Platform Enabling High Performance Grid Processing of Microarray Experiments", 20th IEEE Conf on Computer Based Medical Systems CBMS2007, Slovenia

ANDROMEDA: A MATLAB Automated cDNA Microarray Data Analysis Platform

Aristotelis Chatziioannou[1], Panagiotis Moulos[1]

1 National Hellenic Research Foundation, Institute of Biological Research and Biotechnology, Metabolic Engineering and Bioinformatics Group 48 Vassileos Constantinou ave., 11635 Athens, Greece
{achatzi,pmoulos}@eie.gr
WWW home page:
http://www.eie.gr/nhrf/institutes/ibrb/programmes/metabolicengineering-en.html

Abstract. DNA microarrays constitute a relatively new biological technology which allows gene expression profiling at a global level by measuring mRNA abundance. However, the grand complexity characterizing a microarray experiment entails the development of computationally powerful tools apt for probing the biological problem studied. ANDROMEDA (Automated aND RObust Microarray Experiment Data Analysis) is a MATLAB implemented program which performs all steps of typical microarray data analysis including noise filtering processes, background correction, data normalization, statistical selection of differentially expressed genes based on parametric or non parametric statistics and hierarchical cluster analysis resulting in detailed lists of differentially expressed genes and formed clusters through a strictly defined automated workflow. Along with the completely automated procedure, ANDROMEDA offers a variety of visualization options (MA plots, boxplots, clustering images etc). Emphasis is given to the output data format which contains a substantial amount of useful information and can be easily imported in a spreadsheet supporting software or incorporated in a relational database for further processing and data mining.

1 Introduction

Functional genomics includes the analysis of large datasets derived from various biological experiments. One such type of large-scale experiment involves monitoring the expression levels of thousands of genes simultaneously under a particular condition [1] which has turned out to be a major tool for discovery in biological research. cDNA microarrays constitute a promising high-throughput technology which has become one of the indispensable tools for the inspection of genome-wide

Please use the following format when citing this chapter:

Chatziioannou, A, Moulos, P., 2007, in IFIP International Federation for Information Processing, Volume 247, Artificial Intelligence and Innovations 2007: From Theory to Applications, eds. Boukis, C., Pnevmatikakis, L., Polymenakos, L., (Boston: Springer), pp. 127-136.

changes in gene expression in an organism. Two of the frequent goals of genome-scale gene expression experiments are to identify significant alterations in transcript levels resulting from the exposure of a living system to a test agent at a given dose and time [2] and develop genetic signatures in order to distinguish between health and disease states. Additionally, such high-throughput expression profiling can be used to compare the level of gene transcription in clinical studies conditions in order to: i) identify and categorize diagnostic or prognostic biomarkers ii) classify diseases, e.g. tumours with different prognosis that are indistinguishable by microscopic examination iii) monitor the response to therapy and iv) understand the mechanisms involved in the genesis of disease processes [3].

The key physicochemical process involved in microarrays is DNA hybridization. mRNA is extracted from tissues or cells, reversed-transcribed, labelled with a fluorescent dye, usually Cy3 (green) for the reference sample and Cy5 (red) for the treated sample, and hybridized on the array using an experimental strategy that permits expression to be assayed and compared between appropriate sample pairs. Hybridization and washes are carried out under high stringency conditions to diminish the possibility of cross-hybridization between similar genes. The next step is to generate an image using laser-induced fluorescent imaging. The principle behind the quantification of expression levels is that the amount of fluorescence measured at each sequence specific location is directly proportional to the amount of mRNA with complementary sequence present in the sample analyzed. These images must then be analyzed to locate the arrayed spots and to quantify the relative fluorescence intensities for each element. Even though these experiments do not provide data on the absolute level of expression of a particular gene, they are useful to compare the expression level among conditions and genes (e.g. health vs disease, treated vs untreated) [3, 4].

The ensuing images are used to create a dataset which needs to be preprocessed prior to the subsequent analysis and interpretation of the results. Typical preprocessing steps are background noise correction, filtering procedures to eliminate non-informative genes, the calculation of the logarithmic transformed ratio between Cy5 and Cy3 channels and data normalization. The background correction is intended to adjust for non-specific hybridization such as hybridization of sample transcripts whose sequences do not perfectly match those of the probes on the array [3] and for other systematic or technical issues such as possible artefacts on the arrays, scanner setbacks, washing issues or quantum fluctuations. Other options for background correction constitute for example of using computational techniques that model the distribution of the observed intensity values and estimate the background noise based on mathematical models. The filtering procedures aim at excluding problematic or low in information content array spots and are usually based in processes that use the amount of spot noise or outlier detection to remove genes from further analysis. The ratio between channels of treated and reference samples is a simple measure which can investigate relationships between related biological samples based on expression patterns. Particularly, the $\log_2$ ratio transformation has the advantage of treating expression ratios symmetrically [4]. As another preprocessing step, normalization is considered critical to compensate for systematic differences among genes or arrays and provide appropriate balances in order to derive meaningful biological comparisons. Several reasons for normalization include unequal quantities of RNA, differences in labelling or the fluorescent dyes and systematic biases in the measured expression levels [4]. Typical normalization methods are global mean or median normalization [5], rank invariant normalization [6] and LOWESS/LOESS methods [7]. There exist several methods for normalizing cDNA microarray data and abundant literature is available on the subject [8-13].

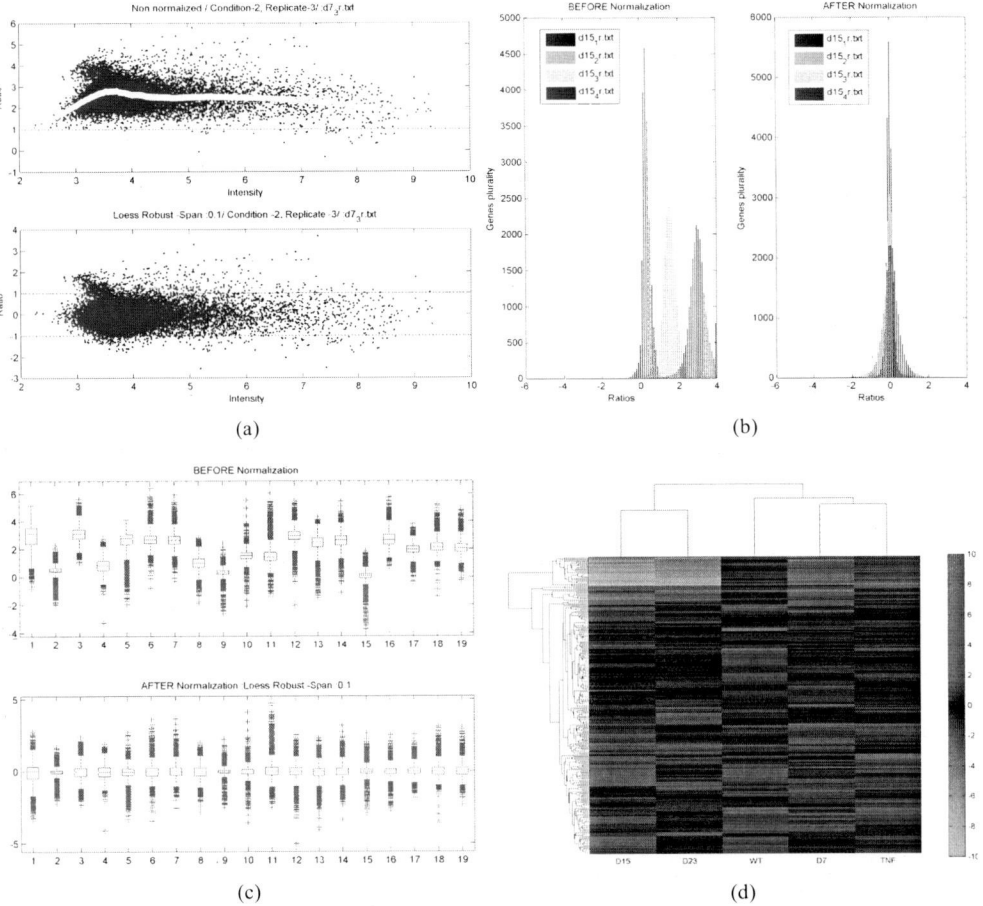

Fig. 1. (a) Example of ratio-intensity plot before (upper panel) and after (lower panel) the application of robust loess normalization with neighbouring span 0.1. The light solid line on the upper panel depicts the normalization curve. These plots display the log ratio (see section 2) for each element on the array as a function of the $\log_2(S_{Cy3}*S_{Cy5})$ product intensities and can reveal systematic intensity dependent effects in the measured log ratio values (b) Example of log ratio distributions for an experimental condition with 4 array replicates. The impact of normalization is profound (c) Example of boxplots before and after the application or robust loess normalization for a set of 19 slides. Boxplots are ideal for visualizing the result of the normalization procedure and the data spread before and after normalization (d) Example of a heatmap generated after hierarchical clustering with average linkage and euclidean distance for a set of 259 DE genes among 5 experimental conditions. Heatmaps are helpful in visualizing distinct gene clusters as well as optically distinguishing different gene groups.

There currently exist several commercial or open source microarray data analysis software packages. However, most of them are either closed black-box tools (e.g. GeneSight™, BioDiscovery Inc., Los Angeles, USA), or completely open architecture [14]. Concerning the open source solutions for microarray data analysis, although a number of software tools have been developed [15-19], a major drawback with most of them is the absence of a predefined analysis protocol leading to a batch process that commences from raw image analysis data and results in sound lists of differentially expressed (DE) genes. An exception to this rule is MIDAS software [20] where the analyst is given the ability to pre-program the analysis steps in a form of a batch procedure and caGEDA [21] which is a web-based analysis tool. Moreover, many of these analysis packages provide only several sets of routines often being of little avail to biologists with small experience in programming or scripting and other software packages which come with a graphical user interface (GUI) lack the ability to read raw data immediately after the image analysis step without certain manual transformation first [22].

The ANDROMEDA pipeline comes to fill these gaps by providing a unified environment implemented in MATLAB to form an analysis batch process, starting from reading raw image analysis software output data and resulting in lists of differentially expressed genes and gene clusters. The program utilizes a set of well defined and widely used gene filtering, normalization, and parametric or non-parametric statistical tests to analyze any number of experimental conditions and replicates and hierarchically cluster the results. Moreover, the pipeline implements additional features such as the *Trust Factor* filtering, condition based imputation of missing values and background correction based on the signal-to-noise ratio of image array spots further discussed in the Features section.

2   Features

ANDROMEDA consists of a user friendly GUI which offers a variety of options to enable different combinations among the analysis steps of a microarray experiment. It is worth noting that while most tools specialize either in data visualization and normalization, or statistical testing and clustering, ANDROMEDA offers the ability to implement all the above in a pre-defined workflow with minimal user interaction through a batch programming plug-in while being capable at the same time of performing the analysis step by step depending on the preferences of the user. Starting from the result files of the image analysis software (GenePix, ImaGene, QuantArray and text tab-delimited file formats currently supported), ANDROMEDA organizes the loaded arrays in internal data structures that will be used from the pipeline for the rest of the analysis.

After importing the data, the analysis starts by background correction to estimate the net signal for each spot, which can be performed in three different ways:

1. Background noise subtraction for each slide of each condition. In that case the net signal $\tilde{S}^{bs}$ for each channel is $\tilde{S}^{bs} = \overline{S} - \overline{B}$, where $\overline{S}$ and $\overline{B}$ are the mean or

median of the spot signal and background respectively and the log ratio between channels is:

$$R_{bs} = log_2 \left(\frac{\overline{S}_{Cy5} - \overline{B}_{Cy5}}{\overline{S}_{Cy3} - \overline{B}_{Cy3}} \right) = log_2 \left(\tilde{S}_{Cy5}^{bs} / \tilde{S}_{Cy3}^{bs} \right)$$

2. Signal-to-noise ratio calculation for each slide of each condition. In that case the net signal $\tilde{S}^{s2n}$ for each channel is $\tilde{S}^{s2n} = \overline{S}/\overline{B}$ and the log ratio between channels is:

$$R_{s2n} = log_2 \left(\frac{\overline{S}_{Cy5}/\overline{B}_{Cy5}}{\overline{S}_{Cy3}/\overline{B}_{Cy3}} \right) = log_2 \left(\tilde{S}_{Cy5}^{s2n} / \tilde{S}_{Cy3}^{s2n} \right)$$

3. No background correction. In that case the log ratio is:

$$R_{nc} = log_2 \left(\overline{S}_{Cy5} / \overline{S}_{Cy3} \right)$$

Notice that in case (1) the log_2 data transformation takes place after background subtraction while in case (2) before background subtraction (immediately seen from basic properties of logarithms). Case (2) takes into consideration the signal-to-noise content of a signal, an established notion in systems theory and image processing [23], thus coming in line with the perception of the experimentalist about the quality of a signal, taking into account its interest in the strength of the signal compared to noise. This might prove critical especially when dealing with weak signal datasets whereas a majority of spot signals is close or even below the background contamination levels.

The identification of poor quality spots that will be excluded from data normalization is performed for each experimental condition in two steps: firstly spots marked as poor manually or by the image analysis software are excluded for every replicate. Then noise sensitive genes are further isolated for each slide replicate of the condition based on three possible filters according to the analyst's preference:

1. A signal-to-noise threshold filter based on the formula $\left(\overline{S}/\overline{N} \right) < BBF$ where BBF stands for Below Background Factor and is a user-defined threshold below which noisy spots are filtered out from the slide.
2. A filter based on the distance between the signal and the background noise distributions: a spot is robust against this filter if its signal and noise distributions abstain from each other a distance which is determined by the signal and noise standard deviations. The sensitive spots to this filter are determined by the inequality $\overline{S} - x\sigma_S^2 < \overline{B} + y\sigma_B^2$, where x and y are user-defined parameters.
3. A custom filter: in this case the investigator is given the ability to create a custom filter utilizing the signal and background means, medians and standard deviations.

In the second step, a t-test (parametric) or Wilcoxon (non-parametric) test verifies that for each spot, the ratio measurements of all condition replicates derive from a normal (or a continuous symmetrical) distribution with mean (median) equal to the average ratio for this spot among all replicates. This test tracks and excludes outliers among the replicate slides of an experimental condition. Array spots sensitive to any of these two tests are marked as non-informative poor quality spots and excluded from the estimation of the normalization curve to alleviate the normalization procedure from the impact of systematic measurement errors.

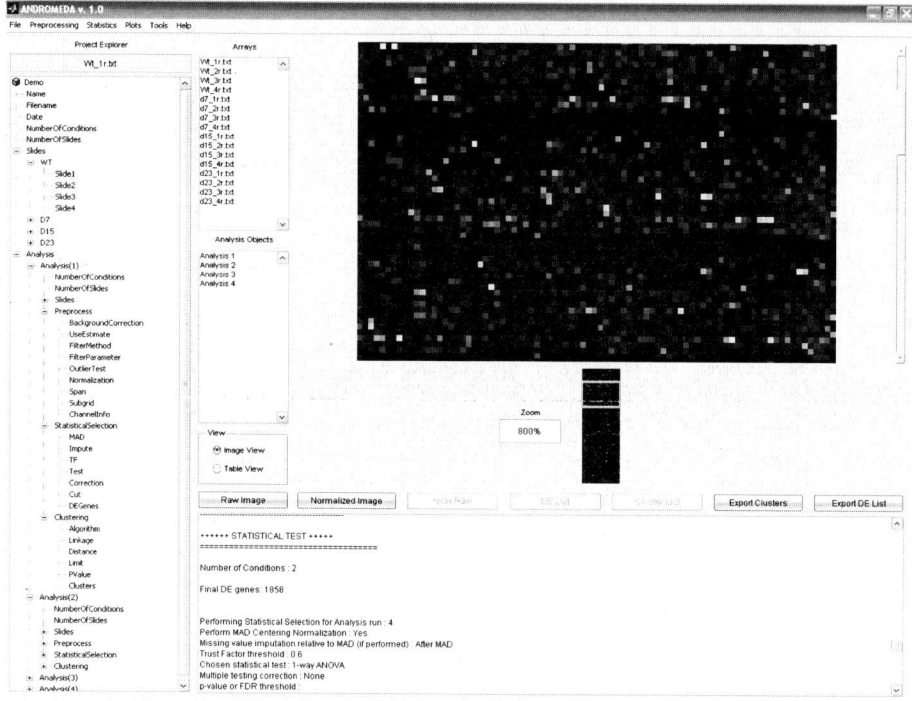

Fig. 2. A snapshot of the ANDROMEDA main window: on the left part of the interface, the project explorer allows the analyst to have a quick look at several dataset and different analyses parameters in the form of a tree. On the right next to the explorer, two lists allow the user to inspect the different arrays of the experiment as well as cycle through different analysis steps followed and display brief reports. Next to the lists on the right, each array can be viewed as an image or table depicting several values such as mean (median) signal and background intensities and their standard deviations, extracted from the image analysis software files. A message box on the bottom part of the GUI displays brief information on the steps followed throughout the analysis while several buttons offer shortcuts to different functionalities such as exporting list of DE genes. Finally, the available menus control the several functionalities as well as the variety of visualization options of the program.

ANDROMEDA continues the analysis by normalizing data on each slide separately (Figure 1a-c). If a subgrid is present on the slides, the user is given the choice to select subgrid normalization to possibly allow considering several spatial dependent properties such as local background noise in the normalization procedure. Currently, six normalization methods are supported: Global Mean, Global Median, Linear Lowess, Robust Linear Lowess, Quadratic Loess and Robust Quadratic Loess. The robust versions of Lowess/Loess [7] perform additional fitting iterations over the dataset while readjusting each point's weight on each pass, so as to mitigate the impact of possible outliers. After the normalization a subset of experimental conditions and slide replicates can be selected while the original data of the whole experiment are stored separately. With this option, the analyst may examine specific conditions or condition combinations and carry out statistical tests without having to repeat the computationally intensive and time consuming part of normalization, especially if the total number of slides is high.

The statistical selection of DE genes starts with the calculation of the Trust Factor (TF) for each gene for all conditions and replicates and is defined for each experimental condition as: $TF = \#Appearances/\#Replicates$. The number of appearances for each gene is determined by the initial filtering steps: for example, if one gene in a specific slide is found sensitive either to the noise filtering condition or to the measurement reproducibility test, then it is marked as absent. If one gene is filtered out from all replicates for a given condition, then the TF for this gene is zero. This gene is then marked as 'unreliable' and is excluded from further analysis. Generally, for a biologically consistent subsequent analysis, no more than 30% of the expression values for a gene should be missing from an experimental condition (TF cutoff to 0.7). Following the TF filtering, a set of 'reliable' genes is obtained for each condition. However, since certain genes are absent from certain replicates the imputation of missing values for a gene is based on the average expression of the remaining present values of the gene of interest from the same experimental condition. Before imputing the missing values the user is given the option to perform Median Absolute Deviation [24] centering normalization to further scale the data for each condition.

The final lists of DE genes are acquired using a parametric (1-way ANOVA, [25]) or non-parametric (Kruskal-Wallis, [26]) statistical procedure, applied on the data after all the filtering and scaling steps among the subset of conditions defined after the normalization. At this point, the user has to specify certain parameters such as the statistical test to be performed or whether to correct or not for multiple statistical testing by controlling the False Discovery Rate [27] level. The final lists are formed in text tab delimited format output and they can be further manipulated effortlessly.

Finally, the DE gene lists obtained through the previous steps can be subjective to hierarchical cluster analysis, depending on the user's preference. The clustering can be performed on genes (rows), replicates (columns) or both (Figure 1d). The linkage algorithms and distance metrics supported are the single, average or complete linkage and the euclidean, standardized euclidean, Pearson correlation coefficient, Mahalanobis, Manhattan, cosine or Spearman's correlation coefficient metric respectively. The output of the cluster analysis is a clustering heatmap and lists containing formed clusters and the respective genes in MS Excel format.

3 Conclusions

The main purpose of ANDROMEDA is to provide to investigators a complete open source and flexible platform for microarray data analysis, implementing all the typical steps of the latter, starting from raw image analysis software output files up to easily interpretable and simple to manipulate gene lists. It aims both at researchers with little or no programming experience by providing a reasonably automated procedure and a user friendly interface for the analysis of microarray experiments and to those with certain expertise on statistical computation by providing completely open source routines which can be adjusted and enriched according to specific requirements. Attention is paid to the output data files which contain additional information on each spot of each slide and can be useful for drawing empirical conclusions as well as constitute key starting points for further investigation. The total procedure time of an experiment depends heavily on the amount of arrays to be analyzed as well as on several other parameters such as the normalization method (e.g. while global median normalization is preformed in less than a second, robust LOESS requires a much larger amount of time due to local data processing). Concerning the program use, apart from the graphical interface, the user can program several analysis rounds through the batch programming module. A snapshot of the program is illustrated in Figure 2 while a sample of the various outputs on Figure 3. ANDROMEDA is also provided as a library of routines which can be used individually or executed through a 'main' routine in the MATLAB command window depending on the investigator's skills.

Slide Pos ReArrayID	Description	Symbol	GenBank	GO	p-value	26611-Cy3	26682-Cy3	27731-Cy3	Mean_Ctrl	Avg_(Not L	Std_Ctrl	CV_Ctrl
18912 A_51_P157677	PDZ and LIM domain 3	Pdlim3	NM_016798	GO:0005515;	1.43E-05	3.705595	4.112176	3.908886	3.908886	15.02076	0.20329	0.05201
20114 A_51_P104747	general transcription factor II H, g	Gtf2h4	NM_010364	GO:0003700;	1.90E-05	0.3013757	0.334892	0.318134	0.318134	1.246717	0.01676	0.05268
16993 A_51_P201945	RIKEN cDNA 4933411K20 gene	4933411	NM_025747	NA	4.25E-05	0.0149991	0.076109	0.045554	0.045554	1.032079	0.03055	0.67074
16008 A_51_P380401	RIKEN cDNA 2310051N18 gene	2310051	AK009937	GO:0004812	6.20E-05	0.5199323	0.489874	0.504903	0.504903	1.419028	0.01503	0.02977
17457 A_51_P278540	melanocyte proliferating gene 1	Myg1	NM_021713	GO:0005615	8.76E-05	0.4079994	0.495628	0.451814	0.451814	1.367759	0.04381	0.09697
14760 A_51_P212053	serine (or cysteine) peptidase inh	Serpinb1	NM_173051	GO:0000004;	8.95E-05	0.7151395	0.78945	0.752295	0.752295	1.68447	0.03716	0.04939
18330 A_51_P264495	phosphoglycerate mutase 2	Pgam2	NM_018870	GO:0003824;	0.000103	9.222468	10.18542	9.703944	9.703944	834.0235	0.48148	0.04962
6572 A_51_P318291	homeodomain interacting protein	Hipk2	NM_010433	GO:0000122;	0.000115	0.6072618	0.604532	0.601803	0.604532	1.520486	0.00273	0.00451
1588 A_51_P107998	RIKEN cDNA 9930013L23 gene	9930013	AK036809	NA	0.000124	0.8881537	0.737595	0.773229	0.799659	1.74069	0.07868	0.0984
2364 A_51_P317788	RIKEN cDNA 1110055N21 gene	Ints5	NM_176843	NA	0.000197	-0.056815	-0.15166	0.038026	-0.05681	0.961384	0.09484	-1.6693
1441 A_51_P495220	casein kinase 1, gamma 1	Csnk1g1	NM_173185	GO:0000166;	0.000215	-0.222053	-0.13621	-0.17913	-0.17913	0.883236	0.04292	-0.23962
13596 A_51_P440743	cadherin EGF LAG seven-pass G	Celsr1	NM_009886	GO:0004871;	0.000232	2.665289	3.102746	2.748885	2.838974	7.155108	0.23223	0.0818
166 A_51_P370700	glutamate oxaloacetate transamir	Got1	NM_010324	GO:0003824;	0.000239	3.436163	2.847107	3.141635	3.141635	8.825238	0.29453	0.09375
22351 A_51_P510997	ATPase, Cu++ transporting, beta	Atp7b	NM_007511	GO:0000166;	0.000277	1.193671	1.076985	1.310358	1.193671	2.287341	0.11669	0.09775
14671 A_51_P124315	cDNA sequence BC034076		BC03407	NM_177649	NA	0.000305	3.891627	3.67011	3.780869	3.780869	13.74532	0.11076	0.02929
6576 A_51_P282394	mitochondrial ribosomal protein S	Mrps28	NM_025434	GO:0003723;	0.000363	2.045372	1.932279	2.115032	2.030894	4.086581	0.09223	0.04541
4819 A_51_P264671	procollagen, type XI, alpha 2	Col11a2	NM_009926	GO:0005198;	0.000375	-0.05406	-0.18263	-0.11834	-0.11834	0.921244	0.06429	-0.5432
1903 A_51_P163867	protein phosphatase 4, regulatory	Ppp4r1	NM_146081	GO:0005488	0.000422	-0.148718	-0.58589	-0.36731	-0.36731	0.775229	0.21859	-0.59511
10984 A_51_P232889	pellino 1	Peli1	NM_023324	NA	0.000431	-0.804246	-1.07086	-0.96503	0.512266	0.14155	-0.14668	
17090 A_51_P513785	CCCTC-binding factor	Ctcf	NM_007794	GO:0003676;	0.000532	0.0146753	-0.13792	-0.06162	-0.06162	0.958188	0.0763	-1.23816
13365 A_51_P300986	NA		NP377814	NA	0.000734	2.537802	1.74924	2.143521	2.143521	4.418391	0.39428	0.18394
18803 A_51_P171700	phosphatidylethanolamine binding	Pebp1	NM_018858	GO:0000166;	0.000844	1.923194	1.923548	1.906894	1.917879	3.778671	0.00951	0.00496
4003 A_51_P416660	CDC14 cell division cycle 14 hom	Cdc14b	NM_172587	GO:0004721;	0.000965	0.7283452	0.635406	0.681876	0.681876	1.604224	0.04647	0.06815
7171 A_51_P444874	nemo like kinase	Nlk	NM_008702	GO:0000166;	0.000997	-0.607607	-0.86572	-0.73666	-0.73666	0.600127	0.12905	-0.17519
1666 A_51_P253593	RIKEN cDNA 1700008O03 gene	1700008	XM_133454	NA	0.001074	0.8349389	0.722111	1.071445	0.876165	1.83549	0.17828	0.20348

Fig. 3. A snapshot from a DE gene list output from ANDROMEDA where the DE genes found from the statistical procedures described in the text are reported together with several annotation elements as well as raw and normalized expression values and statistical measurements concerning the genes of each experimental condition (p-values, coefficient of variation, trust factor).

Regarding to future versions, additional features such as the support of more image analysis software formats plus model based background noise estimation will be integrated. Another goal which is currently being realized is the parallelization of the ANDROMEDA towards a powerful grid application being able to handle experiments with a vast amount of experimental conditions and large number of replicates through a simple web interface.

References

1. M. Babu, in: Computational Genomics: Theory and Applications, edited by R. Grant (Horizon Press, 2004).
2. B.A. Rosenzweig, P.S. Pine, O.E. Domon, S.M. Morris, J.J. Chen and F.D. Sistare, Dye Bias Correction in Dual-Labeled cDNA Microarray Gene Expression Measurements, *Environ Health Perspect* **112**(4), 480-487 (2004).
3. A.L. Tarca, R. Romero and S. Draghici, Analysis of Microarray Experiments of Gene Expression Profiling, *Am J Obstet Gynecol* **195**(2), 373-388 (2006).
4. J. Quackenbush, Microarray Data Normalization and Transformation, *Nat Genet* **32**, 496-501 (2002).
5. M. Bilban, L.K. Buehler, S. Head, G. Desoye and V. Quaranta, Normalizing DNA Microarray Data, *Curr Issues Mol Biol* **4**(2), 57-64 (2002).
6. G.C. Tseng, M.K. Oh, L. Rohlin, J.C. Liao and W.H. Wong, Issues in cDNA Microarray Analysis: Quality Filtering, Channel Normalization, Models of Variations and Assessment of Gene Effects, *Nucleic Acids Res* **29**(12), 2549-2557 (2001).
7. W.S. Cleveland, E. Grosse and W.M. Shyu, in: Statistical Models in S, edited by J.M. Chambers and T.J. Hastie (Wadsworth & Brooks/Cole Dormand, J.R., 1992).
8. X. Cui, M.K. Kerr and G.A. Churchill, Transformations for cDNA Microarray Data, *Stat Appl Genet Mol Biol* **2**, Article4 (2003).
9. B.P. Durbin, J.S. Hardin, D.M. Hawkins and D.M. Rocke, A Variance-Stabilizing Transformation for Gene-Expression Microarray Data, *Bioinformatics* **18**, S105-S110 (2002).
10. D.B. Finkelstein, R. Ewing, J. Gollub, F. Sterky, S. Somerville and J.M. Cherry, in: Methods of Microarray Data Analysis, edited by L. S.M. and K.F. Johnson (Kluwer Academic, Cambridge, MA, 2002) 57-68.
11. P. Hegde, R. Qi, K. Abernathy, C. Gay, S. Dharap, R. Gaspard, J.E. Hughes, E. Snesrud, N. Lee and J. Quackenbush, A Concise Guide to cDNA Microarray Analysis, *Biotechniques* **29**(3), 548-550, 552-544, 556 passim (2000).
12. J. Quackenbush, Computational Analysis of Microarray Data, *Nat Rev Genet* **2**(6), 418-427 (2001).
13. Y.H. Yang, S. Dudoit, P. Luu, D.M. Lin, V. Peng, J. Ngai and T.P. Speed, Normalization for cDNA Microarray Data: A Robust Composite Method Addressing Single and Multiple Slide Systematic Variation, *Nucleic Acids Res* **30**(4), e15 (2002).
14. R.C. Gentleman, V.J. Carey, D.M. Bates, B. Bolstad, M. Dettling, S. Dudoit, B. Ellis, L. Gautier, Y. Ge, J. Gentry, K. Hornik, T. Hothorn, W. Huber, S. Iacus, R. Irizarry, F. Leisch, C. Li, M. Maechler, A.J. Rossini, G. Sawitzki, C. Smith, G. Smyth, L. Tierney, J.Y. Yang and J. Zhang, Bioconductor: Open Software Development for Computational Biology and Bioinformatics, *Genome Biol* **5**(10), R80 (2004).
15. A. Buness, W. Huber, K. Steiner, H. Sultmann and A. Poustka, Arraymagic: Two-Colour cDNA Microarray Quality Control and Preprocessing, *Bioinformatics* **21**(4), 554-556 (2005).

16. J. Dietzsch, N. Gehlenborg and K. Nieselt, Mayday--a Microarray Data Analysis Workbench, *Bioinformatics* **22**(8), 1010-1012 (2006).
17. N. Knowlton, I.M. Dozmorov and M. Centola, Microarray Data Analysis Toolbox (Mdat): For Normalization, Adjustment and Analysis of Gene Expression Data, *Bioinformatics* **20**(18), 3687-3690 (2004).
18. R. Pieler, F. Sanchez-Cabo, H. Hackl, G.G. Thallinger and Z. Trajanoski, Arraynorm: Comprehensive Normalization and Analysis of Microarray Data, *Bioinformatics* **20**(12), 1971-1973 (2004).
19. D. Venet, Matarray: A Matlab Toolbox for Microarray Data, *Bioinformatics* **19**(5), 659-660 (2003).
20. A.I. Saeed, N.K. Bhagabati, J.C. Braisted, W. Liang, V. Sharov, E.A. Howe, J. Li, M. Thiagarajan, J.A. White and J. Quackenbush, TM4 Microarray Software Suite, *Methods Enzymol* **411**(134-193 (2006).
21. S. Patel and J. Lyons-Weiler, Cageda: A Web Application for the Integrated Analysis of Global Gene Expression Patterns in Cancer, *Appl Bioinformatics* **3**(1), 49-62 (2004).
22. A. Chatziioannou, P. Moulos, V. Aidinis and F. Kolisis, Andromeda: A Pipeline for Versatile 2-Colour cDNA Microarray Data Analysis Implemented in Matlab, (submitted to *Bioinformatics*, 2007).
23. S. de Jong and F. van der Meer *Imaging Spectrometry: Basic Principles and Prospective Applications* (Kluwer Academic, 2002)
24. J.W. Tukey *Exploratory Data Analysis* (Addison-Wesley, Reading, MA, 1977)
25. M.K. Kerr, M. Martin and G.A. Churchill, Analysis of Variance for Gene Expression Microarray Data, *J Comput Biol* **7**(6), 819-837 (2000).
26. W.J. Conover *Practical Nonparametric Statistics* (Wiley, 1980).
27. Y. Benjamini and Y. Hochberg, Controlling the False Discovery Rate: A Practical and Powerful Approach to Multiple Testing, *J R Statist Soc* **57**, 289-300 (1995).

Mining Interesting Clinico-Genomic Associations: The HealthObs Approach

George Potamias[1], Lefteris Koumakis[1], Alexandros Kanterakis[1], Vassilis Moustakis[1,3], Dimitrsi Kafetzopoulos[2], and Manolis Tsiknakis[1].

1 Institute of Computer Science (ICS)
2 Institute of Molecular Biology & Biotechnology (IMBB)
Foundation for Research & Technology – Hellas (FORTH)
Vassilika Vouton, P.O. box 1385, 71110 Heraklion, Crete, Greece
3 Technical University of Crete, Department of Production Engineering &
Management, 73100 Chania, Crete, Greece
{potamias,koumakis,kantale,moustaki,tsiknaki}@ics.forth.gr,
kafetzo@imbb.forth.gr

Abstract. HealthObs is an integrated (Java-based) environment targeting the seamless integration and intelligent processing of distributed and heterogeneous clinical and genomic data. Via the appropriate customization of standard medical and genomic data-models HealthObs achieves the semantic homogenization of remote clinical and gene-expression records, and their uniform XML-based representation. The system utilizes data-mining techniques (association rules mining) that operate on top of query-specific XML documents. Application of HealthObs on a real world breast-cancer clinico-genomic study demonstrates the utility and efficiency of the approach.

1 Introduction

As the number of electronic clinical records and respective data repositories increases, the seamless integration of the respective data repositories coupled with knowledge discovery operations offer the potential for the automated discovery of valuable clinical knowledge. Furthermore, the completion of the human genome drives us to the post-genomics era. In this environment the newly raised scientific and technological challenges push for trans-disciplinary team science and translational research. As it is noted by J. Grimson: '... *Patient empowerment fuelled by the Internet coupled with post genomics will ultimately lead to a health system which focuses more on promoting wellness rather than on treating illness ... Such a system must be centred on the patient (citizen) and their health status and management. The existence of a longitudinal Electronic Health Care Record is fundamental to bringing about this paradigm shift in the healthcare system*' [11].

Please use the following format when citing this chapter:

Potamias, G., Koumakis, L., Kanterakis, A., Moustakis, V., Kafetzopoulos, D., Tsiknakis, M., 2007, in IFIP International Federation for Information Processing, Volume 247, Artificial Intelligence and Innovations 2007: From Theory to Applications, eds. Boukis, C., Pnevmatikakis, L., Polymenakos, L., (Boston: Springer), pp. 137-145.

The vision is to compact major diseases, such as cancer, on an *individualized* diagnostic, prognostic and treatment manner. This requires not only an understanding of the genetic basis of the disease – acquired, for example, from patient's gene expression profiling studies [4, 13, 21], but also the correlation of this data with knowledge normally processed in the clinical setting. Coupling the knowledge gained from genomics and from clinical practice is of crucial importance and presents a major challenge for on-going and future clinico-genomic trials [15]. Such *evidential* knowledge will enhance health care professionals' decision-making capabilities, in an attempt to meet the raising evidence-based medicine demand.

Recently, and in the context of three research projects – PrognoChio (http://www.ics.forth.gr/~analyti/PrognoChip/isl_site/index.html, [6]), INFOBIOMED (www.infobiomed.net, [10]), and ACGT (http://www.eu-acgt.org, [15]), we have designed and implemented an integated clinico-genomics environment [7]. The environment is enhanced by a *Mediation* infrastructure through which linkage and integration of patients' clinical and genomic (e.g., nicroarray gene-expression) data is achieved [2]. The clinical information systems being utilized are components of an integrated clinical systems' infrastructure built in the region of Crete, Greece [16]. These systems are: (a) *Onco-Surgery* information system – manages information related to patient identification and demographic information, medical history, patient risk factors, family history of malignancy, clinical examinations and findings, results of laboratory exams (mammography, ultrasound, hematological etc.), pre-surgical and post-surgical therapies, as well as therapy effectiveness and follow-up; and (b) *Histo-Pathology* information system – manages information related to patients samples' histopathologic evaluation and TNM staging (tumor size, lymph node involvement, and metastatic spread). Engaged CISs comply with relevant medical information and data models, such as: SNOMED CT® (http://www.snomed.org/), ICD (http://www.cdc.gov/nchs/ icd9.htm), and LOINC® (http://www.regenstrief.org/loinc/). Data and information exchange between the two CIS is based on the HL7 (Health Level 7) messaging standard (http://www.hl7.org). The experimental study presented in this paper (section 4) deploys the two CIS to store and manage patients' clinico-histopathology information and data drawn from an anonymized public domain clinico-genomic study [13]. In this respect we are not confronted with ethical, legal and security issues (even if the whole infrastructure provides high-level security services).

With the help of the *Mediator*, the biomedical investigator can form clinico-genomic queries through the web-based graphical user interface of the Mediator and translates them into an equivalent set of local sub-queries, which are executed directly against the constituent databases (i.e., clinical and genomic/microarray information systems). Then, results are combined for presentation to the user and/or transmission to further analysis.

Access to distributed and heterogeneous data sources and collection of respective data items are not end in itself. What is desirable is the exploitation of data, hence the possibility for exporting useful and comprehensible conclusions. In this context we have designed and developed an integrated clinico-genomic knowledge discovery scenario enabled by a multi-strategy data-mining approach. The scenario is realized by the smooth integration of three data-mining techniques: clustering, association rules mining and feature selection [3,14]. In this scenario, clustering is performed on gene-expression datasets in order to induce indicative clusters of genes, called *Metagenes*. Clustering is performed with *discr_k-means* – a revision of the k-means algorithm that primarily identifies clusters of co-regulated *binary*-valued genes. To overcome the error-prone variance of gene-expression levels, gene-expression values are *discretized* (following a data pre-processing discretization step) into two nominal values: 'low' and 'high'. Putting it in more molecular biology terms, the 'low' and 'high' gene-expression levels correspond to 'DOWN'- and 'UP'-regulated status of the genes, respectively. The discr_k-means algorithm resembles similar approaches presented in [17] and [20]; for a more detailed description of the discr_k-means algorithm, please refer to [3,14]. After convergence of discr_k-means, each metagene is linked with respective (patient) samples and obeys a special characteristic: all of its genes exhibit a 'strong' gene-expression profile for all of its linked samples, i.e., exhibit solely 'high' (or, solely 'low') expression levels. Then, the quest is forwarded towards the identification of associations between metagenes and specific clinico-histopathological profiles.

In this paper we focus on the presentation and utilization of an association rule mining system, called HealthObs [5, 8, 12], to discover interesting and indicative association between patients' clinical and genomic gene-expression profiles, i.e., the metagenes. In the next section we present the architectural specifics of HealthObs. Section 3 presents the basic HealthObs operations and functionality. In section 4 we present results of using HealthObs on a real world breast-cancer study. In the last section we conclude and present hints for further research and development.

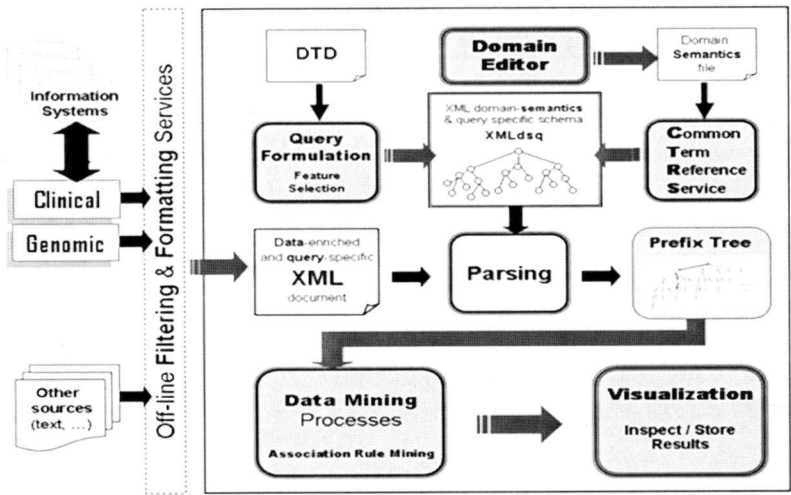

Fig. 1. Architecture and Components of HealthObs

2   Architectural and Operational Set-Up of HealthObs

HealthObs is an integrated system that offers: (i) semantic homogenization of respective distributed and heterogeneous clinical and genomic data sources, (ii) uniform representation of the respective data-items as realized by standard clinical and microarray data-models, and (iii) intelligent processing of XML-formatted documents enabled by the discovery of interesting clinical associations implemented by the customization of association rules mining (ARM) techniques [9,18]. HealthObs offers a population-oriented view on the distributed patients' clinico-genomic information as recorded in respective clinical and genomic/microarray information systems.

Association rules mining [9,18] is among the most advanced and interesting methods for finding interesting patterns and indicative trends in data. The definition of an ARM problem has as follows: Let $I = \{i_1, i_2, ..., i_m\}$ be a set of items. Let D be a set of transactions, where each transaction T is a set of items such that $T \subseteq I$. An association rule is an implication of the form $X \Rightarrow Y$, where $X \subset I$, $Y \subset I$, and $X \cap Y = \varnothing$. The rule $X \Rightarrow Y$ has confidence c in the transaction set D if $c\%$ of transactions in D that contain X also contains Y. The rule $X \Rightarrow Y$ has support s in the transaction set D if $s\%$ of transactions in D contains $X \cup Y$. Given a set of transactions D, the ARM problem is to discover the associations that have support and confidence values higher that the user specified *minimum support*, and *minimum confidence* levels, respectively.

An outline of the reference architecture underlying HealthObs is shown in Figure 1 (above) where, the basic operational modules of the system are also shown. Central to the architecture is a single data-enriched XML file which contains information and data from distributed and heterogeneous clinical and genomic information systems. Accumulation of data and their XML formatting are performed off-line. To this end, the Mediator infrastructure [2] is utilized in order to mediate and query federated clinical and genomic information sources and recall the relevant query-specific data items. For each query, and with the aid of custom made filtering and formatting operations, the respective query-specific XML file is created. HealthObs initiates and base its operations on such data-enriched XML files.

3   Basic Operations and Functionality of HealthObs

Query formulation supports the representation of the inquiry presented to the system. For instance, a user may decide to investigate and assess the confidence of associations between a focused number of clinical and genomic features. For example, between histological/biochemical-tests, such as 'ER' (Estrogen Receptor) status and prognostic features, such as patients' 'METASTASIS' status, on one hand, and genomic features, e,g., 'UP'/'DOWN'-regulated status of specific genes, on the other. In Figure 2, the system's feature-selection/focusing interface is shown. The features to be selected correspond to the instance elements being present in the data-enriched XML file to process.

In Figure 2 note the unique characteristic of HealthObs that relate to the specification of the desired form of 'focused' association rules to induce: rules to induce: (a) if the user only check-tick (☑) a feature, then this feature may or may-not be present in the rule, i.e., not-obligatory feature, (b) if the user not only checks a feature but post an 'IF' (☑, e.g., ER, MG33g9c19) or a 'THEN' (☑, e.g., METASTASIS) tick on it then, the presence of the feature in the association rules is obligatory in the 'IF' or, 'THEN' part of the rule, respectively.

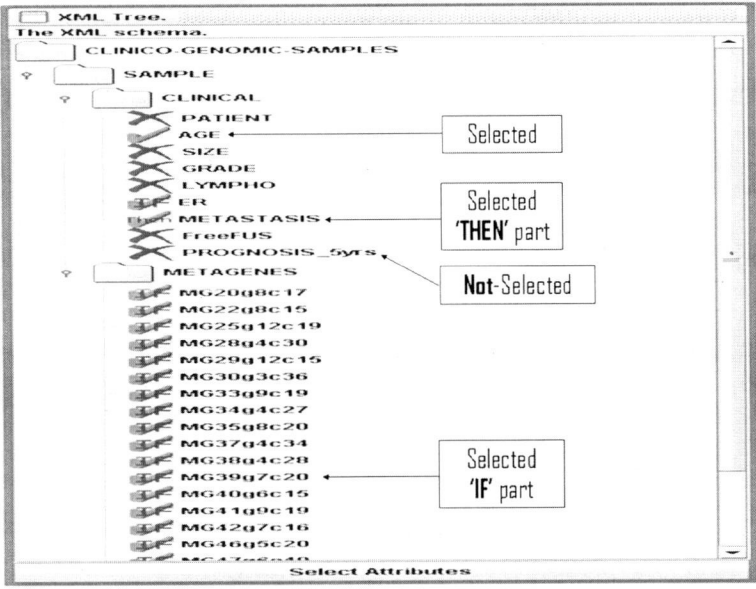

Fig. 2. Feature focusing and query formulation in HealthObs

3.1   Semantic Homogenization

Upon presentation of the inquiry and selection of the respective query features, HealthObs activates the Common Term Reference Service (CTRS) component. CTRS support the placement of the query in context of domain's semantics, e.g., involved medical and genomic nomenclatures and data-models. The SNOMED/CT, ICD and LOINC medical ontologies and nomenclatures (see section 1), as well as the 'Minimum Information About Microarray Experiments' (MIAME, http://www.mged.org/Workgroups/MIAME/miame.html) microarray/gene-expression data-models are utilized. CTRS incorporates (user's) specifications for the semantics of the domain (e.g., valid reference-ranges for lab findings, enabled by the transformation of numerical values to qualitative equivalents or, assignment of continuous gene-expression values to qualitative ones, e.g., into 'high'/'low' expression levels). Activation of the CTRS component results to the creation of an intermediate XML domain semantics and query specific schema ('XMLdsq' tree in Figure 1). XMLdsq is a restriction of the given DTD grammar and helps to: (i) focus the inquiry on the user selected features, and (ii) semantically homogenize the content of the data-enriched XML file. For the editing of the domain-semantics file, and its customization to different domains, we have also developed a special tool, the 'Domain Editor', made operational within the HealthObs environment (for detail see [8]).

3.2   The Prefix-Tree Structure

The recalled query-specific clinical data are kept in the corresponding data-rich XML-documents, and the implemented ARM operations are performed exclusively on top of these documents. The implemented ARM operations rely on the principles of the Apriori algorithm [18]. Adaptation of Apriori-like functionality on top of XML structures is based on a specially devised XML parser enabled by object-oriented search operations. Following RDF/XML techniques, the parser reads/scans the XML document in order to identify composite/atomic observations and homogenize their content (with CCTR service).

In the core of the ARM process is the identification of all frequent itemsets. Usually this is achieved by multiple-scans of the data (in our case, of the XML-document). Thus information-space search operations should be efficient. To enhance on efficiency we rely on a prefix-tree – a special tree-like data structure, that passes the data only once, the *prefix-tree* [1,19]. A prefix-tree structure makes no distinction between internal and leaf nodes. In this structure, nodes do not contain sets, but only information about sets (e.g. counters). Each edge in the tree is labelled with an item, and each node contains the information for the set of items labelling the edges of its path to the root. Prefix-trees store both frequent sets and candidate sets in the same tree.

4   HealthObs in Practice

The utility of HealthObs system was assessed byn applying it on a real-world breast-cancer study [13]. This study profiles the expression of ~24800 genes on 78 breast-cancer patients. The aim was to reveal (potentially) interesting and indicative *individualized* (i.e., target-population oriented) *clinico-genomic profiles*.

Characterization and classification of a disease, and prediction of respective patients' clinical outcome could be performed with reference either to solely clinico-histopathological patient profiles (CHPPs or, clinical phenotypes) -the clinical classification of the disease or, to solely genomic (i.e., microarray gene-expression) patient profiles (GEPPs or, genomic phenotypes) – provided that specific and reliable gene-markers are available. If this presents the decision-making track in the course of a clinico-genomic research trial, the most challenging task is the *knowledge discovery* track which works in a more-or-less inverse way. That is, starting from observable clinico-histopathological disease states the quest targets the identification of respective molecular signatures or, gene-markers able to discriminate between the different disease states.

Based on the central-dogma of molecular biology, CHPPs could be fully 'shaped' and *causally determinable* by respective GEPPs. In this setting, the quest is forwarded towards the following target: *"which clinico-histopathology phenotypes relate and how with which gene-expression phenotypes?"* Such a discovery-driven scenario falls into the *individualized* medicine context -GEPPs may be utilised to 'screen' respective CHPPs, to refine the clinical decision-making process, and finally identify specific patients groups (i.e., cohorts) as more suitable for specific clinical follow-up procedures. The whole endeavour aims to the identification of *abductive* and *inductive* inferential 'rules'.

As we have already mentioned (see section 1) we have designed and developed a *Mediation* infrastructure to recall patients' clinical and gene-expression data from respective clinical and microarray information systems [2]. With the utilization of a clustering operation – realized by the customization of k-means clustering technique on categorical data [3,14], we induce indicative clusters of genes, called *Metagenes* that meet a special characteristic: all of its genes exhibit a 'strong' gene-expression profile for all of its linked samples, i.e., exhibit solely 'high'/'UP'-regulated or, solely 'low'/'DOWN'-regulated expression levels. For example, with 'MG39g7c20=DOWN' we denote a cluster with id=39 ('MG39'), which includes 7 genes ('g7') and covers 20 cases ('c20'), and for all 20 cases all the respective genes exhibit a DOWN value (i.e., are down-regulated or, exhibit 'low' expression levels). A total of 22 such metagenes were induced when the following genes' pre-filtering was applied: p-value ≤ 0.01 and a 2-fold difference in at least 5 samples (similar filtering was applied in the original reference study [13]).

HealthObs was called to induce associations between the induced metagene-values and respective clinical feature-values for the available set of 78 patient samples. The target clinical feature was set to 'METASTASIS' (in the reference breast-cancer study metastasis is considered as 'YES' ('good') or 'NO' ('bad') if it occurred in less than five years or not, respectively. A total of 32 association rules were induced (22 concluding to 'METASTASIS=NO', and 10 to 'METASTASIS=YES') when the following parameters were applied: min-sup = 13% (i.e., at least 10 samples), and min-conf = 60%. By visual inspection of the rules (offered by HealthObs's graphical interface), we were able to identify some interesting associations with potential clinical decision-making value.

For example, one of the rules is:

$$ER=pos \quad \Rightarrow \quad METASTASIS=NO$$
Confidence=**63%**, Support: **63%** = **49** cases

Another, related with the above, rule that was induced is:

$$ER=pos \quad \& \quad MG39g7c20=DOWN \quad \Rightarrow \quad METASTASIS=NO$$
Confidence=**100%**, Support: **13%** = **10** cases

ER (Estrogen Receptor) factor possesses a distinct prognostic value for breast-cancer patients. In a 'positive' ('pos') ER state the prognosis is considered as good (i.e., no metastasis). The first rule, above, validates partially this, i.e., it is true in 63% of the cases. With the inclusion of gene-expression information and knowledge the evidence of a good prognosis could be improved. This is what the second rule states and suggests: with the knowledge that all genes in metagene MG39g7c20 are in 'DOWN'-regulated state then, the good prognosis is definite (i.e., 100% confident). Note that the second rule covers just 10 cases, less than the 49 cases (~ 9%) covered by the first rule. This could be considered as an approach to *individualization* of prognosis in the context of a *molecular medicine* environment. There are other association rules induced by HealthObs that cover other cases. For example the rule below engages two metagenes, is also 100% confident, and covers another sub-population of 7 cases:

$$ER=pos \quad \& \quad MG9g6c22=UP \quad \& \quad MG38g4c28=UP \quad \Rightarrow \quad METASTASIS=NO$$
Confidence=**100%**, Support: ~**9%** = **7** cases

Of course the findings are valid for the specific case-study that refers to a limited set of samples. Further evaluation and validation of results depends on the initiation of specific and targeted clinico-genomic trials that acquire adequate numbers of (statistically stratified) patients' samples. The running times for the discr-k_means and the ARM component of HealthObs were 13 and 3 seconds, respectively; the figures are indicative for the efficiency of the whole approach and of the respective clustering and ARM/HealthObs implementations.

5 Conclusions

We have presented a methodology for mining distributed and heterogeneous clinical and genomic data sources implemented within the context of the HealthObs environment. HealthObs represents an integrated platform with inter-operating software components that offers: (i) semantic homogenization of heterogeneous data resources, (ii) operationalization of ARM operations on-top of XML-formatted clinico-genomic data items, and (iii) flexible query-formulation and mining operations. Preliminary results on applying HealthObs on a real-world clinico-genomic (breast-cancer) study demonstrate the utility of the approach.

Our future research and development plans include: (a) design and development of appropriate human computer interfaces, accompanied with user-profiling capabilities for the personalized delivery of the results, (b) experimentation with other clinico-genomic domains and assessment of the clinical/genomic validity of the results, (c) incorporation of other data-mining operations (e.g., rule discovery), and (c) implementation of 'active-query' capabilities where, discovered clinico-genomic associations from pre-selected records are tested for potential differences and deviations so that, specific alarms could be broadcasted to the interested clinical researcher.

References

1. A. Amir, R. Feldman R., and R. Kashi, A new and versatile method for association generation, *Information Systems* 2, 333-347, (1997).
2. A. Analyti, H. Kondylakis, D. Manakanatas, M. Kalaitzakis, D. Plexousakis, and G. Potamias, Integrating Clinical and Genomic Information through the PrognoChip Mediator, *Lecture Notes in Bioinformatics* **4345**, 250-261, (2006).
3. D. Kanterakis, G. Potamias, Supporting Clinico-Genomic Knowledge Discovery: A Multistrategy Data Mining Process, *Lecture Notes in Computer Science* **3955**, pp. 520-524 (2006).
4. F. Cardoso, Microarray technology and its effect on breast cancer (re)classification and prediction of outcome, *Breast Cancer Res.*, **5**, 303-304, (2003).
5. G. Potamias and V. Moustakis, Knowledge Discovery from Distributed Clinical Data Sources: The Era for Internet-Based Epidemiology, in: 23rd Annual International Conference of the IEEE Engineering in Medicine and Biology Society, (2001), pp. 3638- 3641 vol.4.
6. G. Potamias, A. Analyti, D. Kafetzopoulos, M. Kafousi, T. Margaritis, D. Plexousakis, P. Poirazi, M. Reczko, Y. Tollis, E. Sanidas, E. Stathopoulos, M. Tsiknakis, and S. Vassilaros, Breast Cancer and Biomedical Informatics: The PrognoChip Project, in: Proceedings of the 17th IMACS World Congress Scientific Computation, Applied Mathematics and Simulation, Paper T3-I-68-1066.

7. G. Potamias, D. Kafetzopoulos, and M. Tsiknakis, Integrated Clinico-Genomics Environment: Design and Operational Specification, *Journal for Quality of Life Research* (JQLR), **2**(1), pp. 145-150 (2004).
8. G. Potamias, L. Koumakis, and V. Moustakis, Mining XML Clinical Data: the HealthObs System. *Ingénierie des Systèmes d'Information* **10**(1), pp. 59-79 (2005).
9. H. Mannila, H. Toivonen, and A.I. Verkamo, Efficient algorithms for discovering association rules, in: KDD-94: AAAI Workshop on Knowledge Discovery in Databases, (2001), pp. 181-192, 1994.
10. H.P. Eich, G. de la Calle, C. Diaz, S. Boyer, A.S. Pena, B.G. Loos, P. Ghazal, and I. Bernstein, Practical Approaches to the Development of Biomedical Informatics: the INFOBIOMED Network of Excellence. *Stud Health Technol Inform.*, **116**, pp. 39-44, (2005).
11. J. Grimson, Delivering the electronic healthcare record of the 21st century, *International Journal of Medical Informatics* **64**, pp. 111-127 (2001).
12. L. Koumakis, HealthObs: Health Observatory. An integrated system of data mining and knowledge discovery over distributed and heterogeneous clinical sources, Department of Computer Science, University of Crete MSc thesis (in Greek), 2004.
13. L.J. van 't Veer, et al., Gene expression profiling predicts clinical outcome of breast cancer, *Nature* **415**, pp. 530-536 (2002).
14. M. May, G. Potamias, and S. Rüping, Grid-based Knowledge Discovery in Clinico Genomic Data, *Lecture Notes in Bioinformatics* **4345**, pp. 219-230 (2006).
15. M. Tsiknakis, D. Kafetzopoulos, G. Potamias, A. Analyti, K. Marias, and A. Manganas, Building a European biomedical grid on cancer: the ACGT Integrated Project, *Stud Health Technol Inform.*, **120**, pp. 247-258, (2006).
16. M. Tsiknakis, D. Katehakis and, S. Orphanoudakis, An open, component-based information infrastructure for integrated health information networks, *International Journal of Medical Informatics* **68**(1-3), pp. 3-26 (2002).
17. O.M. San, V. Huynh, and Y. Nakamori, An alternative extension of the k-means algorithm for clustering categorical data, *Int. J. Appl. Math. Comput. Sci.* 14(2), pp. 241-247 (2004).
18. R. Agrawal, H. Manilla, R. Srikant, H. Toivonen, and I. A. Verkamo, Fast discovery of association rules, in: Advances in Knowledge Discovery and Data Mining, (AAAI/MIT Press, 1995), pp. 307-328.
19. R.J. Jr. Bayardo, Efficiently mining long patterns from databases, *SIGMOD Record* **27**(2), pp. 85-93 (1998).
20. S. Gupta, S. Rao, and V. Bhatnagar, K-means Clustering Algorithm for Categorical Attributes, *Lecture Notes in Computer Science* **1676**, pp. 203-208 (1999).
21. S.K. Gruvberger, M.Ringnér, P. Eden, A. Borg, M. Ferno, C. Peterson, and P.S Meltzer, Expression profiling to predict outcome in breast cancer: the influence of sample selection, *Breast Cancer Res.* **5**(1), pp. 23-26 (2003).

Patient Fall Detection using Support Vector Machines

Charalampos Doukas , Ilias Maglogiannis , Philippos Tragas , Dimitris
Liapis , Gregory Yovanof
University of the Aegean
Athens Information Technology

Abstract This paper presents a novel implementation of a patient fall detection
system that may be used for patient activity recognition and emergency
treatment. Sensors equipped with accelerometers are attached on the body of
the patients and transmit patient movement data wirelessly to the monitoring
unit. The methodology of support Vector Machines is used for precise
classification of the acquired data and determination of a fall emergency event.
Then a context-aware server transmits video from patient site properly coded
according to both patient and network status. Evaluation results indicate the
high accuracy of the classification method and the effectiveness of the
proposed implementation.

1 Introduction

The telemonitoring of human physiological data, in both normal and abnormal
situations of activity, is interesting for the purpose of emergency event detection or
long term data-storage for later diagnosis or for the purpose of medical exploration.
In the case of elderly people living on their own, there is a particular need for
monitoring their behavior. The first goal of this surveillance is the detection of major
incidents such as a fall, or a long period of inactivity in a part of their area. The early
detection of fall is an important step to alert and protect the subject, so that serious
injury can be avoided. Fall detection is an important part of human body movement
analysis; it is considered as an area of increasing importance and interest to
practitioners, researchers, and health industry and most importantly, it is vital for
indication of emergency cases. Accelerometers have been proposed as a practical,
inexpensive and reliable method for monitoring ambulatory motion in elderly

Please use the following format when citing this chapter:

Doukas, C., Maglogiannis, I., Tragas, P., Liapis, D., Yovanof, G., 2007, in IFIP International Federation for Information
Processing, Volume 247, Artificial Intelligence and Innovations 2007: From Theory to Applications, eds. Boukis, C.,
Pnevmatikakis, L., Polymenakos, L., (Boston: Springer), pp. 147-156.

subjects for the detection and prediction of falls. Robust classification of motion and postures from accelerometer data enable the development of more reliable methods for monitoring long term change in physiological indicators such as parameters of gait, balance, energy expenditure and general well-being.

This paper presents a patient fall detection platform based on accelerometer data. Body sensors collect the movement data and transmit them wirelessly to the monitoring unit. Appropriate data classification using Support Vector Machines 19, can classify the recorded movement into three categories; fall, walk and run. Then the deployment of additional context awareness based on the previous activity detection may enable the proper coding and transmission of video images from the patient to remote monitoring units (i.e alarm triggering and high quality video transmission). The rest of the paper is organized as follows; Section 2 discusses related work in the context of patient activity and fall detection. Section 3 describes the acquisition of the patient movement data using sensors, whereas Section 4 presents that data classification using Support Vector Machines. The whole system architecture is described in Section 5 and Section 6 presents the evaluation results. Finally, Section 7 concludes the paper.

2   Related Work

Although the concept of patient activity recognition with focus on fall detection is relatively new, there exists related research work, that may be retrieved from the literature (1-16). Information regarding the patient movement and activity is frequently acquired through visual tracking of the patient's position. In 6 and 15 overhead tracking through cameras provides the movement trajectory of the patient and gives information about user activity on predetermined monitored areas. Unusual inactivity (e.g., continuous tracking of the patient on the floor) is interpreted as a fall. Similarly, in 10 omni-camera images are used in order to determine the horizontal placement of the patient's silhouettes on the floor (case of fall). Success rate for fall detection is declared at 81% for the latter work. Head tracking is used in 13 in order to follow patient's movement trajectory with a success rate of fall detection at 66.67%. The aforementioned methods that detect falls based on visual information of the user require capturing equipment and thus are limited to indoor environment usage. In addition, some of the methods require also the a-priori knowledge of the area structure (e.g., obstacles, definition of floor, etc.), or user information (e.g., height in 10). A different approach for collecting patient activity information is the use of sensors that integrate devices like accelerometers, gyroscopes and contact sensors. The decrease of sensors size and weight, in conjunction with the introduction of embedded wireless transceivers allows their pervasive placement on patients and the transmission of the collected movement information to monitoring units wirelessly. The latter approach is less depended on the patient and environmental information and can be used for a variety of applications for user activity recognition (1, 3, 9). Regarding fall detection, authors in 2, 7, 8, 12 use accelerometers, gyroscopes and tilt sensors for movement tracking. Collected data from the accelerometers (i.e., usually rotation angle or acceleration in the X, Y and Z axis) is used in order to verify the placement of the patient and time occupation in rooms and detect abrupt movement that could be associated with fall. Detection is performed using predefined thresholds 1, 3, 4, 7 and association between current position, movement and acceleration 2, 8, 12. Finally, area sensors have been used in order to track and analyze patient movement; authors in 11 describe a vibration-based detector that can detect falls based on the vibration caused on the floor. In 5 infrared sensors are used that provide thermal information regarding the patient's location and movement. The latter approaches do not require from the user to wear or carry sensor devices, however they demand more expensive equipment to be installed on the surrounding environment.

Most of the related work based on accelerometers for fall detection, focuses on the elderly and may not be used for general classification of the patient movement activity or usage in younger ages (e.g. interpretation of running has not been assessed against falling). In addition, detection is usually performed through predefined thresholds and thus results can be depended to the movement patterns of the users. The presented system is using a state of the art classification methodology, the Support Vector Machines, for data classification and fall detection. The proposed system may be used for a variety of patient activity recognition since it can successfully distinguish movement between run and fall. In addition it is not biased by the movement pattern or the physiology of a specific patient (i.e. it can perform successfully with movement data from different individuals) and it does not apply restrictions to the user's environment (e.g., it can be used in outdoor environments as well). A context-aware framework deployed within the system enables the proper transmission of video images from the patient in case of emergency events, optimizing the whole telemonitoring procedure.

3   Patient Movement Data Acquisition

This section provides information on the acquisition and pre-processing of the patient movement data. The MC13192 [2] sensor has been used in our system. The latter contains a 2.4 GHz wireless data transceiver RF reference design with printed circuit antenna, which provides all hardware required for a complete wireless node using IEEE 802.15.4 (ZigBee) 17 packet structure. It includes an RS232 port for interface with a personal computer, background debug module for in-circuit hardware debug, four switches and LEDs for control and monitoring, a low-power, low-voltage MCU (MicroController Unit) with 60KB of on-chip Flash which allows the user flexibility in establishing wireless data networks and two 3D Accelerometers for X, Y and Z axis. Fig. 1 shows the SARD ZigBee node 18. ZigBee has been chosen as communication technology for a number of reasons:

- Low cost and very low power consumption: its data rate is at 250 kbps and its power consumption is 30mA in Transmit mode and only 3μA in StandBy mode respectively. A ZigBee node can thus have a very long battery life (2-3 years with a AA cell).

- Low complexity that makes the protocol ideal for integration on sensor nodes.
- Higher range compared to Bluetooth (up to 100 meter).
- Can be used for automatic creation of mesh networks.
- Contains built-in security measures.

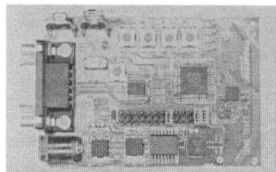

Fig. 1. The SARD ZigBee node. The node acts as both receiver and transmitter. The RS232 interface provides connectivity with the monitoring device (e.g., a laptop or a PDA) when the node is used as receiver. The transmitter is attached on user and sends data through the ZigBee wireless protocol.

The user's foot has been selected for acquiring movement data due to the fact the majority of human movements require the movement of the feet at one of the three axes (i.e. X, Y and Z). Thus the placement of the sensor on the foot allows the collection and association of accelerometer data with a wider range of human activity (e.g., walk, run, lie, etc.) The acquired data contain information about the patient's movement in the context of acceleration in the X, Y and Z axis and are transmitted wirelessly to the monitoring node. Fig. 2 illustrates an association between acceleration data on the X, Y and Z axes for the cases of normal movement, fall and run.

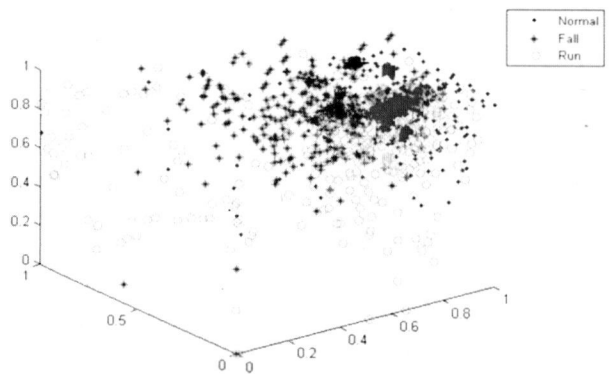

Fig. 2. Graphical association of the acceleration data on the X, Y and Z axis for three different movement types; Normal (i.e. walk), Fall and Run. Values have been normalized to [0,1].

4   Data Classification using Support Vector Machines

This Section provided information regarding the classification method used, parameters and data modeling. The Support Vector Machines (SVMs) is a popular algorithm for data classification into two classes 19, 20. SVMs allow the expansion of the information provided by a training data set as a linear combination of a subset of the data in the training set (support vectors). These vectors locate a hypersurface that separates the input data with a very good degree of generalization. The SVM algorithm is based on training, testing and performance evaluation, which are common steps in every learning procedure. Training involves optimization of a convex cost function where there are no local minima to complicate the learning process. Testing is based on the model evaluation using the support vectors to classify a test data set. Given a training set of instance-label pairs:

$$(x_i, y_i), i = 1, \ldots, l \ where \ x_i \in R^n \ and \ y \in \{1, -1\}^l$$

The SVM require the solution of the following optimization problem:

$$\min_{w, b, \xi} \frac{1}{2} w^T w + C \sum_{i=1}^{l} \xi_i \ , \qquad \text{Equation 1}$$

subject to $y_i (w^T \phi(x_i) + b) \geq 1 - \xi_i, \ \xi i \geq 0,$ \qquad Equation 2

The training vectors x_i can be mapped into a higher dimensional space by the function φ. Then SVM finds a linear separating hyperplane with the maximal margin in this higher dimensional space. $C > 0$ is the penalty parameter of the error term. Furthermore, $K(x_i, x_j) \equiv \phi(xi)^T \phi(xj)$ is called the kernel function. The most commonly used kernels are the following:

- Linear: $K(x_i, x_j) = X_i^T x_j$
- Polynomial: $K(x_i, x_j) = (\gamma x_i^T x_j + r)^d, \gamma > 0$
- Radial Basis Function (RBF): $K(x_i, x_j) = e^{(-\gamma \|xi - xj\|^2)}, \gamma > 0$
- Sigmoid: $K(x_i, x_j) = \tanh(\gamma x_i^T x_j + r)$

where γ, r and d are kernel parameters.
In order to make an efficient selection of the most suitable kernel type for the presented platform, the aforementioned kernel types have been validated against input data from the accelerometer sensors. Three classification classes have been defined according to corresponding movement cases; fall, run and walk. A SVM train model has been created from the latter data using the tool presented in 21. The input data has the following form:

Class_ID X Y Z,

where Class_ID $\in [1,3]$ and represents the movement case (i.e. 1 for walk, 2 for run and 3 for fall), X the acceleration value in the X axis, Y the acceleration value in Y axis and Z the acceleration value in Z axis respectively. For simplicity, acceleration values were normalized to [0,1]. The same data have been used in order to verify the accuracy of each kernel. Fig. 3 illustrates the accuracy of each kernel type for different C values. As results indicate, the RBF kernel behaves much better in terms of accuracy (approaches 98.2% accuracy for C=1000) for proper classification of the test data into the three defined classes, and thus has been selected for data classification in the presented platform. A second experiment was conducted in order to evaluate the RBF kernel's performance against different γ values. Fig. 4 presents the accuracy results for a range of γ value between [1,100].

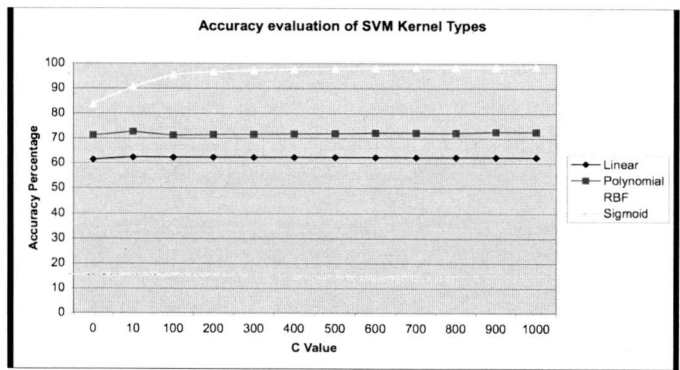

Fig. 3. Accuracy Evaluation of different SVM Kernel types for different C values. X axis represents the C value range between [1, 1000] and the Y axis the accuracy percentage.

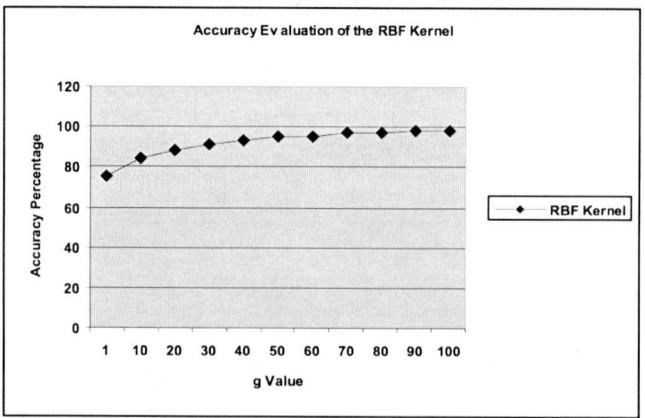

Fig. 4. *Accuracy Evaluation of the RBF kernel for different g values.*

Based on the aforementioned results, RBF with C=1000 and γ=100 was selected for creating the classification (i.e. train) model of the platform.

5   The System Architecture

The presented system follows the architecture illustrated in Fig. 5. Accelerometer data are collected through the sensor attached on the user's foot and are transmitted wirelessly to the monitoring node. The data is properly transformed in a suitable format for the classifier and the classification phase begins. Based on a predefined classification model (i.e. train model), the patient status is detected (i.e. emergency status when fall detected, normal status otherwise). A network status monitoring module determines the quality of the underlying network infrastructure and decides for the proper coding and transmission of the patient video images using H.263 22 video compression.

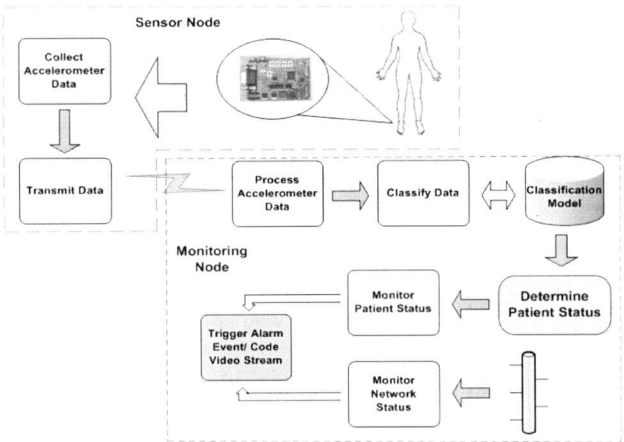

Fig. 5. Platform Architecture and Data interaction between the sensor and monitoring node.

6   Fall Detection and Evaluation Results

In order to evaluate the efficiency and accuracy of the presented platform in the context of detecting patient falls, three different experiments were conducted; two volunteers wearing the sensors devices described in Section 3 performed three combinations of movement types; a) simple walk, b) simple walk and fall, c) simple walk and run. The classification model with parameters and data described in Section 4 was used in order to validate the acquired accelerometer data. Each acceleration value in X, Y and Z axis was validated runtime and a corresponding movement type was associated with it. Based on the number of sequential occurrence of a specific movement type, decision regarding a patient fall is taken. In order to improve the accuracy of the latter decision, Kalman filtering 23, 24 has been applied on the sequence of the movement type association of each acceleration data set.

Fig. 6 represents the classification results from the conducted experiments using the trained SVM model. Blue lines represent original results whereas purple lines results after applying Kalman filtering. Actual run and fall events are also annotated on the diagrams. As it is indicated, Kalman filtering improves the overall detection by smoothing the sequential occurrences of run or fall events respectively. A threshold t =10 has been selected for determining the occurrence of a fall or run event from the total sequence of classified movement types (i.e. if sequential occurrence of fall movement types > 10 then a fall is detected). Using the aforementioned classification and the latter threshold value, fall events were detected with an average accuracy of 98.2% for both users, whereas run events were successfully detected at 96.72%.

7   Conclusions

In this paper a platform for detecting patient falls is presented. User movement is monitored using sensor devices that provide information regarding the acceleration in the X, Y and Z axis. Proper data classification based on Support Vector Machines provides fall detection with accuracy up to 98.2%. Fall detection indicates an emergency status for the patient. In conjunction to network status awareness proper patient video image coding and transmission is applied optimizing this way the telemonitoring procedure. Future work might include the enhancement of the platform with fall detection using computer vision processing of the patient's site for even more accurate results.

References

1.   Noury N., Herve T., Rialle V., Virone G., Mercier E., Morey G., Moro A., and Porcheron T., Monitoring behavior in home using a smart fall sensor and position sensors, Annual International Conference on Microtechnologies in Medicine and Biology, 607-610 (2000).
2.   Noury N., A smart sensor for the remote follow up of activity and fall detection of the elderly, 2nd Annual International Conference on Microtechnologies in Medicine and Biology, 314-317 (2002).
3.   Prado M., Reina-Tosina J., and Roa L., Distributed intelligent architecture for falling detection and physical activity analysis in the elderly, 24th Annual IEEE EMBS Conference, 1910-1911 (2002).
4.   Fukaya K., Fall detection sensor for fall protection airbag, 41st SICE Annual Conference, 419-420 (2002).
5.   Sixsmith A., and Johnson N., A smart sensor to detect the falls of the elderly, IEEE Pervasing Computing, 3 (2), 42-47 (2004).

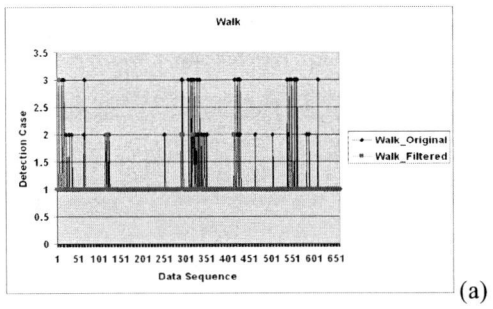

(a)

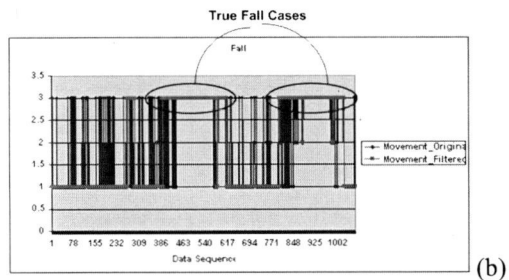

(b)

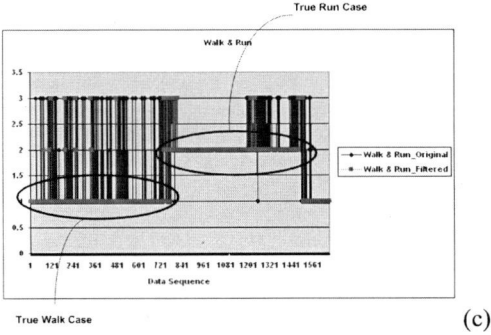

(c)

Fig. 6. Classification results based on the SVM trained model for three different types of movement: (a) simple walk, (b) walk and fall, (c) walk and run. X axis represents the acceleration data sequence and Y axis the corresponding movement type (i.e. 1 for walk, 2 for run and 3 for fall). Light lines represent original results whereas dark lines results after applying Kalman filtering. Actual run and fall events are annotated on the diagrams.

6. Nait-Charif, H. and McKenna, S.J., Activity summarisation and fall detection in a supportive home environment, 17th International Conference on Pattern Recognition ICPR 2004, 323-236 (2004).
7. Hwang, J.Y. Kang, J.M. Jang, Y.W. and Kim, H.C., Development of novel algorithm and real-time monitoring ambulatory system using Bluetooth module for fall detection in the elderly, 26th Annual International Conference of the IEEE Engineering in Medicine and Biology Society, 2204-2207 (2004).

8. Suhuai Luo, and Qingmao Hu, A dynamic motion pattern analysis approach to fall detection, 2004 IEEE International Workshop on Biomedical Circuits and Systems, 1-8a (2004).

9. Shuangquan Wang, Jie Yang, Ningjiang Chen, Xin Chen, and Qinfeng Zhang, Human activity recognition with user-free accelerometers in the sensor networks, International Conference on Neural Networks and Brain, 1212-1217 (2005).

10. S.-G. Miaou, Pei-Hsu Sung, and Chia-Yuan Huang, A Customized Human Fall Detection System Using Omni-Camera Images and Personal Information, 1st Transdisciplinary conference on Distributed Diagnosis and Home Healthcare, 39-42 (2006).

11. Alwan, M. Rajendran, P.J. Kell, S. Mack, D. Dalal, S. Wolfe, M. and Felder, R. A Smart and Passive Floor-Vibration Based Fall Detector for Elderly, 2nd Information and Communication Technologies Conference, ICTTA 06, 1003-1007 (2006).

12. Allen, F.R. Ambikairajah, E. Lovell N.H. and Celler, B.G., An Adapted Gaussian Mixture Model Approach to Accelerometry-Based Movement Classification Using Time-Domain Features, 28th Annual International Conference of the IEEE Engineering in Medicine and Biology Society, 3600-3603 (2006).

13. Rougier, C. Meunier, J. St-Arnaud, A. and Rousseau, J., Monocular 3D Head Tracking to Detect Falls of Elderly People, 28th Annual International Conference of the IEEE Engineering in Medicine and Biology Society, 6384 - 6387, (2006).

14. Cao, X.B. Chen, D. Qiao, H. and Xu, Y.W., An Evolutionary Support Vector Machines Classifier for Pedestrian Detection, 2006 IEEE International Conference on Intelligent Robots and Systems, 4223-4227 (2006).

15. Jansen Bart, and Deklerck Rudi, Context aware inactivity recognition for visual fall detection, 2006 Pervasive Health Conference and Workshops, 1-4 (2006).

16. Gaura, E.I., Rider, R.J., Steele, N., and Naguib R.N.G., Neural-network compensation methods for capacitive micromachined accelerometers for use in telecare medicine, IEEE Transactions on Information Technology in Biomedicine, 5, (3), 248-252 (2001).

17. The IEEE 802.15.4 ZigBee wireless technology; http://www.zigbee.org

18. The SARD sensor node; http://www.freescale.com

19. Christianini N, and Shawe-Taylor J, *An introduction to support vector machines.* (Cambridge University Press, 2000).

20. Schölkopf B: Statistical learning and kernel methods. [http://research.Microsoft.com/~bsc].

21. Chih-Chung Chang and Chih-Jen Lin, LIBSVM : A library for support vector machines, 2001. Software available at http://www.csie.ntu.edu.tw/~cjlin/libsvm

22. The ITU H.263 compression standard, available in http://www.itu.int/itudoc/itu-t/rec/h/

23. Sasiadek J.Z., and Khe J., Sensor fusion based on fuzzy Kalman filter, 2nd International IEEE Workshop on Robot Motion and Control, 275-283, (2001).

24. Mohinder S. Grewal, Angus P. Andrews, *Kalman Filtering* (Second Edition), (John Wiley & Sons, 2001).

A web-based service for improving conformance to medication treatment and patient-physician relationship

Nikolaos Riggos, Ilias Skalkidis, George Karkalis, Maria Haritou, Dimitris Koutsouris
Biomedical Engineering Laboratory
National Technical University of Athens,
9 Iroon Polytechniou Str., Zografou Campus, 157 73
Athens, Greece
Tel: (+30)210-7722269
nriggos@biomed.ntua.gr
WWW home page: http://www.biomed.ntua.gr

Abstract. The proposed service is a health-related web portal serving a twofold purpose: Reminding the patient of important tasks related to a long-term treatment, such as medication intake, clinical encounters, follow-up actions etc., as well as tightening the patient-physician relationship through bidirectional communication. The physician is able to register and review patient-related information through a user-friendly web-based interface, assign medication treatment plans, examination plans etc. The patient receives notifications about the treatment plan through several means, including Short Message Service (SMS) and e-mail. The common web-based space shared by the patient and the physician enables the bidirectional exchange of observations or comments about the treatment, publishing additional guidelines augmenting the treatment outcome, reporting side-effects etc. The implementation of the service is based on MS SQL Server Notification Services technology and we believe that is has the potential to improve adherence to the medication plans, especially in the case of long-term therapy.

1 Introduction

The success of drugs in controlling many of the illnesses associated with old age, means that people can continue to enjoy full and independent lives in the community providing that they comply with their prescribed medications. Unfortunately, many older people suffer from a number of different chronic conditions each of which requires a separate type of medication. Consequently, significant numbers need to

Please use the following format when citing this chapter:

Riggos, N., Skalkidis, I., Karkalis, G., Haritou, M., Koutsouris, D., 2007, in IFIP International Federation for Information Processing, Volume 247, Artificial Intelligence and Innovations 2007: From Theory to Applications, eds. Boukis, C., Pnevmatikakis, L., Polymenakos, L., (Boston: Springer), pp. 157-162.

administer several drugs during the course of a day. In an institutional care setting such as a hospital or nursing home, responsibility for taking the correct medication at the correct time lies with the medical and nursing personnel. When the patient returns home, professional help is not generally available at the times when the drugs must be administered. There is therefore a risk that the medication may be forgotten, the wrong dose will be taken or that the wrong medication will be taken. These risks are especially relevant to older people whose cognitive abilities may be diminishing and those who are suffering from any degree of confusion.

Despite wide recognition and documentation of its existence, patient noncompliance to prescribed medication regimens continues to be a prevalent problem. Stewart and Cluff have stated that the percentage of patients making medication errors in the self-administration of prescribed medications, with few exceptions, has ranged between 25 and 95 per cent [1]. The most frequently cited errors relate to dosage, frequency of administration, and drug identification. Several studies have shown that over half of elderly patients do not take their drugs as prescribed, [2,3] and the percentage of all patients who make errors is probably between 25% and 59%[1]. Many of these patients may not clearly understand their regimens, [4] and about 4-35% of patients misuse their drugs to such an extent that they endanger their health [1]. Furthermore, the lack of effective communication between physicians and patients about medications may be an important reason why patients do not follow medical advice [5]. According to Kanjanarat et. al., "Most preventable adverse drug events occur in the prescribing stage of the medication-use process and have been attributed to inappropriate prescribing decisions and inappropriate monitoring" [6]. It is therefore evident that a complete solution that helps both the physicians and the patients reduce medication errors is needed.

The application presented at this paper is a user friendly web based portal, designed specifically to provide reminder services to the patient as well as monitoring and archiving services to the physician tightening the patient-physician relationship through bidirectional communication.

2   Application Description

The most appropriate way to describe this application is by describing the roles of the three distinct users of the system.

2.1   The administrator

The administrator is responsible for the administration of all the users and the system in general. The administrator is the only user that can create a "doctor user", change a user password or delete a user.

2.2   The Doctor

The doctor has the option to create a user account for the patient and prescribe a specific medication from a list of drugs available to him (Figure 1). The doctor can edit a medication schedule, indicating the frequency of the drug intake, the dose and the specific time a reminding notification will be sent to his patient. He also has the option to choose whether the notification will be sent via an SMS and/or an e-mail. Additionally the doctor can create a new scheduled examination specifying the date and time this examination will occur, as well as the number of days he would like his patient to be notified in advance. Finally the doctor is able to add explanatory comments on every parameter of a medication schedule, making it easier for the patient to remember and follow his instructions.

Figure 1. The Doctor can choose a drug from the database using a search engine

2.3   The Patient

When the patient logins into the system, he can view a summary of the information related to him. These include the doses of drugs to be taken in the next 24 hours, all active medication regimens, a full history of medication plans completed and any scheduled appointments created by the doctor. Everything is presented in a clear and concise manner with extra detail coming up to the screen if a specific element is clicked (Figure 2). The patient can insert comments regarding a specific medication plan, drug or dose at any time, providing feedback to his doctor. If any new entry is recorded a notification is sent to the doctor.

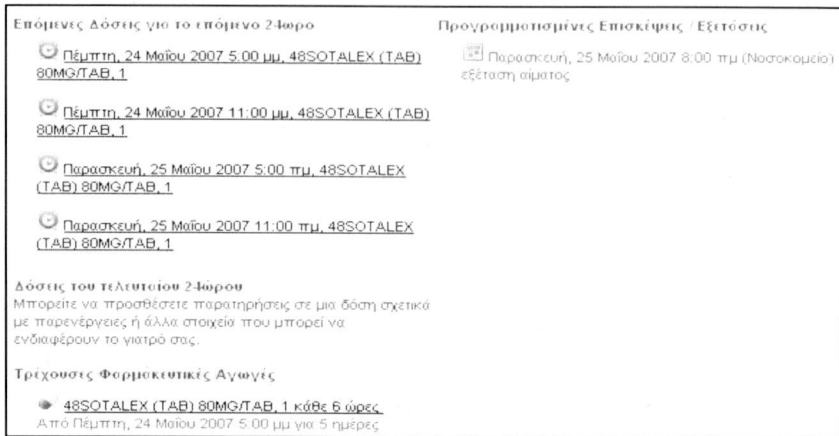

Figure 2. The patient details screen

3   System Architecture

The system architecture is largely based on MS SQL Server Notification Services technology [8] (Figure 3). Notification Services is a programming framework for building applications that send notifications to subscribed users, and a server that hosts the applications. The user is required to subscribe to the service by specifying triggering events when the notification should be generated and sent to the user. This is accomplished through a subscription management interface library, developed using subscription management objects supplied with Notification Services. A web service is built upon the subscription management interface exposing its functionality. The web application uses this web service wrapper to add user subscription information to the Notification Services Database. Notification Services stores the subscriber and delivery information in a central Notification Services' database and it stores individual subscriptions in application-specific databases. This allows applications to share the global subscriber data while separately storing subscriptions for each application.

Notification Services handle the final delivery of notifications through the use of delivery channels, which can be thought of as pipes to delivery services. The delivery channels package the notifications into protocol packets and then send them to the delivery service that handles the final delivery. An e-mail delivery channel is included as an internal component of the Notification Services and its functionality was used as provided by the framework. Additionally, Notification Services provide a mechanism for implementing custom delivery channels. Using this mechanism, a custom SMS delivery channel and an SMS Web Service were built in order to communicate with the Clickatell Bulk SMS Gateway, which handles the sending of the SMS to the users.

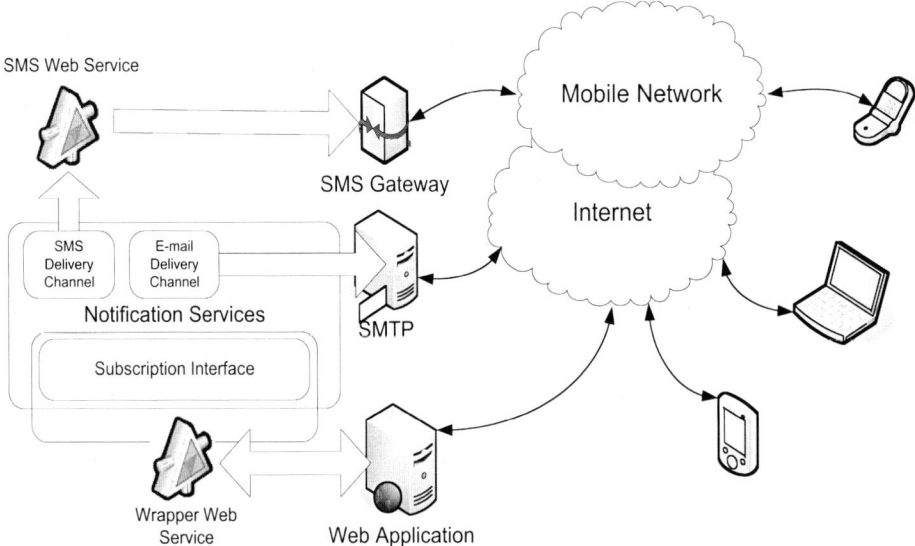

Figure 3. Overall System Architecture

4   Discussion

In an attempt to promote better compliance by decreasing medication errors related to dosage, frequency of administration and drug identification, various devices have been utilized. A variety of simple "pill organizers" and "unit-dose" medication systems are widely available in stores. In addition, more sophisticated devices such as human voice recordings, telephone services, and beeping watches or key chains can be used to remind the person to take medications at designated times [9]. The platform we propose goes one step further, using existing and state-of-the-art technologies, such as the .NET framework, Web Services and MS SQL Server Notification Services providing to the patient and the physician a user friendly tool that can offer notification services to both the patient and the doctor. The common web-based space shared by the patient and the physician enables the bidirectional exchange of observations or comments about the treatment, publishing additional guidelines, augmenting the treatment outcome, reporting side-effects etc. The application takes full advantage of the powerful characteristics nowadays web technologies have to offer, utilizing a system that can be accessed by any terminal (mobile or not) using a web browser without the need to purchase any additional devices. The authors of this paper believe that in the future this platform could be integrated with a system that uses Artificial Intelligence algorithms to detect errors regarding the medication plans issued to the patients, mining knowledge from the physician and patient reports.

Acknowledgments: This work has been co-funded
- ➤ 70% by the European Union (EU) – European Regional Development Fund (ERDF)
- ➤ 30% by the Hellenic Republic – Ministry of Development – General Secretariat for Research & Technology (GSRT)

in the framework of Measure 4.2 of the Op. Pr. Competitiveness – 3rd Community Support Programme

References

1. R. B. Stewart, and L. E.Cluff, Review of medication errors and compliance in ambulant patients, *Clin. Pharmacol. Ther*, **13**, 463 (1972).
2. I. Wandless, and J. W. Davie Can drug compliance in the elderly be improved? *British Medical Journal*, **1**, 359-361 (1977).
3. D. Schwartz, M. Wang, L. Zeitz, M.E. Goss., Medication Errors Made by Elderly Chronically Ill Patients, *American Journal of Public Health*, **52**, 2018-2019 (1962).
4. D. M. Parkin, *British Medical Journal*, **2**, 686 (1976).
5. S.W. Fletcher, R.H. Fletcher, D.C. Thomas, C. Hamann, Patients' understanding of prescribed drugs, *Journal of Community Health*, **4** (3), 183-189 (1979)
6. P. Kanjanarat, A.G. Winterstein, T.E. Johns, R.C. Hatton, R. Gonzalez-Rothi, and Segal R. Nature of preventable adverse drug events in hospitals: a literature review. *Am J Health Syst Pharm*. **60**:(17), 1750–1759 (2003)
7. Clickatell Bulk SMS Gateway (June 11, 2007); http://www.clickatell.com
8. Microsoft SQL Server Notification Services (June 12, 2007); http://www.microsoft.com/technet/prodtechnol/sql/2000/evaluate/sqlnsto.mspx
9. C.A Miller., Teaching Older Adults Medication Self-Care, *Geriatric Nursing* **25** (5), 318-319 (2004)

Section 4

AI in Business and Finance

Informed Agents
Integrating Data Mining and Agency

John Debenham and Simeon Simoff

University of Technology,
Sydney, Australia
{debenham,simeon}@it.uts.edu.au

Summary. We propose that the key to building informed negotiating agents is to develop a form of agency that integrates naturally with data mining and information sources. These agent's take their historic observations as primitive, model their changing uncertainty in that information, and use that model as the foundation for the agent's reasoning. We describe an agent architecture, with an attendant theory, that is based on that model. In this approach, the utility of contracts, and the trust and reliability of a trading partner are intermediate concepts that an agent may estimate from its information model.

1 Introduction

The architecture of informed agents is designed to integrate naturally with information sources are their associated uncertainty. That is, we integrate:

- data mining — real-time data mining technology to tap information flows from the marketplace and the World Wide Web, and to deliver timely information at the right granularity.
- trading agents — intelligent agents that are designed to operate in tandem with the real-time information flows received from the data mining systems.

This paper describes an e-trading system that integrates these three technologies. The e-Market Framework is available on the World Wide Web[1]. This project aims to make informed automated trading a reality, and develops further the "Curious Negotiator" framework [1]. The data mining systems that have been developed for mining information both from the virtual institution and from general sources from the World Wide Web are described in Sec. 2. Intelligent agent that are built on an architecture designed specifically to handle real-time information flows are described in Sec. 3. Sec. 4 concludes.

2 Data Mining

We have designed information discovery and delivery agents that utilise text and network data mining for supporting real-time negotiation. This work has addressed the

---

[1] http://e-markets.org.au

Please use the following format when citing this chapter:

Debenham, J., Simoff, S., 2007, in IFIP International Federation for Information Processing, Volume 247, Artificial Intelligence and Innovations 2007: From Theory to Applications, eds. Boukis, C., Pnevmatikakis, L., Polymenakos, L., (Boston: Springer), pp. 165-173.

central issues of extracting relevant information from different on-line repositories with different formats, with possible duplicative and erroneous data. That is, we have addressed the central issues in extracting information from the World Wide Web. Our mining agents understand the influence that extracted information has on the subject of negotiation and takes that in account.

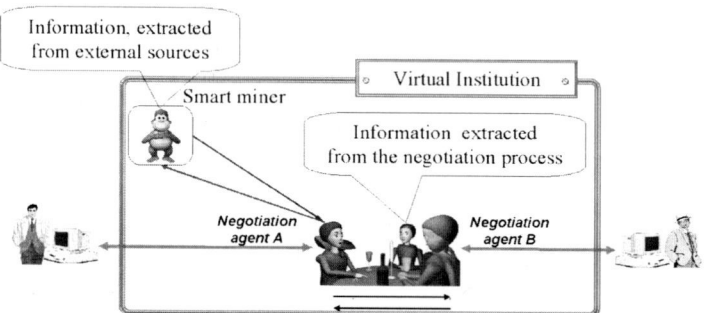

Fig. 1. The information that impacts trading negotiation

Real-time embedded data mining is an essential component of the proposed framework. In this framework the trading agents make their informed decisions, based on utilising two types of information (as illustrated in Figure 1): first, information extracted from the negotiation process (i.e. from the exchange of offers), and, second, information from external sources, extracted and provided in condensed form.

The embedded data mining system provides the information extracted from the external sources. The system complements and services the information-based architecture developed in [2] and [3]. The information request and the information delivery format is defined by the interaction ontology. As these agents operate with negotiation parameters with a discrete set of feasible values, the information request is formulated in terms of these values. As agents proceed with negotiation they have a topic of negotiation and a shared ontology that describes that topic. As the information-based architecture assumes that negotiation parameters are discrete, the information request can be formulated as a subset of the range of values for a negotiation parameter. The collection of parameter sets of the negotiation topic constitutes the input to the data mining system. Continuous numerical values are replaced by finite number of ranges of interest.

The data mining system initially constructs data sets that are "focused" on requested information, as illustrated in Figure 2. From the vast amount of information available in electronic form, we need to filter the information that is relevant to the information request. In our example, this will be the news, opinions, comments, white papers related to the five models of digital cameras. Technically, the automatic retrieval of the information pieces utilises the universal news bot architecture presented in [4]. Developed originally for news sites only, the approach is currently being extended to discussion boards and company white papers.

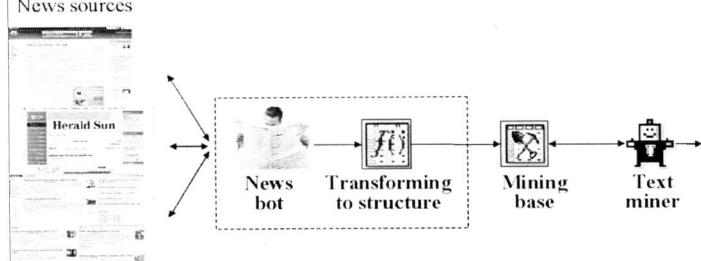

Fig. 2. The pipeline of constructing "focused" data sets

The "focused" data set is dynamically constructed in an iterative process. The data mining agent constructs the news data set according to the concepts in the query. Each concept is represented as a cluster of key terms (a term can include one or more words), defined by the proximity position of the frequent key terms. On each iteration the most frequent (terms) from the retrieved data set are extracted and considered to be related to the same concept. The extracted keywords are resubmitted to the search engine. The process of query submission, data retrieval and keyword extraction is repeated until the search results start to derail from the given topic.

The set of topics in the original request is used as a set of class labels. In our example we are interested in the evidence in support of each particular model camera model. A simple solution is for each model to introduce two labels — positive opinion and negative opinion, ending with ten labels. In the constructed focused data set, each news article is labelled with one of the values from this set of labels. An automated approach reported in [4] extends the tree-based approach proposed in [5].

Once the set is constructed, building the "advising model" is reduced to a classification data mining problem. As the model is communicated back to the information-based agent architecture, the classifier output should include all the possible class labels with an attached probability estimates for each class. Hence, we use probabilistic classifiers (e.g. Naïve Bayes, Bayesian Network classifiers [6] without the min-max selection of the class output [e.g., in a classifier based on Naïve Bayes algorithm, we calculate the posterior probability $\mathbb{P}_p(i)$ of each class $c(i)$ with respect to combinations of key terms and then return the tuples $< c(i), \mathbb{P}_p(i) >$ for all classes, not just the one with maximum $\mathbb{P}_p(i)$. In the case when we deal with range variables the data mining system returns the range within which is the estimated value. For example, the response to a request for an estimate of the rate of change between two currencies over specified period of time will be done in three steps: (i) the relative focused news data set will be updated for the specified period; (ii) the model that takes these news in account is updated, and; (iii) the output of the model is compared with requested ranges and the matching one is returned. The details of this part of the data mining system are presented in [7]. The currently used model is a modified linear model with an additional term that incorporates a news index Inews, which reflects the news effect on exchange rate. The current architecture of the data mining system in the e-market environment is shown in Figure 5. The $\{\theta_1, \ldots, \theta_t\}$ denote the output of the system to the information-based agent architecture.

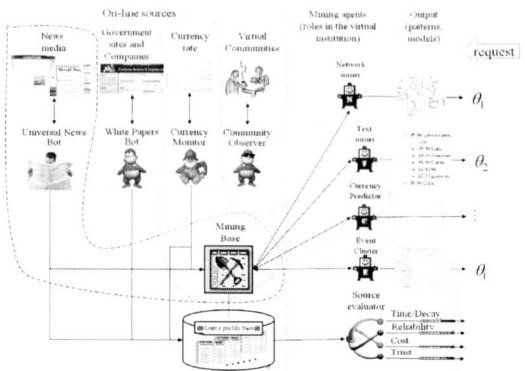

Fig. 3. The architecture of the agent-based data mining system

3 Trading Agents

We have designed a new agent architecture founded on information theory. These "information-based" agents operate in real-time in response to market information flows. We have addressed the central issues of trust in the execution of contracts, and the reliability of information [3]. Our agents understand the value of building business relationships as a foundation for reliable trade. An inherent difficulty in automated trading — including e-procurement — is that it is generally multi-issue. Even a simple trade, such as a quantity of steel, may involve: delivery date, settlement terms, as well as price and the quality of the steel. The "information-based" agent's reasoning is based on a first-order logic world model that manages multi-issue negotiation as easily as single-issue.

Most of the work on multi-issue negotiation has focussed on one-to-one bargaining — for example [8]. There has been rather less interest in one-to-many, multi-issue auctions — [9] analyzes some possibilities — despite the size of the e-procurement market which typically attempts to extend single-issue, reverse auctions to the multi-issue case by post-auction haggling. There has been even less interest in many-to-many, multi-issue exchanges.

The generic architecture of our "information-based" agents is presented in Sec. 3.1. The agent's reasoning employs entropy-based inference and is described in [2]. The integrity of the agent's information is in a permanent state of decay, [3] describes the agent's machinery for managing this decay leading to a characterization of the "value" of information. Sec. 3.2 describes metrics that bring order and structure to the agent's information with the aim of supporting its management.

3.1 Information-Based Agent Architecture

The essence of "information-based agency" is described as follows. An agent observes events in its environment including what other agents actually do. It chooses to represent some of those observations in its world model as beliefs. As time passes, an agent may not be prepared to accept such beliefs as being "true", and qualifies those representations with epistemic probabilities. Those qualified representations of prior observations are the agent's *information*. This information is primitive — it is the agent's representation of its beliefs about prior events in the environment and about the other agents prior actions. It is independent of what the agent is trying to achieve, or what the agent believes the other agents are trying to achieve. Given this information, an agent may then choose to adopt goals and strategies. Those strategies may be based on game theory, for example. To enable the agent's strategies to make good use of its information, tools from information theory are applied to summarize and process that information. Such an agent is called *information-based*.

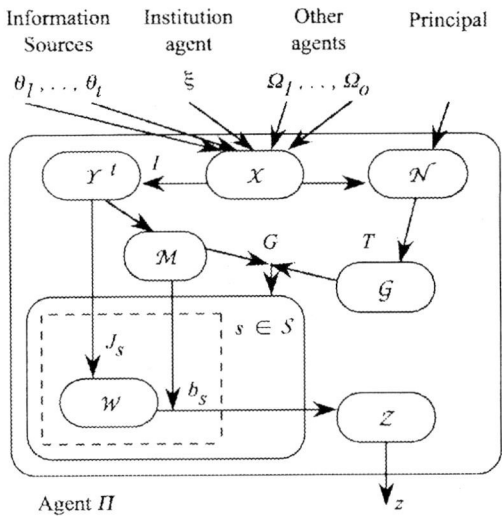

Fig. 4. Basic architecture of agent Π

An agent called Π is the subject of this discussion. Π engages in multi-issue negotiation with a set of other agents: $\{\Omega_1, \cdots, \Omega_o\}$. The foundation for Π's operation is the information that is generated both by and because of its negotiation exchanges. Any message from one agent to another reveals information about the sender. Π also acquires information from the environment — including general information sources —to support its actions. Π uses ideas from information theory to process and summarize its information. Π's aim may not be "utility optimization" — it may not be aware of a utility function. If Π *does* know its utility function *and* if it aims to optimize its utility *then* Π may apply the principles of game theory to achieve its aim. The information-based approach does not to reject utility optimization — in general, the selection of a goal and strategy is secondary to the processing and summarizing of the information.

In addition to the information derived from its opponents, Π has access to a set of information sources $\{\Theta_1, \cdots, \Theta_t\}$ that may include the marketplace in which trading takes place, and general information sources such as news-feeds accessed via the Internet. Together, Π, $\{\Omega_1, \cdots, \Omega_o\}$ and $\{\Theta_1, \cdots, \Theta_t\}$ make up a multiagent system. The integrity of Π's information, including information extracted from the Internet, will decay in time. The way in which this decay occurs will depend on the type of information, and on the source from which it was drawn. Little appears to be known about how the integrity of real information, such as news-feeds, decays, although its validity can often be checked — "Is company X taking over company Y?" — by proactive action given a cooperative information source Θ_j. So Π has to consider how and when to refresh its decaying information.

Π has two languages: $\mathcal{C}$ and $\mathcal{L}$. $\mathcal{C}$ is an illocutionary-based language for communication. $\mathcal{L}$ is a first-order language for internal representation — precisely it is a first-order language with sentence probabilities optionally attached to each sentence representing Π's epistemic belief in the truth of that sentence. Fig. 4 shows a high-level view of how Π operates. Messages expressed in $\mathcal{C}$ from $\{\Theta_i\}$ and $\{\Omega_i\}$ are received, time-stamped, source-stamped and placed in an *in-box* $\mathcal{X}$. The messages in $\mathcal{X}$ are then translated using an *import function* I into sentences expressed in $\mathcal{L}$ that have integrity decay functions (usually of time) attached to each sentence, they are stored in a *repository* $\mathcal{Y}^t$. And that is all that happens until Π triggers a goal.

Π triggers a goal, $g \in \mathcal{G}$, in two ways: first in response to a message received from an opponent $\{\Omega_i\}$ "I offer you €1 in exchange for an apple", and second in response to some need, $\nu \in \mathcal{N}$, "goodness, we've run out of coffee". In either case, Π is motivated by a need — either a need to strike a deal with a particular feature (such as acquiring coffee) or a general need to trade. Π's goals could be short-term such as obtaining some information "what is the time?", medium-term such as striking a deal with one of its opponents, or, rather longer-term such as building a (business) relationship with one of its opponents. So Π has a trigger mechanism T where: $T : \{\mathcal{X} \cup \mathcal{N}\} \rightarrow \mathcal{G}$.

For each goal that Π commits to, it has a mechanism, G, for selecting a strategy to achieve it where $G : \mathcal{G} \times \mathcal{M} \rightarrow \mathcal{S}$ where $\mathcal{S}$ is the strategy library. A *strategy* s maps an information base into an action, $s(\mathcal{Y}^t) = z \in \mathcal{Z}$. Given a goal, g, and the current state of the social model m^t, a strategy: $s = G(g, m^t)$. Each strategy, s, consists of a *plan*, b_s and a *world model* (construction and revision) *function*, J_s, that constructs, and maintains the currency of, the strategy's *world model* W_s^t that consists of a set of probability distributions. A *plan* derives the agent's next action, z, on the basis of the agent's world model for that strategy and the current state of the social model: $z = b_s(W_s^t, m^t)$, and $z = s(\mathcal{Y}^t)$. J_s employs two forms of entropy-based inference:

- Maximum entropy inference, J_s^+, first constructs an *information base* $\mathcal{I}_s^t$ as a set of sentences expressed in $\mathcal{L}$ derived from $\mathcal{Y}^t$, and then from $\mathcal{I}_s^t$ constructs the world model, W_s^t, as a set of complete probability distributions using maximum entropy inference[2].

- Given a prior world model, W_s^u, where $u < t$, minimum relative entropy inference, J_s^-, first constructs the incremental information base $\mathcal{I}_s^{(u,t)}$ of sentences derived from those in $\mathcal{Y}^t$ that were received between time u and time t, and then from W_s^u and $\mathcal{I}_s^{(u,t)}$ constructs a new world model, W_s^t using minimum relative entropy inference.

3.2 Valuing Information

A chunk of information is valued first by the way that it enables Π to do something. So information is valued in relation to the strategies that Π is executing. A strategy, s, is chosen for a particular goal g in the context of a particular representation, or environment, e. One way in which a chunk of information assists Π is by altering s's world model W_s^t — see Fig. 4. A model W_s^t consists of a set of probability distributions: $W_s^t = \{D_{s,i}^t\}_{i=1}^n$. As a chunk of information could be "good" for one distribution and "bad" for another, we first value information by its effect on each distribution. For a model W_s^t, the *value* to W_s^t of a message received at time t is the resulting decrease in entropy in the distributions $\{D_{s,i}^t\}$. In general, suppose that a set of stamped messages $X = \{x_i\}$ is received in $\mathcal{X}$. The *information* in X at time t with respect to a particular distribution $D_{s,i}^t \in W_s^t$, strategy s, goal g and environment e is:

$$\mathbb{I}(X \mid D_{s,i}^t, s, g, e) \triangleq \mathbb{H}(D_{s,i}^t(\mathcal{Y}^t)) - \mathbb{H}(D_{s,i}^t(\mathcal{Y}^t \cup I(X)))$$

for $i = 1, \cdots, n$, where the argument of the $D_{s,i}^t(\cdot)$ is the state of Π's repository from which $D_{s,i}^t$ was derived. The environment e could be determined by a need ν (if the evaluation is made in the context of a particular negotiation) or a relationship ρ (in a broader context). It is reasonable to aggregate the information in X over the distributions used by s. That is, the information in X at time t with respect to strategy s, goal g and environment e is:

$$\mathbb{I}(X \mid s, g, e) \triangleq \sum_i \mathbb{I}(X \mid D_{s,i}^t, s, g, e)$$

and to aggregate again over all strategies to obtain the value of the information in a statement. That is, the *value of the information* in X with respect to goal g and environment e is:

---

[2] Given a probability distribution $\mathbf{q}$, the *minimum relative entropy distribution* $\mathbf{p} = (p_1, \ldots, p_I)$ subject to a set of J linear constraints $\mathbf{g} = \{g_j(\mathbf{p}) = \mathbf{a_j} \cdot \mathbf{p} - c_j = 0\}, j = 1, \ldots, J$ (that must include the constraint $\sum_i p_i - 1 = 0$) is: $\mathbf{p} = \arg\min_{\mathbf{r}} \sum_j r_j \log \frac{r_j}{q_j}$. This may be calculated by introducing Lagrange multipliers $\boldsymbol{\lambda}$: $L(\mathbf{p}, \boldsymbol{\lambda}) = \sum_j p_j \log \frac{p_j}{q_j} + \boldsymbol{\lambda} \cdot \mathbf{g}$. Minimising L, $\{\frac{\partial L}{\partial \lambda_j} = g_j(\mathbf{p}) = 0\}, j = 1, \ldots, J$ is the set of given constraints $\mathbf{g}$, and a solution to $\frac{\partial L}{\partial p_i} = 0, i = 1, \ldots, I$ leads eventually to $\mathbf{p}$. Entropy-based inference is a form of Bayesian inference that is convenient when the data is sparse [10] and encapsulates common-sense reasoning [11].

$$\mathbb{I}(X \mid g, e) \triangleq \sum_{s \in \mathcal{S}(g)} \mathbb{P}(s) \cdot \mathbb{I}(X \mid s, g, e)$$

where $\mathbb{P}(s)$ is a distribution over the set of strategies for goal g, $\mathcal{S}(g)$, denoting the probability that strategy s will be chosen for goal g based on historic frequency data. and to aggregate again over all goals to obtain the (potential) information in a statement. That is, the *potential information* in X with respect to environment e is:

$$\mathbb{I}(X \mid e) \triangleq \sum_{g \in \mathcal{G}} \mathbb{P}(g) \cdot \mathbb{I}(X \mid g, e) \tag{1}$$

where $\mathbb{P}(g)$ is a distribution over $\mathcal{G}$ denoting the probability that strategy g will be triggered based on historic frequency data.

4 Conclusions

A demonstrable prototype e-Market system permits both human and software agents to trade with each other on the World Wide Web. The main contributions described are: the broadly-based and "focussed" data mining systems, and the intelligent agent architecture founded on information theory. These technologies combine to give the foundation for our vision of the marketplaces of tomorrow.

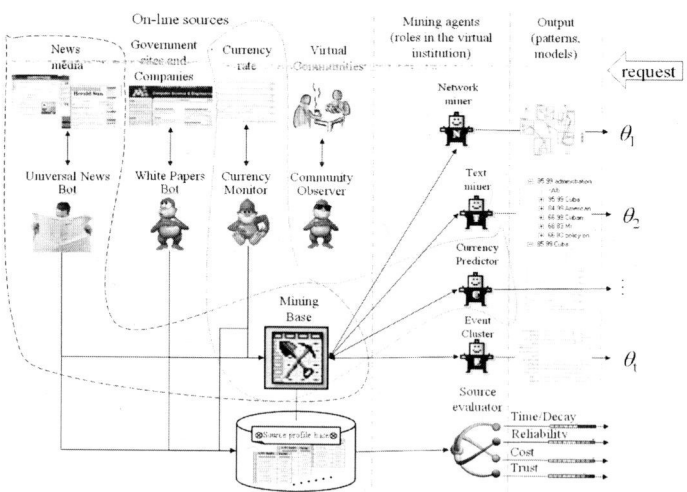

Fig. 5. The architecture of the agent-based data mining system

The implementation of these components is described in greater detail on our e-Markets Group Site[1]. The implementation of the data mining systems is notable for the way in which it is integrated with the trading agents — this enables the agents to dynamically assess the integrity of the various information sources. The implementation of the trading agents is greatly simplified by the assumption that preferences for each individual issue are common knowledge and are complementary for each a pair of traders [12]. This assumption, together with the use of coarse discrete representations of continuous variables, reduces the number of possible worlds and simplifies the minimum relative entropy calculations.

References

1. Debenham, J., Simoff, S.: An e-Market Framework for Informed Trading. In Carr, L., Roure, D.D., Iyengar, A., Goble, C., Dahlin, M., eds.: proceedings 15th International World Wide Web Conference, WWW-2006, Edinburgh, Scotland (2006)
2. Debenham, J.: Bargaining with information. In Jennings, N., Sierra, C., Sonenberg, L., Tambe, M., eds.: Proceedings Third International Conference on Autonomous Agents and Multi Agent Systems AAMAS-2004, ACM Press, New York (2004) 664 – 671
3. Sierra, C., Debenham, J.: An information-based model for trust. In Dignum, F., Dignum, V., Koenig, S., Kraus, S., Singh, M., Wooldridge, M., eds.: Proceedings Fourth International Conference on Autonomous Agents and Multi Agent Systems AAMAS-2005, Utrecht, The Netherlands, ACM Press, New York (2005) 497 – 504
4. Zhang, D., Simoff, S.: Informing the Curious Negotiator: Automatic news extraction from the Internet. In: Proceedings 3rd Australasian Data Mining Conference, Cairns, Australia (2004) 55–72
5. Reis, D., Golgher, P.B., Silva, A., Laender, A.: Automatic web news extraction using tree edit distance. In: Proceedings of the 13th International Conference on the World Wide Web, New York (2004) 502–511
6. Ramoni, M., Sebastiani, P.: Bayesian methods. In: Intelligent Data Analysis. Springer-Verlag: Heidelberg, Germany (2003) 132–168
7. Zhang, D., Simoff, S., Debenham, J.: Exchange rate modelling using news articles and economic data. In: Proceedings of The 18th Australian Joint Conference on Artificial Intelligence, Sydney, Australia, Springer-Verlag: Heidelberg, Germany (2005)
8. Faratin, P., Sierra, C., Jennings, N.: Using similarity criteria to make issue trade-offs in automated negotiation. Journal of Artificial Intelligence 142 (2003) 205–237
9. Debenham, J.: Auctions and bidding with information. In Faratin, P., Rodriguez-Aguilar, J., eds.: Proceedings Agent-Mediated Electronic Commerce VI: AMEC. (2004) 15 – 28
10. Cheeseman, P., Stutz, J.: On The Relationship between Bayesian and Maximum Entropy Inference. In: Bayesian Inference and Maximum Entropy Methods in Science and Engineering. American Institute of Physics, Melville, NY, USA (2004) 445 – 461
11. Paris, J.: Common sense and maximum entropy. Synthese 117 (1999) 75 – 93
12. Sierra, C., Debenham, J.: Information-based agency. In: Proceedings of Twentieth International Joint Conference on Artificial Intelligence IJCAI-07, Hyderabad, India (2007) 1513–1518

Agents Methodologies for e-Chartering Market design

Manolis Sardis, Ilias Maglogiannis
University of the Aegean, Department of Information & Communication
Systems Engineering, Samos, Greece,
WWW home page: http://www.icsd.aegean.gr
emails: sardis@aegean.gr, imaglo@aegean.gr

Abstract. Electronic business and agents are among the most important and exciting areas of research and development in information and communication technology, with considerable potential impact and opportunities for the Maritime sector. This paper proposes the design of a Multi-Agent system for Internet Virtual Chartering Markets (MAVCM). The MAVCM system applies for business-to-business transactions in Maritime markets, and provides mechanisms for Internet-based chartering informational and transactional services. The lifecycle of the proposed system offers a solution for efficiently handling the processes involving a charterer who owns the cargo and employs a shipbroker to find a shipowner to deliver the cargo for a certain freight rate. The objective is to enable Maritime market participants to electronically charter, trade and transport cargos based on information and transactions over Internet via their software agents.

1   Introduction

Electronic business (e-business) can be defined as the process of sharing business information, maintaining business relationships, and conducting business transactions by means of information and communication technologies [1]. With the advent of Internet-based business-to-business (B2B) electronic markets, real opportunities for online transactions have opened up. The Maritime industry has started to recognize the importance of internet and of the electronic markets. Lower costs and less response time are some of the benefits when compared to the traditional procedures operated by humans. However, the most promising Internet-based electronic markets [3], in Maritime are found in the B2B environment where they act as or intermediaries (middlemen) between ships and cargoes [8], [3]. The agent technology can provide a new way of analyzing, designing, and implementing such electronic markets. The use of software agents has mostly been directed towards applications that support business-to-consumer (B2C) transactions [2].

Please use the following format when citing this chapter:

Sardis, M., Maglogiannis, I., 2007, in IFIP International Federation for Information Processing, Volume 247, Artificial Intelligence and Innovations 2007: From Theory to Applications, eds. Boukis, C., Pnevmatikakis, L., Polymenakos, L., (Boston: Springer), pp. 175-185.

However, another important domain is the automation of business transactions that occur in B2B electronic markets. Despite the growing number of electronic markets, conducting electronic transactions is still not trivial. Different obstacles exist such as slow response time, lack of implementation between practical and electronic transactions, poor Web business plan and security problems in critical transactions between a seller and a buyer. A lack of explicit legal provisions on B2B e-markets and the (un)fair commercial practices. The result is a lack of transparency in business transactions. According to the literature, it is accepted that agent technology has the ability to address some of these obstacles [3].

Within this context, this paper proposes the design of a multi-agent system of a Virtual Chartering Market (VCM), called Multi-Agent VCM (MAVCM). The MAVCM system is an Internet e-commerce system for B2B transactions in Maritime chartering markets, providing mechanisms for Internet-based chartering of a vessel for cargo transportation, after an e-investigation and an e-negotiation procedure carried on by agents and web based technologies. Our scope is to overcome traditional chartering limitations using the MAVCM platform. However, designing multi-agent based systems is a complex and demanding task, and so far many standardized design methodologies have been established. Some of such methodologies are Gaia [4], MESSAGE [5], TROPOS [6], and ROADMAP [7]. All of these methodologies share the idea that a multi-agent system may be viewed as an organized society of individual agents with their roles and different kinds of interactions among them specified according to specific protocols that are related to the roles of the interacting agents. The new Gaia proposal [4] is specially significant when used for the analysis and design of an open multi agent system. The success of the Unified Modeling Language (UML) in unifying many different object-oriented approaches as well as the fact that Agent UML (AUML) [9], [12], [13] is considered as a natural starting point for modeling in a very rich and expressive way the Agents Interaction Protocols (AIP), that constitute a central aspect for open multi-agent systems, led to the idea of applying AUML to the design of MAVCM. The goal of this paper is to describe the analysis and the design of a global multi-agent e-Chartering system using multi-agent technologies.

The paper is composed of three parts. In the first part we analyze the business process of the Maritime chartering, the participating actors and their roles. Also the business transactions that occur and their constraints and requirements are presented. In the second part, the information technology solutions based on agent state of the art methodologies and technologies are introduced based on Maritime chartering procedures and requirements. The third part analyzes the design of the e-Chartering system that improves all the traditional methods of the Maritime chartering and brokering procedures giving add-on for the Maritime community using the proposed technologies.

2   The Charter Market

The charter market is by no means a unified and homogenous one. It consists of a number of distinct, separate markets, which are neither interdependent nor clearly and sharply set apart. These features favor the creation of diversiform and heterogonous tendencies in the context of the charter market as a whole. According to the international bibliography pertaining to the subject as well as to the shipping practice, the charter market is divided in categories based on the following criteria: the type of ship, the type and nature of the bulk to be carried, the geographical distribution of Maritime commercial transportation and the sea areas where ships are certified to operate, the duration of the charter period and the type of charter. The key parameters of every charter are the type of ship and that of cargo.

2.1   Charter market key players and processes

The involved actors of the chartering procedure are the following:
1. *Shipowner*, can be a person or a firm owning one or more ships.
2. *Charterer*, the owner of the cargo (*Cargo owner*) is also the representative of the cargo interest in the charter party.
3. *Shipbroker*, can be a chartering owner's broker, negotiating the terms for the charter of a ship on behalf of a charterer or a shipowner respectively. He can also act as a loading broker whose business is to attract cargoes to the ships of his principal, or as sale and purchase broker, negotiating on behalf of a buyer or seller of a ship.
4. *Chartering broker*, an intermediate between shipowners with ships available for charter and charterers who wish to charter them to transport cargo in.

2.2   Communication network between chartering participants

Global events (financial, political, social etc.) influence the freight rates as well as the position occupied by the company in the field of competition in shipping. Information is exchanged between shipowners, brokers and charterers concerning matters such as ships' and cargo's demand and supply. It is obvious that the quality and the quantity of information exchanged between professionals of the shipping field depend largely on the sort of communication the persons involved have and the according cost/fees they pay for accessing that info. The main resources that bring chartering info are, (1) centers of information concerning the shipping market (Baltic Exhange [8], Bimco, Lloyds of London, etc.), (2) different types and forms of Information (Market reports, Fixture reports, Cargo Orders, Indications, etc.), (3) sources of Information (Chartering negotiations, Maritime institutions, shipping institutes and professional unions, research centers, publishing houses specializing in shipping, the Internet). The 'family' type relationships are an obstacle for medium and small companies to participate with, or almost, the same rules in chartering market.

2.3   MAVCM requirements based on e-Chartering market

According to the free market rules (bulk shipping), the procedure until the signing of the chartering market includes the following stages. The *stage of investigation*, during which the seller, buyer or charterer seeks the appropriate vessel in order to carry the cargo, and the shipowner charterer is looking for the appropriate cargo to carry in his/her ship. At this stage, the charterer and the shipowner make their entry in the market by manifesting their interest which is expressed in the drafting of an "order" and of a "position list". The *stage of negotiation* features all dealings between the carrier and the cargo owner aiming to conclude a charter party. Finally, the *follow up stage*, where the charterer and the shipowner have agreed on freight rate details and they proceed to carry the cargo by sea or to put the ship at the charter's disposal to that effect. The promise in question is undertaken in exchange for a fee termed *freight* or *hire*.

2.4   Order and Position

The charterer penetrates the market manifesting his/her interest by putting together an *order*. The *order* is drawn up in conformity with the type of chartering in view (voyage charter, consecutive voyage charter, time charter, bareboat charter, charter of affreightment). When the shipowner makes an entry in the market manifesting his/her interest by putting a *position*. The *position* usually contains information dealing with the ship type and characteristics, how and where the owner wishes to charter it, the period during which the vessel will be chartered, etc. The key target of the negotiations in chartering is the fixing of the freight rate.

3   Applying Gaia and A-UML in e-Chartering Market

The Gaia methodology models multi agents systems from the macro (societal) level to the micro (agent) level. The Gaia methodology [4] comprises three major phases: *analysis*, *architectural design* and *detailed design*. The first phase, *analysis*, assumes that the application requirements have already been compiled. This phase is concerned with the collection and organization of the system specification. In the *architectural design* phase, the organizational structure is defined in terms of its topology and regime control, and the interaction model and role model are completed. The last phase, *detailed design*, is concerned with detailing the agent model, which consists of mapping the identified roles to agent classes and instances, and the services model, which are the blocks of activities in which the agents will engage. The specifications of agents with their roles and the interactions among them and with the environment, are not enough to capture the complex and emergent behavior derived from many self interested agent applications. The complexity of the MAVCM system infrastructure, as stated in section two, needs additional effort for modeling the organizational structure as well as the organizational rules. Agent UML (AUML) builds on the acknowledged success of UML in supporting industrial-strength software engineering. The core part of AUML is the Agent Interaction Protocol (AIP) [30] that constitutes a central aspect for open MAS, specified by means of protocol diagrams. Protocol diagrams extensions to UML include agent roles, multithreaded lifelines, extended message semantics, parameterized nested protocols, and protocol templates. The proposed MAVCM solution for e-Chartering is specified using Gaia methodology and replacing the preliminary interaction model with the AUML notation. The following paragraphs analyze the design considerations of this platform and describe the methodology used.

3.1   MAVCM requirements

The initial scope of this architecture is to provide mechanisms for the implementation of the following functions: *stage of investigation, stage of negotiation* and the *follow up stage*. The structure should be generic enough to suit different supervisory applications, and should provide means for the integration of diverse tools and techniques. An additional requirement is that this architecture provides means for the future expansion of the functions. The FIPA-ACL [14] agent communication language will be the linking language between different implementations of the MAVCM platform, on any FIPA compliant platform. It should be noted that this paper is presenting only the first two main stages (analysis, design). The implementation phase, where different technologically approaches found in literature [17], [18], [19], [20] for MAS systems and electronic markets are under research for the MAVCM platform.

3.2   The environmental model

Gaia methodology suggests a general approach to model the MAS environment. This environment is represented in terms of abstract computational resources that can be detected and changed by the agents. In MAVCM, the resources of interest are the vessel information depicted as POSITION and the cargo information depicted as ORDER in "Fig. 1".

3.3   Organizational structure

MAVCM is organized by federations, or domains, according to different services provided. The integration of different tools and techniques is achieved through the mapping of their capabilities into the agent roles and by the implementation of agent wrappers. MAVCM domains are organized differently depending on the case. Each agent is responsible for each shipowner or cargowner. Agents of the same port are controlled and organized based on their Broker functionality. The agent organization for each port is controlled by an agent Broker. The Broker is responsible for the manipulation and the agent peer collection in which all members have the same level of authority. The Broker also controls other resources such as Maritime News, forums info, Web Services which for the specific port are important parameters for the investigation phase of the e-Chartering procedure. The internal structure of agents and Brokers is analyzed in more detail in "Fig. 2", where internal

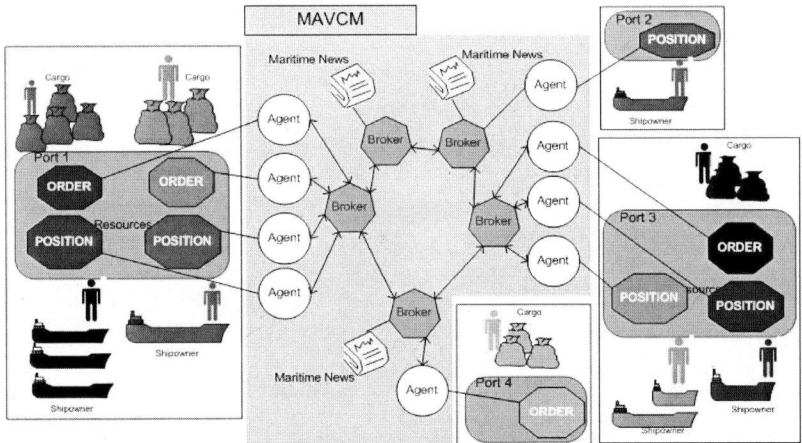

Fig. 1, MAVCM organization structure

relationships and dependencies are presented. The MAVCM architecture was divided according to the different services provided, grouped by domains. Each service domain, in turn, may comprise other domains. At the highest level of abstraction, the system is sub-divided into six service domains: *agent platform services* (APS), *information services* (IS), *investigation services* (INVS), *data collection* (DC), *negotiation services* (NS) and *contract services* (CS). The APS module is responsible for providing the communication infrastructure with naming and yellow pages services. Contains the a*gent controller* (AC) module, which is responsible for controlling the agent interactions and the process communication with each other in the multi-agent system [10]. The *directory facilitator* (DF) is a yellow pages service in which agents may register their services (to offer them to other agents), and search for services offered by other agents. Therefore, it has the following functions: *register*, *deregister*, *modify* and *search* [14]. The IS module is responsible for the storage and retrieval of information when it is required by users and other agents. Also it supports the end user with the *user interface* (UI) to accomplish the necessary actions for the e-Chartering procedures. The core module for the MAVCM platform is the INVS module, which includes the modules *investigation manager* (INVM), *data analysis* (DA) and *algorithms for best solution* (ABS). The purpose of these modules is to collect and analyze data from the available data sources of the MAVCM platform and then, by analyzing them through the ABS module, to offer the best scenario(s) at the MAVCM registered user. The *data collection* (DC) module is responsible for the data collection, the *data management* (DM) module, from the end users ORDERs or POSITIONs and from external resources (yellow pages, Maritime web services, etc.) through the functionality of the *external resources management* (ERM) module.

When the user has found data scenarios, then the NS module is responsible for the negotiation procedures with the data providers. This module includes the necessary control tools for secure multi-user negotiations (e-auctions) and data exchange with history keeping and user transactions storage capabilities. The *behavioral–phase model controller* (BPMC) [21] is responsible for the negotiation stages and

MAVCM AGENT MODULES		
Information Services (IS) User Interface (UI) User Database (UD)	**Agent Platform Services (APS)** Agent Controller (AC) Directory Facilitator (DF)	**Negotiation Services (NS)** Behavioral - phase model Controller (BPMC) Protocol Management (PM)
Investigation Services (INVS) Investigation Manager (INVM) Data Analysis (DA) Algorithms for best solution (ABS)	**Data Collection (DC)** Data management (DM) External resources management (ERM)	**Contract Services (CS)** Contract Management (CM) Security Controller (SC)

Fig. 2. MAVCM agent's internal modules

procedures, by controlling the involved agents interactions and inform the MAVCM user for automatic or semi-automatic status of the negotiation before the finalization of the negotiation. The *protocol management* (PM) module is controlling the interactions protocol between different agents that are participating in the MAVCM platform. Based on the chartering procedures, the final step for a web user will be implemented using the *contact services* (CS) module where the final decisions between two negotiated parties will be finalized by the creation of the electronic contract during the *follow up stage*. This module structure will include all the tools for contract creation and digital signing through the *security controller* (SC) module responsible for the security part of the contracts.

This MAVCM platform organization provides a balance of flexibility and control to facilitate the inclusion of future functionalities like in the *user information* (UI) module, where web functionality will inform the user for Maritime cargo changes and opportunities on vessel market.

3.4   Role model

Agent roles represent the tasks that the system needs to perform. Each agent in the system may have the capability to perform one or more roles. It is possible, for example, to have one agent performing both the *data collection* role and the *investigation* role. Additionally, there may be multiple agents performing the same role, providing redundancy mechanisms and adding flexibility to the system, as for instance, it is possible to instantiate multiple agents for the *user interface* role, with different views of the system for different purposes when the user is a shipowner or a charterer. According to Gaia, a role can be viewed as an abstract description of an entity's expected function and is defined by four attributes, namely, *responsibilities*, *permissions*, *activities*, and *protocols*. A role model represents the functions that are expected in the system. For the MAVCM platform twelve roles have been identified: User Interface (UI), User Database (UD), Investigation Manager (INVM), Data Analysis (DA), Algorithms for Best Solution (ABS), Agent Controller (AC), Directory Facilitator (DF), Data Management (DM), External Resources Management (ERM), Behavioral Phase Model Controller (BPMC)/Protocol Management (PM), Contract Management (CM) and Security Controller (SC). "Table 1".

Responsibilities determine functionality and, as such, are perhaps the key attribute associated with a role. *Responsibilities* are divided into two types: *liveness* that describe those states of affairs that an agent must bring about, given certain environmental conditions, and *safety* properties which are invariants. An acceptance state of affairs is maintained across all states of execution. The atomic components of a *liveness* expression are either *activities* or *protocols*. *Activities* are actions performed by agents that do not require interaction with others. *Protocols* are actions that involve interactions with others. In order to distinguish between these two types of actions, *activities* appear underlined in the role model.

Finally, *permissions* are the 'rights' associated with a role, they identify the resources that are available to that role in order to realize its responsibilities. For example, in the INVM Role the Investigation agent has to search zero or more times for POSITIONs or ORDERs elements in other Brokers agents or agents that belong to the same agent domain and then update the AC state or the agent records in DM.

Protocols and *activities* described in the organizational rules are not explicitly mentioned in the role models [15].

Table 1. Role Model Using Gaia

Role Schema: Investigation Management (INVM)
Description: This role is responsible for performing the search functionality between the Broker agents of MAVCM based on specific user requirements of a shipowner or a cargo owner. Its functionality will be separated first in local domains (eg. same port) and then in more ports' Brokers. Also is responsible to maintain and interact with other Broker agents and perform as an intermediate agent.
Protocols and Activities: SearchBrokers, SearchDomainAgents, UpdateState, UpdateAgentRecords
Permissions: SearchAgentConnected, SearchAgentMetadata, SearchBrokerConnected, SearchBrokerMetadata
Responsibilities   **Liveness:** INVM=(SearchBrokers^w.UpdateState | SearchDomainAgents^w.UpdateAgentRecords)   **Safety:**

3.5   Services model

The Services model represents the services associated with each agent role. The agent role is defined by the list of protocols, activities and responsibilities. Table 2 is presenting the services models for the Investigation Management Role of the MAVCM platform.

Table 2, Services Model

Service Schema: Investigation Management Role (INVM)				
Service	**Inputs**	**Outputs**	**Pre- Condition**	**Post- Condition**
SearchBrokers	Search Criteria for Broker information	Broker list	Connection with Brokers	True
SearchDomainAgents	Search Criteria for Domain	Agent list	Connection with DMs agents	True
UpdateState	New state from investigation procedure	New state updated	Connection with ACs agents	True
UpdateAgentRecords	New record from agents	New record updated	Connection with ACs agents	True

3.6   Interaction model

The Interaction Model consists of a set of protocol definitions. The objective of the Interaction Model is to represent the dependencies and relationships between the various roles in the MAVCM platform by utilizing protocol definitions. More attention is paid to the nature and purpose of the interaction than to the sequence of execution steps. Using the Gaia methodology, one can distinguishes the characteristics that are considered extrinsic in order to minimize the impact of changes in the organizational structure and to enable roles to be repeated in systems with different structures. The Manager assumption that will control the INVM module behavior is an example of an extrinsic characteristic. Gaia models have been combined with AUML [16] sequence diagrams for the additional detailing of agent interactions.

3.7   Agent model

The specification of the agents in MAVCM depends on the tools that compose the solution. Each tool has different capabilities that are associated with different agent roles, thus the definition of the agent model can only be further detailed when the MAVCM conceptual architecture is realized into implementation architecture. For the MAVCM prototype implementation, each role will be mapped to one agent class. This mapping results in a simple agent model with a total of thirteen agent classes as represented in Table 3.

Table 3. Agent model

Role	Class	Instances
UI	User Interface	Zero or more
UD	User Database	Zero or more
INVM	Investigation Manager	One or more
DA	Data Analysis	One
ABS	Algorithms for Best Solution	Zero or more
AC	Agent Controller	One
DF	Directory Facilitator	One
DM	Data Management	Zero or more
EDM	External Resources Management	Zero or more
BPMC	Behavior Phase Model Controller	One or more
PM	Protocol Management	One or more
CM	Contract Management	One or more
SC	Security Controller	One or more

Our aims were to analyze and design a system that could transform the 'human' chartering procedure into a dynamic and electronic automated system that could implement as much as possible of the human procedures and methodologies that humans perform during the Maritime chartering. This proposed solution gives add-on benefits to chartering procedure as it vastly increases customer reach and visibility. Promotes new relationships in a cost-effective fashion. Allows saving time finding quality service cargo providers and shippers. Competitive negotiation promotes market-driven pricing to save money and create healthy e-negotiation transactions. Utilizes the internet to allow Shipowners and Cargo owners to negotiate cargo shipments and available service across any geography and any mode of transport.

4   Conclusions

The organization of MAVCM into functional domains and roles provides a clear coordination of agents inside its domains and facilitates the integration of additional functionalities such as security issues and management of more than one community of MAVCM systems. Our aim was to design an architecture based on Gaia methodologies and AUML that first will describe with an analytic way the chartering human procedures and second to enable the integration of different tools and functionalities that will describe in more detail chartering procedures for specific vessels and cargo types. The main contribution of this research is the transformation of the chartering Maritime market procedures, into an electronic format, where until now most of them are done manually by humans. The identification of the chartering procedures and necessary functions and then the design of a system based on these market requirements using information technology tools over the web is an add-on. The actors of the e-Chartering procedures will be implemented by multi-agents that support the creation of virtual chartering markets, electronic negotiations and the construction of electronic contracts between a shipowner and a cargo owner. The implementation of the proposed system is under research. Negotiation and e-auctions procedures and techniques will be analyzed in more detail. Agent software development framework suites like the JADE [10] platform, and SALSA [11] framework will be evaluated for the implementation of the MAVCM platform.

5   References

1.   Zwass, V. (1996). Electronic commerce: Structures and issues. International Journal of Electronic Commerce vol. 1(1), 3-23.
2.   He, M. and Leung, H. (2002). Agents in e-commerce: State of the art. Knowledge and Information Systems vol. 4, 257-282.
3.   Maamar, Z. (2002). Association of users with software agents in e-commerce. Electronic Commerce Research and Applications vol. 1, 104-112.
4.   Zambonelli, F., Jennings, N., and Woolddridge, M., "Developing Multiagent Systems. The Gaia Methodology". ACM Transactions on Software Engineering and Methodology, Vol 12, No 3, (pp. 417-470), July 2003.
5.   Caire, C., Garrijo, F., Gomez, J., Pavon, J., Leal, F., et al., "Agent oriented analysis using MESSAGE/UML". Proceedings of Agent-Oriented Software Engineering –AOSE 01, Canada, May, 2001.
6.   Guinchiglia, F., Mylopoulos, J., and Perini A., "The Tropos Software Development Methodology: Processes, Models and Diagrams", Proceedings of Agent-Oriented Software Engineering (AOSE-2002),Bologna, Italy, July 2002.
7.   Juan, T., Pearce, A. and Sterling, L., "ROADMAP: Extending the Gaia Methodology for Complex Open Systems". Proceedings of Autonomous Agents and Multi-Agent Systems – AAMAS '02 (pp. 3-10), Bologna, Italy, July 15-19, 2002.
8.   Baltic Exchange, available from http://www.balticexchange.com
9.   AUML Home Page, available from http://www.auml.org
10.   JADE Home Page, 2004, available from http://jade.tilab.com

11. Marcela Rodriguez, Jesus Favela, "A Framework for Supporting Autonomous Agents in Ubiquitous Computing Environments", Book Autonomous Agents for Ubiquitous Collaborative Environments, Springer Berlin / Heidelberg, Volume 2313/2002, 2002

12. J. Odell, V. D. Parunak, and B. Bauer. "Extending UML for Agents". In: Wagner, G.,Lesperance, Y. and Yu, E. Proceedings of the Second Workshop on agent-Oriented Information systems (AOIS'00), iCue Publishing , pp. 3-17, 2000.

13. J. Odell, V. D. Parunak, and B. Bauer. "Representing Agent Interaction Protocols in UML ", In Proceedings of the First International Workshop on Agent-Oriented Software Engineering (AOSE'01), Springer Verlag, 121-140.

14. FIPA (Foundation for Intelligent Physical Agents), http://www.fipa.org.

15. Chengqi Zhang, Chunsheng Li, 'An Agent-Based Framework for Petroleum Information Services from Distributed Heterogeneous Data Resources', (APSEC'02), IEEE, 2002.

16. M. Huget, "Agent UML Notation for Multiagent System Design", IEEE Internet Computing, 2004.http://www.fipa.org/specs/fipa00029/SC00029H.html

17. Michael Berger, Steffen Rusitschka, Dimitri Toropov, Michael Watzke, Marc Schlichte, "Porting Agents to Small Mobile Devices-The Development of the Lightweight Extensible Agent Platform", 2003.

18. F. Bellifemine, A. Poggi, G. Rimassa, "Developing multi agent systems with a FIPA-compliant agent framework". In Software Practice & Experience", John Wiley & Sons, Ltd. vol no. 31, pp. 103-128, Feb. 2001.

19. Youyong Zou, Tim Finin, Li Ding, Harry Chen, Rong Pan, "Using Semantic Web technology in Multi-Agent Systems: a case study in the TAGA trading agent environment", In Proceedings of the 5th international Conference on Electronic Commerce (Pittsburgh, Pennsylvania, September 30- October 03, 2003). ICEC '03, vol. 50. ACM Press, New York, NY, 95-101.

20. J.M. Vidal, P. Buhler, and C. Stahl, "Multiagent systems with workflows", IEEE Internet Computing, 8(1):76–82, January/ February 2004.

21. Jing Han, Ming Li , Lei Guo, "Soft Control on Collective Behavior of a Group of Autonomous Agents By a Shill Agent", Journal of Systems Science and Complexity, Springer Boston, Vol 19, Number 1 / March, 2006, Pages54-62.

Applications of Nature-Inspired Intelligence in Finance

Vasilios Vasiliadis , and Georgios Dounias

University of the Aegean, Dept. of Financial Engineering and
Management, Management & Decision Engineering Laboratory,
31 Fostini Str., GR-821 00, Chios, GREECE,
tel: +30-2271-0-35454(35483), fax: +30-2271-0-35499,
23100045@fme.aegean.gr, g.dounias@aegean.gr,
WWW home page: http://decision.fme.aegean.gr

Abstract. A great variety of complex real-life problems can be sufficiently
solved by intelligent nature-inspired methods which can be considered part of
artificial or computational intelligence. These newly introduced techniques
have proven their important role on many successful implementations, mostly
related to optimization problems. The basic reason for their success is that they
imitate the way that real-life networks and other biological systems function
and evolve in order to solve problems in different domains. Such systems can
be found in the human brain (neurons), or can be observed in the natural world
in the form of ant colonies, flocks of birds, as well as in other examples taken
from the microcosm such as the human immune system. In this paper, we try
to briefly present popular nature-inspired techniques, ant colony optimization
and particle swarm optimization, and also to clarify the significance and
appropriateness of nature-inspired intelligent approaches for solving complex
financial optimization problems. A short discussion in included for a number
of selected financial decision making applications, i.e. forecasting of financial
distress, multi-stage portfolio optimization, credit scoring, investment
decisions and capital investment planning.

Please use the following format when citing this chapter:

Vasiliadis, V., Dounias, G., 2007, in IFIP International Federation for Information Processing, Volume 247, Artificial
Intelligence and Innovations 2007: From Theory to Applications, eds. Boukis, C., Pnevmatikakis, L., Polymenakos, L.,
(Boston: Springer), pp. 187-194.

1   Introduction

In the recent years, both global economy and technology have advanced rapidly. A clear effect of this is the fact that new problem domains have been created, difficult to handle with standard approaches. New techniques are required, usually computer assisted, that offer effective and premium solutions with the least computational effort. However, it is indicative that new nature-inspired techniques have arose aiming at solving complex optimization problems. Nature-inspired intelligent systems mimic the way in which biological systems and real-world networks function in order to discover solutions in difficult optimization problems. Such examples are the function of the human brain (neural networks), the process through which an ant colony searches for its food, etc.

In literature there is a variety of engineering, medical, managerial or financial applications, suitable to be handled through nature-inspired approaches. In production and manufacturing, the key issue is usually to determine the optimal parameters in product planning. An important point is often the optimization of the time distributed in each workstation.

In medical domains, nature-inspired techniques are appropriate in making predictions for certain health problems, based on specific disease characteristics corresponding to decision variables. Finally, financial problems are of great importance. We deal with these kinds of problems later in this paper.

The present work mainly focuses on the description of two varieties of optimization algorithms. Their common characteristic is that both are based on the way in which biological systems behave.

The first method is ant colony optimization, an approach that mimics the way in which a colony of ants searches for its food. Ants search for food at random. After they have found a possible source, they return to their colony depositing pheromone in all the way. Other ants realize this chemical product. The power of pheromone is a function of the quality of the food and the distance between the nest and the source of food. The second algorithm is particle swarm optimization. It imitates the way in which a flock of birds migrates. Each bird has a certain speed and direction, as if a vector. All birds communicate with each other and finally decide to adopt the direction of the one that has the best position according to their final destination. In the next section, we depict in more detail the way that the two algorithmic approaches work in principle.

The paper is organized as follows: In section 2, a brief description of the optimization algorithms is given. In section 3, we present some of the financial applications successfully solved by these approaches. In the final section, we propose future trends and research perspectives of nature-inspired approaches, not only in the financial domain, but in other domains as well.

2 Popular nature-inspired optimization algorithms

2.1 Ant colony optimization

Ant colony optimization (ACO) algorithms were first introduced by M. Dorigo in the early 1990's [8,12,13]. The development of these algorithms was inspired by the observation of ant colonies. Ants' behavior is governed by the goal of colony survival rather than being focused on the survival of individuals. The philosophy of these optimization algorithms stems from the ants' foraging behavior, and in particular, how ants can find shortest paths between food sources and their nest. When searching for food, ants initially explore the area surrounding their nest in a random manner. While moving, ants leave a chemical pheromone trail on the ground, which can be smelled by other members of the colony. Other ants tend to choose, in probability, paths marked by strong pheromone concentrations. As soon as an ant finds a food source, it evaluates the quantity and the quality of the food and carries some of it back to the nest. During the return trip, the quantity of pheromone that an ant leaves on the ground may depend on the quantity and quality of the food. These pheromone trails will guide other ants to the food source. It has been shown that the indirect communication between the ants via pheromone trails-known as stigmergy-enables them to find shortest paths between their nest and food sources.

In general, the ACO approach attempts to solve an optimization problem by iterating the following steps:

- Candidate solutions are constructed using a pheromone model, that is, a parameterized probability distribution over the solution space;
- The candidate solutions are used to modify the pheromone values in a way that is deemed to bias future sampling toward high quality solutions;

Finally, the pheromone update aims to concentrate the search in regions of the search space containing high quality solutions.

2.2 Particle swarm optimization

The first particle swarm optimization (PSO) algorithm was proposed by Kennedy and Eberhart in 1995 [14,10]. It is a biologically inspired algorithm which models the social dynamics of bird flocking. A large number of birds flock synchronously, change direction suddenly, scatter and regroup iteratively, and finally perch on a target. The PSO algorithm facilitates simple rules simulating bird flocking and serves as an optimizer for continuous nonlinear functions. The attractiveness of the PSO algorithm is due to features like natural metaphor, stochastic move, adaptivity, and positive feedback.

The general principles of the PSO algorithm are outlined as follows:

- *Particle representation*: The particle in the PSO is a candidate solution to the underlying problem and move iteratively about to the solution space.
- *Swarm*: The PSO explores the solution space by flying a number of particles, called swarm.
- *Personal best experience and swarm's best experience*: The PSO enriches the swarm intelligence by storing the best positions visited so far by every particle. In particular, each particle remembers the best position among those it has visited and the best position by its neighbors.
- *Particle movement*: The PSO is an iterative algorithm according to which a swarm of particles flies about the solution space until the stopping criterion is satisfied.

Stopping criterion: The PSO algorithm is terminated with a maximal number of iterations or the best particle position of the entire swarm cannot be improved further after a sufficiently large number of iterations.

3   Financial applications

The aforementioned nature-inspired optimization algorithms have been recently (2006) used, among others, in a variety of applications of the financial domain. A first issue that has been studied is the forecasting of financial distress for companies [1]. Due to the radical changing of the global economy, a more precise forecasting of corporate financial distress helps provide important judgment principles to decision-makers. Although financial statements reflect a firm's business activities, it is very challenging to discover critical information from these statements.

In this study, an evolutionary approach with modularized evaluation functions, which extracts the set of critical financial ratios and integrates more evaluation functions modules to achieve a better forecasting accuracy by assigning distinct weights, is introduced to forecast financial distress. PSO and genetic algorithms (GA) will be the evolutionary algorithms and logistic regression, discriminant analysis and neural networks will be the evaluation modules. In conclusion, it appears that the use of the proposed approach achieves better forecasting accuracy with a minimum critical consideration of financial ratios than using conventional statistical techniques. Furthermore, more integrated evaluation modules would achieve better forecasting accuracies in our approach.

Credit scoring is another issue of great importance both for the academic and the business society [2]. Numerous modeling techniques have been developed in order to tackle this problem. The use of the particle swarm optimization described above, introduces a quite original approach. The algorithm is used in order to train a neural network. This hybridized algorithm is used in order to evaluate the creditability of real-world cases. There are two advantages from this approach. Firstly, the neural network, which comes from the parameterization process of the optimization algorithm, has better decision making ability. Secondly, we can comment on the classification ability of the network, which is improved greatly.

Another application is a multistage stochastic financial optimization problem [3]. Multistage stochastic financial optimization manages portfolio in constantly changing financial markets by periodically rebalancing the asset portfolio to achieve return maximization and/or risk minimization. Particle swarm optimization is used for the decision-making process in order to solve the multi-stage portfolio optimization problem. The performance of the algorithm is demonstrated by optimizing the allocation of cash and various stocks in a weighted index.

There are two more recent works based on the topic of portfolio optimization [18,19]. In [18], a particle swarm optimization algorithm was applied to the construction of optimal risky portfolios for financial investments. Constructing an optimal risky portfolio is a high-dimensional constrained optimization problem where financial investors look for an optimal combination of their investments among different financial assets with the aim of achieving a maximum reward-to-variability ratio (Sharpe ratio). A particle swarm solver is developed and tested on various restricted and unrestricted risky investment portfolios. The particle swarm solver demonstrates high computational efficiency in constructing optimal risky portfolios consisting of a small number of assets. In [19], apart from including stocks in the portfolio, bonds are also taken as potential assets for investment.

Another application of particle swarm optimization algorithm to financial problems is the construction of a decision making model that generates one-step forward investment decisions for stock markets. In this case, the optimization algorithm is hybridized with a neural network [4,17,21]. The neural network is used to make the analysis of daily stock returns and to calculate one day forward decision for the purchase of the stocks. Subsequently the PSO algorithm is applied in order to select the "best" ANN for the future investment decisions and to adapt the weights of other networks towards the weights of the best network. The experimental investigations were made considering different forms of decision-making model, i.e. different number of ANN, ANN inputs, sliding windows, and commission fees. One of the central problems in financial markets is to make the profitable stocks trading decisions using historical stocks' market data [21]. In order to achieve this, a decision making method, which is based on the application of neural networks and swarm intelligence technologies is presented. This model generates one-step-ahead investment decisions. In brief, the analysis of historical stock prices variations is made using single layer NN, and subsequently the Particle Swarm Optimization algorithm is applied in order to select global best NN for the future investment decisions and to adapt the weights of other networks towards the weights of the best network.

An application of the ant colony optimization algorithm for the capital investment planning problem is given in [7]. Capital investment planning is a periodic management task that is particularly challenging in the presence of multiple objectives as trade-offs have to be made with respect to the preferences of the decision-makers. The underlying mathematical model is a multi-objective combinatorial optimization problem. One way to tackle this problem is first to determine the set of all efficient portfolios and then to explore this set in order to identify a final preferred portfolio. The ant colony optimization algorithm is developed in order to find efficient portfolios as it is impossible to enumerate all of them within a reasonable computation time for practical problems. Firstly, a neighbourhood search routine is added to ACO to improve its performance. Then a taboo search and variable neighbourhood search procedure are developed. The multi-objective integer linear programming model of the capital investment planning problem is adopted. There are two sets of constraints in the model. The first set restricts each feasible portfolio to contain no more than a given maximum (or no less than a given minimum) number of projects out f a certain subset. The second set of constraints deals with resource limitations. Results of this study indicated that the performance of ACO can be remarkably improved by supplementing it with a neighbourhood search routine. The improved ACO provides the best solution and is less parameter-sensitive than other procedures.

The topic of time series analysis and data processing in general is of great financial importance [6,15]. In [15], a recurrent neural network is trained with a new learning algorithm in order to predict a number of missing values from a certain time series. This training algorithm is based on a hybrid of particle swarm optimization and evolutionary algorithm. By combining the searching abilities of these two global optimization methods, the evolution of individuals is no longer restricted to be in the same generation, and better performing individuals may produce offspring to replace those with poor performance. The trained RNNs are able to predict the missing values in the time series with minimum error.

Another important issue in the field of financial management is the modeling of time series, as well as the prediction and forecasting ability of the model [16,22,23]. In [16], an attempt to represent the seemingly chaotic behavior of stock markets by using flexible neural networks is made. Again, the parameters of the neural network are optimized using genetic programming and particle swarm optimization algorithms. In [22], a time series forecasting methodology and its application to generate one-step-ahead predictions for two daily foreign exchange spot rate time series is presented. The methodology draws from the disciplines of chaotic time series analysis, clustering, artificial neural networks and evolutionary computation. In brief, clustering is applied to identify neighborhoods in the reconstructed state space of the system; and subsequently neural networks are trained to model the dynamics of each neighborhood separately. Again, the training techniques used are an evolutionary and a particle swarm optimization algorithm. Finally, in [23], the special issue of forecasting exchange rates is analyzed. A flexible neural tree is proposed for the forecasting process. Based on the pre-defined operator sets, a flexible neural tree model can be created end evolved. The structure of this technique is developed using the extended compact genetic programming and the free parameters embedded in the neural tree are optimized by particle swarm optimization algorithm.

4   Conclusions

As we can see from the above applications, particle swarm optimization algorithms are used in most cases. In addition, the role of these algorithms is to optimize the parameters of the model used to perform a certain financial task (portfolio selection, forecasting). In most cases, swarm intelligence was complementary to neural networks. However, these new nature-inspired techniques have the ability to select the optimal parameters of the model under considerations. This surely leads to better results than using traditional approaches.

Future perspectives can be divided into two categories. Firstly, there could be an improvement in technical aspects of the aforementioned methodologies. More specifically, the communication topology of the particles in the particle swarm optimization algorithm can be changed dynamically and not remain fixed. Also, the investigation of the relationship between the weighting function and the premature convergence of PSO might be a challenging task. Other, more general technical issues are the use of alternative methods or more detailed versions of the new nature-inspired techniques, larger data sets (might give better estimations) etc. The second category has to do with several alternative scenarios as far as certain applications are considered. For example, in decision making problems, we can allow for more frequent trading possibilities, in the capital investment planning, more projects might be included in the company's portfolio etc.

To summarise, we can comment that nature-inspired optimization techniques might become the next step in effectively facing optimization problems. Standard methodologies sometimes lack the abilities and the efficiency of nature inspired intelligent algorithms. Moreover, nature-inspired methods can effectively be used in production, manufacturing, medical applications etc. As general future directions in the financial domain, we can indicate several problems that can be addressed by these algorithms. For example, an interesting issue is the investigation of whether there exists any relationship between national economies, stocks, rates, exchange rates etc., in other words to discover whether there exist profitable opportunities for investment.

References

1. P. C. Ko, P. C. Lin, An evolution based approach with modularized evaluations to forecast financial distress, Knowledge – Based Systems (19), 84 – 91 (2006)
2. L. Gao, C. Zhou, H.B. Gao, Y.R. Shi, Credit scoring model based on Neural Network with particle swarm optimization, Advances in Natural Computation, 76 – 79 (2006)
3. J. Sun, W.B. Xu, W. Fang, Solving multi–period financial planning problem via quantum – behaved particle swarm algorithm, Computational Intelligence, 1158 – 1169 (2006)
4. J. Nenortaite, R. Simutis, Development and evaluation of decision – making model for stock markets, Journal of global optimization, 1 - 19 (2006)
5. J. S. Lee, S. Lee, S. Chang, B.H. Ahn, A comparison of GA and PSO for excess return evaluation in stock markets, Artificial Intelligence and Knowledge Engineering Applications : A Bio – inspired approach, 221 – 230 (2005)
6. S. S. Weng, Y. H. Liu, Mining time series data for segmentation by using Ant Colony Optimization, European Journal of Operational Research (173), 921 – 937 (2006)
7. C. Stummer, M.H. Sun, New multi – objective metaheuristic solution procedures for capital investment planning, Journal of Heuristics, 183 – 199 (2005)

8. C. Blum, Ant Colony Optimization: Introduction and recent trends, Physics of life Reviews, 353 – 373 (2005)
9. E. Elmeltagi, T. Hegazy, D. Grierson, Comparison among five evolutionary – based optimization algorithms, Advanced Engineering Informatics (19), 43 – 53 (2005)
10. Y. Dong, J. Tang, B. Xu, D. Wang, An application of swarm optimization to nonlinear programming, Computers and Mathematics with Applications (49), 1655 – 1668 (2005)
11. D.N. Jeyakumar, T. Jayabarathi, T. Raghunathan, Particle swarm optimization for various types of economic dispatch problems, Electrical Power & Energy systems (28), 36–42 (2006)
12. M. Dorigo, L. M. Gambardella, Ant colonies for the traveling salesman problem, Biosystems 43(2),73–81 (1997)
13. M. Dorigo, V. Maniezzo, A. Colorni, Ant system: optimization by a colony of cooperating agents, IEEE Trans SystMan Cybern 26(1), 29–41(1996)
14. P. Y. Yin, Particle swarm optimization for point pattern matching, Journal of Visual Communication & Image Representation, 143-162 (2006)
15. X. Cai, N. Zhang, G. K. Venayaagamoorthy, D. C. Wunsch II, Time series prediction with recurrent neural networks trained by a hybrid PSO-EA algorithm, Neurocomputing 70, 2342-2353 (2007)
16. Y. Chen, J. Yang, B. Yang, A. Abraham, Flexible Neural Trees Ensemble for Stock Index Modeling
17. J. Nenortaite, A particle swarm optimization approach in the construction of decision-making model, Information Technology and Control 1A (36) (2007)
18. G. Kendall, Y. Su, A particle swarm optimization approach in the construction of optimal risky portfolios, Artificial Intelligence and Applications (2005)
19. T. Fischer, A. Roehrl, Risk and performance optimization for portfolios of bonds and stocks (2003)
20. T. Fischer, A. Roehrl, Optimization of performance measures based on Expected Shortfall (2005)
21. J. Nenortaite, R. Simutis, Stocks' Trading System Based on the Particle Swarm Optimization Algorithm, Springer-Verlag, Heidelberg, 843-850 (2004)
22. N. G. Pavlidis, D. K. Tasoulis, M. N. Vrahatis, Financial Forecasting Through Unsupervised Clustering and Evolutionary Trained Neural Networks, IEEE (2003)
23. Y. Chen, L. Peng, A. Abraham, Exchange Rate Forecasting using Flexible Neural Networks

Staff Performance Appraisal using Fuzzy Evaluation

Nureize Arbaiy and Zurinah Suradi
Information System Department, Faculty of Information Technology
and Multimedia, University of Tun Hussein Onn Malaysia, Locked Bag
101, Parit Raja, Batu Pahat, Johor, Malaysia
{nureize, zurinah}@uth.edu.my
WWW home page: http://fatekma.uthm.edu.my

Abstract. Most organizations use performance appraisal system to evaluate the effectiveness and efficiency of their employees. In evaluating staff performance, it usually involves awarding numerical values or linguistic labels to their performance. These values and labels are used to represent each staff's achievement by reasoning incorporated in the arithmetical or statistical methods. However, the staff performance appraisal may involve judgments which are based on imprecise data especially when human (the superior) tries to interpret another human (his/her subordinate) performance. Thus, the scores awarded by the appraiser are only approximations. From fuzzy logic perspective, the performance of the appraisee involves the measurement of his/her ability, competence and skills, which are actually fuzzy concepts that can be captured in fuzzy terms. Accordingly, fuzzy approach can be used to handle these imprecision and uncertainty information. Therefore, the performance appraisal system can be examined using Fuzzy Logic Approach and this was carried out in the study. The study utilized hierarchical fuzzy inference approach since performance evaluation comprises of four criteria; namely work achievement, skill knowledge, personal quality, and community services. The output of the study provides the ranking for staff performance. From this study, it is expected that reasoning based on fuzzy models will provide an alternative way in handling various kinds of imprecise data, which often reflected in the way people think and make judgments.

1   Introduction

Performance appraisal may be defined as a structured formal interaction between a subordinate and his/her superior. It usually embraces of a periodic interview, in which the work performance of the subordinate is examined and discussed. The appraisal also triggers to identify weaknesses and strengths as well as opportunities

Please use the following format when citing this chapter:

Arbaiy, N., Suradi, Z., 2007, in IFIP International Federation for Information Processing, Volume 247, Artificial Intelligence and Innovations 2007: From Theory to Applications, eds. Boukis, C., Pnevmatikakis, L., Polymenakos, L., (Boston: Springer), pp. 195-203.

for improvement and skills development. In most cases, performance appraisal system is used by managers to evaluate the management of the effectiveness and efficiency of employees and/or other resources within the organization [1]. It is a tool that can create competitive advantages amongst employees. In the Malaysian Public Services, each staff is being evaluated through a performance appraisal system that was designed to be a systematic annual process which involved evaluating employee's set targets (SKT), perceived behavior evaluation and work achievement during the year of evaluation. Here, each departmental targeted activities, programs and projects were decided upon, in reference to predetermined overall organizational policy and strategies agreed upon at the beginning of the year of evaluation. And, the appraisal focuses upon the integration and achievement of individual targets, behavior and performance at work as compared to the goals of the organization.

Performance appraisals are mainly used for judgmental and developmental purposes [2] in order to make good administrative decisions. Performance measures are meant to provide more complete information about an entity's performance. Organizations rely on supervisors to sort out how well individuals under their supervisions perform. The hope is that supervisors can disentangle the effects of job changes, collective action, luck and their own likes and dislikes, to make an accurate judgment of how well individuals have performed over a period of time. However, this hope is rarely realized, the appraisers (or the supervisors) bring their own biases and information-processing problems to the task of performance appraisal, thus the appraisal are often flawed. Therefore, the evaluation given may involve information of uncertainty and subjectivity.

In most staff performance evaluation, the process usually involves awarding numerical values or linguistic labels to staff performance. These values and labels are used to represent the staff's achievement by reasoning using arithmetical or statistical methods. In general, those methods can be classified using nominal score and single numerical score. These numerical scores may refer to another numerical interval-value that refers to a certain category of achievement, which is equivalent to100 percent value. However, in most cases, the evaluation of staff performance may be influenced by the appraiser's experience, sensitivity and standard(s). Thus, the scores awarded by the appraiser are only approximations and there is an inherent vagueness in the evaluation. However, if we looked into the evaluation using fuzzy logic approach, the performance of the appraisee involves the measurement of ability, competence and skills, which are fuzzy concepts that may be captured in fuzzy terms. Consequently, fuzzy logic approach can be implemented to manage the uncertainty information involved in performance evaluation.

This paper is divided into four sections. First, the introduction briefly describes the topic of this paper. Second, the approach and methods in this study were explained. This section includes some related work. The third section discusses the result of this study and the final section concludes the study.

2   Method

Decision making is a process of problem solving that involves pursuing of goals under constraints. The outcome is a decision that should result in an action [3]. This is a difficult process due to the factors such as incomplete and imprecise information subjectivity, linguistics, which tend to be present to a lesser or greater degree. As knowledge involved in appraisal evaluation is an approximate and fuzzy logic has been successfully used for approximate reasoning in such cases, its application becomes significant to manage the uncertainty in the evaluation system.

The design of fuzzy system mainly involved two operations of knowledge base derivation and the selection of the fuzzy inference process to perform the fuzzy reasoning [4]. The successful development of a fuzzy model for a particular application domain is a complex multi-step process, in which the designer is faced with a large number of alternative implementation strategies [5]. Fuzzy logic addresses such applications perfectly as it resembles human decision making with an ability to generate precise solutions from certain or approximate information. The advantage of fuzziness dealing with imprecision fit ideally into decision systems; the vagueness and uncertainty of human expressions are well modeled in the fuzzy sets, and a pseudo-verbal representation, similar to an expert's formulation, can be achieved [6].

Fuzzy approach has been used to evaluate many type of performances such as product and marketing, finance, education and more. [7] suggest a new learning achievement evaluation strategy in student's learning procedure. That study aimed to overcome conventional approaches' shortcomings that can consider such vague factors as complexity, importance, and difficulty. [8] applied Fuzzy Multiple Criteria Decision Making to evaluate feasible developmental strategies in regard to the needs of manufacturers, government and consumers. In accordance, this study is also concerned with the Fuzzy Logic which mainly aims to manage the uncertainty information and human-like reasoning and approached the domain problem.

2.1   Fuzzy System

Fuzzy system generally involves three phases of fuzzification, fuzzy inference and defuzzification [9]. The SKT evaluation comprises of four criteria; namely work achievement, skill knowledge, personal quality, and community services. The fuzzy linguistic for these criteria chosen are identified as *competent, need improvement, proficient* or else. The input value is mapped into the membership function graph to obtain the confidence value of that particular input variable. The real value that is supplied into the system is converted to linguistic variables. Linguistic variables are assigned to several systems' input. Table 1 tabulates the linguistic variables for several system inputs.

Table 1: Fuzzy Set Definition

Fuzzy Variables		Fuzzy Set Linguistic Term
Input	Work Achievement	*{needs improvement, meet expectation,, competent}*
	Skill Knowledge	*{needs improvement, medium, proficient}*
	Personal Quality	*{poor, fair, good}*
	Community Service	*{not active, average, fair}*
Output	Appraisal's Mark	*{needs improvement, meet expectation,, exceed expectation}*

The elements of a fuzzy set are mapped to a universe of memberships values, X to the interval [0, 1] [10] or $\mu_A(x)$: X → [0, 1]. Membership function is denoted by $\mu_{a(}x)$. If X is a universe of membership values and x is an element of X, then a fuzzy set A is represented by A= {(x, $\mu_A(x)$)}, x∈X. For this system, several membership functions were drawn for corresponding variables. The x-axis represents the variable while the y-axis represents the confidence value ranges from 0 to 1.0. The trapezoidal function was used to represent the linguistic variable.

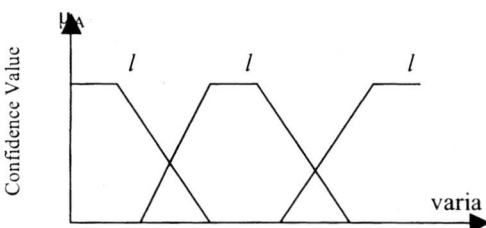

Figure 1: Trapezoidal Membership Function

From figure 1, $\Pi(x0, x1, x2, x3) = \begin{cases} 0 & x < x_0 \\ (x - x_0)/(x_1 - x_0) & x_0 \leq x \leq x_1 \\ 1 & x_1 \leq x \leq x_2 \\ (x - x_2)/(x_3 - x_2) & x_2 \leq x \leq x_3 \\ 0 & x > x_3 \end{cases}$

General trapezoid membership function graph drawn for this system variable is illustrated in Fig 1. From the membership function graph, a confidence value for each label will be retrieved from x- axis to y-axis.

2.2   Fuzzy Inference

Fuzzy inference engine resembles human reasoning in its use of approximate information and uncertainty to generate decisions. It consists of rules, facts and conclusions. The fuzzy production rules connect premises with conclusions, condition with action. In this inference, expert's knowledge and experience was acquired and formulate accordingly to develop the appropriate rule to perform the system. The fuzzy inference can be implemented using the if-then statements or Fuzzy Associative Memory (FAM). The if-then implementation is the same as that executed in expert system except that it involves the linguistic variables. Rules are simplified in fuzzy associative memory (FAM) tables to make the system easier to evaluate each set of rules. The single inference structure is shown as Fig 2-a. Therefore, as more than one attribute of inputs are involved in this system, then a hierarchical inference structure is needed (Fig.2-b).

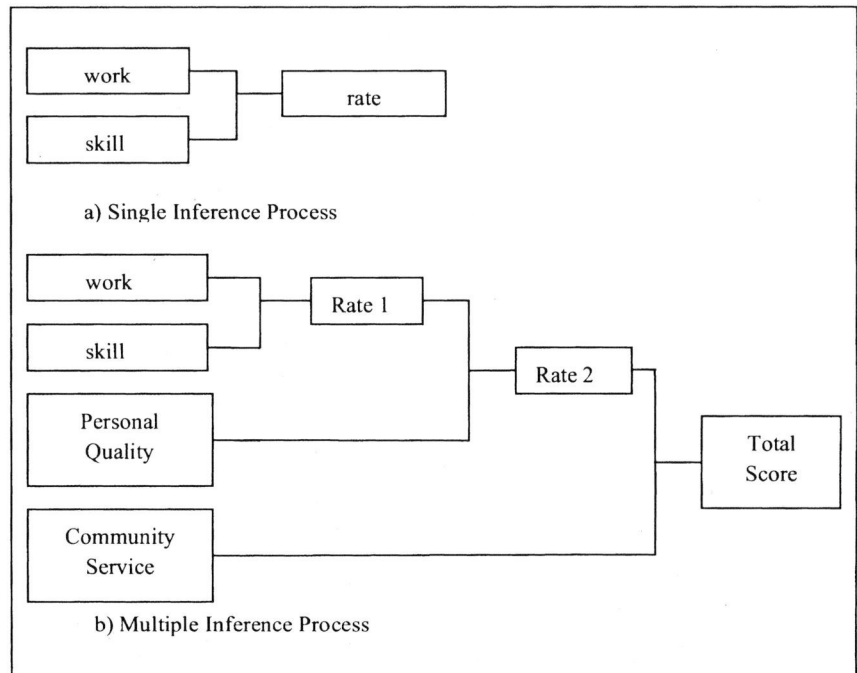

Figure 2: Fuzzy Inference Structure

Such fuzzy rules are represented as given below.

IF work_achievement is 'poor' AND skill is 'poor' THEN appraisal_ rate is 'need improvement'

IF work_achievement is 'poor' AND skill is 'satisfactory' THEN appraisal_ rate is 'need improvement'

IF work_achievement is 'poor' AND skill is 'proficient' THEN appraisal_ rate is 'meet expectation'

This fuzzy rule determines the decision embedded into the system engine, and should be validated from domain expert. Moreover, the human linguistic term involves in fuzzy rules enable the human-like fuzzy reasoning.

2.3   Defuzzification

Defuzzification or decomposition involves finding a value that best represents the information contained in the fuzzy set. The implementation of defuzzification is important in order to transform the linguistic terms back into crisp interpretation. The Defuzzification process yields the expected value of the variable for a particular execution of a fuzzy model. In fuzzy models, there are several methods of Defuzzification that describe an expected value for the final fuzzy state space could be derived [10].

There are a number of Defuzzification methods such as Centre of Gravity, Centre of Sums and Mean of Maxima. However, the system in this study only focuses on centre of gravity technique. The implementation of gravity technique is as modeled in eq 1.

$$\mu^* = \frac{\sum_{i=1}^{n} u_i * \mu_{out}(u_i)}{\sum_{i=1}^{n} \mu_{out}(u_i)} \qquad (1)$$

The output is calculated as

$$output = \frac{Lw_{11} + Lw_{12} + Mw_{13} + Lw_{21} + Mw_{22} + Mw_{23} + Mw_{31} + Mw_{32} + Hw}{\sum_{w_i}^{9} i = 1}$$

Equation (2)

H represent as *Excellent*, M as *meet_expectation* and L as *need_improvement* respectively. In short, {H, M, L} are a fuzzy label (linguistic) used to represent the fuzzy variables.

3.   Implementation and Results

This section focuses on the implementation of Fuzzy Appraisal Evaluation System prototype and it is separated from the existing performance system. However it is assumed that the input parameter for this system is observed from the existing system. This application consists of fuzzy system components, which have been discussed above. The architecture of the system is illustrated as in Fig 3.

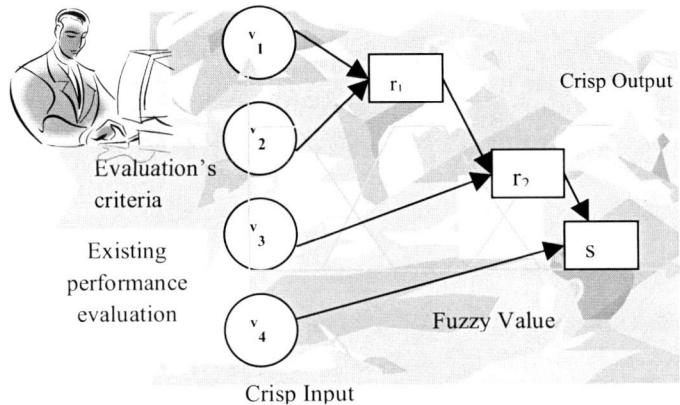

Figure 3: Fuzzy System Architecture for Appraisal Evaluation

This system uses four parameters as its system input. The input value actually should be observed from existing evaluation tool. However this study only focuses on the fuzzy system engine only, and assumed that the value is observed from the existing evaluation tool. So, it not does cover the details criteria for each group of input parameters. All inputs that are in the form of crisp value, will be processed throughout fuzzification phase, fuzzy inference and defuzzify the fuzzy value into crisp value for user presentation. As a prototype, this fuzzy system was developed using Microsoft Visual Basic (VB) 6.0 to test the fuzzy engine. Since VB provide easy programming facility, it was used as a platform to develop fuzzy engine as it consumed less time for coding task.

In practice, the 2-dimensional graph is used to represent a decision diagram using a total score accumulated from various criteria that be evaluated. The diagram can be illustrated in the Fig. 4 and is known as a singleton function. Consequently, the decision of forecasting staff's achievement will falls into specific conditions, which have a rigid boundary. Clearly the decision is based on crisp values which are rather rigid.

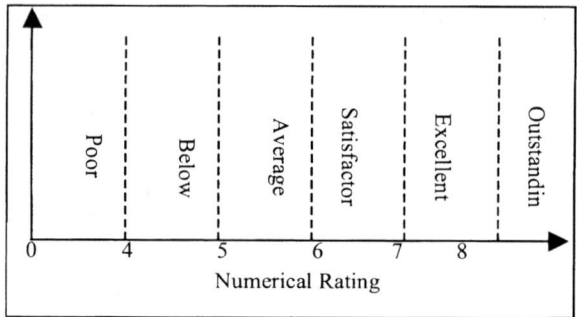

Figure 4: Example of Performance Decision

Based on the current practice, appraisal's evaluation for staff involves several criteria. Marks accumulated from the criteria then will be judge into single decision. For example, if the accumulated marks is above 85 than the staff will have an excellent result from the appraisal evaluation. In this study, several linguistic labels for each criterion are proposed. This study explores the evaluation process using more than one attributes. From the findings, if more than one attributes involved, the less rigid 3-dimensional decision graph was produced.

Although fuzzy logic eases the mapping problem, more programming effort was involved. To this end, fuzzy technique has definitely eases the mapping process. As a result, it produces more meaningful information to the user as well as improving the efficiency of handling uncertainty. Also, a fuzzy approach was used in order to accumulate the marks and assist the decision. Although fuzzy logic eases the mapping problem, more programming effort was involved. To this end, fuzzy technique has definitely eases the mapping process. As a result, it produces more meaningful information to the user as well as improving the efficiency of handling uncertainty.

However, the success of the system especially on the fuzzy engine relies much on the experience of selecting membership function and mainly the fuzzy knowledge base. The more expert knowledge involved and validated the rules and membership function, then the more reliable its end result. Thus, as expert systems rely on expert knowledge, fuzzy system also needs expert experience to strengthen the decision rules and capable to handle imprecise value in its reasoning.

4.   Discussion and Conclusion

This study focuses on the implementation of fuzzy logic approach in the staff appraisal system. Therefore it emphasizes on the mapping of uncertainty data in performance measurement system into fuzzy values which consist of labels and confidence values. The mapping process is essential in this study since if erroneous membership function and rules were chosen, it may yield a flawed output. In future, it is urge that this system may be implemented in a web based version and incorporate with the existing evaluation system. Furthermore, others artificial intelligence techniques can be used in this study. For instance, expert system may be used to enhance the explanation facilities, or neural network technique to forecast the potential of staff performances. Finally, it is expected that reasoning based on fuzzy models will provide an alternative way in handling various kinds of imprecise data, which often reflected in the way people think and make judgments. It is important to point out that the aim of the proposed system is not to replace the current system of evaluating performance but it may be used to strengthen and improve the present system of evaluation by providing additional information for appraiser to make decision in performance evaluation and management of resources in an organization.

References

1. Armstrong, M. and Baron, A. (1998). Performance Management: The New Reality, London: Institute of Personnel and Development
2. Schweiger, I. and Sumners, G.E. (1994). Optimizing the Value of Performance Appraisals
3. Chan, D.C.K., Yung, K.L., Ip, A.W.H. (2002). An Application of fuzzy sets to process performance evaluation, Integrated Manufacturing Systems, 237-246.
4. Cordon, O., Herera, F., and Peregrin, A. (1999). Looking for the best Defuzzification method features for each implication operator to design accurate fuzzy model, Department of Computer Science and Artificial Intelligent, Spain.
5. Garibaldi, J.M. and Ifeachor, E.C. (1999). Application of simulated Annealing Fuzzy Model Tuning to Umbilical Cord Acid-base Interpretation, *IEEE Transactions on Fuzzy Systems*, Vol.7, No.1.
6. Hasiloglu, A.S., Yavuz, U., Rezos, S. and Kaya, M.D. (2003). A Fuzzy Expert System for Product Life Cycle Management, International XII, Turkish Symposium on Artificial Intelligence and Neural Networks.
7. Sunghyun, W and Jinil, K. (2001) Learning Achievement Evaluation Strategy Using Fuzzy Membership Function, 31st ASEE/IEEE Frontiers in Education Conference
8. Tzeng, G.H., Teng, J.Y., Chang, S.L., and Lin, C.W. (2001) Fuzzy Multi-Criteria Evaluation Method for Developmental Strategies Of Hybrid Electric Vehicles, World Energy Council 18th Congress, Buenos Aires.
9. Zimmerman, H.J. (1996). Fuzzy Set Theory and Its Application, Third ed. Kluwer Academic Publishers, Boston, MA.
10. Nasution, H., (2002). Design Methodology of Fuzzy Logic Control, UTM

Extraction of Cause Information from Newspaper Articles Concerning Business Performance

Hiroyuki Sakai[1] and Shigeru Masuyama[1]

Department of Knowledge-based Information Engineering, Toyohashi University of
Technology, 1-1 Hibarigaoka, Tempaku-cho, Toyohashi-shi, Aichi 441-8580, Japan
(sakai,masuyama)@smlab.tutkie.tut.ac.jp

Abstract. We propose a method of extracting cause information from
Japanese newspaper articles concerning business performance. Cause
information is useful for investors in selecting companies to invest. Our
method extracts cause information as a form of causal expression by
using statistical information and initial clue phrases automatically. Our
method can extract causal expressions without predetermined patterns
or complex rules given by hand, and is expected to be applied to other
tasks or language for acquiring phrases that have a particular meaning
not limited to cause information. We compared our method with our
previous method originally proposed for extracting phrases concerning
traffic accident causes and experimental results showed that our new
method outperforms our previous one.

1 Introduction

We propose a method of extracting cause information from Japanese newspaper articles concerning business performance. Our method extracts phrases
implying cause information, e.g. "自動車の売上げが好調 (*zidousya no uriage ga
koutyou*: Sales of cars were good)" or "鉄管の売上げが不振 (*tekkan no uriage ga
husin*: Sales of iron tubes were down)". Here, we de ne a phrase implying cause
information as a "causal expression". Cause information is useful for investors in
selecting companies to invest. Collecting information concerning business performance is a very important task for investment. If the business performance
of a company is good, the stock price of the company will rise. Moreover, cause
information of the business performance is also important, because, even if the
business performance is good, the stock price will not rise if the main cause is
the recording of an extraordinary pro t not related to core business (e.g. pro t
from sales of stocks). This is also the case for the bad business performance.
However, since there are a number of companies that announce business performance, acquiring their all cause information manually is a considerably hard
task. First, our method extracts articles concerning business performance from
newspaper corpus as a preparation. Next, our method extracts causal expressions automatically from these articles by using statistical information and 2

Please use the following format when citing this chapter:

Sakai, H., Masuyama, S., 2007, in IFIP International Federation for Information Processing, Volume 247, Artificial
Intelligence and Innovations 2007: From Theory to Applications, eds. Boukis, C., Pnevmatikakis, L., Polymenakos, L.,
(Boston: Springer), pp. 205-212.

initial clue phrases. Here, the "clue phrases" are de ned as phrases frequently modi ed by causal expressions.

As related work for extracting phrases that have a particular meaning, Rilo et al. proposed a method for learning extraction patterns for subjective expressions by applying syntactic templates made by hand to the training corpus[5]. Khoo et al. proposed a method for extracting cause-e ect information from a newspaper text and a method for extracting causal knowledge from a medical database by applying patterns made by hand[2][3]. Kanayama et al. proposed a method for extracting a set of sentiment units by using transfer-based machine translation engine replacing the translation patterns with sentiment patterns[1]. Morinaga et al. proposed a method for collecting and analyzing people's opinions about target products from Web pages by using an evaluation-expression dictionary and syntactic property rules learned manually from training examples[4]. However, to construct a complete list of complex rules or patterns manually, which is the case of the above methods, is a time-consuming and costly task. Moreover, the rules and the patters made by hand may be domain-speci c and can not be applied to other tasks. In contract, our method uses statistical information and only 2 initial clue phrases consisting of 2 words as an initial input. The domain-speci c dictionaries, predetermined patterns, complex rules made by hand are not needed. Hence, our method is expected to be applied to other tasks or language for acquiring phrases that have a particular meaning not limited to cause information (e.g. opinion information, reputation information) by changing an initial input. We preliminarily proposed a method for extracting phrases concerning traffic accident causes by using statistical information and initial clue phrases[6]. However, our previous method could not attain high precision if inappropriate phrases are extracted. In this paper, we also propose a method for eliminating inappropriate phrases automatically and, by introducing it, our new method attains high precision.

2 Extraction of articles concerning business performance

As a preparation, our method extracts articles concerning business performance from newspaper corpus by using Support Vector Machine (SVM) [7].

2.1 Feature selection

As training data, we manually extract $2,920$ articles concerning business performance as positive examples and $2,920$ articles not concerning business performance as negative examples from Nikkei newspapers published in 2000. Here, some of words contained in the positive examples are used as features of SVM. The method for extracting content words e ective as features is as follows:

First, our method calculates score $W(t_i, S_p)$ of word t_i contained in positive example set S_p and score $W(t_i, S_n)$ of word t_i contained in negative example set S_n by the following Formula 1.

$$W(t_i, S_p) = P(t_i, S_p)H(t_i, S_p), \tag{1}$$

where, $P(t_i, S_p)$ is the probability that word t_i appears in positive example set S_p and $H(t_i, S_p)$ is the entropy based on the probability $P(t_i, d)$ that word t_i appears in document $d \in S_p$. The entropy $H(t_i, S_p)$ is calculated by the following Formula 2:

$$H(t_i, S_p) = -\sum_{d \in S_p} P(t_i, d) \log_2 P(t_i, d), \ P(t_i, d) = \frac{tf(t_i, d)}{\sum_{d \in S_p} tf(t_i, d)}, \tag{2}$$

where, $tf(t_i, d)$ is the frequency of word t_i in document d. Next, our method compares $W(t_i, S_p)$ with $W(t_i, S_n)$. If score $W(t_i, S_p)$ is larger than $2W(t_i, S_n)$, word t_i is extracted as a feature of SVM. By introducing Entropy $H(t_i, S_p)$, a large score is assigned to a word that appears uniformly in each document contained in positive example set S_p. For example, when word t_i is contained only in one document, $H(t_i, S_p) = 0$. Although such a word t_i may be an important word for the document, it may be an irrelevant word for positive example set S_p. Hence, word t_i with small entropy value should not be extracted as a feature. However, Formula 1 may assign a large score to a general word not relevant to business performance. Such a general word may also be assigned a large score in the negative example set. Hence, in our method, not only $W(t_i, S_p)$, a score in positive example set S_p, but also $W(t_i, S_n)$, a score in negative example set S_n, are calculated and compared.

3 Extraction of causal expressions

Our method extracts causal expressions from articles concerning business performance extracted by the method described in Section 2. Here, a causal expression is a part of a sentence consisting of some "*bunsetu*'s" (a *bunsetu* is a basic block in Japanese composed of several words). Our method extracts causal expressions by using "clue phrases", i.e. phrases modi ed by causal expressions frequently. For example, a causal expression concerning good business modi es clue phrase "が好調 (*ga koutyou*: is good)" and a causal expression concerning bad business modi es clue phrase "が不振 ([*ga husin*: is down)" frequently in Japanese. Our method extracts an expression that consists of a clue phrase and a phrase that modi es it as a causal expression. Hence, if many clue phrases e ective for extracting causal expressions is acquirable, causal expressions are extracted automatically. However, it is hard to acquire many clue phrases e ective for extracting causal expressions by hand. Hence, our method also acquires such clue phrases automatically from a set of articles concerning business performance.

3.1 Acquisition of clue phrases

Our method for acquiring clue phrases is as follows.

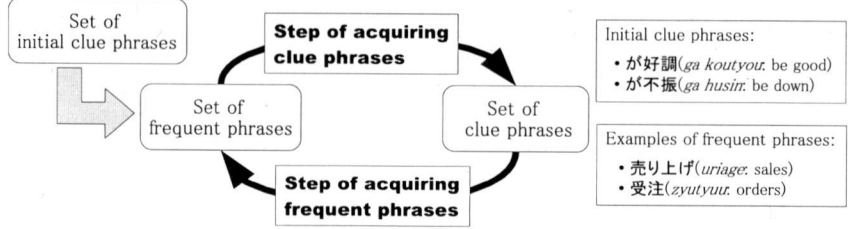

Fig. 1. Outline of our method

Step 1: Input some initial clue phrases and acquire phrases that modify them. Here, we use two clue phrases, "が好調 (*ga koutyou*: be good)" and "が不振 (*ga husin*: be down)", as initial clue phrases.

Step 2: Extract phrases appearing frequently in a set of the phrases acquired in Step 1 (e.g. 売り上げ (*uriage*: sales)). In this paper, such phrases extracted in Step 2 are de ned as "frequent phrases".

Step 3: Acquire new clue phrases modi ed by the frequent phrases.

Step 4: Extract new frequent phrases from a set of phrases that modify the new clue phrases acquired in Step 3. This step is the same as Step 2.

Step 5: Repeat Steps 3 and 4 until predetermined times or neither new clue phrases nor new frequent phrases are extracted.

An outline of the method is illustrated in Figure 1.

3.2 Extraction of Frequent phrases

The method for extracting "frequent phrases" from a set of phrases that modify clue phrases is as follows.

Step 1: Acquire a *bunsetu* modifying a clue phrase and eliminate a case particle from the *bunsetu*. Here, the *bunsetu* is de ned as c.

Step 2: Acquire frequent phrase candidates by adding *bunsetu* modifying c to c. (See Figure 2.)

Step 3: Calculate score $S_f(e, c)$ of frequent phrase candidate e containing c by the following Formula 3.

Step 4: Adopt e assigned the best score $S_f(e, c)$ in the set of frequent phrase candidates containing c as the frequent phrase.

Score $S_f(e, c)$ is calculated by the following Formula 3:

$$S_f(e, c) = -f_e(e, c)\sqrt{f_p(e)}\log_2 P(e, c), \tag{3}$$

where, $P(e, c)$ is the probability that frequent phrase candidate e containing c appears in the set of articles concerning business performance. $f_e(e, c)$ is the number of frequent phrase candidate e's containing c. $f_p(e)$ is the number of *bunsetu*'s that compose e. Here, $P(e, c) = f_e(e, c)/Ne(c)$, where, $Ne(c)$ is the total number of frequent phrase candidates containing c in the set of articles concerning business performance.

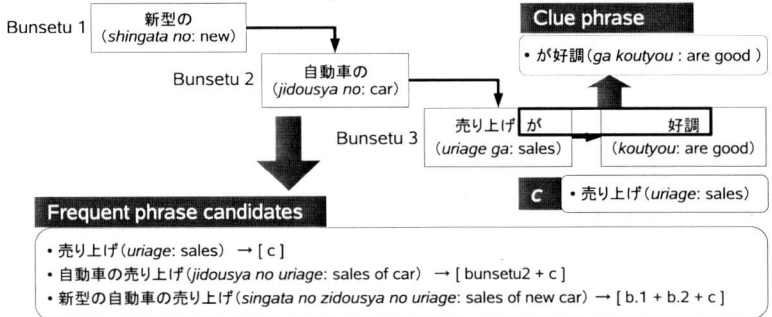

Fig. 2. Examples of frequent phrase candidates

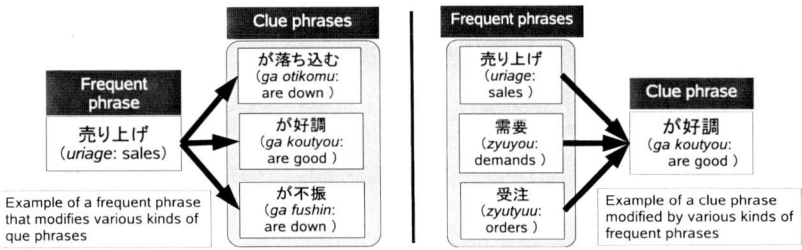

Fig. 3. Example of an appropriate frequent phrase and an appropriate que phrase

3.3 Selection of frequent phrases

The frequent phrases extracted from a set of phrases that modify clue phrases may contain inappropriate ones. Hence, our method selects appropriate frequent phrases from them. Here, our method calculates entropy $H(e)$ based on the probability $P(e, s)$ that frequent phrase e modifies clue phrase s and selects frequent phrases assigned entropy $H(e)$ larger than a threshold value. Entropy $H(e)$ is used for reflecting "variety of clue phrases modified by frequent phrase e". If entropy $H(e)$ is large, frequent phrase e modifies various kinds of clue phrases and such a frequent phrase is appropriate. (See Figure 3.) The entropy $H(e)$ is calculated by the following Formula 4.

$$H(e) = - \sum_{s \in S(e)} P(e, s) \log_2 P(e, s), \quad P(e, s) = \frac{f(e, s)}{\sum_{s \in S(e)} f(e, s)}, \quad (4)$$

where, $S(e)$ is the set of clue phrases modified by frequent phrase e and $f(e, s)$ is the number of frequent phrases e's that modifies clue phrase s in the set of articles concerning business performance. The threshold value is calculated by the following Formula 5.

$$T_e = \alpha \log_2 |N_s|, \quad (5)$$

where, N_s is the set of clue phrases used for extracting frequent phrases and α is a constant ($0 < \alpha < 1$).

3.4 Acquisition of clue phrases

The method for acquiring new clue phrases from frequent phrases is as follows.

Step 1: Extract a *bunsetu* modi ed by frequent phrase e.

Step 2: Acquire clue phrase s by adding a case particle contained in the frequent phrase e to the *bunsetu*.

Step 3: Calculate entropy $H(s)$ based on the probability $P(s, e)$ that clue phrase s is modi ed by frequent phrase e.

Step 4: Select clue phrase s assigned entropy $H(s)$ larger than a threshold value calculated by the Formula 5. (In this case, N_s is a set of frequent phrases used for extracting clue phrases.)

Here, entropy $H(s)$ is introduced for selecting appropriate clue phrases and is calculated by the following Formula 6 (See Figure 3.).

$$H(s) = - \sum_{e \in E(s)} P(s, e) \log_2 P(s, e), \qquad (6)$$

where, $P(s, e)$ is the probability that clue phrase s is modi ed by frequent phrase e and $E(s)$ is the set of frequent phrases that modify clue phrase s.

3.5 Elimination of inappropriate clue phrases

Finally, our method eliminates inappropriate clue phrases by using statistical information in the set of articles concerning business performance and the set of articles not concerning business performance. The method for eliminating inappropriate clue phrases is as follows. First, our method calculates score $W(s, S_p)$ of clue phrase s in set S_p of articles concerning business performance and score $W(s, S_n)$ of clue phrase s in set S_n of articles not concerning business performance by the following Formula 7.

$$W(s, S_p) = P(s, S_p) H(s, S_p), \qquad (7)$$

where, $P(s, S_p)$ is the probability that a sentence containing clue phrase s appears in S_p, and $H(s, S_p)$ is the entropy based on the probability $P(s, d)$ that a sentence containing s appears in document $d \in S_p$. Next, our method compares $W(s, S_p)$ with $W(s, S_n)$. If score $W(s, S_p)$ is smaller than $2W(s, S_n)$, clue phrase s is eliminated as an inappropriate clue phrase. Moreover, inappropriate frequent phrases are also eliminated by applying this method to frequent phrases. Here, clue phrases and frequent phrases containing numbers are also eliminated to prevent extracting sale proceeds as a causal expression.

4 Evaluation

We implemented our method. Our method extracted $20,880$ newspaper articles concerning business performance from Nikkei newspapers published from

Table 1. Recall and precision of causal expression acquisition

α	num. of clue phrases	Precision (%)	Recall (%)
0.5	12	85.7	1.25
0.4	139	77.7	12.8
0.3	922	77.7	66.0
0.2	3381	63.7	80.1

Table 2. Comparison between our method and previous method

	num. of clue phrases	Precision (%)	Recall (%)
our new method	922	77.7	66.0
our previous method	938	70.5	64.6

2001 to 2005 and extracted causal expressions from them. We employ ChaSen[1] as a Japanese morphological analyzer, and CaboCha[2] as a Japanese parser and SVM^{light}[3] as an implementation of SVM. First, we evaluated our method for extracting articles concerning business performance. We manually selected 1, 136 articles concerning business performance from Nikkei newspapers published from 2001 to 2005 as a correct data set, and calculated precision and recall. As a result, our method attained 93.7% recall and 88.6% precision, respectively. Next, we evaluated our method for extracting causal expressions. We manually extracted 559 causal expressions from 131 articles concerning business performance as a correct data set. Moreover, we extracted causal expressions by our method from the same 131 articles and calculated precision and recall. Here, a causal expression extracted by our method is correct if it contains a causal expression extracted as the correct data set. Table 1 shows the results. Here, α is a parameter used for determining a threshold value in Formula 5. For con rming the e ectiveness of our method, we compared our method with our previous method[6], which was originally developed for extracting phrases concerning traffic accident causes. Note that our new method is a one that improves our previous method for eliminating inappropriate clue phrases and inappropriate frequent phrases. Table 2 shows the results.

5 Discussion

Experimental results shown in Table 2 suggest that our new method outperforms our previous method. The reason why our new method outperforms our previous method is that our new method can e ectively eliminate inappropriate clue phrases than our previous method due to improvement of process for eliminating inappropriate clue phrases. Our new method and our previous

---

[1] http://chasen.aist-nara.ac.jp/hiki/ChaSen/

[2] http://chasen.org/~taku/software/cabocha/

[3] http://svmlight.joachims.org

method process the step of acquiring clue phrases and the step of acquiring frequent phrases, iteratively. If many inappropriate clue phrases are included in the set of clue phrases for acquiring frequent phrases, many inappropriate frequent phrases may be acquired. Hence, the process for eliminating inappropriate clue phrases is important for improving the performance. For example, "になる (*ni naru*: become)", which is an inappropriate clue phrase, is acquired as a clue phrase by our previous method. However, it is not acquired by our new method. "になる (*ni naru*: become)" is contained in not only the set of articles concerning business performance but also the set of articles not concerning business performance. Hence, it is not acquired by the method shown in Section 3.5, which is introduced only into our new method.

6 Conclusion

We proposed a method for extracting phrases implying cause information from Japanese newspaper articles concerning business performance. First, our method extracts articles concerning business performance from newspaper corpus. Next, our method extracts causal expressions from them by using statistical information and initial clue phrases. We evaluated our method and it attained 77.7% precision and 66.0% recall, respectively. In addition to this, we compared our method with our previous method[6] by experiments and the experimental results showed that our new method outperforms our previous one.

References

1. Kanayama, H., Nasukawa, T. and Watanabe, H.: Deeper sentiment analysis using machine translation technology, *Proceedings of the 20th COLING*, pp. 494–500 (2004).
2. Khoo, C. S., Korn lt, J., Oddy, R. N. and Myaeng, S. H.: Automatic Extraction of Cause-E ect Information from Newspaper Text Without Knowledge-based Inferencing, *Literary and Linguistic Computing*, Vol. 13, No. 4, pp. 177–186 (1998).
3. Khoo, C. S., Chan, S. and Niu, Y.: Extracting Causal Knowledge from a Medical Database Using Graphical Patterns, *Proceedings of the 38th ACL*, pp. 336–343 (2000).
4. Morinaga, S., Yamanishi, K., Tateishi, K. and Fukushima, T.: Mining product reputations on the Web, *Proceedings of Eighth ACM SIGKDD Int. Conf. on KDD2002*, pp. 341–349 (2002).
5. Rilo , E. and Wiebe, J.: Learning Extraction Patterns for Subjective Expressions, *Proceedings of the 2003 Conference on Empirical Methods in Natural Language Processing (EMNLP)*, pp. 105–112 (2003).
6. Sakai, H., Umemura, S. and Masuyama, S.: Extraction of Expressions concerning Accident Cause contained in Articles on Traffic Accidents, *Journal of Natural Language Processing*, Vol. 13, No. 4, pp. 99–124 (2006(in Japanese)).
7. Vapnik, V.: *Statistical Learning Theory*, Wiley (1999).

A fast parallel algorithm for frequent itemsets mining

Dora Souliou, Aris Pagourtzis, and Panayiotis Tsanakas *

School of Electrical and Computer Engineering
National Technical University of Athens
Heroon Politechniou 9, 15780 Zografou, Greece
{dsouliou, panag}@cslab.ece.ntua.gr, pagour@cs.ntua.gr

Abstract. Mining frequent itemsets from large databases is an important computational task with a lot of applications. The most known among them is the market-basket problem which assumes that we have a large number of items and we want to know which items are bought together. A recent application is that of web pages (baskets) and linked pages (items). Pages with many common references may be about the same topic. In this paper we present a parallel algorithm for mining frequent itemsets. We provide experimental evidence that our algorithm scales quite well and we discuss the merits of parallelization for this problem.

Keywords: *parallel data mining, association rules, frequent itemsets, partial support tree, set-enumeration tree.*

1 Introduction

The market-basket problem is described as follows: a database D of transactions is given, each of which consists of several distinct items. The goal is to determine association rules of the form $A \Rightarrow B$, where A and B are sets of items (itemsets).

In order to determine validity of a rule $A \Rightarrow B$, two quantities are taken into account: the *confidence* of the rule, which is the fraction $freq(A \cup B)/freq(A)$, where $freq(I)$ is the number of transactions that contain itemset I, and the *support* of the rule, which is equal to $freq(A \cup B)$. The *support* of the rule is usually called frequency. One is usually interested in rules the frequency of which is above a threshold t and the confidence of which is above another threshold c. Once we have found which itemsets have frequency larger than t it is only a matter of simple calculations to find rules whose confidence exceeds c. Therefore, a fundamental ingredient of discovering association rules is the generation of all itemsets the frequency of which exceeds threshold t; from now on, we will call such itemsets *t-frequent* or simply *frequent*.

Several sequential methods for computing frequent itemsets have been proposed in the literature [3], [8], [11]. Sequential algorithms however, can not cope with very large databases. In that case parallelization techniques seem to be necessary [4], [14], [13], [9]. In this paper we implement a new parallel algorithm named PMP (Parallel Multiple Pointer) which achieves a satisfactory speedup and is particularly adequate for certain types of data sets.

The paper is organized as follows. In section 2 we give a brief description of the sequential algorithm on which our parallel algorithm is based. In section 3 we present the parallel algorithm. In section 4 we give experimental results that demonstrate the efficiency on certain datasets. Conclusions and directions for future work are discussed in the last section.

* This research is supported by the PENED 2003 Project (EPAN), co-funded by the European Social Fund (75%) and National Resources (25%).

Please use the following format when citing this chapter:

Souliou, D., Pagourtzis, A., Tsanakas, P., 2007, in IFIP International Federation for Information Processing, Volume 247, Artificial Intelligence and Innovations 2007: From Theory to Applications, eds. Boukis, C., Pnevmatikakis, L., Polymenakos, L., (Boston: Springer), pp. 213-220.

2 The Sequential Algorithm

The main difficulties in computing frequent itemsets are related to two factors: the number of transactions and the number of items. When the number of transactions increases each scan of the database becomes time consuming. A large number of items on the other hand, implies many possible itemsets and this means delays on computations and increased requirements on memory space. Some known algorithms [11], [8] in the area gave an answer to the first problem by using structures in which the database is stored in a more compact form. For the second problem techniques have been developed for reducing the number of itemsets that need to be examined e.g the well known A-priori Algorithm [3].

The sequential algorithm that we use as a basis for our parallel algorithm makes use of a structure called *Partial Support Tree* (or P-tree for short), introduced in [8], in which the whole database is stored in one scan. It is a set enumeration tree [12] that contains itemsets in its nodes. These itemsets represent either whole transactions of database D or common prefixes of transactions of D. An integer is stored in each tree node which represents the partial support of the corresponding itemset I, that is, the number of transactions that contain I as a prefix. The construction of the P-tree was described in [8]; a more detailed description can be found in [7].

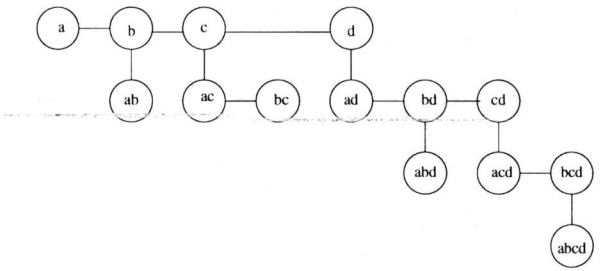

Fig. 1. An example of T-tree.

The sequential algorithm that we use for parallelization uses a second tree structure, namely the T-tree on the nodes of which candidate frequent itemsets are stored. This structure was introduced in [6] and algorithms that use it are presented in [10]. Here we propose a modification of this structure as follows: each node of the tree in the initial structure had two pointers. The first one points to the right sibling and the second one to the lexicographically smaller child. In the modified T-tree we use more than one pointers to the children. Figure 1 shows a T-tree for items a,b,c and d. For example, the node with label "d" would have one pointer to the node "ad" in the initial structure. In the proposed structure it may have up to two pointers more: one that points to the node "bd" and one that points to the node "cd". The number of pointers depends on the desired tradeoff between memory space and running time.

We give here some details of how the algorithm calculates the itemset frequencies. The algorithm traverses the P-tree and for each node visited, all subsets of this node with k items are generated (k is the current level of the T-tree). For each such itemset the nodes of the T-tree are visited in order to find the itemset. If it is found, the frequency of the node that contains the itemset is increased by the partial support of the current node of the P-tree. Suppose for example that we visit the node "abef" of the P-tree with partial support 12 and that the current level of the T-tree is three. The subsets with 3 items of "abef" are "abe", "abf", "aef", and "bef". In order to find "abe" we visit the following nodes of the T-tree "e", "be", "abe". If "abe" is found, we increase its frequency by 12.

3 The Parallel Algorithm (PMP)

Algorithm PMP (* Parallel Multiple Pointer *)

distribute the database D to the processors in a round-robin manner;
let d_j denote the part of D assigned to processor p_j;
in each processor p_j **in parallel do**
　　build local P-tree from local database d_j;
　　(* *1st level construction* *)
　　for each node I of the local P-tree
　　　　compute all subsets of I with *1 item*;
　　　　for each $I \in L_1$ frequency($\{I\}$)++;　　　　(*L_1 is the first level of T-tree *)

　　(* *Global synchronized computation* *)
　　for $i := 1$ **to** *nitems* **do**　　　　　　　　(* *nitems* = number of items *)

　　　　total_frequency($\{i\}$):= parallel_sum$_{j=1}^{nprocs}$ local_frequency$_j$($\{i\}$);　　(* *nprocs* = number of processors *)

　　(* *Local computation continues* *)
　　for $i := 1$ **to** *nitems* **do**
　　　　if total_frequency($\{i\}$) $\geq t$ **then** append $\{i\}$ to L_1;　　(* *all processors obtain the same list L_1* *)

　　$k:=2$;
　　while L_{k-1} not empty and $k \leq nitems$ **do**
　　　　(* *k-th level construction* *)
　　　　set L_k to be the empty list;
　　　　for each itemset $I \in L_{k-1}$ **do**
　　　　　　for each item $x_i >$ last item of I **do** $I' := I \cup x_i$;
　　　　　　　　insert I' into C_k;
　　　　　　　　update pointers for I';
　　　　for each node J of the local P-tree
　　　　　　compute all subsets s of J with k *items*
　　　　　　for each s go down to the level k of T-tree and
　　　　　　　　if s is found then frequency($\{s\}$)++;
　　　　for all itemsets $I_k \in C_k$ **do**
　　　　　　get local_frequency$_j$($\{I_k\}$) from local P-tree;
　　　　(* *Global synchronized computation* *)
　　　　for all itemsets $I_k \in C_k$ **do**
　　　　　　total_frequency(I_k):= parallel_sum$_{j=1}^{nprocs}$(local_frequency$_j$(I_k));
　　　　(* *Local computation continues* *)
　　　　for all itemsets $I_k \in C_k$ **do**
　　　　　　if total_frequency($\{I_k\}$) $\leq t$
　　　　　　　　then delete I_k from L_k and update pointers;
　　　　$k := k + 1$;
　　(* *end of while-loop* *)

Fig. 2. The Parallel Algorithm

In this section we give a detailed description of the new parallel algorithm. Our approach follows the ideas of a parallel version of A-priori, called Count Distribution, which was described by Agrawal and Shafer [4]; the difference is, of course, that

PMP makes use of two tree structures P-tree for storing the database and T-tree for storing the frequent itemsets.

In the beginning, the root process distributes the database transactions to the processors in a round-robin fashion; then, each of the processors creates its own local P-tree based on the transactions that it has received. Next, each processor traverses each local P-tree and for each node visited produces all subsets with 1 item. For each such item the algorithm traverses the T-tree in order to find it and increase its frequency. When all the nodes of the P-tree have been visited the local frequencies have been calculated. The calculation of total frequencies of singletons takes place as follows. Each processor sends the local frequencies and an appropriate parallel procedure (MPI All_reduce function) sums total frequencies. This function is used to make calculations in an efficient way. The result is distributed to all processors so that each one ends up with the same list L_1 of singletons. Following each processor visits the nodes of L_1 and removes all infrequent singletons. In this step each processor has the same list of frequent singletons. During k-level computation (for each $k \geq 2$), all processors first generate the same list of candidate itemsets C_k from the common list L_{k-1}. Then the same procedure as that followed for the first level allows each processor to obtain the total frequencies for all itemsets of C_k, and finally to derive list L_k by removing infrequent itemsets of C_k.

A detailed description of the algorithm is given in Figure 2.

4 Numerical Results

Our experimental platform is an 8-node Pentium III dual-SMP cluster interconnected with 100 Mbps FastEthernet. Each node has two Pentium III CPUs at 800 MHz, 256 MB of RAM, 16 KB of L1 I Cache, 16 KB L1 D Cache, 256 KB of L2 cache, and runs Linux with 2.4.26 kernel. We use MPI implementation MPICH v.1.2.6, compiled with the Intel C++ compiler v.8.1. The experiments presented below study the behavior of the algorithm in terms of running time and parallel efficiency.

We have implemented our parallel algorithm (PMP) using synthetic datasets generated by the IBM Quest generator, described in [3]. We have generated our datasets using the following parameters:

- D: the number of transactions
- N: the number of items
- T: the average transaction length

We have used four synthetic datasets in our experiments, with number of transactions varying from 100K to 500K and number of items between 100 and 200; For the datasets with 100 items the average transaction length that we used was 10 ($T = 10$ 10 items per transaction) while for the itemsets with 200 items the average transaction length was 20. We have chosen relatively small minimum frequency threshold values varying from 0.1% to 1%.

In Figures 3 and 4 we observe the time performance of the algorithm for number of transactions 100, 200K, 300K and 500, number of items 100 and threshold values 0.1%, 0.5% and 1%.

We observe that in most cases PMP algorithm is a time efficient algorithm. For the dataset D100KN100T10 PMP gives satisfactory results for every number of processors and every threshold value. For the dataset D200KN100T10 the results show that the algorithm achieves a good time performance with the exception of one processor and threshold values 200 and 1000. For the datasets with 300K or 500K transactions and 100 items the algorithm scales well enough with the same

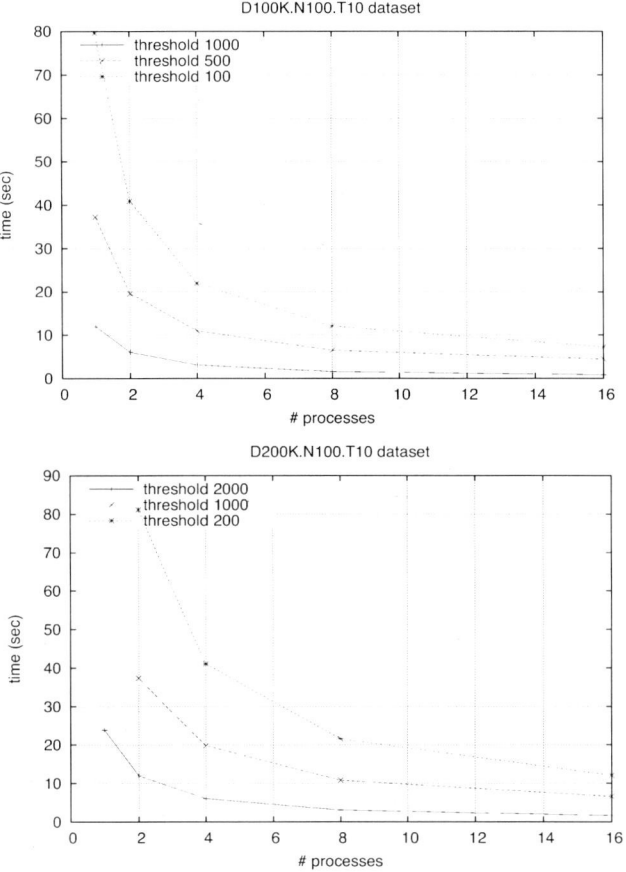

Fig. 3. Time performance for datasets D100K.N100.T10 and D200K.N100.T10

exception which now expands to two processors. This drawback is due to the inefficient memory space which slows down the computations. The same remarks could
be made in Figure 5. The two tree structures are space consuming and that is the
main reason for not getting satisfactory results in cases of one or two processors.
On the other hand the PMP algorithm behaves equally well when the number of
processors increases and that renders the parallelization meaningful. This is more
obvious in Figure 6, and in Figure 7 where we can see speedups even above 90%.
Our technique is efficient when the P-tree fits into the local memory of each processor. If it is not possible due to the limited number of processors our technique
would require special customization in order to reduce disk accesses.

5 Conclusions

In this work we have developed and implemented the Parallel Multiple Pointer
algorithm and investigated the efficiency of this parallelization technique. The use of
P-tree and T-tree has facilitated the process of computing frequencies. This process
is further accelerated by the use of parallelization. In particular, each processor
handles a part of the database and creates a small local P-tree that can be kept in
memory, thus providing a practicable solution when dealing with extremely large
datasets.

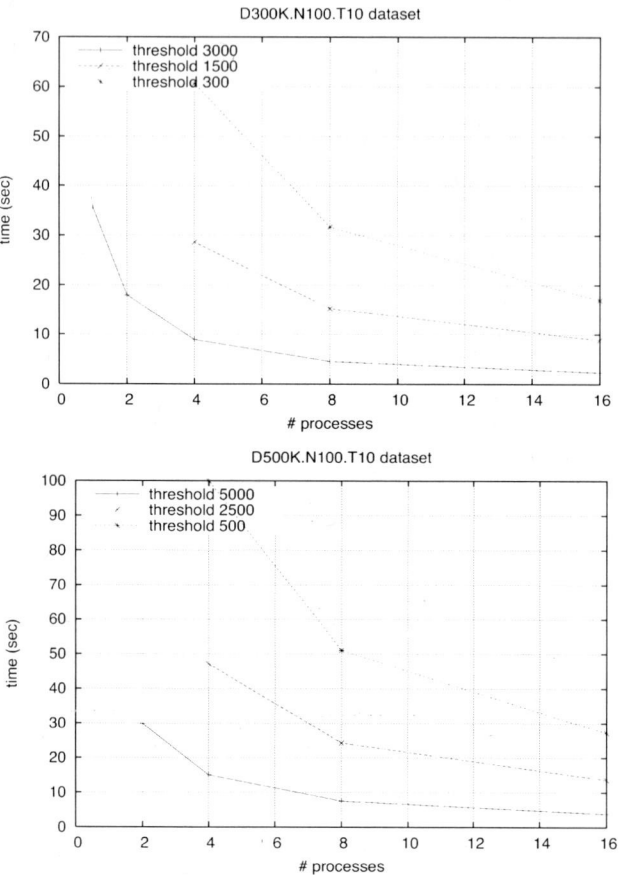

Fig. 4. Time performance for datasets D300K.N100.T10 and D500K.N100.T10

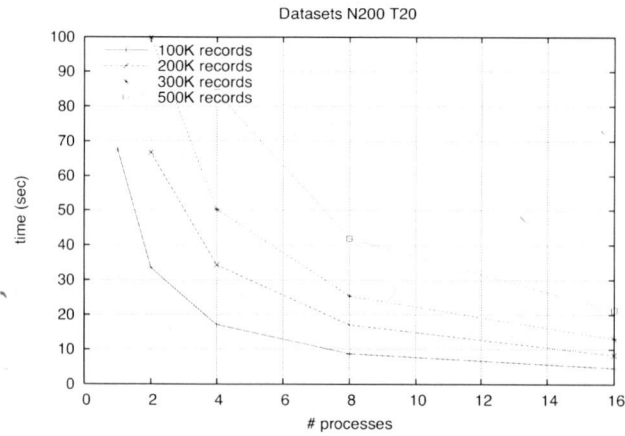

Fig. 5. Time performance for datasets with 200 items and average transaction length 20

We have implemented the algorithm using message passing, with the help of the Message Passing Interface (MPI). Experiments show that the above described parallel strategy is generally competitive. However the time efficiency sometimes

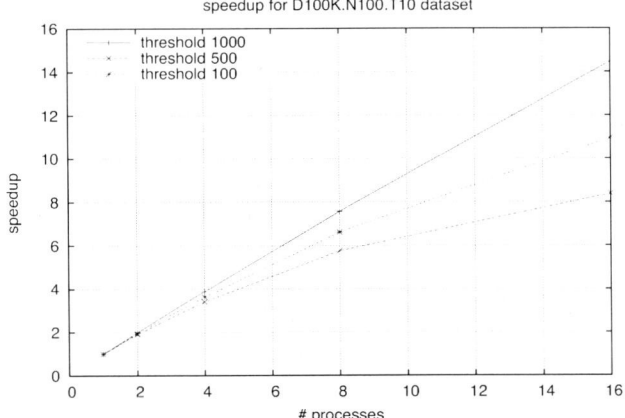

Fig. 6. Speedup obtained by PMP for dataset D100K N100 T10.

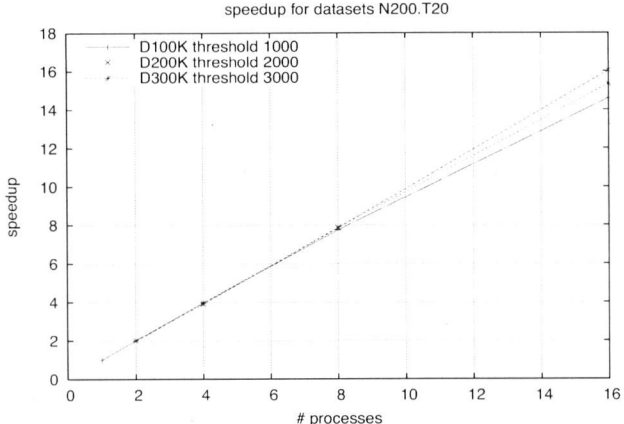

Fig. 7. Speedup obtained by PMP for datasets with 100 items.

causes problems in memory space. An answer to this problem could be the reduction on the number of pointers used to construct the T-tree. This could cause delays on frequency computations but it is necessary when the datasets used are extremely large and the needs in memory space are increased. An interesting research direction is therefore to fine tune the number of pointers used in the T-tree structure in order to balance the needs in space and time.

References

1. S. Ahmed, F. Coenen, and P.H. Leng: A Tree Partitioning Method for Memory Management in Association Rule Mining. In Proc. of Data Warehousing and Knowledge Discovery, 6th International Conference (DaWaK 2004), Lecture Notes in Computer Science 3181, pp. 331–340, Springer-Verlag 2004.
2. R. Agrawal, T. Imielinski, and A. Swami. Mining Association Rules between Sets of Items in Large Databases. In Proc. of the 1993 ACM SIGMOD Conference on Management of Data, Washington DC, pp. 207–216 1993.
3. R. Agrawal and R. Srikant. Fast Algorithms for mining association rules. In Proc. VLDB'94, pp. 487–499 1994.

4. R. Agrawal and J.C. Shafer. Parallel Mining of Association Rules. *IEEE Transactions on Knowledge and Data Engineering* 8(6), pp. 962–969, 1996.
5. R. J. Bayardo, Jr. and R. Agrawal. Mining the Most Interesting Rules. In Proc. of the Fifth ACM SIGKDD International Conference on Knowledge Discovery and Data Mining, pp. 145–154, 1999.
6. F. Coenen, G. Goulbourne, and P. Leng. Computing Association Rules using Partial Totals. In L. De Raedt and A. Siebes eds, *Principles of Data Mining and Knowledge Discovery* (Proceedings of the 5th European Conference, PKDD 2001, Freiburg), Lecture Notes in AI 2168, Springer-Verlag, Berlin, Heidelberg: pp. 54–66 2001.
7. F. Coenen, G. Goulbourne, and P. Leng. Tree Structures for Mining Association Rules. *Data Mining and Knowledge Discovery*, pp. 25–51, 8 2004
8. G. Goulbourne, F. Coenen, and P. Leng. Algorithms for Computing Association Rules using a Partial-Support Tree. *Journal of Knowledge-Based Systems* pp. 141–149, 13 2000.
9. F. Coenen, P. Leng, and S. Ahmed. T-Trees, Vertical Partitioning and Distributed Association Rule Mining. In Proc. of the 3rd IEEE International Conference on Data Mining pp. 513–516, ICDM 2003.
10. F. Coenen, P. Leng, A. Pagourtzis, W. Rytter, D. Souliou. Improved Methods for Extracting Frequent Itemsets from Interim-Support Trees. In Proc. of AI 2005.
11. J. Han, J. Pei, Y.Yin, and R. Mao. Mining Frequent Patterns without Candidate Generation: A Frequent-Pattern Tree Approach. *Data Mining and Knowledge Discovery*, pp. 53–87, 8 2004.
12. R. Raymon. Search Through Systematic Search Enumeration. In Proc. of the 3rd Internaltional Conference on Principles of Knowledge Representation and Reasoning, pp. 539–550 1992.
13. D. Souliou, A. Pagourtzis, N. Drosinos, P. Tsanakas. Computing Frequent Itemsets in Parallel Using Partial Support Trees. In Proceedings of 12th European PVM/MPI Conference (Euro PVM/MPI 2005), Sorrento (Naples), Italy, Lecture Notes in Computer Science 3666, pp. 28-37, Springer-Verlag 2005
14. Osmar R. Zaine Mohammad El-Hajj Paul Lu. Fast Parallel Association Rule Mining without Candidate Generation. In Proc. of ICDM 2001.

Section 5

Applications of AI in Industry and Daily Round

Genetic Algorithms for Municipal Solid Waste Collection and Routing Optimization

Nikolaos V. Karadimas, Katerina Papatzelou and Vassili G. Loumos
National Technical University of Athens,
School of Electrical and Computer Engineering,
Multimedia Technology Laboratory,
Heroon Polytechneiou 9, Zografou Campus, 157 80 Athens, Greece
e-mail:nkaradim@central.ntua.gr, rina310@gmail.com, loumos@cs.ntua.gr

Abstract. In the present paper, the Genetic Algorithm (GA) is used for the identification of optimal routes in the case of Municipal Solid Waste (MSW) collection. The identification of a route for MSW collection trucks is critical since it has been estimated that, of the total amount of money spent for the collection, transportation, and disposal of solid waste, approximately 60-80% is spent on the collection phase. Therefore, a small percentage improvement in the collection operation can result to a significant saving in the overall cost. The proposed MSW management system is based on a geo-referenced spatial database supported by a geographic information system (GIS). The GIS takes into account all the required parameters for solid waste collection. These parameters include static and dynamic data, such as the positions of waste bins, the road network and its related traffic, as well as the population density in the area under study. In addition, waste collection schedules, truck capacities and their characteristics are also taken into consideration. Spatio-temporal statistical analysis is used to estimate inter-relations between dynamic factors, like network traffic changes in residential and commercial areas. The user, in the proposed system, is able to define or modify all of the required dynamic factors for the creation of alternative initial scenarios. The objective of the system is to identify the most cost-effective scenario for waste collection, to estimate its running cost and to simulate its application.

1 Introduction

Nowadays, waste management is one of the main environmental and socio-economic problems, especially in towns and large cities which are densely populated. The rapid and constant growth in urban population led to a dramatic increase in urban

Please use the following format when citing this chapter:

Karadimas, N. V., Papatzelou, K., Loumos, V. G., 2007, in IFIP International Federation for Information Processing, Volume 247, Artificial Intelligence and Innovations 2007: From Theory to Applications, eds. Boukis, C., Pnevmatikakis, L., Polymenakos, L., (Boston: Springer), pp. 223-231.

solid waste production, which in turn forced many municipalities to assess their solid waste management program and examine its environmental and cost-effectiveness in terms of collection, transportation, processing and landfill.

The management of urban solid waste is a hard task since it is necessary to take into account conflicting objectives. Therefore, a multi-criteria urban waste management decision approach is needed. In order for the municipalities to implement sustainable management of urban solid waste, more comprehensive use of data collection and information systems is required. Information technology (IT) gave the development of information systems in waste management a boost. Direct database accessing, in combination with GIS-techniques, provide relevant information for visualization, planning and decision making of regional waste collection (for example planning routes, and forecasting the amount of needed trucks).

The identification of a route for MSW collection trucks is critical since it has been estimated that, of the total amount of money spent for the collection, transportation, and disposal of solid waste, approximately 60-80% is spent on the collection phase [1]. Therefore, a small percentage improvement in the collection operation can result to a significant saving in the overall cost.

The present paper mainly focuses on the collection and transport of solid waste from any loading spot in the area under study. In addition, other factors that affect the whole system will be mentioned and discussed. Of course, this research covers only the routes included in the given area, but can be applied to any other area, simply by changing the input data. Therefore, a framework (schema) for the design and implementation of a solution for the solid waste collection and routing is proposed. According to this schema, the genetic algorithm is introduced and implemented, for defining the optimal collection route. In the end, the results of the GA are also compared with the empirical method that the Municipality of Athens (MoA) uses to collect and transport the solid waste to the landfill site.

This scheme is described in the rest of the paper, first the theoretical and methodological aspects for urban solid waste management and the related work that has been done in this area is described. This is followed by an introduction to the waste management problem in the selected case study area. Thereafter the GA optimization algorithm is introduced and implemented for the area under study. The results of the GA algorithm and its comparison with the present empirical solution that the MoA uses are illustrated and conclusions are discussed.

2   Related Work

In the literature, many methods and algorithms have been used for optimizing routing aspects of solid waste collection networks. Many papers have modeled the optimization problem of urban waste collection and transport as various versions of the Arc Routing Problem (ARP) [2], [3], [4]. Nevertheless, the particular problem has been also modeled as a Vehicle Routing Problem (VRP) in which a set of waste trucks have to serve a set of waste bins minimizing the cost function while being subject to a number of constraints. The characteristics of the vehicles and of the constraints determine the various types of VRPs [5], [6], [7]. However, the speed distributions, from which the travel times can be calculated, are supposed to be known at the beginning of the optimization.

In addition, the routing problem of the solid waste collection process has been treated as a Traveling Salesman Problem (TSP), which can be formulated as finding the minimum of a function representing the route that visits all the nodes of a set, at least once. An Ant Colony System (ACS), a distributed algorithm inspired by the observation of real colonies of ants, has been presented [8], [9], for the solution of TSP and ATSP problems [10], [11]. Viotti et al. [12] introduce a Genetic Algorithm for solving the TSP and present its results. Poser and Awad [13] have developed a methodology based on real genetic algorithm for effectively solving the TSP in the field of solid waste routing system in the large cities.

In this context the problem is reduced to a Single Vehicle Origin Round trip Routing which is similar to the common Traveling Salesman Problem (TSP). The well-known combinatorial optimization problem, in which each waste truck, in this work, is required to minimize the total distance traveled to visit, only once, all the waste bins in its visiting list. In the traditional TSP, the cost of traveling (distance) between two waste bins does not depend on the direction of travel. Hence, the cost (distance) matrix representing the parameters of the problem is symmetric. However, the problem, which this work refers to, is modeled as an Asymmetric TSP (ATSP) problem due to road network restrictions. An ATSP problem considers that the bi-directional distances between a pair of waste bins are not necessarily identical. The ATSP problem can be solved to optimality using various algorithms. Some heuristic procedures for solving the symmetric version of the problem (TSP) can be easily modified for the asymmetric versions, but others are not. The objective of this paper is the application of a Genetic Algorithm for the identification of optimal routes in the case of Municipal Solid Waste (MSW) collection.

3   Case Study

In this research work, a small part of Attica's prefecture (a suburb of Athens) was chosen as the case study area. The MoA has empirically divided its area in about 122 solid waste collecting programs, where in general each one includes approximately 100 waste bins. Any garbage truck that is responsible for the collection of the solid waste in that given area must visit all the bins in order to complete its collection program.

This examined area is about $0.45Km^2$, with a population of more than 8,500 citizens and a production of about 3,800 tones of solid urban waste per year. The data concerning the area under examination was obtained from the pertinent Agency of the MoA. This data includes maps of the examined area with the correspondent annotation (address and numbering labels of streets), the building blocks and the locations of the existing waste bins. The waste bins locations were initially derived from a pilot program that the MoA was using for the allocation of their trucks.

Fig 1 illustrates the loading spots in the area under study (totally 72), in which each loading spot may represent one or more waste bins. The location of these loading spots was defined by the MoA to serve the needs of the present waste collection system. A different placement of the loading spots would assist the proposed model better but this issue is beyond the scope of the present paper. A method for optimal placement of waste bins is described in Karadimas et al. [15].

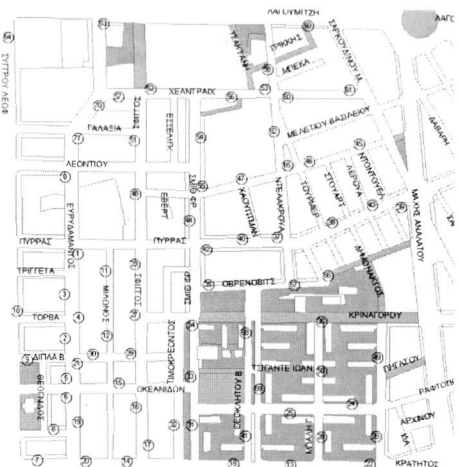

Fig. 1. The 72 dots, in the map of the study area, represent the loading spots that the Municipality presently uses.

Finally, the information stored in the aforementioned database such as the present sequence of the waste collection and transport that the Municipality uses (called the empirical method), has been compared to the derived results of the proposed algorithms in the following sections.

According to the above, the urban solid waste collection and transport is a complex problem with many limitations. Minimization of cost means minimization of collection time and not necessarily choosing the minimal route. In addition, each waste truck is able to collect a specific quantity of solid waste due to its limited waste capacity. So, the collected area, considering all parameters for that part of the problem, should be fragmented to sub programs, in which the produced quantity of solid waste is equal to or less than the capacity of each truck. Therefore, the problem in our case, as mentioned above, can be classified as a Asymmetric Traveling Salesman Problem (ATSP): "Given a set of n loading spots and the transport cost between any loading spots, the ATSP can be stated as the problem of finding a minimal cost closed tour that visits each loading spot only once and bi-directional distances between at least one pair of loading spots are not necessarily identical".

4   Genetic Algorithm Implementation

Genetic Algorithms (GA) were invented by John Holland [14] and his colleagues in the early 1970s and are inspired by Darwin's theory of evolution. GA use genetic operators such as selection, crossover, and mutation for the exploration of solutions to complex problems. Initially, GA randomly yields a population (set of candidate solutions or individuals). Each individual is characterized by certain fitness. In each iteration, a selection of individuals from the entire population takes place according to their fitness values and then the chosen solutions are perturbed (through the mechanisms of crossover or mutation) in order to yield a new generation. This process is repeated for a number of iterations until a predefined termination criterion is satisfied.

In the following paragraphs, the GA implementation is presented for the under study optimization problem. The initial population is randomly produced by GA implementation. **Fig 2** illustrates a snapshot of the GUI for our GA implementation. The candidate solutions which comprise the population are represented as a list showing the order in which the loading spots (nodes) are visited by the waste truck.

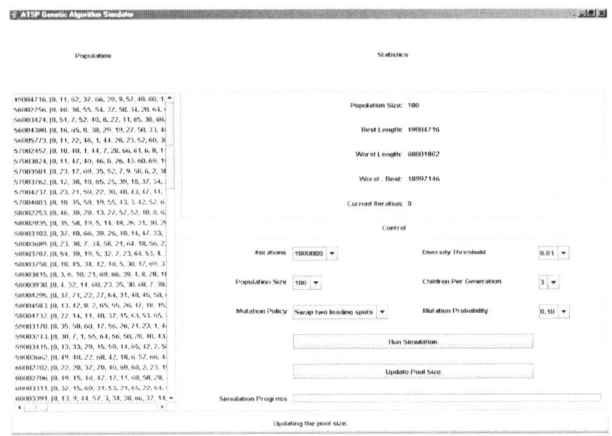

Fig. 2. The Graphical User Interface for the Genetic Algorithm implementation

The objective function is the minimization of the total tour length of the waste truck through a set of loading points. The population in the GA program evolves from one generation (iteration) to the next through the use of genetic operators. Three genetic operators are used in the GA program: Selection, Crossover and Mutation.

During the *selection* operation, the algorithm selects one parent from the top half of the candidate solutions (population) and the other parent from anywhere inside the population. This tends to slightly favor the "fitter" individuals since the candidate solutions of the population are sorted by tour length.

The operation of *crossover* selects two loading spots from inside a tour. Next, the sub-tour of one of the parents (between these two points) is copied directly to the child. The remaining loading spots in the tour are places around the child's sub-tour in the same order that they occur in the other parent.

Finally, in the *mutation* phase, two different functions are used. The user can select the mutation operator of his preference through the user interface. The first method simply reverses a random sub-tour in a given tour. The second randomly selects two loading spots and swaps their positions. Through experimentation, it was discovered that that the second mutation mechanism yielded better results than the first one. To sum up, it is worth mentioning that the values for all the parameters of the GA (iterations, population size, mutation policy, mutation probability, diversity threshold and children per generation) are user configurable and good parameter tuning is essential for the GA to produce satisfactory solutions.

5   Results of Genetic Algorithm

In order to execute the GA, the user should adjust the values of the following six parameters: *Iterations, Population, Children per Generation, Mutation Policy, Mutation Probability* and *Diversity Threshold*. The values of the parameters of this algorithm can be selected from the following set of values:

- *Iterations* $\in$ {100,000, 1,000,000},
- *Population* $\in$ {20, 50, 72, 100, 144, 300},
- *Children per Generation* $\in$ {1, 2, 3, 4, 5},
- *Mutation Policy* $\in$ {Swap two loading spots, Reverse sub tour},
- *Mutation Probability* $\in$ {0, 0.05, 0.1, 0.2, 0.4, 0.8} and
- *Diversity Threshold* $\in$ {0, 0.01, 0.05, 0.1, 0.5}

In order to cover all the possible solutions that the aforementioned parameter settings can produce, there are 3,600 different combinations, which make the testing process even more difficult. The set of values for the GA parameters presented above is common in the literature and this is why they have chosen. Through the process of trial and error the GA has been executed more than 1,200 times in order to find the best parameters values combination. **Table 1** presents the total number of the GA algorithm execution and the acceptable solution (solutions which their values are less than 1,000,000) as well as the number of the solutions which are better than the empirical one. Besides **Fig 3** illustrates the distribution of these solutions (accepted and not accepted) yielded by the GA.

Table 1. The analysis of experimental results for GA.

Num of runs	Not accepted	Accepted		
		Better	Worse	Total
12,000	10,200	450	1,350	1,800

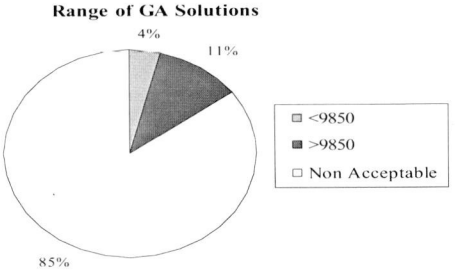

Fig. 3. A pie depicting the range of the solutions yielded by GA.

Eventually, the best result of this algorithm stemmed from the following parameter setting:

- *Iterations*: 200,000,
- *Population*: 100,
- *Children per Generation*: 5,
- *Mutation Policy*:
  - Swap 2 Loading Spots - the 1st 100,000 *iterations* (9,084) and
  - Reverse Subtour - the 2nd 100,000 *iterations* (8,902),
- *Mutation Probability*: 0.1,
- *Diversity Threshold*: 0.01.

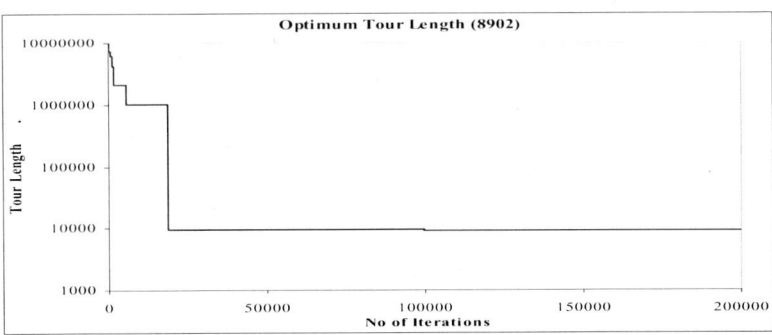

Fig. 4. The best result of the Genetic Algorithm.

Fig 4 illustrates the graphical representation of the best result of GA execution (8,902). The algorithm converges in the first 21,000 iterations and in the following iterations only a slight improvement is achieved. In general, a considerable number of iterations are required in order for the GA to yield satisfactory solutions. Subsequently, the computation time required is sizeable and this was detrimental to the testing. Practically, the algorithm converges at the final optimum solution in approximately 15,000 iterations. Therefore, the algorithm produces good results from the first 10% of the algorithm executions even for the experiments that have been executed for 2,000,000 iterations. That is the reason that the executions of the algorithm have been arranged at 100,000 iterations.

Concluding, Table 2 illustrates the best solution, that GA produce, which has a significantly improvement (9.62%) in comparison to the respective of the empirical method which is currently used by MoA (9,850).

Table 2. The comparison between the best GA solution and the empirical model

Empirical Model (meter)	GA Optimized route (meter)	Improvement (%)
9,850	8,902	9.62%

6   Conclusions

This work focuses on the collection and transport of solid waste from waste bins in the area under study. The Genetic Algorithm is introduced and implemented, for monitoring, simulation, testing, and route optimization of alternative scenarios for a solid waste management system.

The first experiments have shown that applying the GA for the solution of this every day problem – the collection of urban solid waste – can greatly minimize the collection tour length and eventually the total cost in time and money. However, as it was reported above, the particular problem is much more complicated than presented in the current work. The proposed methodology was applied in a region of the MoA which contains a quantity of solid waste equal to the capacity of the waste truck used in this particular area. Therefore, the problem was transformed into a classic TSP problem.

Although the case study covers an area of about 0.45 km^2, 8,500 citizens and over 100 building blocks, to ensure the reliability of the derived results, a future prospect of this work is that the proposed model should be tested in an even more extended area.

References

1.   Municipality Of Athens. Estimation, Evaluation and Planning Of Actions for Municipal Solid Waste Services During Olympic Games 2004. Athens, Greece. (2003)
2.   V. Maniezzo, Algorithms for large directed CARP instances: urban solid waste collection operational support, Technical Report UBLCS-2004-16, (2004).
3.   S.K. Amponsah and S. Salhi, The investigation of a class of capacitated arc routing problems: the collection of garbage in developing countries, *Waste Management* 24, 711-721, (2004).
4.   G. Ghiani, F. Guerriero, G. Improta and R. Musmannod, Waste collection in Southern Italy: solution of a real-life arc routing problem, *Intl. Trans. in Op. Res.* 12, 135-144, (2005).

5. S. Sahoo, S. Kim and B.I. Kim, Routing Optimization for Waste Management, *Interfaces Journal (SCIE)*, *Informs (OR/MS)*, 35(1), 24-36, (2005).
6. B. Bullnheimer, R.F. Hartl, and C. Strauss, Applying the ant system to the vehicle routing problem. In: Osman, I.H., Voss, S., Martello, S. & Roucairol C. (eds): *Meta-Heuristics: Advances and Trends in Local Search Paradigms for Optimization*, (Kluwer Academic Publishers, Dordrecht, The Netherlands, 1998), pp. 109–120.
7. A.V. Donati, R. Montemanni, N. Casagrande, A.E. Rizzoli, and L.M. Gambardella, Time-dependent Vehicle Routing Problem with a Multi Ant Colony System, Technical Report TR-17-03, IDSIA, Galleria 2, Manno, Switzerland (2003).
8. M. Dorigo, V. Maniezzo and A. Colorni, The ant system: optimization by a colony of cooperating agents, *IEEE Transactions on Systems, Man and Cybernetics*, 26(1), 1-13, (1996).
9. M. Dorigo and L.M. Gambardella, Ant Colony System: A Cooperative Learning Approach to the Traveling Salesman Problem, *IEEE Transactions on Evolutionary Computation*, 1(1) (1997).
10. N.V. Karadimas, G. Kouzas, I. Anagnostopoulos and V. Loumos, Urban Solid Waste Collection and Routing: The Ant Colony Strategic Approach. *International Journal of Simulation: Systems, Science & Technology*, 6(12-13), 45-53, (2005).
11. N.V. Karadimas, K. Papatzelou and V.G. Loumos, Optimal solid waste collection routes identified by the ant colony system algorithm, *Waste Management & Research* 25, 139-147, (2007).
12. P. Viotti, A. Pelettini, R. Pomi and C. Innocetti, Genetic algorithms as a promising tool for optimisation of the MSW collection routes, *Waste Management Research*, 21, 292–298, (2003).
13. I. von Poser, A.R. Awad, Optimal Routing for Solid Waste Collection in Cities by Using Real Genetic Algorithm, *Information and Communication Technologies*, ICTTA '06, 1, 221-226, (2006).
14. J.H. Holland, Adaptation in Natural and Artificial Systems: An Introductory Analysis With Applications to Biology, Control, and Artificial Intelligence, MIT Press, 1992. First Published by University of Michigan Press 1975.
15. N.V. Karadimas, O. Mavrantza and V. Loumos, GIS Integrated Waste Production Modelling. IEEE EUROCON 2005- The International Conference on "Computer as a Tool", Belgrade, 22-24 November, pp. 1279-1282. Serbia & Montenegro, (2005).

A Multi-Agent Design for a Home Automation System dedicated to power management

Shadi ABRAS[1], Stéphane PLOIX[2], Sylvie PESTY[1], and Mireille JACOMINO[2]

[1] Laboratoire LIG-Institut IMAG,CNRS, UMR5217,
[2] Laboratoire G-SCOP, CNRS, UMR5528,
46, Avenue Félix Viallet, 38031 Grenoble, France.
Phone: 00 33 4 76 57 50 59, Fax: 00 33 4 76 57 46 02
{Shadi.Abras, Sylvie.Pesty}@imag.fr
{Stephane.Ploix, Mireille.Jacomino}@inpg.fr

Abstract. This paper presents the principles of a Home Automation System dedicated to power management that adapts power consumption to available power ressources according to user comfort and cost criteria. The system relies on a multi-agent paradigm. Each agent, supporting a type of service achieved by one or several devices, cooperates and coordinates its action with others in order to find an acceptable near-optimal solution. The control algorithm is decomposed into two complementary mechanisms: a reactive mechanism, which protects from constraint violations, and an anticipation mechanism, which computes a predicted plan of global consumption according to predicted productions and consumptions and to user criteria. The paper presents a design for the Multi Agent Home Automation System.

1 Introduction

A building is both a place of power consumption and potentially a place of decentralized power production using resources like wind, solar, geothermal, etc. The resort to renewable power resources comes up in homes knowing that buildings represent 47% of the global power consumption [2]. Therefore, the design of a control system which allows the exploitation of different energy resources, while managing globally the power needs and the production capacity of a home, is an upcoming issue.

The role of a Home Automation System dedicated to power management is to adapt the power consumption to the available power resources, and vice verse, taking into account inhabitant comfort criteria. It has to reach a compromise between the priorities of inhabitants in terms of comfort and cost.

Algorithms based on MAS are nowadays used in several areas such as Computer Science or Automatic Control. The design of solutions based on Multi-Agent Systems, which are well suited to solve spatially distributed and open problems, facilitates the design of an intelligent **M**ulti-**A**gent **H**ome **A**utomation **S**ystem

Please use the following format when citing this chapter:

Abras, S., Ploix, S., Pesty, S., Jacomino, M., 2007, in IFIP International Federation for Information Processing, Volume 247, Artificial Intelligence and Innovations 2007: From Theory to Applications, eds. Boukis, C., Pnevmatikakis, L., Polymenakos, L., (Boston: Springer), pp. 233-241.

(*MAHAS*). This paper presents the architecture of a MAHAS and shows why a MAS are particularly well suited for this class of problems.

2 Multi-Agent Home Automation System

A MAHAS consists of agents, each agent supports one type of service (heating, cooking, etc) achieved by one or several devices. The main features of the MAHAS are the following:

- Distributed: the energy resources and devices are independent and spatially distributed.
- Flexible: some devices can accumulate energy (different kinds of heating services) or satisfy with a timed delay the demands of inhabitants (washing service, etc).
- Open: the number of connected resources and devices may vary with time without having to completely redefine the control mechanism.
- Extendable: agents dedicated to new kinds of services may appear.

In MAS, the notion of control involves operations such as coordination and negotiation among agents, elimination of agents and addition of new agents when needed. Depending on weather forecasts, power resource information and inhabitant habits:

- an agent, dedicated to a power source, is assumed to be capable of calculating the future available power production.
- an agent, dedicated to a load, is assumed to be capable of calculating the prediction of power consumption: to determine what are the future power needs taking into account the usual behaviour of inhabitants.

In MAHAS, an additional agent is responsible for broadcasting the computed predicted plans to the other agents.
The structure of the MAHAS is decomposed into two main mechanisms: the reactive mechanism and the anticipation mechanism.

2.1 Reactive mechanism

The reactive mechanism is a short time adjustment mechanism which is triggered when the level of satisfaction of an agent falls below weak values (10% for example). This mechanism, which relies on the negotiation protocol [1], reacts quickly to avoid violations of energy constraints due to unpredicted perturbations and to guarantee a good level of inhabitant satisfaction. Therefore, the reactive mechanism adjusts, with a short sample time, the set points coming from the predicted plan, the device's current state (device satisfaction value) and the constraints and inhabitant criteria.

2.2 Anticipative mechanism

The reactive mechanism is sufficient to avoid constraint violations but a MA-HAS can be improved in order to avoid frequent emergency situations. This improvement is obtained due to the anticipation mechanism. The objective of this mechanism is to compute plans for production and consumption of services in a house. The anticipation mechanism benefits from, on the one hand, some devices are capable of accumulating energy, and on the other hand, some services have a variable date for their execution: some services can be either delayed or advanced. From these preliminary observations, it is possible to imagine that if the device consumption can be anticipated, there is a way to organize it better.

It works on a time window, which corresponds to a sampling period called the anticipative period. This period is greater than the one used by the reactive mechanism (typically 10 times). Because of the large sampling period, it considers average values of energy. This is an advantage when considering prediction because it is difficult to make precise predictions. The predicted set points can be directly transmitted to devices or adjusted by the reactive mechanism in case of constraint violation.

Because the reactive mechanism has been presented in detail in [1], this paper focuses on the anticipative mechanism.

3 M.A.H.A.S modelling

One of the objectives of the MAHAS is to fulfil inhabitant comfort, a notion which can be linked directly to the concept of satisfaction function [5]. Satisfaction functions have been defined for power resources as well as for devices. A satisfaction function is expressed by a function defined from the domain of characteristic variables to the interval $[0, 1]$. In MAHAS, satisfaction characterizes the inhabitant's feeling about a service where zero means "unacceptable" and 1 means "fully satisfied". For example, satisfaction function for a thermal air environment is based on room temperature values (figure 1). For instance, figure 1 can be represented by the set $\{(TMIN(heating), 0), (TPRE(heating), 1), (TMAX(heating), 0)\}$, it is implicitly assumed that before the first abscisse and after the last one, the satisfaction is null. A Home Automation System aims at

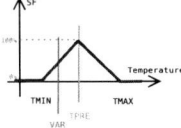

Fig. 1. *Thermal air environment satisfaction function.*

reaching a compromise between the inhabitant requests in terms of comfort and cost while satisfying technological constraints of devices. A MAHAS takes into account the price variation because the energy providers could charge inhabitants for the actual energy production cost in real time. Therefore, a MAHAS aims at minimizing the cost while maximizing the users comfort.

To optimize the criteria, the agents (figure 2) must communicate and cooperate in exchanging messages based on a common knowledge model. As mentioned

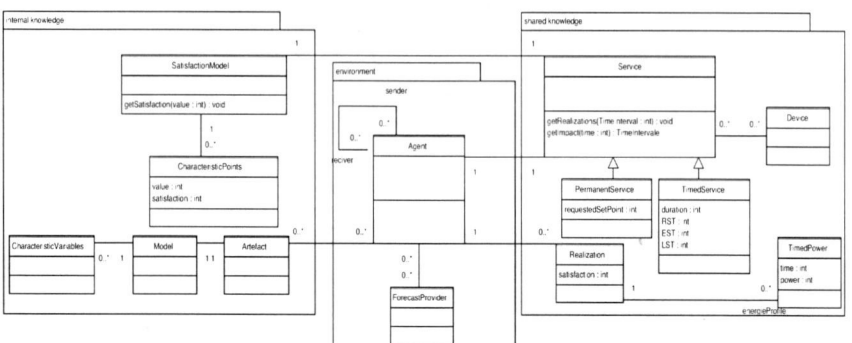

Fig. 2. *MAHAS UML model.*

in section 2, a MAHAS is "open" and "extendable" and because there are many kinds of services in a home, which provide predictions based on specific physical constraints, some knowledge are not shareable. It is indeed very difficult to formalize in a UML class diagram the structure of a general model, which can be composed of differential equations, recurrent equations, state machine, rules or a mix of all. It is all the more difficult that the system is extendable, it is not possible to circumscribe all the possible kinds of models. Just like for humans, some knowledge cannot be formalized in a general way. MAHAS is particularly suited because agents endowed into devices may embed their own knowledge and exchange messages based only on shareable knowledge which can be analysed by all the agents (for example: a power profile of a service represents a series of consumed or supplied powers corresponding to consecutive sampling periods). These shared data have to be formalized in a standardized form. In figure 2, an agent has its internal knowledge that gathers all the data that cannot be formalized in a general manner. Each agent embeds non-shareable piece of knowledge, build up its own representation of its environment, including other agents and interacts with other agents with a protocol [1] that deals with shareable knowledge.

3.1 Agent modelling

In the MAHAS, an agent supports a service $SRV_i \in SRVS$ where $SRVS$ is the set of all services. A service SRV_i may be either a timed service, denoted SRV_i^T , or a permanent service, denoted SRV_i^P, achieved by one or several devices, knowing that a device may also achieve many services.

Modelling of a timed service agent A timed service corresponds to power profiles during a given period; the flexibility of the service comes from the possibility that it may shifted. The internal knowledge of a timed service agent is modeled by:

- a characteristic variable which corresponds to the starting time of the service.
- a behavioral model that defines the possible power profiles once the service has been started.
- a satisfaction function defined from the set of possible starting time to the set of possible satisfaction values. The parameters of the satisfaction function may be gathered in a set of characteristic points: $\{(EST(SRV_i), 0), (RST(SRV_i), 1), (LST(SRV_i), 0)\}$ that represent respectively the earliest (unacceptable satisfaction), requested (fully satisfied) and latest starting times for the timed service.

A realization for a timed service agent represents the shared knowledge about a timed service. It is composed of:

- a power profile: $\Pi = [POW(SRV_i)_0, \ldots, POW(SRV_i)_n]$ where $POW(SRV_i)_j \neq 0$ represents the average power consumption/production (negative/positive) of the service during the kth sampling period. The duration of a service is determined by the length of the power profile $length(\Pi)$.
- a satisfaction value which depends on the starting time of the service.

A realization corresponds to an instantiated power profile denoted: $REAZ(SRV_i^T) = (k, \Pi, \sigma)$, where k is the selected starting sampling period, Π is the power profile and σ is the satisfaction value modelling the inhabitant's feeling about this realization.

Modelling of a permanent service agent A permanent service corresponds to power profiles covering a given period. The flexibility of the service comes from the possibility of adjusting energy allocation from time to time. The internal knowledge of a permanent service agent is modeled by:

- a behavioral model linking the power profile to effect an inhabitant environment.
- a satisfaction function defined from a set of variables computed by the behavioral model to the set of possible satisfaction values. The parameters of the satisfaction function may be gathered in a set of characteristic points.

A realization for a permanent service agent represents the shared knowledge of a timed service. It is composed of:

- a power profile: $\Pi = [\ldots, POW(SRV_i)_k, \ldots]$ where $POW(SRV_i)_k$ represents the average power consumption/production during the kth period.
- a satisfaction value. Even if a realization covers several periods, there is only one value that models the inhabitant resulting satisfaction for the whole considered period: it is usually equal to the minimum of the satisfaction values computed for each period.

A realization corresponds to an instantiated power profile denoted: $REAZ(SRV_i^P) = (k, \Pi, \sigma)$, where Π is a power profile from the sampling period $[k, k + length(\Pi)]$ and σ is a satisfaction value modelling the inhabitant's feeling about this realization.

Let's define the notion of impact of a service for a given sampling period k. It corresponds to the set of realizations for a service SRV_i, which is affected by a change of power affectation at the given time k. For a permanent service, the impact coresponds to $[k - p, k + p]$ where $p \times \Delta$ corresponds to the time response of the related devices. For a timed service, it coresponds to the set of realizations defined at k.

Even if the methods for solving the optimization problem may provide good solutions, they still require long computation times and considerable working memory because the complexity is NP-Hard [4]. A relevant optimization strategy (section 4), exploiting the nature of the Home Automation System problem, is a promising avenue for performance improvement.

4 Optimization strategy

An intelligent power management problem in buildings can be divided into sub-problems involving different agents because, generally, inhabitants do not use their devices most of the time. The basic principle is to divide the whole problem into independent sub-problems then to solve each sub-problem independently in order to find a solution for the whole problem. The advantage of this method is to reduce the complexity of the whole problem which depends on the number of periods for each sub-problem and on the number of devices. When the whole problem is divided into sub-problems, each sub-problem does not involve all of the services (for example: some inhabitants vacuum clean in the morning and not in the evening). Because the number of considered periods in a sub-problem is lower than the number of periods of the whole problem [3], the complexity of solving the sub-problems is less than the complexity of solving the whole problem at once.

The principle of the division of the problem into sub-problems is described in the following procedure:

- procedure *solving of the whole problem*
-     distribute the energy over all periods for all the services according to the inhabitant's satisfaction;
-     *if* insufficient energy for some periods *then*
-       detect sub-problems;
-       determine the time interval for each sub-problem;
-       solve each sub-problem separately;
-       merge the sub-problems solutions to obtain a global plan;
-     *else* a solution according to the inhabitant's satisfaction is selected;
-     *end if*;
- *end procedure*;

This procedure is described in the next sub-sections.

4.1 Energy distribution

The search for the global solution starts by distributing the available energy over all the periods for all the services according to the inhabitant's fully satisfaction where agents provide realizations with a satisfaction value equal to 1 and where agents, dedicated to a power resource, provide one realization that is the best prediction over all periods. When agents has several realizations with a satisfaction equal to 1, the solving agent verifies, using the Bellman-Ford's algorithm, if the agent realizations are acceptable or not according to the available energy. At the end of the energy distribution, if there is enough energy for all devices, the search for a solution is stopped and a solution according to the inhabitant's fully satisfaction is obtained. But if there is not enough energy for all devices, sub-problems will be detected (sub-section 4.2) and then will be solved (sub-section 4.3).

4.2 Determination of the sub-problem interval

When the service agents suppling power have not enough power for all devices, the solving agent sends the periods for which there is not enough energy to all permanent and timed service agents. To obtain independent sub-problems, it is necessary to determine the service influences over theses periods. The principle of the sub-problem interval determination is described as follows:
First, compute the earliest and the latest starting time for the timed services:

– each realization of a timed service agent is characterized by a starting time, an ending time (equal to the starting time plus the length of the power profile).
– each timed service agent sends their intervals to the solving agent.

Each permanent service agent sends its impact to the solving agent.
The solving agent creates several intervals (sub-problem intervals) depending on the number of periods where there is not enough energy.

– The solving agent verifies the intersection between the sub-problem intervals and the earliest and the latest time of the timed services; it chooses the minimum value between the earliest time and the inferior bound of the interval and the maximum value between the latest time and the superior bound of the interval.
– The solving agent adds the impact of the permanent agent to the sub-problem intervals; the fact of adding the impact of permanent service agents increases the interval of the sub-problem but it guarantees that there is no influence on the previous or next periods.
– The solving agent merges two sub-problem intervals if there is an intersection between these two sub-problem intervals.

Then the solving agent sends the sub-problems intervals to all agents.

4.3 Resolution of a sub-problem

The solving agent computes a predicted plan for each sub-problem using the Tabu Search (TS) algorithm [6]. The basic principles of TS for the MAHAS problem are the following: the search for a solution starts from the initial solution found at the energy distribution step. At each iteration, the solving agent decreases the satisfaction interval (for example 5% for each time) and sends it with the best realizations (according to a combination of cost and comfort criteria) at the previous iteration to the agents; agents computes the neighborhood of the realization sent by the solving agent by generating a given number of realizations corresponding to the satisfaction interval. When the solving agent receives the agent realizations, it chooses the realizations that violate the constraints the less as possible. The search is stopped when the collected realizations do not violate the global power constraints and when the global satisfaction has converged. Because the number of realizations corresponding to a satisfaction interval is very high, an agent generates randomly theses realizations corresponding to the satisfaction in performing elementary step from the realization selected by the solving agent at the previous iteration knowing that an agent realization will not be generated and sent twice to the solving agent.

5 Conclusion

This paper has presented the principles of a MAHAS which allows the agents to cooperate and coordinate their actions in order to find an acceptable near-optimal solution for power management. A cooperation mechanism that reduces the problem complexity has been detailed. It has also been shown why autonomous and cooperative agent are particularly well suited for spatially distributed, flexible, open and extendable context such as power management in buildings, in pointing out that there is non shareable knowledge. This feature is a clear improvement over the capabilities provided by current Automatic Controlled Systems. A simulator has been designed and results let imagine a new way for producing and consuming power. The next step is the implementation in a real building.

References

1. Abras, S., Ploix, S., Pesty, S., and Jacomino, M. (2006). A multi-agent home automation system for power managememnt. In *Proceedings of the Third International Conference in Control, Automation, and Robotics, ICINCO 2006*, pages 3–8, Setúbal, Portugal.
2. Fontaine, N. (2003). Livre blanc sur les énergies. *débat national sur les énergies*, http://www.industrie.gouv.fr/energie/politiqu/ploe.htm.

3. Habbas, Z., M. Krajecki and D. Singer (2005). Decomposition techniques for parallel resolution of constraint satisfaction problems in shared memory: a comparative study. *International Journal of Computational Science and Engineering (IJCSE)* **1**(2), 192–206.

4. Garey, M. R. and D. S. Johnson (1979). *Computers and Intractability: A Guide to the Theory of NP-Completeness*. W.H. Freeman and Co. New York, USA.

5. Lucidarme, P., O. Simonin and A. Liégeois (2002). Implementation and evaluation of a satisfaction/altruism based architecture for multi-robot systems. In: *Proceedings of the 2002 IEEE International Conference on Robotics and Automation*. Washington, USA. pp. 1007–1012.

6. N. Koji and I. Toshihide. A tabu search approach to the constraint satisfaction problem as a general problem solver. *European Journal of Operational Research*, 106:599–623, 1998.

Domain of impact for agents collaborating in a baggage handling system*

Kasper Hallenborg

Maersk Mc-Kinney Moller Institute
University of Southern Denmark
Odense M, 5230, Denmark
hallenborg@mmmi.sdu.dk

Abstract. Recognize the frustration of waiting in slow starting queues? Acceleration ramps and reaction times make traffic queues frustrating to many people every day. Similar problems arise in many production and material handling systems.

In this paper we present research activities conducted on a baggage handling system (BHS) of a large airport hub in Asia, where we have applied an intelligent multi-agent based approach to control the flow of bags on the BHS. By exchanging a centralized control system with an agent-based solution, local queues can be avoided or minimized, which increase the overall performance of the BHS.

Through an established community of highly collaborating and coordinating agents, each agent can, based on its relative placement in the topology of the BHS, decide whether it is appropriate to route more bags through this node relative to the overall system load. The agent-based approach not only improves robustness of the system, and utilize the entire BHS in a more convenient and dynamical way, it also include strategies for maximizing capacity of the system.

We present results from ongoing work of developing suitable and proficient algorithms and agent collaboration schemes to increase the performance of the BHS. In this paper we pay special attention to the impact of the relative physical displacement of the agents in the system.

Key words: Multi-agent systems, decision logic, production systems, graphs

1.1 Introduction

For historic reasons (The Denver Airport software scandal) the Airport industry has been rather conservative about introducing new approaches and intelligent control in baggage handling systems.

A baggage handling system (BHS) transfers baggage in major airports between the arrival and departure gates, and from early check-ins. In setup and

---

* This research was supported by The Ministry of Science, Technology and Innovation in Denmark under the IT Cooridor Foundation

---

Please use the following format when citing this chapter:

Hallenborg, K., 2007, in IFIP International Federation for Information Processing, Volume 247, Artificial Intelligence and Innovations 2007: From Theory to Applications, eds. Boukis, C., Pnevmatikakis, L., Polymenakos, L., (Boston: Springer), pp. 243-250.

functionality a BHS is comparable to many manufacturing systems - bags enter the system through various channels, undergo various processing (mainly routing), before it leaves the BHS at the departure gates.

A BHS is a huge mechanical system, usually composed of conveyor-like modules capable of transferring totes (plastic barrels) carrying one bag each[2]. We have researched a BHS for a major airport hub in Asia, with more than 5000 modular components each with a length of 2-9 m running at speeds from 2-7 m/s. The BHS alone can easily be up to 20 km. in total length and may cover an area of up to 600.000 m^2. A BHS should be capable of handling more than 100.000 pieces of baggage every day, and for the researched airport the maximum allowed transfer time is 8-11 minutes for a distance of up to 2.5 km.

1.1.1 Main functionality

The core task of a BHS is transferring bags from A to B, but a highly dynamic environment complicates the control and optimization of capacity in the system. Changes in flight schedules, lost baggage information, and breakdowns are factors, which in combination with peak loads on the system result in queues and delayed baggage. Dischargers at the departure gates are temporarily allocated to one or more flights. Totes carrying bags are discharged (unloaded) when they reach the correct discharger according to their flight destination. Identity and destination of the bags is unknown until scanned at the input facility. After discharge the empty tote continues on the BHS back to the input facility sharing the conveyor lanes with other full totes. Thus routing of empty totes clearly impact the performance of the BHS. As no reliable model exists for arrival of bags to the system, and given the complexity of the BHS and time constraints of travelling bags (5-12 min as allowed max. transfer time) makes exact off-line scheduling impossible. Because totes or DCVs in many systems have to stop or slow down when discharging or unloading, respectively, the capacity for that lane section goes down, and a queue can accumulate behind the discharger, therefore more dischargers are often allocated to the same flight in order to distribute the load on the entire BHS. Traditionally the control software of the BHS is built on a simple reliable centralized approach based on static shortest paths of the system. Each pre-calculated route between toploaders and dischargers are given a route number and when the destination of a bag is known by the system, it follows that route until it reaches the destination.

Thus the structure, complexity and task make it an appropriate candidate for a decentralized agent-based control system with local observations.

1.1.2 MAS technology

MAS technology, which spawned from artificial intelligence as DAI (Distributed Artificial Intelligence) [?], offers an approach to decompose complexity of systems into a number of collaborating autonomous agents. System-wide tasks are

---

[2] Some BHSs are based on AGV-like telecars, which autonomously run on the BHS

solved partly by subtasks in the individual agents, which are coordinated and aligned through their interaction patterns. Interaction schemes and communication protocols for agents can be specified or programmed in an ad-hoc or domain specific manner, but to increase common understanding and platform independence, FIPA provides a set of specifications for interaction protocols supporting both negotiation and co-ordination between agents [?].

1.1.3 DECIDE project

Our research case of the BHS is conducted in collaboration with the company installing and producing the BHS, FKI Logistex. This case is part of a larger research project called DECIDE, which focus on promoting and proving the appropriateness of multi-agent based control in production and manufacturing systems. Major Danish manufactures are among the other partners of the consortium: Lego, Grundfos, Bang and Olufsen (B&O), and Odense Steel Shipyard.

1.2 System setup

Recent years advancement in computer performance has made it possible to do realistic real-time simulations of very complex environments. The ability to continuously interact with the simulation model during operation creates a perfect off-site test-suite for the control-software, which emulates the real BHS.

Together with another consortium partner, Simcon, the BHS company FKI Logistex has created an emulation model of the researched BHS using the Auto-Mod simulation and modeling package [?][3]. One of the strong advantages of using AutoMod is concurrent communication with the model identical to the connection between the control server and the PLCs in the real hardware. Thus the control software cannot see the difference, if it is connected to the emulation model or the real hardware. A snapshot of the emulation model is shown in the figure 1.1. It shows the area with input facilities for terminal 3 of the airport.

1.2.1 Modeling with agents

In abstract form the BHS can be understood as a directed graph of connected nodes, which represent elements of the real BHS, where it is possible to load, unload, or redirect the totes (toploading, discharging, merging, and diverting elements). Given the layout of the BHS no practical arguments exists for making decisions for a tote between nodes of the graphs. Thus an intuitive approach to decompose the decision logic to a multi-agent system is to place agents in each node corresponding to diverters, mergers, toploaders, dischargers, etc.

---

[3] AutoMod is a de-facto standard for systems analysis of manufacturing and material handling systems.

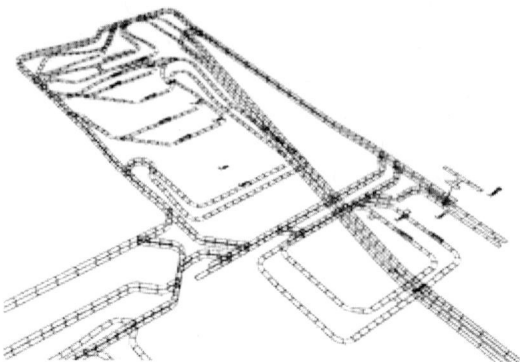

Fig. 1.1. Snapshot of the input area of the investigated BHS

If the design of the agents is simple and intuitive, the modeling of the associations and collaborations between the agents are far more complex. Ideally, with respect to generality and simplicity in the design of the agents and control software, the domain of observation for each agent should only span the edges from the agent's node to the next node in the graph (input and output lanes of conveyors at each node). But for some decisions, agents require more information about the current status of the load on the entire system, e.g. when deciding between alternative dischargers far from the current location.

Forced by both economical and architectural constraints of the airport, the layout of the BHS would usually have a rather low density of lanes and alternative routes compared to communication networks or traffic systems. The low density of connections in the graphs and the limited number of alternatives routes, makes the BHS less appropriate for intelligent network routing algorithms, such as ant-based control by Schoonderwoerd et al. [?] or AntNet by Di Caro and Dorigo [?]. Another important difference between communication strategies and the flow of bags in the BHS, is that a package can always be resubmitted in a package-switched network, that is not an option in the design of a BHS. In contrast to traffic control systems the BHS is actual aware of the correct destination for a tote, as soon as the bags enters the BHS, which makes it more attractive to use more system-wide collaboration of the agents. This could be achieved by assisting the local node agents with a number of mediator agents, which can be queried by local agents about information of routes through the entire system in order to discover, which agents to collaborate and negotiate with. Mediator agents can become a bottleneck or single-point-of-failure points of the system. Another approach is to profile each agent with some relevant knowledge of the topology of the BHS. We have successfully worked with both approaches with no significant difference, besides a lager communication overhead in a mediator based solution.

The important aspect is not how an agent discovers other agents to collaborate and negotiate with in order to route a current tote correctly, but which impact these different agents should have on the decision in the local agent.

As all destinations somehow can be reached from anywhere in the system, one could argue that the status and load of every node in the system should be considered at every decision point, but then complexity increases exponentially, and is both practical impossible and inappropriate for performance reasons. For capacity and space utilization reasons a BHS is often built with 2 or more layers of conveyors vertically displaced. Dischargers placed above each other are usually allocated to the same flight, because an even distribution of totes to two dischargers copes with the lower capacity of dischargers compared to traditional lane elements (discharging is 2 times slower than average lane speed). Due to cost there is only few locations (2-3), where you can go from one layer to another. Thus making the right decision at these points is far more important than minor redirection on the same layer - similar to the importance of taking the right exit on a highway compared to turns in a denser road system of a city.

In the following section we will present different strategies used for different type of decisions in the BHS, to illustrate the importance of considering the domain of impact on the agent's decision logic.

1.3 Agent strategies

The primary reason for exchanging the conventional control software with an agent-based approach is to decrease complexity and minimize dependencies in the control logic of the BHS. A multi-agent solution allows more advanced strategies to be used because the control logic of each node is simple, and altogether both capacity and robustness should be increased.

The basic building block in the strategies of the agents are simple observations of the local neighborhood of each agent - status or queue observations. Each node agent in the BHS collects information about the status of its local domain, which means the conveyor lanes to the previous and the following nodes in the graph. The information collected expose values of a edge/lane, such as the number of totes per element, the average delay for totes, and the average urgency of bags, which means how close a bag is to its departure (in time).

1.3.1 Overtaking urgent bags

An example of a collaborating strategy, which has a little impact on the domain of neighboring mergers and diverters, allows urgent bags to overtake non-urgent bags, by detouring non-urgent bags. Consider a typical layout of a discharging area in figure 1.2. The bottom lane is a fast forward transport line, the middle a slower lane with the dischargers and the upper lane is the return path. A diverter (in the bottom lane) has the option to detour non-urgent to the middle lane to give way for urgent baggage in the transport line. If there is no load on the system all totes follows the shortest path. When the routes merge again at the mergers in the middle lane, it will give higher priority to totes from the merging leg with the most urgent baggage.

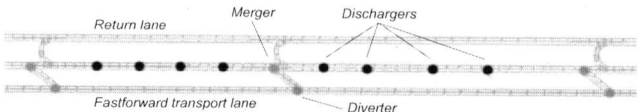

Fig. 1.2. Snapshot of the BHS layout with indication of diverters, mergers, and dischargers

The urgency observation in a node agent is composed of two custom fuzzy sets created from standard hedges [?], which are biased towards a desired neutral point of urgency. Then urgency of a bag goes exponentially up as it approaches departure, and turns negative if it has more than 20 min. to departure. Thus likelihood of detouring is directly given from the urgency information.

The strategy presented above allows urgent baggage to overtake baggage that have plenty of time to departure, is an example of a strategy, where the domain of impact only range between two succeeding nodes of the graph. Experiments showed impressive results without extending the domain of impact.

The strategy for returning empty totes to tote stackers, which are located close to the toploaders, is an example of collaboration between agents, where the domain is much broader and many agents participate. The full status of each tote stacker is, similar to the urgency status of the nodes, composed of fuzzy sets, which secures that the request for empty totes increases exponentially, when the tote stacker is almost empty. Besides the status of the tote stacker also the distance to the tote stacker should be considered, it gives no sense to route an empty tote to the other end of the BHS, if another tote stacker is very close, unless the far one is almost empty. Also the load on the node agents along the route to the tote stackers could influence the decision, as it would be preferred to send empty totes along a route, where they do not obstruct the way for full totes. The load status of the nodes is therefore taken into account as weight in the choice of the destination for the empty tote, similar to how the load status of nodes agents are considers in the strategy for saturation management presented in the next section.

1.3.2 Saturation management and the WIPAC curve

Saturation management is a strategy with the purpose of avoiding queues at all by minimizing the load on the system in critical areas. The issues on acceleration ramps and reaction times mentioned in the beginning result in the characteristics of the BHS known as the work in-progress against capacity curve (WIPAC), which is further described in [?]. In principle it states that the capacity of the systems goes dramatically down, if the load on the system exceeds a certain threshold value - the system more or less end up in a deadlock situation where everything get stocked. The curve is dynamical, due to the various load on the system, and maximum cannot be calculated exactly. Thus the strategy is to quickly respond to minor observations, which indicates that the maximum has been reached, and then block inputs to the area. The strategy is simply to block a toploader if routes from the toploader are overloaded and let the system resolve. Queues close to the toploader are most critical, as the toploader has great impact on filling up those queues, whereas parts of the route far from the toploader could have been resolved before the new totes arrive. Instead of blocking the toploader, we can just slow down the release of new totes using the following fraction of full speed for the toploader.

$$v_\tau \frac{\sum_i w_i q_i}{w_i} = v_\tau \frac{\sum_i \frac{\alpha}{d_i} q_i}{\sum_i \frac{\alpha}{d_i}} \qquad (1.1)$$

where v_τ is the full speed of the toploader, and w_i are weights of the queue statues, q_i, along the routes. The weight is given by a coefficient α and the distance from the toploader d_i. Queue status is a number between 0 and 1, where 1 indicates no queue. The effect of the saturation management strategy is clearly documented by the graph in figure 1.3, and the domain of impact by other agents is almost system-wide for this strategy as well.

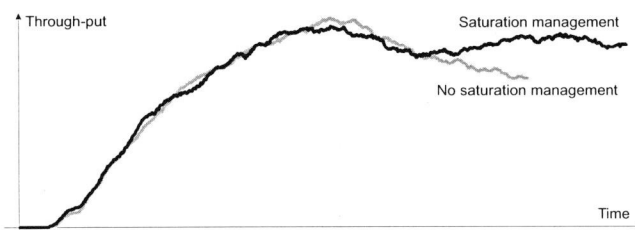

Fig. 1.3. Result of a test scenario with and without saturation management

1.4 Conclusion and future work

Is this paper we have presented important research contributions from the DE-CIDE project about multi-agent based control of a baggage handling system (BHS) in a major airport hub in Asia. The agent-based approach has spread the decision and control logic of the system to a large number of collaborating agents and replaced a complex centralized control structure. It has enabled new strategies and observations in the local agents to increase robustness, capacity, and throughput of the BHS. Special attention has been given to the domain of impact on the decision logic and collaboration among the agents, which varies depending on the strategy.

We continue our research on the BHS and will develop more new strategies for the agents, and increase their mutual collaboration to maximize the utilization of the BHS during peak times. We will try to avoid the use of mediator agents and rely on roles and profiles. Ideally a swarm of local agents would provide a general setup that easily can be ported to other systems. During the research we will pay special attention to develop abstract and general design methodologies for the topological domain of impact for agent collaborations.

References

1. Weiss, G., ed.: Multiagent Systems - A modern approach to distributed artifical intelligence. MIT Press (1999)
2. : FIPA - The Foundation of Intelligent Physical Agents. http://www.fipa.org/ (2006)
3. Brooks Software: Automod - simulation and modeling software. http://www.brookssoftware.com (2006)
4. Schoonderwoerd, R., Holland, O., Bruten, J., Rothkrantz, L.: Ant-based load balancing in telecommunication networks. Adaptive Behaviour (5) (1996) 169–207
5. Caro, G.D., Dorigo, M.: Antnet: A mobile angents approach to adaptive routing. Technical Report IRIDIA/97-12, Université Libre de Bruxelles, Belgium (1997)
6. Negnevitsky, M.: Artificial Intelligence A Guide to Intelligent Systems. 2 edn. Addison Wesley (2005)
7. Kragh, A.: K-Netvrksmodeller til Analyse af FMS Anlg. PhD thesis, Informatics and Mathematical Modelling, Technical University of Denmark (1990)

Prediction of the collapse modes of PVC cylindrical shells under compressive axial loads using Artificial Neural Networks

Angelos P. Markopoulos , Dimitrios E. Manolakos , and Nikolaos M. Vaxevanidis

National Technical University of Athens,
Manufacturing Technology Division
9 Iroon Polytechniou Avenue, 15780, Athens, Greece
E-mail: manolako@central.ntua.gr,
WWW home page: http://users.ntua.gr/manolako
2 Department of Mechanical Engineering Teachers, Institute of
Pedagogical and Technological Education, N. Heraklion Attikis, Greece,
E-mail: vaxev@central.ntua.gr

Abstract. In the present paper Artificial Neural Networks (ANN) are applied in order to predict the buckling modes of thin-walled PVC tubes under compressive axial forces. For the development of the models the neural network toolbox of Matlab® was applied. The results show that these models can satisfactorily face these problems and they constitute not only a fast method, compared to time consuming experiments, but also a reliable tool that can be used for the studying of such parts which are usually employed as structural elements for the absorption of the energy of an impact, in automotive and aerospace applications.

1 Introduction

Due to technological, managerial and legal implications, nowadays, there is an increased interest in the field of safety and protection of the passengers in the case of a car accident. Therefore, automotive industries are focused even more on the damages that a collision imposes on the vehicle. The simulation and the analysis of a vehicle crash are extremely complicated due to the simultaneous interaction of many elements. The various components are structural elements of plain geometric shape, such as thin-walled tubes, cones etc., designed to absorb the impact energy by deforming plastically, thus protecting the passengers, the vehicle and the load.

For the determination of the energy absorption capacity and the response of these elements a simulative test, i.e. the axial crash of thin-walled components is used; by

Please use the following format when citing this chapter:

Markopoulos, A. P., Manolakos, D. E., Vaxevanidis, N. M., 2007, in IFIP International Federation for Information Processing, Volume 247, Artificial Intelligence and Innovations 2007: From Theory to Applications, eds. Boukis, C., Pnevmatikakis, L., Polymenakos, L., (Boston: Springer), pp. 251-258.

this way the deformation characteristics of the components are identified [1-3]. The combined influence of component's geometry and material on their behavior during the crash is of utmost importance. Moreover, the static or dynamic nature of loads should be taken into account. Most of the cases are studied using static analysis, since it is proven that phenomena occurring under dynamic loads are similar to the ones observed under static loading. The overall behavior of the structure depends on the plastic deformation of whole or part of the structure. Taking into account all these factors, the importance and the necessity for further research in that area, in order to fully understand the phenomena involved, become obvious.

The present paper deals with the modeling of the collapse of PVC cylindrical shells under the effect of compressive axial forces, using ANN models. This type of artificial intelligence is applied to a great number of areas of technology, especially for problems where the input and output values cannot be directly connected by simple equations, as in the case of manufacturing [4, 5]. Therefore, the topic studied in this paper is quite challenging since the connection between input and output values is rather complicated. Note that to the authors' knowledge, applications of ANN to crashworthy response are very few, if any. As far as the structure of the paper is concerned, first an overview of the plastic deformation of cylindrical shells and a brief description of neural networks is given. Then the experiments performed in order to acquire the data for the training of the neural network are described. Finally, the neural network models and their results are presented and discussed thoroughly.

2   Plastic deformation of cylindrical shells

Thin-walled shells collapse plastically under the effect of compressive loads and create folds (buckles) when the stress at a point exceeds the critical yield point. The phenomenon of folding can be analyzed into two phases: the pre-buckling and the post-buckling phase. The post-buckling phase is the one that contributes the most to energy absorption, therefore is the one that will be analyzed the most hereafter.

In the post-buckling phase the shell is plastically deformed, resulting to the creation of buckles and its progressive collapse; the characteristic fluctuation of the axial force is caused by the formation of these buckles. The points of maximum and minimum stress in a stress-strain curve, obtained from the compression of a tube, are respectively the points where the buckling starts and ends. The transitional point at the beginning of the shell's plastic collapse describes the maximum load that the shell can withstand. However, in the dynamic analysis of the collapse of tubes the evaluation of capability of energy absorption of the shell is more important than the value of the maximum load.

There is a variety of modes by which a shell may collapse; the occurrence of a mode depends upon geometric parameters such as the ratios D/t (diameter / thickness), L/D (length / diameter) and the properties of the material. In general, the following collapse modes are identified:

(a) Concertina mode: The cylindrical shell, under the effect of the external load, collapses at the shape of concertina with successive axisymmetric folds of length equal to 2h, i.e., buckling wave length; this mode was studied by Alexander [6]. Models for concertina mode have been also proposed by Jones and Abramowicz [7] and Gupta and Velmurugan [8].

(b) Diamond mode: The shell collapses in a non-symmetrical way formatting successive non extensible triangular or trapezoid lobes. The shape of its cross-section can be changed in elliptical, triangular, square and generally polygonal shape resembling the form of a diamond. This buckling mode has been studied extensively by Johnson et al. [9].

(c) Mixed mode: Initially the shell collapses in concertina mode but after the formation of a number of axisymmetric lobes, diamond collapse takes place. The characteristic curve of axial load-axial displacement of mixed mode is a combination of the characteristic curves of concertina and diamond mode; see [1].

(d) Euler buckling: The shell behaves like a bending strut. The work that is absorbed by the shell when Euler buckling occurs is minimal comparing with the work absorbed when other collapse modes take place. Therefore, it is desirable to avoid this particular mode.

(e) Other modes: In this category other collapse modes, such as tilting of the shell's axis, are included. Shearing of one or both ends of the shell that are in contact with the plates may occur, leading to the displacement of one end.

As it has already been mentioned, the mode that a shell develops when it collapses depends upon the material and its geometrical characteristics, namely the thickness (t), the diameter (D) and the length (L). Actually, the collapse mode for a given material depends upon the ratios t/D and L/D [2]. It has been established that shells with small length and large thickness collapse in concertina mode, while shells with large length and small thickness collapse in diamond mode. The transitional area between these two modes has not been clearly determined [1, 2]. Nevertheless, other collapse modes may occur during the compaction of the tubes. The model developed in the present paper is capable of determining the collapse mode when the geometrical and material characteristics of the tube are given.

3   Experimental results

Shells of PVC were examined; the geometrical dimensions of the shells, i.e. the ratios t/D and L/D, where t, D and L are the thickness, the outer diameter and the length of each tube respectively were considered as variables. The compression was performed between two steel parallel plates, by using an Instron universal testing machine. The plates' velocity was about 10 mm/min. In order to cover a wide range of values, 24 experiments were carried out ranging between $0.0470 \leq t/D \leq 0.1410$ and $0.92 \leq L/D \leq 3.94$. For each experiment the collapse mode was identified and logged.

4   ANN models

For the development of the ANN models the neural networks toolbox of Matlab® was used. In this program the creation of neural networks is simplified by using a small amount of commands; the program has a data base with functions, algorithms and commands for this purpose. For an insight to the ANN method and Matlab®, Refs [10, 11] are suggested.

The model presented aims to the prediction of the collapse mode of a tube made from PVC when the t/D and L/D ratios are given. This implies that the two ratios are the input data of the models and the collapse mode the output. Due to the fact that the collapse mode is not an arithmetic value and therefore it cannot be inserted into the program, a substitution becomes necessary; numerals 1, 2, 3 and 4 which stand for Diamond mode, Mixed mode, Concertina mode and Euler buckling, respectively, are introduced.

After the determination of the size of the input and output layers the number of the hidden layers and the neurons within these layers must be decided. This task is accomplished by a trial procedure where different architectures are tested and the one providing the best possible results is finally selected. It is already known that a more complicated than needed network has a reduced generalization capability, since it is characterized by complicated relations. Therefore trials are constrained in models having one or two hidden layers. In the case of one hidden layer models, they are created and tested having 2, 3, 4, 5, 6, 7, 8 and 9 neurons at the hidden layer. In the case of two hidden layers, the models are created having 2, 3, 4, 5, 6, 7 and 8 neurons at the first layer and 3, 4, 5, 6, 7 and 8 at the second hidden layer and all combinations between them are tested; a total of 56 models created. Similarly to the case of selecting the number of hidden layers and their neurons number, for selecting training algorithms trials are made. The training algorithms that are used in the models are the back-propagation algorithm with variable training rate and use of momentum factor and the Levenberg-Marquardt algorithm. Therefore, in total 112 models are created and tested.

As activation function in the hidden layers the hyperbolic tangent sigmoid transfer function was used. It is defined as a strictly increased function, which maintains balance between linear and non-linear behavior and its use provides the opportunity of forming non-linear relations, resulting to the potential of solving non-linear problems.

For the improvement of generalization of the suggested neural network the early stopping technique was used. In this method the existing data are separated in three subsets. The first subset consists of the training vectors, which are used to calculate the gradient and to form the weight factors and the bias. The second subset is the validation group. The error in that group is observed during training and likewise training group normally decreases during the initial phase of training. However, when the network begins to adjust the data more than needed, the error in that group raises and when that increase is continued for a certain number of repetitions, training stops in order to avoid over-fitting. Finally, the third subset is the test group and its error is not used during training. It is used to compare the different models and algorithms.

The selection of each group's data must be representative and uniform. The training group is the biggest and the test group the smallest among the groups. During the training it is possible to watch the change of the MSE of each group versus the epochs graphically. It is known that the original values given to bias and weight factors are chosen randomly each time a network is trained. So training ends up each time in different values of these factors and hence in different error values. For that reason training of each model takes place more than one time; each model is trained five times in order to clearly determine whether a model truly converges to a low value or it is a false value, because e.g. the model was trapped in a local minimum of the function. The mean value of the MSE for these 5 repetitions is calculated and by comparing this mean value the more appropriate one is chosen; that is the model with the lowest mean MSE value in the test group. The error in the test group is more indicative of the generalization capability of the model.

5   Results and Discussion

In Figs 1 (a) and (b) the mean MSE of the training and test groups of all the models trained with the back propagation and the Levenberg-Marquardt algorithm are presented. For the recognition of the models a kind of code is adopted. The models are named according to their architecture, by 1 or 2 numbers depending on the number of the hidden layers they have, where each number is the amount of neurons in the corresponding layer. Furthermore, the numbers are accompanied by letters, by gdx or lm, depending on the training algorithm used for their training, where the first one corresponds to the back-propagation and the second to the Levenberg-Marquardt algorithm. For example the 5-gdx model is the one with one hidden layer with 5 neurons trained with the back-propagation algorithm and the 6-8-lm model has two hidden layers with 6 and 8 neurons respectively, trained with the Levenberg-Marquardt algorithm.

From these charts the model with the minimum test group MSE is selected as the optimal model. It can be seen that this model is the 7-lm. In particular, the repetition with the lower test MSE among the 5 values is the one saved and used for the simulation.

In general, the MSE of the models built was relatively small. Models trained with the back-propagation algorithm result to greater errors than those trained with the Levenberg-Marquardt algorithm. Models trained using Levenberg-Marquardt algorithm and have one hidden layer with 5 or more neurons in it, result to errors similar between them with the smallest to be the 7-lm. Nevertheless, models with two hidden layers also provided accepted results, considering that the particular problem which was simulated using neural networks is quite complicated. The creation of a single network for the simulation of two materials with different properties and behavior concerning to crash reaction, is another factor that makes the procedure of finding relations between the variables even harder and more complicated.

The number of epochs needed to complete the training of each model was small, while by comparing the algorithms used, training with Levenberg-Marquardt algorithm required fewer epochs to complete training. This is expected, since it is known that the particular algorithm has the larger convergence speed. Furthermore, a criterion of maximum epochs was used when programming the models and the limit was set to 600 epochs. In all cases, training was not terminated using the criterion of maximum number of epochs, since none of the trials needed more than 600 epochs to complete, which is attributed, mainly, to the use of the early stopping technique. More specifically, Levenberg-Marquardt algorithm, in most of the cases completed training after 10-20 epochs, while the maximum number of epochs needed was 71. Training using the back-propagation algorithm ranged in higher levels and the larger testing occurred after 143 epochs.

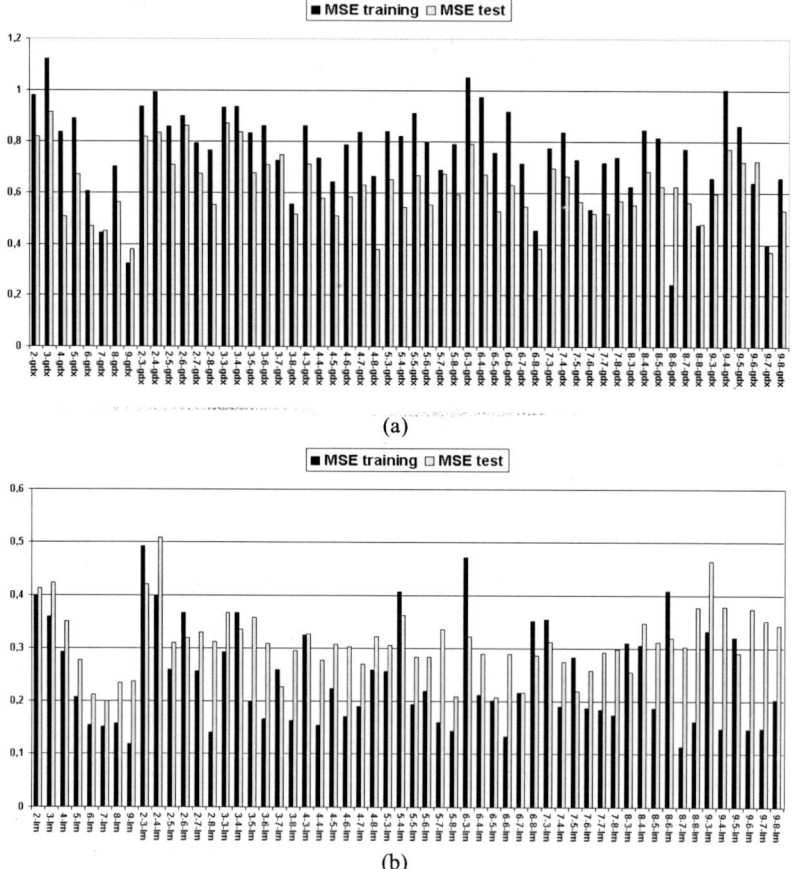

Fig. 1. Mean value (of the five trainings) of the MSE of training and test groups of models trained using (a) the back-propagation and (b) the Levenberg -Marquardt algorithm.

Note, that the desired output values of the model are integers from 1 to 4, implying that the numbers resulting from a model are automatically rounded to the nearest integer in order to provide the output. When the program was tested with values that were not inserted in any of the three groups provided during training it predicted correctly the value corresponding to a collapse mode.

With the results of the trained ANN classification charts for collapse modes for PVC cylindrical shells can be constructed, which indicate the areas of collapse modes and the transitional borders from one mode to another, see Fig 2.

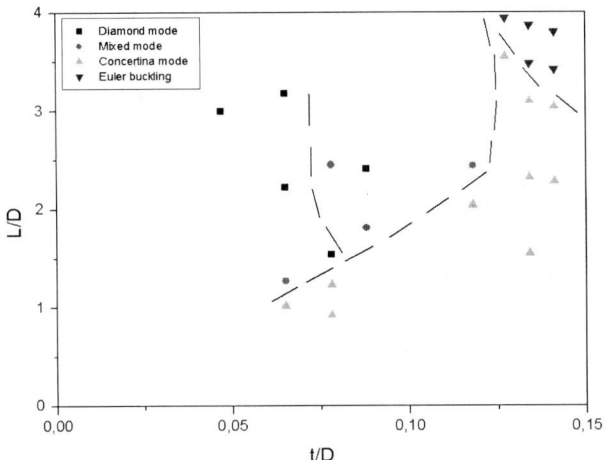

Fig. 2. Classification chart for collapse modes of PVC tubes.

By observing the charts the following conclusions can be drawn: the diamond mode is favored when the t/D ratio is small and the L/D ratio increases. For medium values of the ratios mixed mode is favorable and for even larger ratio values the Euler buckling takes place. In the other regions concertina mode prevails. The classification charts presented here are consistent with others already reported in the relative literature [1, 12].

6   Conclusions

In the present paper neural network models were proposed which can successfully predict the collapse mode of cylindrical shells subjected to axial compressive forces. When the collapse mode of a particular shell is known the mean load that the shell can withstand may be analytically calculated. These shells are mainly used as energy absorbing devices during a potential impact or crash and are of utmost importance for automotive industries.

Taking into account the results of the neural networks models, many points mentioned in the theory were confirmed. Particularly, as it was expected, models trained using the Levenberg-Marquardt algorithm resulted into smaller error in shorter time than the ones trained with the back-propagation algorithm.

The development of neural networks using Matlab® is relatively simple using a small amount of commands. Furthermore, training of the models using the early stopping technique has a very small duration; the maximum is a few seconds, for all training algorithms. Training becomes even faster when the Levenberg-Marquardt algorithm is used.

The network's results are considered very good for the particular application since the network is quite complicated. In many cases the collapse mode varies, even only with a minimal alteration of one of the input variables. Moreover, sometimes there is not a particular sequence in the way that collapse modes change and that makes the simulation of the network even harder. However, according to the results obtained, the proposed ANN may be considered a reliable tool for predicting collapse modes. It is expected that models such as the one suggested here can reduce the cost of product development by reducing time and amount of experiments needed.

References

1. A.G. Mamalis and D.E. Manolakos, *Deformation Characteristics of Crashworthy Components* (VDI, 1989).
2. K.R.F. Andrews, G.L. England and E. Ghani, Classification of the axial collapse of cylindrical tubes under quasi-static loading, *International Journal of Mechanical Sciences*, Vol. **25**, No. 9-10, 687-696 (1983).
3. S.R. Guillow, G. Lu and R.H. Grzebieta, Quasi-static axial compression of thin-walled circular aluminium tubes, *International Journal of Mechanical Sciences* **43**, 2103-2123 (2001).
4. G. Dini, Literature database on applications of artificial intelligence methods in manufacturing engineering, *Annals of the CIRP*, **46** (2), 681-690 (1997).
5. A. Markopoulos, N.M. Vaxevanidis, G. Petropoulos and D.E. Manolakos, Artificial Neural Networks Modeling of Surface Finish in Electro-Discharge Machining of Tool Steels, *Proc. of ESDA 2006, 8th Biennial ASME Conference on Engineering Systems Design and Analysis*, Torino, Italy (July 4-7, 2006).
6. J.M. Alexander, An Approximate analysis of the collapse of thin cylindrical shells under axial loading, *Quart. Journal of Mech. And Applied Math.*, Vol. XIII, Pt. 1 (1960).
7. N. Jones and W. Abramowicz, Static and dynamic axial crushing of circular and square tubes, *In: S.R. Reid "Metal forming and Impact Mechanics"*, Oxford, Pergamon Press, p. 225 (1985).
8. N.K. Gupta and R. Velmurugan, Consideration of internal folding and non-symmetric fold formation axi-symmetric axial collapse round tubes, *Int. J. Solid Structures*, Vol. **34**, 2611-2630 (1997).
9. W. Johnson, P.D. Soden and S.T.S. Al-Hassani, Inextensional Collapse of thin-walled tubes under axial compression, *J. Strain Analysis*, Vol. **12**, No. 4 (1977).
10. S. Haykin, *Neural networks, a comprehensive foundation* (Prentice Hall, 1999).
11. H. Demuth and M. Beale, *Neural networks toolbox for use with Matlab*, (User's guide 2001).
12. A.A.A. Alghamdi, Collapsible impact energy absorbers: an overview, *Thin- Walled Structures*, Vol. **34**, No. 2, 189-213 (2001).

Section 6

Applications of AI in Communications and Networks

An Intelligent CASE Tool for Porting
Mobile Java Applications

Ioannis T. Christou , Sofoklis Efremidis , Aikaterini Roukounaki ,and
Marios Anapliotis
Athens Information Technology, 19.5 km. Markopoulou Ave.
19002 Peania, Greece
{ichr,sefr,arou}@ait.edu.gr
WWW home page: http://www.ait.edu.gr
2 INTRALOT S.A., 64 Kifissias Ave., Maroussi 15125, Greece
anapliotis@intralot.com
WWW home page: http://www.intralot.com

Abstract. Today, many mobile device vendors offer their own versions of the
Connected (Limited) Device Configuration (CLDC 1) and Mobile Information
Device Profile (MIDP 2, 3) of the Java 2 Mobile Edition (J2ME 4). In
addition, depending on the device characteristics they offer device-specific or
series-specific libraries and APIs extending or complementing those specified
in the standard CLDC and MIDP. As a result, porting a Java application
written for one device to another is often a very tedious and time-consuming
task for the developers. We present *SeqFinder*, an intelligent CASE tool for
assisting the porting of Java mobile applications. *SeqFinder* eases the porting
task by automatically generating all minimal method invocation sequences that
lead to an object of a specific type, thus relieving the programmer of the effort
to manually search the manufacturer-provided SDK Java archives to find how
to accomplish a particular task, for example, how to initiate data transfer
through a socket or an HTTP connection.

1   Introduction

It is an unfortunate fact that the promise of Java 5 as a "write once, run everywhere"
language proved to be overly optimistic in the mobile phone market-place. This is by
no means a criticism on the language itself, as Java is probably the best-suited
language for writing applications for mobile phones and mobile information devices
in general, but rather a realization that the extreme variation in those devices'
characteristics necessitated different versions of the language specifically tailored to
these devices. Undoubtedly, the area with the most variations in the offered APIs is
the Graphical User Interface, but as different devices support different features and

Please use the following format when citing this chapter:

Christou, I. T., Efremidis, S., Roukounaki, A., Anapliotis, M., 2007, in IFIP International Federation for Information
Processing, Volume 247, Artificial Intelligence and Innovations 2007: From Theory to Applications, eds. Boukis, C.,
Pnevmatikakis, L., Polymenakos, L., (Boston: Springer), pp. 261-270.

offer the corresponding APIs for developers to take advantage of, there is a wide
range of capabilities of different devices and, correspondingly, of the APIs
supporting them.

Less known is the fact that even standardized APIs such as the connectivity API
that allows access to the Internet and servers and services available over HTTP or
socket protocols are often poorly implemented by the device manufacturers and
cause serious porting problems to application developers. As an example, consider
the trivial standard code snippet for connecting from a Mobile Information Device
applet (MIDlet) via HTTP to an HTTP server.

```
// mMessageItem defined before
HttpConnection hc = null;
InputStream in = null;
String url = getAppProperty("URL");
try {
  hc = (HttpConnection)Connector.open(url);
  in = hc.openInputStream();
  int contentLength = (int)hc.getLength();
  byte[] raw = new byte[contentLength];
  int length = in.read(raw);
  in.close();
  hc.close();
  // Show response to the user
  String s = new String(raw, 0, length);
  mMessageItem.setText(s);
}
catch (IOException ioe) {
  mMessageItem.setText(ioe.toString());
}
```

In certain phone models the previous code will not work, as their virtual machine
does not implement the openInputStream method of the HttpConnection
class that returns null instead, effectively not conforming to the MIDP
specification. Instead, the method openDataInputStream is implemented,
which works as expected.

To further complicate things, many (early) phone models that claimed to support
the MIDP specification had serious bugs in the built-in Kilobyte Virtual Machine
(KVM) especially regarding synchronization issues, thread management, and
memory management. These defects combined make writing complex applications
for such devices at times a daunting task.

Porting of existing applications from one device type to another (of the same or
different vendor) is an equally complicated process. The particularities of the APIs as
well as the KVM and MIDP implementations of the concerned device types have to
be taken into account, making porting a time consuming and tedious process.
Typically, application developers and/or application porters need to try several
alternative sequences of object constructions and method invocations for establishing
a successful connection. Any tools that could assist to the (semi)automatic

generation of such alternative code fragments will be of immense help to the application porters.

To reduce developer time for porting applications to a new mobile device type we have developed *SeqFinder*, a tool that automatically generates all possible code sequences that lead to a specified target, i.e., an object of a certain type as specified by the developer, for example the initiation of a successful data transfer. Note that by code sequences we mean sequences of constructor and method invocations and/or retrievals of field values. The tool generates a separate MIDlet for each sequence of Java statements that leads to a reference to such an object. Each sequence element is either a declaration and initialization of a primitive type such as `int i1 = 0;` or a (possibly static) method invocation such as

```
Connection o1 = Connector.open(s1, i1, b1);
```

For any method invocation that requires references to class objects, the generated sequence includes a valid such reference in a previous line. This is accomplished by recursively generating objects of the type of the calling object and the parameters of the target method.

The automatic generation of all such sequences and their embedding in appropriately wrapped Java code so as to be compile-able and testable MIDlets can help the developer quickly find how to use the APIs provided by the manufacturer in order to accomplish a particular task, such as reading data from the network or sending data to a server.

1.1   Related Work

Several tools and environments for targeting of applications for various families of mobile devices have been proposed and a number of them are in widespread use. All of them focus on the targeting chores from a given code base but do not provide support for developing such a code base at first place.

J2MEPolish 6, 7 is a freely available, powerful toolset that heavily relies on a database of devices containing their specific characteristics, which are taken into account in the targeting process. The mechanism used for targeting is based on the same kind of pre-processing as C. The approach taken by J2MEPolish is feature-driven, i.e., application targeting is governed as specified by the pre-processing directives that take into account the characteristics of the device of interest as recorded in the device database. Otherwise, the tools do not provide functionalities for dynamically developing sequences of "winning" method invocations which will lead to a successful target, e.g., successful transfer of data over an HTTP connection.

The j2me-device-db 8 project started out as a project aiming to create a database of mobile phone characteristics and even bugs, but developed to a set of tools for developing mobile applications via the use of pre-processor directives very similar in nature to J2MEPolish.

Tira Jump 9 (latest release 3) is another software solution that simplifies project planning and, in addition, enables the efficient deployment of content across a range of diverse mobile devices. It employs an extensive knowledge-base that registers most device specificities. The integrated workflow and robust digital asset management systems create an end-to-end solution that simplifies the process, enhances consistency, quality and controls mobile content deployment on a global scale. The Jump Developer Desktop (JDD) manages the adaptation and optimization of reference applications to support new handsets. The tool is available in two versions:

- The JDD Java Edition (based on Eclipse) provides the key interface to the Jump Transformation Engine (JTE) when adapting Java applications.
- The JDD BREW Edition is a Microsoft Visual Studio .NET add-in and adapts BREW 10 applications.

Tira Jump 3 is built around the concept that between any two mobile devices there exists a finite set of differences. Consequently, the platform makes use of a reference device and contains, maintains and updates differences between every supported target device and the reference device. For each difference it provides a series of adaptation instructions to convert content from one device format to the other.

The Jump Transformation Server supplies the device plug-ins and performs the conversion of the Java or BREW application or the ringtone, screensaver or wallpaper. Similar to J2MEPolish, the Tira Jump tools allow for targeting of mobile applications to a range of mobile devices but do not provide methodological support for developing sequences of "winning" method invocations leading to a successful target.

Relevant to the *SeqFinder* algorithm development is perhaps work on hypergraph shortest paths 11, for indeed it is possible to model the problem domain as a hypergraph in the following way: every type in the SDK of the mobile device can be considered as a node, and every public method or field of the SDK can be considered as a Back-feed arc connecting the type of the class declaring the method and the types of each argument of the method to the type of the object the method returns. The problem is then one of computing all minimal different paths of reaching a desired object in this graph starting from primitive types. This model does not take into account inheritance and polymorphism issues but may yield fruitful results in the near future.

2   System Description

SeqFinder operates on a data repository (e.g., a relational database) that contains all the necessary information about the classes that are available on a specific mobile device. *SeqFinder* takes as input the type of an object that the developer wishes to construct and returns all minimal code sequences targeted for this specific device that produce such a reference in the format of valid Java code that can be automatically compiled and executed for testing purposes. The generated Java code sequences contain tool-default values for variables and arguments of primitive types and for the construction of any intermediate objects.

These sequences are fed into a specially designed GUI for fine tuning by the developer. The GUI allows the developer to quickly and intuitively interact with each of the above sequences to fill out the placeholders that contain the generated tool-default values and, as a result, to generate a set of Java files that can be executed directly on the Java-enabled mobile device. Among the generated Java programs those that succeed in successfully transferring data though a connection are tagged as the "winners".

In this section, we present a recursive algorithm that produces all possible sequences of method invocations that, eventually, result in an object of a given type starting from primitive Java type variables.

Input to the Algorithm: The algorithm presented below takes as input

- the type of an object to be constructed by a sequence of method invocations, and
- a unique key that identifies the devices, at which these code sequences are targeted.

Output of the Algorithm: Vector of all minimal distinct sequences of steps leading to a reference to an object of the requested type (specified target by the developer). The produced reference can be of the requested type or of any of its subtypes or its supertypes (in this case casting is necessary). These sequences are invariant with respect to values given to primitive types (e.g., int variables' values do not matter in this program, and each primitive type is assumed to have a unique default value to be assigned whenever such a variable is created). To avoid looking for all the infinite sequences of code segments that arise when multiple objects from the same type can be constructed, we introduce the constraint that only one object of each non-primitive type can be constructed in any given sequence. We also ignore any methods or fields whose type belongs in the same class hierarchy with the class, in which they belong (i.e. is any of the supertypes or subtypes of this specific type).

Finally, *the developers are able to impose two kinds of limitations on the generated code sequences. First, they can limit the maximum length of the code sequences that SeqFinder generates. Second, they can exclude certain packages, classes and members from the generated code sequences*, meaning that they can force SeqFinder to ignore any member that involves in any way the use of these packages, classes of members.

2.1   Auxiliary Data Structures

Our algorithm makes use of auxiliary data structures and methods as described in this subsection.

1. A method newName is provided that receives the name of a type (e.g. int or java.lang.Integer) as a parameter and returns

    a.   the argument with the 'l' appended to it, if the type is not a primitive type

    b.   a new (unique) name, otherwise.

2. Java source-code-level object definitions and initializations of the form

```
        T o1 = (TT) o2.m(a1, .., an);
```

are represented by the following data structure:

```
Command {
    String objType;
    String objName;
    String realType;
    String CCOName;        // called class obj. name
    String CCType;         // called class type
```

```
String memberName;   // called class member name
Vector<Parameter> paramList;
// paramList has the name-type pairs of method's
```
args
```
}
```
where
   a.   type T is represented by objType,
   b.   object o1 is represented by objName,
   c.   type TT is represented by realType
   d.   object o2 is represented by CCOName,
   e.   the type of o2 is represented by CCType,
   f.   method m is represented by memberName, and
   g.   the names and types of the parameters are represented by paramList.
   In case method m is a static method, the value of CCOName member is equal to
CCType. If m is a field and not a method, then paramList is null. If m is a
constructor, then CCOName is null.
   3. Method descriptions are represented by the following data structure
```
CommandStruct {
   boolean isStatic;
   String type;
   String CCType;
   String memberName;   // type of each method parameter
   Vector<String class_type> PTypes;
}
```
where
   a.   isStatic is true, if the member is static,
   b.   type is the member's type,
   c.   CCType is the type of the object on which the method is invoked or
        whose field is accessed,
   d.   memberName is the name of the member,
   e.   PTypes is the types of the parameters
In case the member is actually a field, PTypes is null.
   4. A method findAllMembersOfType is provided that, given a type C,
returns *all* members (fields, methods, constructors) of classes contained in the data
repository that return an object of the requested type or of any of its supertypes or
subtypes. This method returns also members whose type is an array type with
elements of the required type.
   5. A method findIncomplete is provided that, given a vector of Commands
v and an initially empty vector of strings tv, returns the first Command object in v
that is incomplete. An incomplete Command is one, whose called object or one of its
parameters have not already been defined in any of the Command objects that appear
before v is not of primitive type or string This is determined by searching through
the Command objects before v for an objType that belongs to the class hierarchy
of the type of the specific object.
   Effectively, the findIncomplete method identifies the first use of a yet
undefined object in the sequence of Commands under construction; such an object

has to be eventually defined and initialized. The method also fills vector `tv` with two strings, the first is the type name of the object that has been identified in `v` (the value of `CCType` in `Command` or the value of the `PType` member in the `Pair<., .>` in `paramList`), and the second is the name of the object itself (the value of `CCOName` or `PName` in the `Pair<., .>`). If no Command object has a name in the command that is not defined below in vector `v`, then `null` is returned.

3   The Generator Algorithm

The output of the algorithm is a *vector of vectors of* Commands. Each one of these vectors of commands describes a sequence of steps that lead to an object of the requested type. The algorithm assumes that the user may have specified a set of packages, classes and members that should be ignored, as well as the maximum length (maximumLength) of the generated code sequences.

```
vector SEQ(Commands, ObjectType, ObjectName) {
  CommandStructs=findAllMembersOfType (ObjectType);
  create new empty vector called result;
  foreach CommandStruct in CommandStructs {
    if CommandStruct has excluded packages,
              clases or members
      continue;
    create the corresponding Command c;
    create a new vector v containing all the Commands + c;
    add v to the result;
  }
  foreach v in result {
    incompleteCommand=findIncomplete (v,tv);
    if incompleteCommand is NOT null {
      if v.size == maximumLength {
        remove v from result;
        do not move forward in result;
      }
      type = tv[0];
      name = tv[1];
      result' = SEQ(v, type, name);
      if result' is NOT empty {
        replace v in result with result';
        do not move forward in result;
      }
    }
  }
  return result;
}
```

Each Command object represents a Java statement of the form `int i1 = 0;` or more complex statements such as

```
java.util.Hashtable java_util_Hashtable1 =
                    new java.util.Hashtable();
```

or A A1=SomeObjectRef.someMethod(C c1); and so on. Static methods of the form

```
javax.microedition.io.Connection
 javax_microedition_io_Connection1=
 javax.microedition.io.Connector.open(s1);
```

are of course also expressible.

A Command object captures in its objType data member the name of the class A in the statement above. The name of the object reference A1 is captured in objName. The name of the type of the object reference SomeObjectRef is captured in CCType, while the name SomeObjectRef itself is stored in CCOName. The name of the method invocation someMethod is stored in the memberName data member and similarly the name of the type and reference of each argument is stored in the data member paramList.

The algorithm accepts as an input a partially incomplete sequence of Commands and it attempts to locate all the possible ways to complete it (in terms of the specific object type that it receives as a parameter). For this reason, it locates all Java statements that return an object of the desired type (or of any of its supertypes or subtypes) and creates a separate vector of Commands for each one of them, which consists of the received code sequence followed by the new Command. The algorithm then computes recursively for each name that appears in each of the newly generated code sequences and that has not been defined already in this sequence all code sequences that will define this name, and prefixes them with the current sequence. It then replaces the current sequence in the result vector with the expanded code sequences, resulting in all code sequences that can be used to obtain a reference to the requested type.

It is important to notice the way newName(type) works according to its specification. This method always returns the same name when the input is a non-primitive type. This limits the code sequences constructed to sequences that create only one object for each different type considered. This is not a serious limitation of the program and it avoids the otherwise almost inevitable infinitude of different possible code sequences. To clarify why this is the case consider two classes A and B. Class A has a unique constructor A(B b) and there is no other way in the program to obtain a reference to an A object. Class B on the other hand has two constructors, B(int i) and B(A a). Now if we want to find all code sequences leading to an A object, the last line of each such sequence has to be A A1 = new A(B1) where B1 is an object of type B. Apparently, there are two ways to obtain an object B. One is by having a statement of the form B B1 = new B(i); where i is an int variable and the other is by having a statement of the form B B1 = new B(A2); where A2 is an object of type A. If the name A2 is not "unified" with A1, then we must find all ways of creating an A object again and add them to our current code sequences, which leads to infinitely long object creations of the following form in reverse:

```
A A1 = new A(B1);
B B1 = new B(A2);
```

```
A A2 = new A(B2);
B B2 = new B(A3);
. . .
```

To further simplify the things, *SeqFinder allows only for one object from any class hierarchy to exist in a sequence.* In other words, if an object of class A has been created in a Command of a specific command sequence, then no other object of this specific type or of any of its subtypes or supertypes will be created in this code sequence. The already created object can be used in all of the above mentioned cases.

4   Computational Results

As shown in Table 1, the system is capable of finding all valid sequences of 2 or less method invocations leading to a `java.io.InputStream` object reference in less than 16 minutes on a commodity MACBook laptop running at 2Ghz the MAC OS X Operating System and Java JDK 1.6. The response times, even though they are not real-time, still present huge time-savings to developers who previously had to spend *more than two days* in order to make a single network-centric Poker game to establish connections and exchange data with the game server. It is also interesting to note how the number of different code sequences for obtaining a `Connection` object reference jumps from 35 in the case of two-step sequences to 201 different sequences of length 3. The length 3 sequences of course include the length 2 sequences. The table also shows some other first results of running the system.

Table 1. Experimental Results.

Object Type	Number of Steps	Response Time	Number of Sequences
java.io.InputStream	2	15 min	164
java.io.DataInputStream	2	16 min	292
Javax.microedition.io.Connection	2	5 min	35
Javax.microedition.io.Connection	3	6 min	201

5   Conclusions and Future Directions

We presented *SeqFinder*, a tool that automatically generates all sequences of Java method invocations leading to an object reference of a given type (or any of its sub-types). This tool helps mobile application porting and development tasks as it relieves its user (application developer) from the cumbersome task of having to search a manufacturer-specific APIs for functionality described in possibly non-existing or just poor java-docs. It does so by emulating the actual process by which developers approach this task (bottom-up), i.e., by letting the user automatically search for all classes that support a "connect" method, or to directly find all possible ways to get a `java.io.OutputStream` object that can use to send data through the network.

In certain cases, the number of sequences generated can be overwhelming. In addition, the user currently has to know (or guess) what values to assign to the primitive data types variables. For these reasons, we are currently experimenting with machine learning techniques to offer a more intelligent user-interface that will help the user choose quickly the code sequence (by sorting them in a "likelihood-index") and primitive values combination that are most likely to be successful at performing a particular task. This sorting would be performed by examining previous test sequences generated and tested. The tests would then have resulted in "success" or "failure" which, if recorded, can lead to a training set of labeled examples. Standard supervised classification techniques can then be used to infer the likelihood of a proposed sequence to be a winning sequence and from this information any vector of all possible sequences can be "intelligently" sorted.

References

1. Connected Limited Device Configuration (CLDC), JSR 30, JSR 139, http://java.sun.com/products/cldc/

2. Mobile Information Device Profile (MIDP), JSR 37, JSR 138, http://java.sun.com/products/midp/

3. Ortiz, C.E. and Giguere, E., Mobile Information Device Profile for Java 2 Micro Edition: The ultimate guide to creating applications for wireless devices, John Wiley and Sons, Inc., New York, NY, 2001.

4. The Java ME Platform, http://java.sun.com/javame/index.jsp

5. Gosling, J., Joy, B., Steele, G., and Bracha, G., The Java Language Specification, Second Edition, Addison-Wesley, Reading, MA, 2000.

6. Virkus, R., Pro J2ME Polish: Open Source Wireless Java Tools Suite, Apress, Berkeley, CA, 2005.

7. J2MEPolish, http://www.j2mepolish.org/

8. The j2me-device-db project. http://j2me-device-db.sourceforge.net/pmwiki/

9. Tira Jump 3, http://www.tirawireless.com/

10. Binary Runtime Environment for Wireless, http://brewx.qualcomm.com/

11. Gallo, G., Longo, G., Nguyen, S., and Pallottino, S., Directed Hypergraphs and Applications. Discrete Applied Mathematics, 42:2–3, 177–201, 1993.

A Knowledge-based Service Creation and Execution Framework for Adapting Composite Wireless IP Services

Spyros Tombros , Dimitrios Vergados , Ioannis Anagnostopoulos , and
Christoforos Kavadias
APEX AG, Bundesgasse 16, Bern, CH-3011, Switzerland
stombros@apexag.com.

Department of Information and Communication Systems Engineering
University of the Aegean Karlovassi, Samos, GR-832 00, GREECE,
email: vergados@aegean.gr; janag@aegean.gr

Teletel S.A., 124 Kifisias Avenue, Athens, GREECE
c.kavadias@teletel.gr @teletel.gr

Abstract. Wireless services infrastructures beyond 3G are evolving into highly complex and heterogeneous network environments embracing a multitude of different wireless internet access technologies, terminal types and capabilities, different bearer services, core/access network configurations, along with a wide range of application-related functions. Further to this reality, service operators are confronted with increasingly demanding users, becoming more and more aware of their needs. Thus, the main objective of this research work is to pave the way to novel service creation and execution systems beyond 3G, allowing the mobile user to build her/his own highly personalised composite wireless services.

1 Introduction

Mobile service providers have already begun to offer composite wireless services as vehicular route assistance and navigation services, location-sensitive advertising services, presence services, etc. These services typically consist of a combination of elementary component services (e.g. establishment of a bearer channel, a file transmission, user position acquisition, etc) [1]. However, presently there is no direct or indirect way for the user to personalise the most significant services component such as the service logic, (the logic for selecting the elementary components of a composite wireless service) and mandating the way that these resources (elementary component services) are utilised in a coordinated manner. This paper aims at the definition of novel, user-centric service creation and execution systems able to

Please use the following format when citing this chapter:

Tombros, S., Vergados, D., Anagnostopoulos, I., Kavadias, C., 2007, in IFIP International Federation for Information Processing, Volume 247, Artificial Intelligence and Innovations 2007: From Theory to Applications, eds. Boukis, C., Pnevmatikakis, L., Polymenakos, L., (Boston: Springer), pp. 271-278.

identify and autonomously exploit knowledge from the user's needs for the synthesis, deployment, and persistent adaptation of highly personalised composite wireless internet services. The scope is to valorize existing wireless infrastructure investments by radically increasing the value of services in terms of personalisation, and contributing towards the realisation of novel schemes for rapid and automated mobile services creation, deployment and early validation. For this purpose, the paper proposes and defines a knowledge-based, ontology-driven approach for wireless internet composite services conceptualisation and synthesis, and introduces a modular and scalable architecture and accompanying tools serving the creation and deployment of adaptive composite wireless services.

2 State of the Art

As wireless services have started to penetrate into a wide range of everyday-life aspects (work, entertainment, health, safety, etc), wireless service operators need to cope with increasingly divergent user requirements and challenges pertaining to the personalization of the delivered services. Wireless services are still built in an "one-size-fits-all" manner, typically addressing the "specific" requirements of identified broad categories of users, while services personalisation has been limited to simple service-parameterisation. There is no direct or indirect way for the user to cause the adaptation of the most significant services component: the service logic, i.e. the logic for selecting the elementary components of a composite wireless service and mandating the way that these resources are utilised in a coordinated manner. The main problem of current service creation and execution systems [2] is their inability to support different needs of individual users. Hence, there is an evident need for a consolidated approach that will allow the effective capturing of the knowledge pertaining to wireless user requirements and 'wants' and the capabilities of the wireless service-execution infrastructures, and enable the exploitation of this knowledge for the synthesis, and deployment of personalized wireless composite services.

2.1   Objectives

This paper makes use of novel approaches in the field of wireless services specification and creation using the concept of the composite wireless service, which consists of a combination of component wireless services. The proposed generic architecture is consisted of several entities, which their roles and relations are depicted in Figure 1 and described below.
- The Service Synthesis Centre (SSC) hosts the intelligence required for the management of Service Synthesis functions, the identification of the users' needs, and the generation of valid service specifications.
- The Customer Profile and Services Data Store (CSDS) entity provides the means for retrieving data required for service synthesis from the multitude of possible sources (HLR/HSS, SDP, BCCS, etc), and mapping the data onto the

ontological models used for Service Synthesis in order to be accessed in a straightforward manner by the SSC.

Services deployment involves the Service Deployment and Execution Centre (SDEC), which generate on the basis of implementation domain service specifications received from the SSC, the self-adaptive software modules (self-adaptive SW agents that implements the wireless composite service logic, and the installation and integration of the SW into the execution environment of the Wireless Composite Services Execution Server (WCES). During service execution the SDEC is capable of redesigning and reactivating SW agents on the basis of the information provided through interactions with the agents and/or knowledge available within the SDEC.

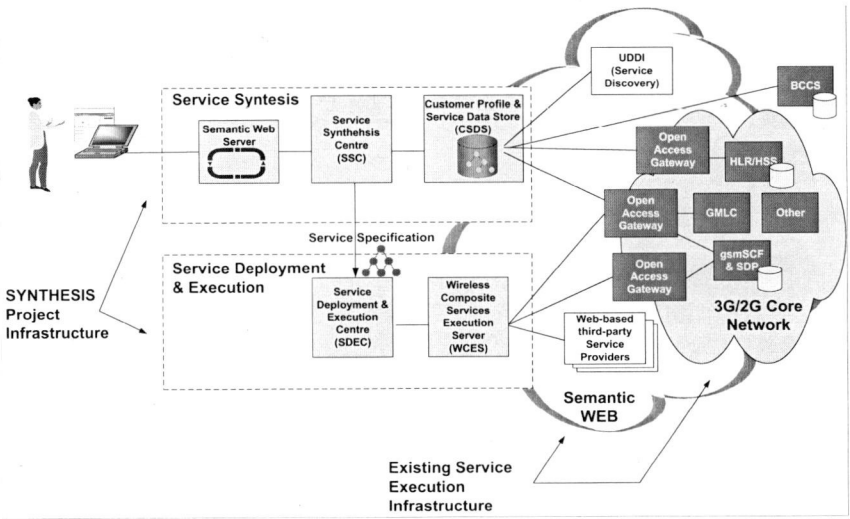

Figure 1: The proposed generic architecture

2.2   Composite Wireless Services Functional Requirements

Our approach makes use of and extend state-of-the-art approaches emerging in the field of wireless services creation and execution: a composite wireless service consists of a combination of component wireless services [4]. A component wireless service can be: a fundamental wireless service that cannot be partitioned into separately identifiable services – for example identify a location, obtain vehicular travel information, transmit/receive a file, etc, a utility service that implements a function within a particular composite service sequence and acts as the binding between fundamental wireless services – for example, invoke a composite service sequence, execute a pause, assign a parameter value, etc, another composite wireless service.

The composite wireless service consists of continual iterations of these three services, in the following sequence, until the destination is reached: a) Determines the present location and provide it to the wireless terminal. If the present location is the same as the destination, inform the user and cease the iteration of services, b)

Computes the least time-consuming route from the present location to the designated destination. If the route has changed, alert the user, of a new route and its directions, c) Retrieves traffic information for the route's regions and determine if traffic delays, such as those due to an accident, would ensue. If traffic delays exist ahead, repeat step (b) with the updated delay information; otherwise, proceed to step (a). The logic of the composite service is executed at an application server, which is called Wireless Composite Services Execution Server (WCES). More specifically service synthesis involves the user and the service synthesis environment interacting for the production of a personalised and valid service specification. This specification should be consistent with the capabilities of the service execution platforms in use, the user profile and subscription status information stored in the multitude of mobile services data infrastructure (HLR/HSS, SDP, BCCS databases, etc), and user context information (e.g. location) retrieved from the network using open access interfaces (OSA). On the other hand, service deployment involves the generation of the self-adaptive software module implementing the wireless composite service logic (self-adaptive SW agent) and its installation and integration into the execution environment of the Wireless Composite Services Execution Server. During composite service logic execution, the Wireless Composite Services Execution Server needs to interact with the mobile user terminal (typically through the use of an OSA gateway or in a proprietary manner using the GPRS service), and also a set of other application servers that belong to external third-party service providers. In this case (navigation service), third party providers include a route estimation (navigation) provider, and a traffic information provider (e.g. state police traffic information server).

3   The Proposed Architecture

Service synthesis is the process resulting into the production of service specifications to be exploited by the advanced service deployment and execution infrastructure. Service synthesis consists of an iterative procedure for progressively collecting user needs and building valid service specifications. The Service Synthesis Centre (SSC) hosts the intelligence required for the management of Service Synthesis functions and the generation of valid service specifications. The SSC cooperates with a Semantic Web Server for handling interactions with the user and capturing user-perspective service descriptions (user needs).

The paper defines adequate ontology models that provide the means for the valid conceptualisation, and specification (instantiation) of composite wireless services. Furthermore, these ontology models provide the means for the communication among the Service Synthesis entities. Additionally, Customer and Business Domain ontological models will be used to effectively represent knowledge pertaining to what the customer wants and can have as a subscriber, while in parallel the Implementation Domain ontological models will be used to effectively represent knowledge pertaining to the capabilities, functionality, and behaviour of existing wireless service execution platforms. On the other hand, service synthesis has to be consistent with static and dynamically changing information pertaining to capabilities of the underlying service execution platforms, capabilities of available third-party providers, present user context (e.g. location), user profile and subscription status, etc, that should be accessed on demand and/or is stored in the multitude of mobile infrastructure (legacy) databases (HLR/HSS, SDP, BSSC, etc). The Customer Profile and Services Data Store (CSDS) entity provides the means for retrieving this data from the multitude of possible sources, and mapping the data onto the ontological models used for Service Synthesis in order be accessed in a straightforward manner by the SSC. In this sense, the Customer Profile and Services Data Store (CSDS) will be capable of providing a single harmonised interface to the SSC, for accessing data required for the production of valid service specifications.

Service deployment involves the Service Deployment and Execution Centre (SDEC) generating – on the basis of implementation-domain service specifications received from the SSC – the self-adaptive software modules (self-adaptive SW agents) implementing the wireless composite service logic, and the installation and integration of the SW into the execution environment of the Wireless Composite Services Execution Server. Further, the service deployment phase involves the generation of the user-terminal SW to be downloaded and installed on the terminal specifically for this service. Finally, service execution involve the Wireless Composite Services Execution Server cooperating with the mobile user terminal and also a set of other application servers that belong to external third-party service providers.

3.1 The Ontology-driven framework for service synthesis

Ontologies include machine-usable definitions (specifications) of basic concepts (e.g. user, subscription, elementary service, composite service, etc) and the relationships among them. Using ontologies, applications can be "intelligent," in the sense that they can more accurately work at the human conceptual level. These ontologies should be expressed in the standardised W3C Web Ontology Language (OWL) [3], [5]. OWL makes use of the XML syntax and is part of the growing stack of W3C recommendations related to the Semantic Web. The proposed schema develops and utilises two types of ontological models. On the first type the main purposes of the Customer and Business Domain ontological models represent knowledge pertaining to what the customer needs and can have as a subscriber. Conversely, the main purpose of the Implementation Domain ontological models highlight in a generic manner knowledge pertaining to the capabilities, functionality, and behaviour of existing wireless service execution platforms.

3.2 Services Synthesis Infrastructure and Techniques

Service synthesis is the process resulting into the production of service specifications to be exploited by the advanced service deployment and execution infrastructure. Service synthesis is performed at the Service Synthesis Centre (SSC). In the context of the proposed architecture the Service Synthesis Centre cooperates with a Semantic Web Server for handling interactions with the user and identifying user-perspective

service descriptions (user needs). Furthermore, the Customer Profile and Services
Data Store (CSDS) provide to the SSC a single harmonised interface for accessing
data required for the production of valid service specifications. The ontology models
provide the means for the communications between the entities of the Service
Synthesis infrastructure, while Service Synthesis consists of an iterative procedure
for progressively collecting user requirements and building valid service
specifications. A high-level description of the Service Synthesis process is depicted
in the Figure 2.

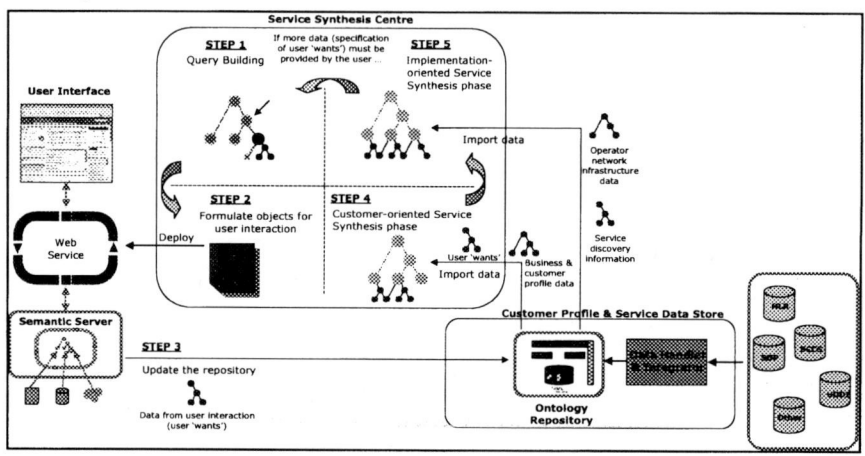

Figure 2: High-level Description of Generic Service-Synthesis Flow

More specifically, a service synthesis iteration process engages the following
main steps: i) A query is built for requesting description of user needs. This query
can be constructed on service triggering (initial query) or at an intermediate stage
after determining that further information on the user needs is required from the user
side, ii) The SSC, using a web-service, formulates and deploys the objects that serve
the specific interaction with the user, iii) The user provides the requested input and
the instantiations of the relevant ontological models are updated accordingly, iv)
Customer-oriented Service Synthesis takes place. The SSC captures and validates -
at the business and customer level - man-to-machine specifications for a wireless
composite service and v) Implementation-oriented Service Synthesis takes place.
The SSC maps and validates customer and business domain concepts onto the
implementation domain. Data pertaining to user context (location, terminal
capabilities, connectivity options, etc), and service discovery (e.g. availability and
capabilities of third-party service providers) is imported for this purpose from the
Customer Profile and Service Data Store.

3.3 Service deployment and execution techniques

Service deployment involves the Service Deployment and Execution Centre (SDEC)
generating the self-adaptive software modules (self-adaptive SW agents) [6]
implementing the wireless composite service logic and the installation and

integration of the SW into the execution environment of the Wireless Composite Services Execution Server. Further, the service deployment phase involve the generation of the user-terminal SW to be downloaded and installed on the terminal, specifically for this service. During service execution the SDEC is capable of redesigning and reactivating SW agents on the basis of the information provided through interactions with the agents and/or knowledge available within the SDEC.

In overall, SW adaptation at the wireless composite services execution server and the user terminal is to be performed at three levels. In the first level SW components based on the interactions with their environment (network service execution environment) are self-adapted. The next level re-designs and re-constructs the adaptive SW components (agents) at the Service Deployment and Execution Centre on the basis of the feedback received from the adaptive SW agents. Finally, in the last level, re-design and re-construction of adaptive SW components at the Service Deployment and Execution Centre after a new conceptual service specification has been requested and received from the Service Synthesis Centre, is performed.

Self adaptive software agents are dynamic entities, thus they are capable of discovering a need for change - for additional knowledge and/or functionality on the basis of their analysis of specific situations. The SDEC is capable of redesigning and reactivating agents on the basis of the information provided by agents and/or knowledge available within the SDEC. Specifically, the self-adaptive SW components implementing the logic of composite wireless services will have an explicit model that it will be aware of their sub-components, their external environment and their specifications. In addition, the SW components throughout this model, will be able to monitor and control their sub-components in order to reconfigure their functions at run-time. Finally, SW components will be able to communicate with the SDEC for reporting performance bottlenecks and implementation deficiencies.

3.4 Service creation, deployment and execution tools and infrastructure

The Service Deployment and Execution Centre (SDEC) hosts the intelligence required for constructing the adaptive SW agents installed on the Wireless Composite Services Execution Servers and user terminals, monitoring the performance of service execution, determining whether SW agents are not performing as they should, and therefore proceed in a new implementation design and deployment, retrieving information from the CPS pertaining to the dynamically changing service execution environment, user context, and discovery of alternative service providers and requesting from the Service Synthesis Centre a new service specification. The implementation of the adaptive SW agent execution environment is based on the OSGi service platform [7]. This platform specifies a standard environment which allows multiple, Java-based components, called bundles, to run in a single Java Virtual Machine (JVM) securely. The JAVA environment is selected by the OSGi alliance as the OSGi execution environment. The proposed approach can utilise one of the J2SE and J2ME, execution environments [8]. The service creation SW will be able to exploit the Semantic Web Enabled Web Services

(SWWS) exposed by the Semantic Server, for effectively adapting the service creation interface during the course of service synthesis.

4   Conclusions

This paper proposed a generic approach and architecture addressing the realisation of novel, user-centric service implementation and execution systems able to capture and autonomously exploit knowledge of user requirements for the synthesis, deployment, and persistent adaptation of highly personalised composite wireless services. To target the goals of this approach, a knowledge-based, ontology-driven approach for wireless composite services conceptualisation and synthesis introduced involving the specification of adequate ontological models and of the techniques and algorithms for capturing and exploiting this knowledge pertaining to user needs, business-domain processes, customer profile, and services-implementation-domain concepts. The proposed modular and scalable architecture will effectively interact with existing wireless services execution environments, and data storage infrastructures. The prototypes of the entities introduced, comprising the proposed architecture, namely the Service Synthesis Centre (SSC), Service Deployment and Execution Centre (SDEC), Customer Profile and Services Data Store (CSDS) and Wireless Composite Services Execution Server (WCES), ensuring at the same time their interoperability.

References

1.   Z. Maamar, Q. Z. Sheng, and B. Benatallah. On Composite Web Services Provisioning in an Environment of Fixed and Mobile Computing Resources. Information Technology and Management Journal, Special Issue on Workflow and E-Business, Kluwer Academic Publishers, 2003.
2.   F. Curbera, M. Duftler, R. Khalaf, W. Nagy, N. Mukhi, and S. Weerawarana. Unraveling the Web Services Web: An Introduction to SOAP, WSDL, and UDDI. IEEE Internet Computing, 6(2), March/April 2002.
3.   S. Kouadri Most'efaoui, and B. Hirsbrunner. Towards a Context Based Service Composition Framework. In Proceedings of The First International Conference on Web Services , Las Vegas, Nevada, USA, June, 2003.
4.   Benatallah, B. Sheng, Q. Z. Dumas, M., "The Self-Serv Environment for Web Services Composition", IEEE INTERNET COMPUTING, vol 7, pp 40-48, 2003.
5.   Sean Bechhofer. OWL Web Ontology Language: Parsing OWL in RDF/XML. W3C Working Group Note, World Wide Web Consortium, January 2004.
6.   Jeff Gray, Raymond Klefstad, Marjan Mernik;"Adaptive and Evolvable Software Systems: Techniques, Tools, and Applications"; Proceedings of the 37th Hawaii International Conference on System Sciences, 2004.
7.   Open Service Gateway Initiative, www.osgi.com.
8.   Roger Riggs, Antero Taivalsaari, Mark VandenBrink, "Programming Wireless Devices with the JavaTM 2 Platform, Micro Edition", Addison-Wesley, 2001.

Efficient Fair TDMA Scheduling In Wireless Multi-Hop Networks

Aggeliki Sgora , Dimitrios J. Vergados , ,and Dimitrios D. Vergados
University of the Aegean
Department of Information and Communication Systems Engineering
Karlovassi, Samos, GR-83200,Greece
{asgora; vergados}@aegean.gr

School of Electrical and Computer Engineering
National Technical University of Athens
GR-15773 Zografou, Athens, Greece
djvergad@telecom.ntua.gr

Abstract. Wireless multihop networks have recently been conceived as a networking paradigm. Several algorithms may be found in the literature for scheduling TDMA transmissions for these networks. These algorithms try to determine the optimal scheduling, in order to increase the capacity and reduce the delay for a given network topology. However, to our best knowledge, no TDMA scheduling algorithms have been developed, that take into consideration the traffic requirements of the active flows of the multihop network. At the same time, the fairness of a network is closely related to the scheduling scheme. In this research effort, we propose an intelligent algorithm that can schedule the transmissions in a fair manner, taking into account the communication requirements of the active flows of the network.

1   Introduction

A wireless multihop network is a network, where communication between two-end nodes is carried out by hopping over multiple short wireless links. In such a network, each node not only sends/receives packets to/from adjacent nodes, but also acts as a router and forwards packets on behalf of other nodes. Wireless multihop networks have many applications, including data monitoring, formation of community and indoor home networks and broadband access network to the Internet. In addition, wireless multihop networks provide wide coverage, as well as, high data rates. The interest in wireless multihop networks has also been increased due to their

Please use the following format when citing this chapter:

Sgora, A., Vergados, D. J., Vergados, D. D., 2007, in IFIP International Federation for Information Processing, Volume 247, Artificial Intelligence and Innovations 2007: From Theory to Applications, eds. Boukis, C., Pnevmatikakis, L., Polymenakos, L., (Boston: Springer), pp. 279-286.

relatively low deployment costs, since they do not require an infrastructure and complicated network preplanning.

However, despite these advantages, some weaknesses still appear in multi-hop networks. Fairness has been found to be limited in multi-hop networks. Regarding, the spatial-temporal congestion variation, the topology of wireless multi-hop networks and the medium access control protocols that have been designed for single-hop networks, are responsible for severe unfairness in these networks.

In this paper, we focus our study on the medium access control protocols and we propose an algorithm that can schedule the transmissions in a fair manner, taking into consideration the communication requirements of the active flows of the network.

The rest of the paper is organized as follows: Section II discusses the related work, while Section III presents the network model. In Section IV the proposed algorithm is presented and in Section V an illustrative example is given. Finally, Section VI concludes the paper.

2   Related Work

The most popular medium access control scheme for wireless multihop networks is the IEEE 802.11 DCF [1], which uses the CSMA algorithm and has numerous disadvantages like high overhead, increased access delay, high jitter and limited QoS capabilities. Furthermore, 802.11 can not overcome the Exposed Terminal problem. The application of TDMA can overcome all these issues. However, a solution for the NP complete Broadcast Scheduling Problem (BSP) [2] is needed for using TDMA in wireless multihop environment. Several TDMA scheduling algorithms may be found in the literature. [2-7].

More specifically, Ephremides et al [2] in order to solve the problem propose a heuristic algorithm that assumes that each Mobile Station (MS) has knowledge of two hops away connectivity. A priority rule is used to select an eligible MS to transmit in slot i. The selected MS sends a broadcast message to inform the other MSs that it is using slot i. The algorithm progresses in a way that allows as many MSs as possible to transmit in each slot. However, it does not ensure fair slot allocations among all MSs and it is not topology-transparent [6]. Also, the authors in [3] propose an approximation algorithm based on Mean Field Annealing (MFA) to solve the scheduling problem and to can achieve maximum channel utilization, as well as, lower delay. More specifically, the authors map the channel utilization to be maximized and the interference-free constraints onto an energy function, and then the MFA procedure is applied to searching for the optimal solutions. Numerical results have shown that the proposed algorithm can find the shortest interference-free frame schedule, while providing the maximum channel utilization. However, the algorithm does not consider the traffic requirements of the active flows of the multihop network. Also, the MFA equations may be also a time consuming process. Salcedo-Sanz et al. [4] propose a mixed neural-genetic algorithm as a solution to the broadcast problem. The proposed algorithm solves the broadcast scheduling problem in two stages: during the first stage finds a feasible frame length able to satisfy interference constraints and to guarantee the transmission of every radio station once per frame; the second stage tackles the maximization of the throughput for a given frame length. For the first stage, a discrete Hopfield neural network (HNN) is used and for the second stage, we apply a combination of a HNN and a genetic algorithm (GA). Simulation results show that the proposed algorithm obtains optimum frame lengths and better transmission packings than MFA. However, in this paper only per node fairness is considered. The authors in [5] propose a centralized scheduling algorithm using a modified genetic algorithm (GA), called the genetic-fix algorithm. Particularly, the authors formulate the broadcast scheduling problem as an unconstrained optimization problem. Then, the genetic-fix algorithm is to obtain a conflict-free broadcast assignment where the frame length is close to minimum within a reasonable time. The main advantage of this algorithm at each repetition the search space is reduced. However, the algorithm does not take into consideration the per-flow fairness requirements. Also, in [8] a distributed approach was proposed. In our previous work [7], we proposed an algorithm for overcoming the NP-complete Broadcast Scheduling Problem that appears in TDMA ad-hoc networks. Simulation results showed that the proposed algorithm is superior than the MFA one and equivalent to the mixed neural-genetic algorithm [4] for most of the tested network topologies in terms of delay and throughput, whereas the new algorithm is far superior in terms of fairness. However, the traffic requirements are not considered. In this paper, we propose an algorithm that can schedule the transmissions in a fair manner, taking into consideration the communication requirements of the active flows of a wireless multihop network.

3   Network Model

We consider a wireless multihop that consists of a set of N nodes. Every transmission of a node is broadcasted over the wireless channel, and all nodes located close to the transmitting node can receive the transmission, where as far away nodes cannot receive the transmission. Nodes that can transmit with each other are called neighboring nodes. Furthermore, the receiving nodes can only receive one transmission at a time without errors, and nodes cannot transmit and receive packets at the same time.

We assume that multiple access in the wireless channel is achieved by TDMA. All nodes in the wireless multihop network must have at least one transmission opportunity within each TDMA frame. The TDMA frame consists of a number of TDMA slots. The number of slots in each TDMA frame is called the frame length. More than one wireless multihop nodes may transmit in every TDMA slot without collision, if they do not have any common neighbors. The purpose of TDMA scheduling is to determine the slots used by every node for transmitting its packets, in a way that ensures collision avoidance and at the same time minimizes the delay each node experiences, and maximized the total network capacity in a fair manner.

If we represent all nodes in the a wireless multihop network as vertices of a graph with edges between neighboring nodes then there are no collisions in the network, if the distance of all transmitting nodes in the graph is at least two hops. So the broadcast scheduling problem is to determine how to schedule every node of the network into the appropriate slot, so that maximum capacity is achieved in the shortest possible frame length. As shown in [2], broadcast scheduling is an NP-complete problem.

4   Description of the Proposed Algorithm

Two stations can use in the same slot if they have no common neighbors. Therefore, we consider the one–hop neighboring table A, where

$$A_{i,j} = \begin{cases} 1 & \text{if node i and j are neighbors, or } i = j \\ 0 & \text{otherwise} \end{cases} \tag{1}$$

We represent the set of nodes transmitting during timeslot k as S_k. Consider the vector C, which helps to determine if a new node may collide with the slot, where

$$C_i = \sum_{j \in S_k} A_{i,j} . \tag{2}$$

If node $k \notin S_k$ and there is at least one node $l \in S_k$, where k and l have z as a common neighbour, then $A_{z,l} = A_{z,k} = 1$. Therefore, $C_z \geq 1$ and $\vec{A}_k \cdot \vec{C} > 0$.   On the contrary, if

$$\vec{A}_k \cdot \vec{C} = 0 \tag{3}$$

there is no $l \in S_k$ that has a common neighbour with node k and consequently node k can be added to the slot. This technique is an easy test to determine if a node collides with a node in the TDMA frame, and reduces the complexity of the algorithm.

We also consider the Flow table F, where

$$F_{i,j} = \begin{cases} 1 & \text{if node i transmits data on behalf of flow j} \\ 0 & \text{otherwise} \end{cases} \tag{4}$$

In order to produce the desired schedule, all nodes in the network are tested in a specific order. If equation (3) is true for the tested node (k), then the node is added to the slot; otherwise it is not added and the next node is tested. When all nodes in the network are tested, then the first time slot is produced. The nodes are re-ordered, and the nodes are re-tested to produce the second timeslot. This procedure is repeated until every node in the network has transmitted as many times as it needs according to the number of flows it participates.

Obviously, the set of nodes in every slot is determined by the order by which the nodes are tested. Since the objectives of the algorithm are fairness we created a weight vector $\vec{W}$, where

$$W_i = \sum_{j \in T} F_{i,j} \tag{5}$$

where T is the set of flows in the network. When creating each slot, if b_k is the order of node k, then the nodes are ordered as follows:

If $b_i < b_j$ if $W_i > W_j$. Nodes that transmit in many slots should be checked first, because nodes that participate in few flows have a grater chance of transmitting in a following slot.

After each slot is created, the values in W are updated and the nodes are re-ordered. If a slot has been assigned to node i then W_i is reduced by 1, meaning that now it requires one less slot to fulfill its transmission requirements. Then, the next slots are created until all nodes have fulfill their transmission requirements based on the W_i .

4   An Illustrative Example

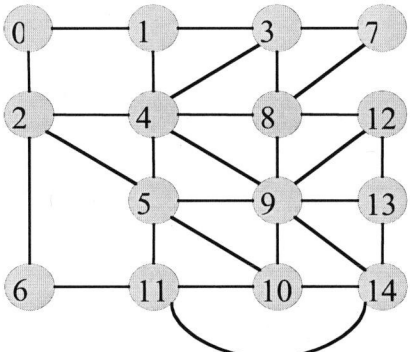

Figure 1. The topology used for the performance evaluation of the algorithm.

In this first approach, we examine the performance of the proposed protocol on a static topology that consists of 15 nodes (Figure 1). In this topology, we randomly selected 6 nodes to be used as sources for the connections, and 6 other nodes to be used as destinations. The sources intend to transmit information to the destinations, and our scheduling scheme will calculate a multihop TDMA schedule, that will be used for organizing the nodes' transmissions, so that no collisions appear, and the frame length is as small as possible. As stated previously, the scheduling scheme will assign the nodes with transmission slots proportionally, depending on the transmission opportunities that each node needs for fulfilling the flows' requirements in a fair manner.

The produced flows are the following:
- Flow 1: 0 -9
- Flow 2: 2-3
- Flow 3: 2-12
- Flow 4: 14 -4
- Flow 5: 7-3
- Flow 6: 6 -14

A shortest path routing protocol was used for obtaining the routes from the sources to the destinations. Note that the shortest path routing algorithm may not always produce the optimal solution, because a different routing could cause a more balanced network, which could result in a shorter frame length. However, this fact is not taken into consideration in this preliminary work, and the shortest paths are used. In future work we will deal with this matter. The routing protocol has produced the following routes:
- Route 1: 0-2-4-9
- Route 2: 2-4-3
- Route 3: 2-4-8-12
- Route 4: 14-9-4
- Route 5: 7-3
- Route 6: 6-11-14

According to the above routes, the corresponding weights (W_i) were calculated using equations (4) and (5). As mentioned in the previous section, the scheduling algorithm will assign slots to the nodes, at a number that is proportional to the transmission opportunities required for fulfilling the active flows' needs, as produced by the routing algorithm. The produced weights are shown in Table 1.

Table I. The corresponding weights that are produced by applying the above routes on the network topology

Node	W_i	
0	1	
2	3	
4	2	
6	1	
7	1	
8	1	
9	2	
11		1
14	1	

After executing the fair scheduling algorithm, the TDMA schedule was produced (Figure 2). Each row represents a separate slot, and each column represents a node. If the cell that is defined by a node (column) and a slot (row) is white, then the node does not transmit in this slot. Otherwise, if the cell is black, the node will transmit in the slot. As we can see, the produces schedule gives the nodes the appropriate slots. In addition, we see that the nodes may transmit simultaneously, as long this doesn't cause a collision. The produced frame length is 8.

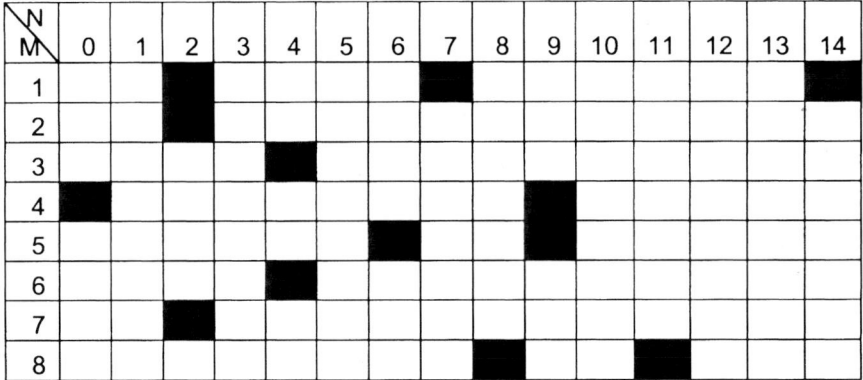

Figure 2. The broadcast schedule for the 14-node-28-edge instance. N and M stand for the number of nodes and the number of time slots, respectively. The black square stands for the transmission of node i in slot j.

5 Conclusions

A wireless multihop network is a network that communication between two end nodes is carried out by hopping over multiple short wireless links. In such network, each node not only sends/receives packets to/from adjacent nodes, but also acts as a router and forwards packets for other nodes. Fairness has been found to be limited in multi-hop networks. The topology of wireless multi-hop networks, in addition to the medium access control protocols that have been designed for single-hop networks, in relation to the spatial-temporal congestion variation are responsible for severe unfairness in these networks. In this paper, we propose an intelligent algorithm that can schedule the transmissions in a fair manner, taking into consideration the communication requirements of the active flows of the network.

References

1. IEEE std. 802.11, "Wireless LAN Medium Access Control (MAC) and Physical Layer (PHY) Specifications", 1999.
2. Ephremides and T. V. Truong, "Scheduling broadcast in multihop radio networks," *IEEE Transactions on Communications*, vol. 38, no. 4, April 1990, pp. 456–460.
3. G. Wang and N. Ansari, "Optimal broadcast scheduling in packet radio networks using mean field annealing," *IEEE Journal on Selected Areas in Communications*, vol.15, no 2, February 1997, pp.250-260.
4. S. Salcedo-Sanz, C. Busono-Calzon, and A.R. Figueiral-Vidal, "A Mixed Neural-Genetic Algorithm for the Broadcast Scheduling Problem", *IEEE Transactions on Wireless Communications*, vol. 2, no 2, March 2003, pp. 277-283.
5. Y. Ngo, and Victor O. K. Li, "Centralized Broadcast Scheduling in Packet Radio Networks via Genetic-Fix Algorithms", *IEEE Transactions on Communications*, vol. 51, no. 9, September 2003, pp. 1439-1441.
6. H. Fattah and C. Leung, "An Overview Of Scheduling Algorithms In Wireless Multimedia Networks", *IEEE Wireless Communications*, October 2002, pp. 76-83.

7.   D. J. Vergados, D. D. Vergados and C. Douligeris, "A new approach for TDMA scheduling in ad-hoc networks", *In the Proceedings of the 10th IFIP International Conference on Personal Wireless Communications (PWC'05)*, Colmar, France, 2005.

8.   Dimitrios D. Vergados, Dimitrios J. Vergados, Christos Douligeris, Spyridon L. Tombros, "QoS-Aware TDMA for End-to-End Traffic Scheduling in Ad-hoc Networks", IEEE Wireless Communications, Vol. 13, No. 5, 2006, pp. 68-74.

ANN Prediction Models for Outdoor SIMO Millimeter Band System

Nektarios Moraitis and Demosthenes Vouyioukas
Mobile Radiocommunications Laboratory, National Technical
University of Athens, 9 Heroon Polytechniou str. 15773, Zografou, Athens,
Greece, morai@mobile.ntua.gr
Dept. of Information and Communication Systems Engineering,
University of the Aegean, Karlovassi 83200, Samos, Greece
dvouyiou@aegean.gr

Abstract. This paper presents the prediction propagation paths of angle of arrivals (AoAs) of a Smart Antenna System in an outdoor environment utilizing Artificial Neural Networks (ANN). The proposed models consist of a Multilayer Perceptron and a Generalized Regression Neural Network trained with measurements of an antenna system consisted of a Single Input Single Output (SISO) system in the millimeter wave band. For comparison purposes the theoretical Gaussian scatter density model was investigated for the derivation of the power angle profile. The proposed models utilize the characteristics of the environment for prediction of the angle of arrivals of each one of the propagation paths and can be applicable for the derivation of SIMO (Single Input Single Output) parameters, such as system capacity. The results are presented towards the average error, standard deviation and mean square error compared with the measurements and they are capable for the derivation of accurate prediction models for the case of AoA in an outdoor millimeter wave propagation environment.

1 Introduction

Smart Antenna Systems [1] and especially MISO (Multiple Input Single Output) [2] or SIMO (Single Input Multiple Output) [3] systems have already been evaluated for the optimization of wireless system performance. The prediction of the field strength is a very complex and difficult task. In most cases, there are no clear line-of-sight (LOS) conditions between the transmitter and the receiver. Generally, the prediction models are classified as empirical [4] or theoretical [5], or a combination of these two [6]. However, the main problem of the classical empirical models is the unsatisfactory accuracy, while the theoretical models lack in computational efficiency.

Please use the following format when citing this chapter:

Moraitis, N., Vouyioukas, D., 2007, in IFIP International Federation for Information Processing, Volume 247, Artificial Intelligence and Innovations 2007: From Theory to Applications, eds. Boukis, C., Pnevmatikakis, L., Polymenakos, L., (Boston: Springer), pp. 287-296.

During last years, Artificial Neural Networks (ANN) have experienced a great development. ANN applications are already very numerous. Classificators, signal processors, optimizers and controllers have already been realized. Although there are several types of ANN's all of them share the following features [7]: exact analytical formula impossible; required accuracy around some percent; medium quantity of data to process; environment adaptation that allows them to learn from a changing environment and parallel structure that allows them to achieve high computation speed. All these characteristics of ANN's make them suitable for predicting field strength in different environments and additionally angle of arrivals (AoA).

The prediction of field strength and AoA can be described as the transformation of an input vector containing topographical and morphographical information (e.g. path profile) to the desired output value. The unknown transformation is a scalar function of many variables (several inputs and a single output), because a huge amount of input data has to be processed. The inputs contain information about the transmitter and receiver locations, surrounding buildings, frequency, etc while the output gives the propagation loss for those inputs. From this point of view, research in propagation loss modeling consists in finding both the inputs and the function that best approximate the propagation loss. Given that ANN's are capable of function approximation, they are useful for the propagation loss and angle of arrival modeling. The feedforward neural networks are very well suited for prediction purposes because do not allow any feedback from the output (field strength or path loss) to the input (topographical and morphographical data).

In this paper, the presented studies develop a number of Multilayer Perceptron Neural Networks (MLP-NN) and Generalized Radial Basis Function Neural Networks (RBF-NN) based models trained on extended data set of propagation path loss measurements taken in an outdoor environment. The smart antenna measurement system was a SISO one where a continuous wave (CW) signal at 60 GHz was transmitted from a fixed base station to a fixed receiver, comprised of one antenna element, rotated in the azimuthal direction recording the multipath components. The signal envelope as a function of time was recorded. The performance of the neural network based models is evaluated by comparing their prediction, standard deviation and mean square error (MSE) between their predicted values and measurements data. Also, a comparison with the results is obtained by applying the Gaussian model.

The remainder of this paper is organized as follows. Section 2 deals with the ANN overview describing and explaining the behavior of the two NN utilized models. In Section 3, an analytically description of the geometry of the measurement environment under consideration is presented along with the measurement procedure. In Section 4, the NN prediction models are implemented analytically describing the implementation method and the prediction results are presented in terms of measured Power Angle Profile (PAP), taking also into consideration the Gaussian model. Finally, Section 5 is devoted to conclusions derived by the prediction procedure.

2   The ANN Overview

2.1   Multilayer Perceptron Neural Network (MLP-NN)

Fig. 1 shows the configuration of a multilayer perceptron with one hidden layer and one output layer. The network shown here is fully interconnected. This means that each neuron of a layer is connected to each neuron of the next layer so that only forward transmission through the network is possible, from the input layer to the output layer through the hidden layers. Two kinds of signals are identified in this network:

- The function signals (also called input signals) that come in at the input of the network, propagate forward (neuron by neuron) through the network and reach the output end of the network as output signals;
- The error signals that originate at the output neuron of the network and propagate backward (layer by layer) through the network.

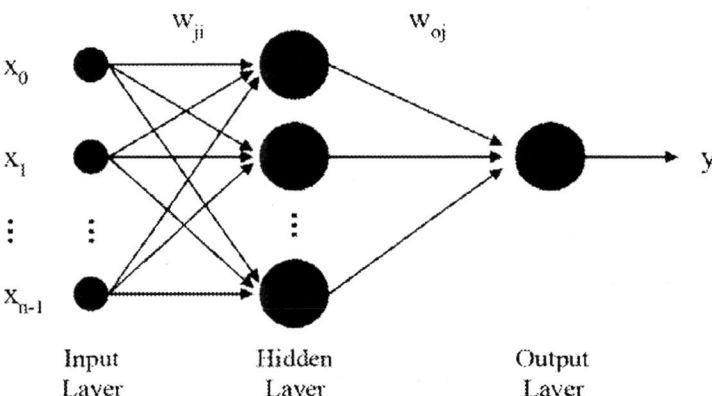

Fig. 1. MLP-NN configuration

The output of the neural network is described by the following equation:

$$y = F_o \left(\sum_{j=0}^{M} w_{0j} \left(F_h \left(\sum_{i=0}^{N} w_{ji} x_i \right) \right) \right) \tag{1}$$

where
- w_{0j} represents the synaptic weights from neuron j in the hidden layer to the single output neuron,
- x_i represents the i-th element of the input vector,
- F_h and F_o are the activation function of the neurons from the hidden layer and output layer, respectively,
- w_{ji} are the connection weights between the neurons of the hidden layer and the inputs.

The learning phase of the network proceeds by adaptively adjusting the free parameters of the system based on the mean square error E, described by Equation (2), between predicted and measured path loss for a set of appropriately selected training examples:

$$E = \frac{1}{2} \sum_{i=1}^{m} (y_i - d_i)^2 \qquad (2)$$

where y_i is the output value calculated by the network and d_i represents the expected output.

When the error between network output and the desired output is minimized, the learning process is terminated and the network can be used in a testing phase with test vectors. At this stage, the neural network is described by the optimal weight configuration, which means that theoretically ensures the output error minimization.

2.2   Generalized Radial Basis Function Neural Network (RBF-NN)

The Generalized Radial Basis Function Neural Network (RBF-NN) is a neural network architecture that can solve any function approximation problem. The learning process is equivalent to finding a surface in a multidimensional space that provides a best fit to the training data, with the criterion for the "best fit" being measured in some statistical sense. The generalization is equivalent to the use of this multidimensional surface to interpolate the test data.

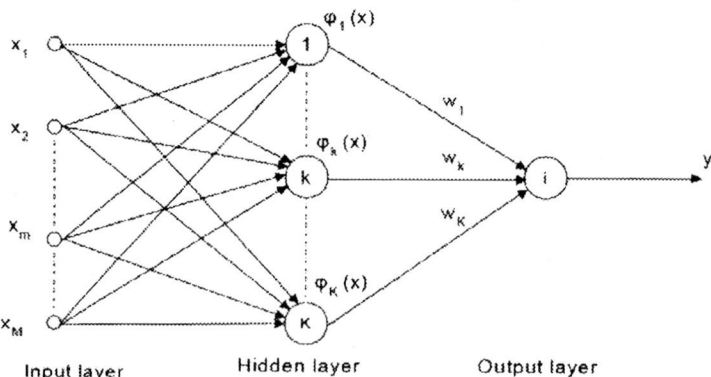

Fig. 2. RBF-NN architecture

As it can be seen from Fig. 2, the Generalized Radial Basis Function Neural Network (RBF–NN) consists of three layers of nodes with entirely different roles:
•   the input layer, where the inputs are applied,

- the hidden layer, where a nonlinear transformation is applied on the data from the input space to the hidden space; in most applications the hidden space is of high dimensionality and
- the linear output layer, where the outputs are produced

The most popular choice for the function φ is a multivariate Gaussian function with an appropriate mean and autocovariance matrix. The outputs of the hidden layer units are of the form:

$$\varphi_k [x] = \exp \left[-\frac{\left(x - v_k^x\right)^T \left(x - v_k^x\right)}{2\sigma^2} \right] \tag{3}$$

when v_k^x are the corresponding clusters for the inputs and v_k^y are the corresponding clusters for the outputs obtained by applying a clustering technique of the input/output data that produces K cluster centers [8]. v_k^x and v_k^y are defined as:

$$v_k^x = \sum_{x(p) \in \text{cluster } k} x(p) \tag{4}$$

$$v_k^y = \sum_{y(p) \in \text{cluster } k} y(p) \tag{5}$$

The outputs of the hidden layer nodes are multiplied with appropriate interconnection weights to produce the output of the GRNN. The weight for the hidden node k (i.e., w_k) is equal to:

$$w_k = \frac{v_k^x}{\sum_{k=1}^{K} N_k \exp \left[-\frac{d\left(x, v_k^x\right)^2}{2\sigma^2} \right]} \tag{6}$$

where N_k is the number of input data in the cluster centre k, and

$$d\left(x, v_k^x\right) = \left(x - v_k^x\right)^T \left(x - v_k^x\right) \tag{7}$$

3   Measurement Environment and Procedure

The measurement took place in a typical urban environment as indicated in Fig. 3. The ground plan is illustrated as well as the transmitter and receiver positions. The first receiver position is 30 m away from the transmitter, whereas the second location is 70 m apart. Both transmitter and receiver terminals were placed at 3 m above the ground. Line-of-Sight (LoS) condition was preserved during the measurement. The street where the measurement took place is 20 m wide, including the pavements. All the indicated buildings have 5 to 6 stories creating a narrow propagation canyon. The buildings are made with concrete and bricks, while all the building facades are covered with plaster and paint. There were also cars parked along both sides of the road, but their height is lower than the direct propagation path between the transmitter and receiver.

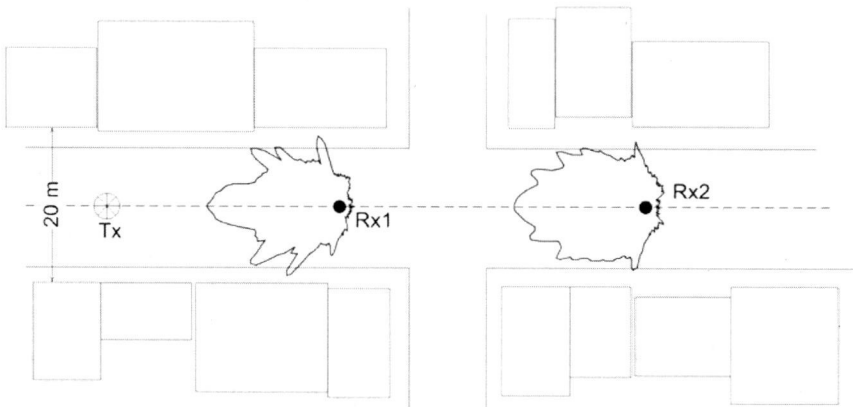

Fig. 3. Measurement environment and superimposed the derived Power Angle Profile.

The measurements were performed by transmitting a continuous wave (CW) signal at 60 GHz, from a fixed base station to a fixed receiver, and recording the signal envelope as a function of time. Details for the measurement setup can be found in [9]. The transmitter output power was 100 mW (+20 dBm). The receiver hardware is located on a trolley, which was stationary at the measurement position. After amplification, the received signal is down-converted to 300 MHz IF and fed to a commercial receiver. The input to the automatic gain control (AGC) of the receiver is then sampled at 2 kHz and the data values were stored to a portable PC. The receiver had a noise floor of -90 dBm. For this measurement, a biconical antenna (omni-directional with 0 dBi gain in azimuth and 36° in elevation) was used as the transmitter antenna, and a horn antenna with 35 dBi gain was used as the receiver antenna. Both antennas are vertically polarized. The half power beamwidth of the horn antenna was 4° in azimuth and 3° in elevation. When a highly directional antenna is used, the system provides high spatial resolution to resolve multipath components with different AoAs.

During the measurements, a mechanically steered directional antenna was used to resolve multipath components. An automated system was used to precisely position the receiver antenna along a linear track and then rotate the antenna in the azimuthal direction. At each position, the receiver antenna is rotated in azimuth from 0 to 360° with a step size of 5° and power was recorded at each of the 72 angular steps. Then, a local average is calculated from the measurement results at 10 different positions along the linear track being λ/2 apart. The local average helps to remove any residual small-scale or time-varying fading that may occur at individual positions. The precisions of the track and spin positions are better than 1 mm and $1°$, respectively.

Consequently, if we know the Power Angle Profile (PAP) of a SISO channel, we can calculate the channel matrix of a SIMO channel multiplying the array response vector at the receiver. The PAP of a SISO channel can be yielded by either PAP measurements between fixed transmit and receive terminals, a properly trained NN model and, a theoretical model (e.g. Gaussian model).

4   Prediction Models' Implementation

The goal of the prediction is not only to produce small errors for the set of training examples but also to be able to perform well with examples not used in the training process. This generalization property is very important in practical prediction situation where the intention is to use the propagation prediction model to determine the angle of arrival of potential transmitter locations for which no or limited measured data are available.

The selection of the set of training examples is very important in order to achieve good generalization properties [7], [10]. The set of all available data is separated in two disjoint sets that are training set and test set. The test set is not involved in the learning phase of the networks and it is used to evaluate the performance of the neural model. An important problem that occurs during the neural network training is the overadaptation that is the network memorizes the training examples and it does not learn to generalize the new situations. In order to avoid overadaptation and to achieve good generalization performances, the training set is separated in the actual training subset and the validation subset, typically 10-20 % of the full training set [7]. In order to make the neural network training process more efficient, the input and desired output values are normalized so that they will have zero mean and unity standard deviation.

Since the purpose is to train the neural networks to perform well for all the routes, we should build the training set including points from the entire set of measurements data. In our applications the neural networks are trained with the Levenberg-Marquardt algorithm, which converges faster than the backpropagation algorithm with adaptive learning rates and momentum. The Levenberg-Marquardt algorithm is an approximation of Newton's method. As an optimization technique is more powerful than the method of gradient descent used in backpropagation algorithm. The Levenberg-Marquardt rule for updating parameters (weights and biases) is given by:

$$\Delta W = \left(J^T J + \mu I \right)^{-1} J^T e \tag{8}$$

where e is an error vector, μ is a scalar parameter, W is a matrix of networks weights and J is the Jacobian matrix of the partial derivatives of the error components with respect to the weights. For large values of μ the $J^T J$ terms become negligible and learning progresses according to $\mu^{-1} J^T e$, which is gradient descent. Whenever a step is taken and error increases, μ is increased until a step can be taken without increasing error. However, if μ becomes too large, no learning process takes place (i.e. $\mu^{-1}J^{T}\mathrm{e}$ approaches zero). This occurs when an error minima has been found. For small value of μ, the above expression becomes the Gaussian-Newton method.

A data set of 406 patterns, that represents 20% from all available patterns, was used for training purpose. A set of 1620 patterns was used to test the model. In order to train the NN model the measured PAP was used. In Table 1, the average error, the standard deviation and the mean square error are presented, obtained from the training set by the proposed Multilayer Perceptron Neural Network and the Generalized Regression Neural Network. Fig. 4 presents the measured Power Angle Profile (PAP) together with the results derived by the MLP-NN and the RBF-NN predictions. As it is evident the results between the measured and the predicted PAP are very good with the Mean Square Error (MSE) equals to 4.9 dB for the MLP-NN model and 2.6 dB for the RBG-NN model. Furthermore, the theoretical Gaussian model for angular profile prediction is utilized for comparison reasons and presented also in Table 1 and Fig. 4. The Gaussian model is given by [11]:

$$PAP(\phi) = \frac{1}{2\pi\sigma_\phi^2} \exp\left[-\frac{\phi^2}{2\sigma_\phi^2} \right] \qquad (9)$$

The measured angular spread σ_ϕ was calculated $240°$ for the first and $260°$ for the second measurement position. Hence the same value will be used in Equation (9). The measured angular spread is calculated by [12]:

$$\sigma_\phi = \sqrt{1 - \frac{\|F_1\|^2}{\|F_2\|^2}}, \quad F_n = \int_0^{2\pi} p(\theta)\exp(jn\theta)d\theta \qquad (10)$$

where F_n (n =1 or 2) is given by [12], and $p(\theta)$ is the measured PAP. The MSE between the measured PAP and the Gaussian model was found equal to 6.4 dB. All the results are summarized in Table 1.

Table 1. Prediction results of the ANN models' implementation

	Model	Average Error [dB]	Standard Deviation [dB]	Mean Square Error [dB]
	RBF-NN	2.0	1.3	2.4
Rx-1	MLP-NN	4.0	2.1	4.5
	Gaussian	5.2	3.2	6.0
	RBF-NN	2.5	1.1	2.8
Rx-2	MLP-NN	4.8	2.0	5.2
	Gaussian	5.5	3.5	6.7

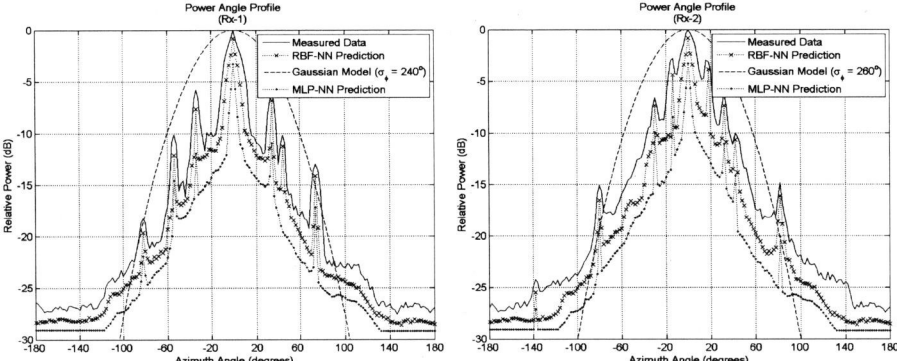

Fig. 4. Comparison between the measured PAP, RBF-NN, MLP-NN prediction, and theoretical Gaussian model for two different receiver's location.

From Fig. 4 it is clear that the prediction of the trained NN models is very good, whereas the best results are yielded by the RBF-NN model. On the other hand the Gaussian model provides greater errors than the other two cases because it is not so accurate, and takes into account a smaller range of azimuth angle.

5   Conclusions

In this paper we examined the applicability of the neural networks for the prediction of angle of arrivals in an outdoor smart antenna system. The data measurements of an outdoor environment using a rotating receiver in the azimuthal direction recording the multipath components at the millimeter wave band of 60 GHz were taken into consideration for training purposes of the NN. Two NN models (RBF and MLP) were considered for the derivation of the prediction models as well as the Gaussian theoretical model is evaluated for comparison purposes. The main advantage of the proposed NN models is that the models should be easily adjusted to specific environments and complex propagation conditions. The knowledge of the Power Angle Profile from the ANN prediction models of a SISO channel can be used for the calculation of the channel matrix of a SIMO channel multiplying the array response vector at the receiver.

The results are depicted in terms of average error, standard deviation and mean square error compared with the measurements and showed very good accuracy. The MSE between the measurements and the NN-models was found 4.9 dB for the MLP-NN model and 2.6 dB for the RBG-NN model. The Gaussian model provides greater errors because it takes into account a smaller range of azimuth angle. High accuracy can be obtained, because the NNs are trained with measurements taking into account buildings characteristics and orientation, thus contain realistic propagation effects considering parameters which are difficult to include in analytic equations. In more specific local cases, the accuracy can be improved by using additional NNs training. Results are always connected with some uncertainty but accuracy is sufficient for prediction purposes.

References

1. J. H. Winters, Smart antennas for wireless systems, *IEEE Personal Commun.*, **5**(1) (1998), 23–27.
2. K. C. Zangi, L.G. Krasny, Capacity-achieving transmitter and receiver pairs for dispersive MISO channels, *IEEE Trans. on Wireless Communications*, **2**(6), 1204 – 1216 (2003).
3. J. K. Tugnait, A multidelay whitening approach to blind identification and equalization of SIMO channels, *IEEE Trans. on Wireless Communications*, **1**(3), 456 – 467 (2002).
4. M. Hata, Empirical formula for propagation loss in land mobile radio services, *IEEE Trans. on Vehicular Technology,* **29**(3), 317-325 (1980).
5. J. Walfisch, H. L. Bertoni, A theoretical model of UHF propagation in urban environments, *IEEE Trans. On Antennas and Propagation,* **36**(12), 1788-1796 (1988).
6. G. K. Chan, Propagation and coverage prediction for cellular radio systems, *IEEE Trans. on Vehicular Technology,* **40**(4), 665-670 (1991).
7. S. Haykin, *Neural Networks: A Comprehensive Foundation*, IEEE Press (McMillan College Publishing Co., 1994).
8. W. Honcharenko, H. L. Bertoni, J. L. Dailing, J. Qian, and H. D. Yee, Mechanisms Governing UHF Propagation on Single Floors in Modern Office Buildings, *IEEE Trans. on Vehicular Technology*, **41**(4), 496-504 (1992).
9. A. Kanatas, N. Moraitis, G. Pantos, and P. Constantinou, Time delay and coherence bandwidth evaluation in urban environment for PCS microcells, *in Proc. IST'02*, 508-512, (2002).
10. C. Christodoulou, and M. Georgiopoulos, *Applications of Neural Networks in Electromagnetics* (Artech House, 2001).
11. R. Janaswamy, Angle and time of arrival statistics for the Gaussian scatter density model, *IEEE Trans. Wireless Commun.*, **1**(3), 488-497 (2002).
12. H. Hu, V. Kukshya, and T. S. Rappaport, Spatial and temporal characteristics of 60-GHz indoor channels, *IEEE J. Select. Areas Commun.*, **20**(3), 620-630 (2002).

Section 7

Intelligent Processing of Audiovisual Content

Gender Classification Based on FeedForward Backpropagation Neural Network

S. Mostafa Rahimi Azghadi , M. Reza Bonyadi and Hamed Shahhosseini
Department of Electrical and Computer Engineering, Shahid Beheshti
University, Evin, Tehran, Iran.
{M_rahimi, M_bonyadi}@std.sbu.ac.ir
Department of Electrical and Computer Engineering, Shahid Beheshti
University, Evin, Tehran, Iran.
H_shahhosseini@sbu.ac.ir

Abstract. Gender classification based on speech signal is an important task in variant fields such as content-based multimedia. In this paper we propose a novel and efficient method for gender classification based on neural network. In our work pitch feature of voice is used for classification between males and females. Our method is based on an MLP neural network. About 96 % of classification accuracy is obtained for 1 second speech segments.

Keywords. Gender classifications, Backpropagation neural network, pitch features, Fast Fourier Transform.

1 Introduction

Automatically detecting the gender of a speaker has several potential applications. In the content of automatic speech recognition, gender dependent models are more accurate than gender independent ones [1]. Also, gender dependent speech coders are more accurate than gender independent ones [2]. Therefore, automatic gender classification can be important tool in multimedia signal analysis systems.

The proposed technique assumes a constraint on the speech segment lengths, such as other existing techniques. Konig and Morgan (1992) extracted 12 Linear Prediction coding Coefficients (LPC) and the energy feature every 500 ms and used a Multi-Layer Perceptron as a classifier for gender detection [3]. Vergin and Farhat (1996) used the first two formants estimated from vowels to classify gender based on a 7 seconds sentences reporting 85% of classification accuracy on the Air Travel Information System (ATIS) corpus (Hemphill Charles et al., 1990) containing

Please use the following format when citing this chapter:

Azghadi, S. M. R., Bonyadi, M. R., Shahhosseini, H., 2007, in IFIP International Federation for Information Processing, Volume 247, Artificial Intelligence and Innovations 2007: From Theory to Applications, eds. Boukis, C., Pnevmatikakis, L., Polymenakos, L., (Boston: Springer), pp. 299-304.

specifically recorded clean speech[4]. Parris and Carey (1996) combined pitch and HMM for gender identification reporting results of 97.3% [5]. Their experiments have been carried out on sentences of 5 seconds from the OGI database. Some studies on the behavior of specific speech units, such as phonemes, for each gender were carried out [6].

This overview of the existing techniques for gender identification shows that the reported accuracies are generally based on sentences from 3 to 7 seconds obtained manually. In our work, speech segments have 1 second length and we obtained 96 % accuracy.

In several studies, some preprocessing of speech is also done, such as silence removal or phoneme recognition.

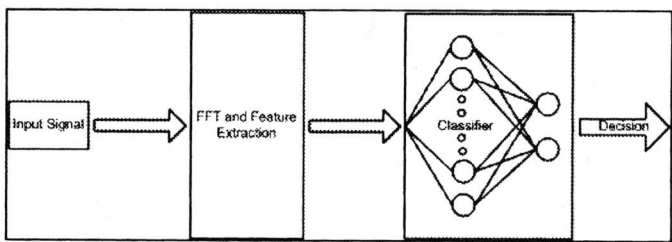

Fig. 1. Gender Classification system Architecture

2   Audio classifier

Our method is based on neural network for classification. Proposed method has 2 parts, after reading data from database tulips1 [7], first part is feature extraction and next part is our classifying based on neural network. Fig. 1 shows our system architecture. Next section describes all parts of our algorithm.

3   Feature extraction

Most important part in classification is feature extraction, because features determine differences between different signals and data. Main features are pitch and acoustic feature. These features are described in the following.

3.1   Pitch features

The pitch feature is perceptually and biologically proved as a good discrimin- ator between males' and females' voices. However the estimation of the pitch from the signal is not an easy task. Moreover, an overlap of the pitch values between male's and female's voices naturally exist, hence intrinsically limiting the capacity of the pitch feature in the case of gender identification, Fig. 2 [1]. Hence, a major difference between male and female speech is the pitch.

In general, female speech has higher pitch (120 - 200 Hz) than male speech (60 - 120 Hz) and could therefore be used to discriminate between men and women if an accurate pitch [5]. By using auread command in MATLAB we read an .au file that consist voice of a male or female. With this command, we can convert an au file to a vector. For example, we read voice of a female in database (candace11e.au) and plot her audio signal in the following   Fig. 3.

3.2. Acoustic features

Short term acoustic features describe the spectral components of the audio signal. Fast Fourier Transform can be used to extract the spectral components of the signal [1]. However, such features which are extracted at a short term basis (several ms) have a great variability for the male and female speech and captures phoneme like characteristics which is not required. For the problem of gender classification, we actually need features that do not capture the linguistic information such as words or phonemes.

4   The Classifier

The choice of a classifier for the gender classification problem in multimedia applications basically depends on the classification accuracy. Some of the important classifier is Gaussian Mixture Models (GMM), Multi Layer Perceptron (MLP), and Decision Tree. In similar training condition MLP has better accuracy in classification [1]. In this paper we used a MLP neural network for classifying, hence we describe a MLP in following, briefly.

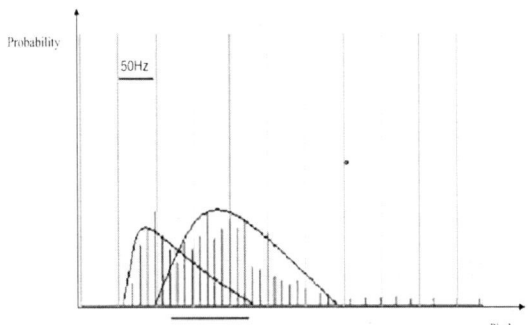

Fig. 2. Pitch Histogram for 1000 seconds of males (lower values) and 1000 seconds of females' speech (higher values). We can see the overlap between two classes.

4.1 Multi Layer Perceptron

MLP imposes no hypothesis on the distribution of the feature vectors. It tries to find a decision boundary, almost arbitrary, which is optimal for the discrimination between the feature vectors. The main drawback for MLPs is that the training time can be very long. However, we assume that if the features are good discriminators between the classes and if their values are well normalized the training process will be fast enough.

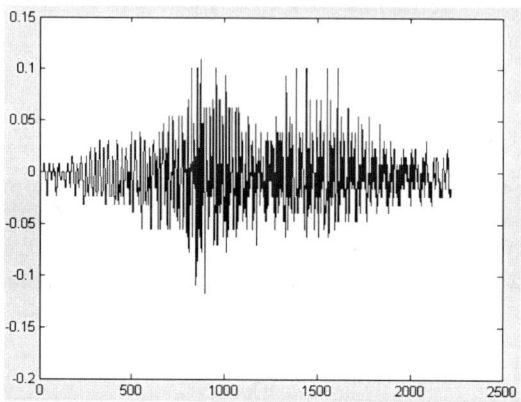

Fig. 3. A female audio signal that plot and show samples of this signal and their values between -0.2 and 0.2.

5   Proposed approach

In our method we processed audio signal that capture from a database (tulips1) contain 96 .au files. In this database every signal has a length about 1 second and we used some of this data for classifier training, and another files used for testing. First, we read 48 sound files that consists 3 males and 3 females, and with these data we train our network. As a classifier we use a multi layer perceptron with one hidden layer, 11 hidden neurons, and 2 output neurons that determine input vector is a male audio sample or female. For training an error backpropagation algorithm is used. First we used trainlm function for training, but for our application and with 1000 epochs for training, this function work very slow and it requires a lot of memory to run. Accordingly, we change Backpropagation network training function to TRAINRP. This function is a network training function that updates weight and bias values according to the resilient backpropagation algorithm (RPROP) and TRAINRP can train any network as long as its weight, net input, and transfer functions have derivative functions. Inputs data to this network are product of some preprocessing on raw data. Also, Transfer functions of layers in our network are default function in MATLAB (tansig). After reading data from database we get a Discrete Fourier Transform from input vectors by FFT(X, N) command. Fast Fourier Transform can be used to extract the spectral components of the signal. This command is the N-point FFT, padded with zeros if X has less than N points and truncated if it has more.

N in our problem is 4096, because with this number of point we can cover input data completely. After that, network training has been started with this vector as an input.

6 Experiments

The database used to evaluate our system consists of 96 samples with about 1 second length and we train our network with 50 percent of its data. Training data are consisting of 3 women' voices, 24 samples and three men, 24 samples (every person said one, two, three and four each of them twice). After training, we tested our classifier with another half of database and 96 % accuracy is obtained in gender classification.

7 Conclusion

The importance of accurate speech-based gender classification is rapidly increasing with the emergence of technologies which exploit gender information to enhance performance. This paper presented a voice-based gender classification system using a neural network as a classifier. With this classifier and by using pitch features we attained 96 % accuracy.

8 Future works

In the future, by using other features and using wavelet instead of Fourier transform or with that, we can get better results and achieve to higher performance. Also combining pitch and HMM for gender classification can be used to improve power of classification. And by dependent to problem, by using other classifier, better result may be obtained.

References

1. Hadi Harb, Liming Chen, Voice-Based Gender Identification in Multimedia Applications, Journal of Intelligent Information Systems, 24:2/3, 179–198, 2005.
2. Marston D., Gender Adapted Speech Coding, Proc 1998 IEEE International Conference on Acoustics, Speech, and Signal Processing, 1998. ICASSP 98, Vol. 1, 12–15, pp. 357–360.
3. Konig, Y. and Morgan, N., GDNN a Gender Dependent Neural Network for Continuous Speech Recognition, International Joint Conference on Neural Networks, 1992. IJCNN, Vol. 2, 7–11, pp. 332–337.
4. Rivarol, V., Farhat, A., and O'Shaughnessy D., Robust Gender-Dependent Acoustic-Phonetic Modelling in Continuous Speech Recognition Based on a New

Automatic Male Female Classification, Proc. Fourth International Conference on Spoken Language, 1996. ICSLP 96, Vol. 2, 3–6, pp. 1081–1084.

5. Parris, E.S. and Carey, M. J., Language Independent Gender Identification, Proc IEEE ICASSP, pp. 685–688.

6. Martland, P., Whiteside, S.P., Beet, S.W., and Baghai-Ravary, Analysis of Ten Vowel Sounds Across Gender and Regional Cultural Accent   Proc Fourth International Conference on Spoken Language, 1996. ICSLP 96, Vol. 4, 3–6, pp. 2231–2234.

7. Quast, Holger, Automatic Recognition of Nonverbal Speech: An Approach to Model the Perception of Para- and Extralinguistic Vocal Communication with Neural Networks, Machine Perception Lab Tech Report 2002/2. Institute for Neural   Computation,   UCSD.   Download   Website: http://mplab.ucsd.edu/databases/databases.html#orator

Hardware Natural Language Interface

C. Pavlatos, A. C. Dimopoulos, G. Papakonstantinou
National Technical University of Athens
Department of Electrical and Computer Engineering
Zografou 15773, Athens
Greece

Abstract. In this paper an efficient architecture for natural language processing is presented, implemented in hardware using FPGAs (Field Programmable Gate Arrays). The system can receive sentences belonging to a subset of Natural Languages (NL) from the internet or as SMS (Short Message Service). The recognition task of the input string uses Earley's parallel parsing algorithm and produces intermediate code according to the semantics of the grammar. The intermediate code can be transmitted to a computer, for further processing. The high computational cost of the parsing task in conjunction with a possible large amount of input sentences, to be processed simultaneously, justify the hardware implementation of the grammar (syntax and semantics). An extensive illustrative example is given from the area of question answering, in order to show the feasibility of the proposed system.

1 Introduction

Natural Language (NL) processing is a very attractive method of human-computer interaction and may be applied to a considerable number of fields such as intelligent embedded systems, intelligent interfaces, learning systems, etc [2], [3]. It is clear that automatically extracting linguistic information from a text can be an extremely powerful method for NL processing systems.

In this paper a hardware natural language interface is presented, using FPGAs (Field Programmable Gate Array). The system can receive sentences belonging to a subset of Natural Languages (NL) from the internet or as SMS (Short Message Service). In Fig. 4 a possible application is shown. Clients of a firm are asking questions which have to be answered very fast. The recognition task of the input string uses Earley's [1] parallel parsing algorithm and produces intermediate code according to the semantics of the grammar. The intermediate code can be transmitted to a computer, for further processing. The high computational cost of the parsing task, in conjunction with a possible large amount of input sentences to be processed concurrently, can dramatically speed-up the processing, due to the hardware

Please use the following format when citing this chapter:

Pavlatos, C., Dimopoulos, A. C., Papakonstantinou, G., 2007, in IFIP International Federation for Information Processing, Volume 247, Artificial Intelligence and Innovations 2007: From Theory to Applications, eds. Boukis, C., Pnevmatikakis, L., Polymenakos, L., (Boston: Springer), pp. 305-313.

implementation of the grammar (syntax and semantics). An extensive illustrative example is given from the area of question answering [4], in order to show the feasibility of the proposed system.

In the example given, the well known parallel parsing algorithm of Early [1], [5] has been used, based on the implementation proposed in [10]. When the syntactic recognition of the input sentence is completed, using the created parse tree, the semantics are evaluated and the FPGA sends the intermediate code generated to an abstract data-management machine that has access to a data-base, in order to produce the final result (answer). The intermediate code consists of commands and their parameters. The FPGA may receive the questions either via internet or via SMS receiver, since both interfaces may be implemented on the FPGA. In the second case an extra device (SMS receiver) is necessary.

The proposed architecture has been implemented in synthesizable Verilog in the XILINX ISE 8.2 [6] environment while the generated source has been simulated for validation, synthesized and tested on a Xilinx SPARTAN 3E FPGA.

2   The Hardware Parser

2.1   Theoretical Background

A Context Free Grammar [7] (CFG) is a quadruple $G = (N, T, R, S)$, where N is the set of non-terminal symbols, T is the set of terminal symbols, R is the set of grammar rules (a subset of $N \times (N \cup T)^*$ written in the form $A \rightarrow \alpha$, where $A \in N$ and $\alpha \in (N \cup T)^*$) and S ($S \in N$) is the start symbol (the root of the grammar). We use capital letters A, B, C... to denote non terminal symbols, lowercases a, b, c... to denote terminal symbols and Greek lowercases α, β, γ... for $(N \cup T)^*$ strings, λ is the null string and $V = N \cup T$ is called vocabulary. $A \rightarrow a$ means that a can derive from A after the application of one or more rules.

Let $S \rightarrow \alpha$, ($\alpha \in T^*$) be a derivation in G. The corresponding derivation (parsing) tree is an ordered tree with root S, leaves the terminal symbols in α, and nodes the rules that are used for the derivation process.

The process of analyzing a string for syntactic correctness is known as parsing. A parser is an algorithm that decides whether or not a string $a_1 a_2 a_3 ... a_n$ (of length n) can be generated from a grammar G and simultaneously constructs the derivation (or parse) tree.

An Attribute Grammar [8] (AG) is based upon a CFG. An AG is a quadruple $AG = \{G, A, SR, d\}$ where G is a CFG, $A = \cup A(X)$ where $A(X)$ is a finite set of attributes associated with each symbol $X \in V$. Each attribute represents a specific context-sensitive property of the corresponding symbol. The notation X.a is used to indicate that attribute a is an element of $A(X)$. $A(X)$ is partitioned into two disjoint sets; the set of synthesized attributes $AS(X)$ and the set of inherited attributes $AI(X)$. Synthesized attributes X.s are those whose values are defined in terms of attributes at descendant nodes of node X of the corresponding semantic tree. Inherited attributes X.i are those whose values are defined in terms of attributes at the parent and (possibly) the sibling nodes of node X of the corresponding semantic tree. The start symbol does not have inherited attributes. Each of the productions $p \in R$ $(p: X_0 \rightarrow X_1 X_2 X_n)$ of the CFG is augmented by a set of semantic rules SR(p) that define attributes in terms of other attributes of terminals and on terminals appearing in the same production. The way attributes will be evaluated depends both on their dependencies to other attributes in the tree and also on the way the tree is traversed. Finally d is a function that gives for each attribute a its domain d (a).

In the case of the illustrative example given in this paper (based on the one of ref. [4]) a subset of NL is given in the formalism of AG where the semantics are described using a synthesized attribute called 'output' for each non-terminal symbol. The only operation for the semantic rules needed, between the attributes of the non-terminals, is *conc (par$_1$, ..., par$_n$)*, which stands for the concatenation of strings *par$_1$, ..., par$_n$* that are values of the attributes of the non-terminal symbols of the syntax rule.

2.2   The Parsing Algorithm

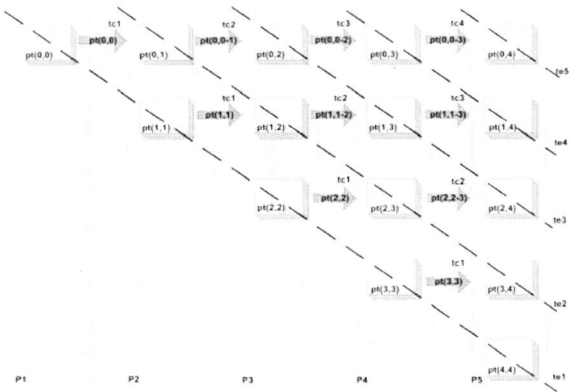

Fig. 1. The parallel architecture for the construction of Parsing Table

The parsing task may be reduced to the procedure of filling a two dimension table (parsing table: pt ()). Chiang & Fu [5] proved that the construction of the parsing table can be parallelized with respect to the length of the input string n, by computing at step k the cells pt(i, j) for which j-i=k≥1. Only the elements on or above the diagonal are used. In [9] a parallel architecture (see Fig. 1) has been presented that uses n+2 elements to compute the parse table in O(n) time where n is the input string length. In each execution step, each processing element P$_j$ is computing one cell pt(i,j) of the column j. At the next execution time P$_j$ is used again to compute the cell that belongs to the same column but is one row higher pt(i-1, j). In addition one processing element is required to control the whole process and one more to handle the attribute evaluation process as shown in Fig. 3. The n elements that are used for the parallel parsing are following the design presented in [10] (see Fig. 2).

After the end of each execution step k (t_{ek}), the computation of one parsing processing element terminates. At the next execution step this processing element should transmit the cells that it has computed, to the next processing (t_{ck}). Each processing element repeatedly calculates a cell, checks if it should transmit some cells and then if it should receive any.

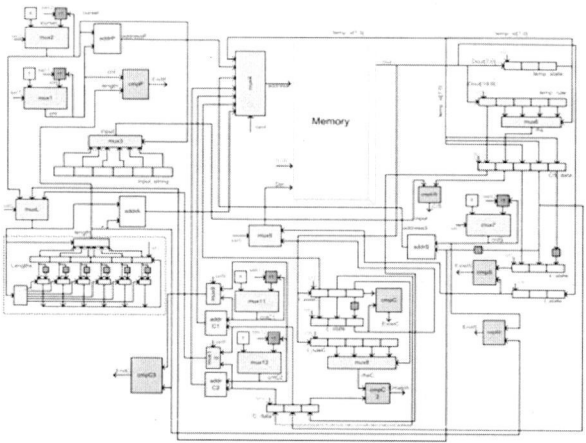

Fig. 2. The architecture of the Processing Element (PE)

2.3   The proposed modifications for the semantic processing

As it must be clear by now, the proposed implementation follows the architecture shown in Fig.3. The proposed architecture is based on the abovementioned CFG parser. The parser handles the recognition task and constructs the parse tree or parse trees in the case of ambiguous sentences. When the parsing process is over, the attributes may be evaluated. For that purpose, an extra module (Semantic Evaluator) has been created, so as to compute the semantics. This module takes as input the parse tree encoded in bit-vectors and gradually traverses it. In each branch (syntactic rule) of the tree, the semantic evaluator executes the corresponding semantic rule, which is nothing more than a concatenation of alpharithmetic strings. The resulting attribute value of the root symbol is the output string that will be transmitted to the abstract data-management machine that has access to a data-base in order to produce the final result (answer). Both parser and Semantic Evaluator are downloaded into the same FPGA board.

The parser module and semantic evaluator module are initialized by the grammar specifications. The resulting source code is downloaded into the FPGA. The latter, takes as input the input string, recognizes it, evaluates the semantics and responds with an intermediate code. In the example given in the next session the intermediate code consisting of commands and their parameters, for the abstract data-management machine. Finally, the abstract data-management machine executes the received commands and provides the user with the final result.

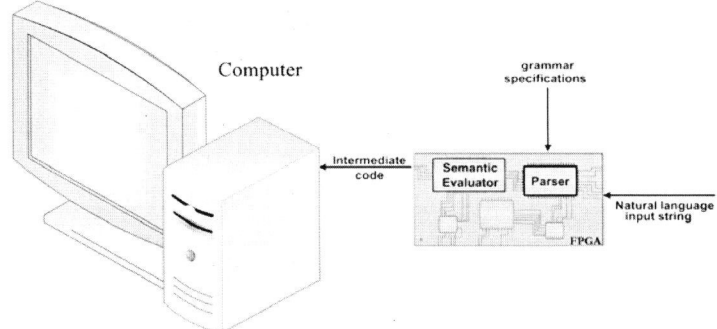

Fig. 3. The proposed architecture

3   An Illustrative Example

In order to show how we can build a natural language interface, using the system proposed, we have chosen a question-answering example [4] from the area of airline flights. In Table 1 an AG is given. The underlying grammar accepts questions concerning airline flights and the semantic rules produce an intermediate code, consisting of commands and their parameters, for an abstract data-management machine that has access to a data-base (Fig. 3), according to the example grammar of Table 1.

The subset of English accepted by the system uses words belonging to classes like: class names, object names, property names e.t.c.

The sentences of the subset of English are questions concerning airline flights and the answer after the processing of the intermediate code by the abstract data-management machine is YES or NO.

In this grammar, the semantics are described using a synthesized attribute called "output" for each non-terminal symbol of the underlying grammar. It contains the generated output string so far. The only operation needed between the attributes of the non-terminals is conc (par1, ... parn), which stands for the concatenation of the contains of par1, ... parn.

An illustrative simple question is:

A FLIGHT DEPARTS FROM ATHENS?

This question can be syntactically analyzed into a noun phrase consisting of a determiner and a common noun and a verb phrase consisting of a verb, a preposition and a proper noun. The determiner corresponds to a quantifier, the common noun to a class name, the verb and the preposition to a relation and the proper noun to an object. The nouns and the verb will be used as parameters by the commands that will be generated. In order to show the exact correspondence between the above question and its semantic interpretation (described by the grammar), they are written one underneath the other as follows:

A FLIGHT   DEPARTS   FROM ATHENS?
(01)INT, (x)   UNIV, (01)STO,   (y)   (z)   CON.

The capital letters strings INT, UNIV, STO and CON are the name parts of commands which use as parameters the symbols enclosed in parentheses. Commas are used in the above illustration to separate a command and its parameters from the others. At this point it should be noted that the program generated must always be executed from right to left. For this reason the parameters combined with each call usually lie at the left of the call and this will be the form used in the explanation that follows.

The first command to be executed in the above example would be CON (z,y). The function of the command CON is to retrieve from the data-base the set of all objects which are related by the binary relation y, which here stands for "DEPARTS", to the object (z), which here stands for "ATHENS", and store it in the buffer. The second command to be executed is STO(01). The function of this command is to store the contents of the buffer into a location of the working data structure. This location is specified by the parameter of this call in this case (01). This call is generated when the main verb phrase structure is recognized. The next call is UNIV(x). The function of this command is to store in the buffer all the objects belonging to the class denoted by the parameter x which here stands for "FLIGHT". The next command is INT(01) which forms the intersection of the sets stores it in the buffer and tests whether it is empty or not. The result of this test determines the correct answer to the question and it is held in a flag-register.

A second illustrative question and its procedural semantic interpretation are:

FLT-1   FLIES FROM ATHENS TO NEW-YORK?
(01)(x)MEM, (01)STO,   (y)   (z)   (w)   COB.

The new commands generated by the above question are COB and MEM. The function of COB is to retrieve from the data base the set of all objects which are related by the ternary relation y, which stands for "FLIES", to the pair of objects z and w, which stand for "ATHENS" and "NEW YORK" respectively. The function of MEM(x,01) is to test whether the object x is a member of the set stored in location 01. The result of this test again determines the correct answer to the question.

More complex questions, like "EACH FLIGHT WHICH IS CONNECTED TO A FLIGHT WHICH BELONGS TO AIRLINE-1 DEPARTS FROM A CITY WHICH IS LINKED TO EACH CITY WHICH BELONGS TO GREECE", can be handled by the proposed grammar. In this question, nested quantified subordinate clauses are used and new commands will be generated according to the grammar.

It can be seen from the above illustration that semantic interpretation can be achieved by establishing a mapping between syntactic structures and semantic components. This mapping can be described formally with the attribute grammar of Table 1. In this grammar the semantics are described using a synthesized attribute called 'output' for each non-terminal symbol of the underlying grammar. The only operation needed between the attributes of the non-terminals is conc (par$_1$, ..., par$_n$), which stands for the concatenation of the contains of par$_1$, ..., par$_n$. In Table 1 the 'output' attribute is represented by 'o' for simplicity.

Table 1. The AG of the example

Non Terminals	PR, NP, VP, QS, W, OB, A, E, SET, REL, AT, NRL, N, CNJ	
Terminals	Object names, Class Names, Relation Phrases, Property Names, Numerical Relations, Numbers, Relative pronouns, Determiners, Conjunction words or symbols	
Syntax Rules		**Semantic Rules**
PR → NP VP		PR.o=conc(NP.o, "01ST0", VP.o)
NP → QS W VP		NP.o=conc(QS.o, "SEL", W.o, VP.o)
NP → QS		NP.o = conc(QS.o, "UNIV")
NP → OB		NP.o = conc("QS" ,OB.o, "01MEM")
QS → A SET		QS.o=(A.o, "01INT", SET.o)
QS → E SET		QS.o= conc(E.o, "01IMP", SET.o)
VP → VP$_1$ VP$_2$ SP		VP.o= conc(VP$_1$.o, VP$_2$.o, SP.o)
VP$_1$ → IP VP$_1$		VP$_1$.o = conc(IP.o,VP$_1$.o)
VP$_1$ → null		
VP$_2$ → SP CNJ VP$_2$		VP$_2$.o = conc("02INT", SP.o, CNJ.o,"02ST0", VP$_2$.o)
VP$_2$ → null		
IP → REL QF W		IP.o = conc(REL.o, QF.o, "SEL", W.o)
SP → REL SB		SP.o = conc(REL.o, SB.o)
SP → AT NRL N		SP.o = conc(AT.o, NRL.o, N.o, "LIM")
SB → QF		SB.o = conc(QF.o,"UNIV")
SB → OB		SB.o = conc(OB.o, "CON")
SB → OB P OB		SB.o = conc(OB.o, P.o, OB.o, "COB")
QF → A SET		QF.o=(A.o, "RAN", SET.o)
QF → E SET		QF.o= conc(E.o, "REA", SET.o)
OB → Object names	e.g. : Athens	OB.o="Athens"
SET → Class Names	e.g.: Flights	SET.o ="Flights"
REL → Relation Phrases	e.g.: Departs from	REL.o ="Departs from"
AT → Property Names	e.g.: Has population	AT.o ="Has population"
NRL → Numerical Relations	e.g.: Larger than	NRL.o ="Larger than"
N → Numbers		
W → Relative pronouns	e.g.: which	W.o ="which"
A → Determiners	e.g.: A	A.o ="A"
E → Determiners	e.g.: Each	E.o ="Each"
CNJ → Conjunction words or symbols	e.g.: And	CNJ.o ="And"

5   Conclusion and Future Work

This work is a part of a project for developing a platform (based on AGs) in order to automatically generate special purpose embedded systems. In this paper, an efficient architecture for natural language processing is presented, implemented in hardware using FPGA. The system can receive sentences belonging to a subset of NL from the internet or as SMS, as it is shown in Fig. 4. The system has been tested with numerous application examples [10] and the speed-up was an order of magnitude on the average. The main contribution of this paper is the proposed model, for implementing in hardware the complete grammar (syntax rules plus semantic rules), for NL applications. Our future work remains focused in implementing the proposed architecture using a faster parser, e.g. the one proposed in ref. [11]. In applications where more complicated semantics are required instead of a simple module, as in the illustrative example, a processor should also be incorporated in the FPGA e.g. MicroBlaze [6] soft-core microprocessor, as proposed in ref. [12].

312   C. Pavlatos, A. C. Dimopoulos, G. Papakonstantinou

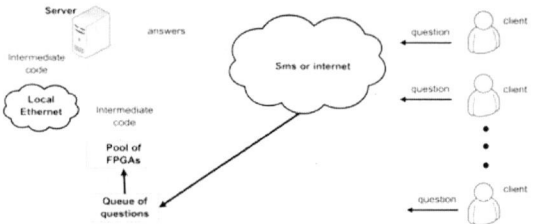

Fig. 4. A real-life application example

Acknowledgements: This work has been funded by the project PENED 2003.This project is part of the OPERATIONAL PROGRAMME "COMPETITIVENESS" and is co-funded by the European Social Fund (75%) and National Resources (25%).

References

1.   J. Earley, "An efficient context–free parsing algorithm", Com.of ACM, 13, pp. 94-102, 1970.
2.   Y. Li, H. Yang and H. V. Jagadish, "NaLIX: an interactive natural language interface for querying XML", Proceedings of the 2005 ACM SIGMOD international conference on Management of data, pp. 900-902, Baltimore, Maryland
3.   A. Yates, O. Etzioni and D. Weld , "A reliable natural language interface to household appliance", Proceedings of the 8th international conference on Intelligent user interfaces, pp. 189 - 196, 2003
4.   J. Kontos and G. Papakonstantinou, "Semantic interpretation of English like questions using procedural components", NATO ASI on on-line mechanized information retrieval systems, Lyngby, Denmark, 1972.
5.   Y. Chiang, K. Fu "Parallel parsing algorithms and VLSI implementation for syntactic pattern recognition", IEEE Trans. Pattern Anal. and Mach. Intell. PAMI-7, 1984
6.   Xilinx Official WebSite,www.xilinx.com
7.   A. Aho, R. Sethi and J. Ullman, "Compilers – Principles, Techniques and Tools", Reading, MA, MADDISON-WESLEY, pp. 293-296. 1986
8.   J. Paaki, "Attribute grammar paradigms -a high-level methodology in language implementation" ACM Computing Surveys, 27(2):196–255, 1995
9.   C. Pavlatos, A. Dimopoulos and G. Papakonstantinou, "An Intelligent Embedded System for Control Applications", Workshop on Modeling and Control of Complex Systems, Cyprus, 2005
10. C. Pavlatos, I. Panagopoulos and G. Papakonstantinou, "A programmable Pipelined Coprocessor for Parsing Applications", Workshop on Application Specific Processors CODES, Stockholm, 2004
11. A. Koulouris, T. Andronikos, C. Pavlatos, A. Dimopoulos, I.Panagopoulos, and G. Papakonstantinou, "Efficient Signal Processing using Syntactic Pattern

RecognitionMethods", International Conference on SIGNAL AND IMAGE PROCESSING ,Honolulu, Hawaii, USA, August 14–16, 2006

12. C. Pavlatos, A. Dimopoulos and G. Papakonstantinou, "An embedded system for the electrocardiogram recognition", EMBEC'05, Prague, Czech Republic, November 2005

Robustness of Non-Exact Multi-Channel Equalization in Reverberant Environments

Fotios Talantzis and Lazaros C. Polymenakos

Athens Information Technology,
19.5 Km Markopoulo Ave.,
Peania/Athens 19002, Greece
{fota,lcp}@ait.edu.gr

Abstract. We consider the revision of a previously derived theoretical framework for the robustness of multi-channel sound equalization in reverberant environments when non-exact equalizers are used. Using results from image model simulations, we demonstrate the degradation in performance of an equalization system as the sound source moves from its nominal position inside the enclosure. We show that performance can be controlled to vary between a lower bound, derived when direct-path equalization is used, and a higher one produced when exact equalization is used.

1 Introduction

Multi-channel sound equalization can be used in a reverberant room whenever a source and receiver cannot be placed close together, for example, in hands-free communication devices. In such an environment, the signal detected by the receiver is distorted by transmission through the room. This distortion can be compensated by using an appropriate inverse filter (equalizer) on each receiver. Because room reverberation is extremely variable, the performance of any acoustic equalizer will be strongly influenced by small changes in either the source or receiver location. Hence, the performance will degrade quickly if either the source or receiver moves.

The assessment of the feasibility of acoustic equalization under reverberant conditions, has been previously addressed in [1] and [2] where we determined the robustness of multi-channel equalization systems, by means of a closed form expression that predicts the equalization error when the source is moved from its nominal position. The work of these papers generalizes the work of *Radlovic et al.* in [4] that only considered one-channel systems. In all of the above, the derivation of the theoretical expressions was based on diffuse field model assumptions as these were presented in [1]. The calculation of the robustness variation for non-exact equalizers cannot be easily parameterized when this model is used. For this reason we need to use a different approach, entirely based on the image model [3]. This is limited in implementation issues but allows for straightforward error calculation for any type of equalization.

In this paper we aim to investigate further these previous studies by considering the robustness of non-exact multi-channel equalizers. Specifically, we investigate the difference between the diffuse and image model and then present a series of experiments

Please use the following format when citing this chapter:

Talantzis, F., Polymenakos, L. C., 2007, in IFIP International Federation for Information Processing, Volume 247, Artificial Intelligence and Innovations 2007: From Theory to Applications, eds. Boukis, C., Pnevmatikakis, L., Polymenakos, L., (Boston: Springer), pp. 315-321.

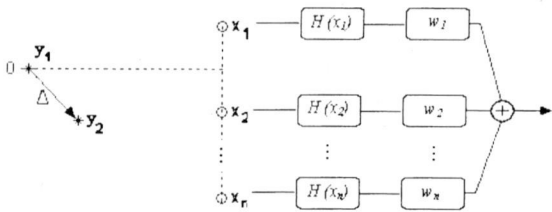

Fig. 1. Block diagram of a N-channel equalization system with the source placed at the origin $\mathbf{y}_1 = [0, 0, 0]^T$ and N receivers placed at positions $\mathbf{x}_n, n = 1, \ldots, N$.

for the expected degradation in performance when the source moves from its nominal position (where the multi-channel non-exact equalizer performs well). We also consider the effect of design parameters such as the number of receivers and the geometry of the receiver array, as well as the range of order of images we decide to equalize. We thereby provide design guidelines for the parameters of a practical design of a multi-channel equalizer. Note again, that we are not specifically concerned with how to design such equalizers; rather, our focus is on the fundamental question of whether the performance of multi-channel non-exact equalizers is robust enough to make them feasible in a time-varying environment where the source location cannot be fixed.

2 Methodology

Consider a source located in a reverberant room at a position $\mathbf{y}_1$, which we hereafter refer to as the *nominal source position*. Without loss of generality we assume a cartesian coordinate system with $\mathbf{y}_1 = [0, 0, 0]^T$ at the origin. Let $G(\mathbf{y}_1, \mathbf{x}_n)$ denote the complex steady-state transfer function from $\mathbf{y}_1$ to a receiver located at the arbitrary position $\mathbf{x}_n$.

Although $G(\mathbf{y}_1, \mathbf{x}_n)$ is a function of frequency, to simplify notation we will not express this frequency dependence explicitly. Assume that the transmission path between $\mathbf{y}_1$ and $\mathbf{x}_n$ is equalized by a causal equalizer $H(\mathbf{x}_n)$ that is chosen to equalize a specific range of order of images i.

Now, consider the general N-channel equalization system shown in Fig. 1, in which the signal at the nth receiver is filtered by an equalizer $H(\mathbf{x}_n)$, and is weighted by a scalar constant w_n (one obvious choice for the scalar weights is $w_n = 1/N, \forall n$). These filtered and weighted signals are then summed to form the output signal.

Without loss of generality, assume that the causal delay on each equalizer is the same, i.e., $\tau_n = \tau_0, \forall n$. Ideally, with the source in the nominal position, the overall transfer function from the source to the equalizer output is a delay, which we will set to τ_0 (again, without loss of generality).

Assume the source moves to a position $\mathbf{y}_2$ that is a distance Δ from the nominal position $\mathbf{y}_1$, i.e., $\Delta = \|\mathbf{y}_1 - \mathbf{y}_2\|$. One can quantify the sensitivity of this multi-channel equalization system in terms of the *mean squared error* (MSE) function, defined as

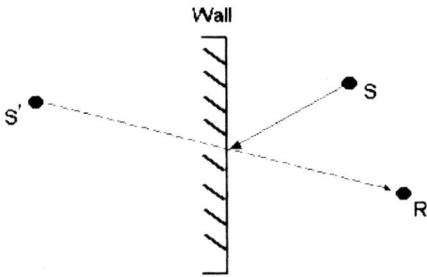

Fig. 2. Image model representation. The signal received by receiver R is transmitted from source S which the model replaces by a "mirror" image S'

$$\text{MSE}(\Delta) \triangleq E\left\{\left|\sum_{n-1}^{N} w_n G(\mathbf{y}_2, \mathbf{x}_n)H(\mathbf{x}_n) - e^{j2\pi f\tau_0}\right|^2\right\},\tag{1}$$

where $\mathbf{y}_2$ is the displaced source position and f the frequency of the signal. Hence, Eq. (1) measures the expected degradation in performance when the source moves a distance Δ from the nominal position *in an arbitrary direction*.

The modelling of reverberation is necessary for the simulation of the above setup. As mentioned before, in this discussion we used the image model to validate the robustness. In contradiction with the diffuse field approach image model calculations allow for direct inclusion or disclusion of any set of order of images. The image model considers a simple geometrical model of the room depending on the assumption that the dimensions of reflective surfaces in the room are large compared to the wavelength of the sound. Consequently, we may model the sound wave as a ray normal to the surface of the wavefront, which reflects specularly.

The image model considers that the reflected ray may be constructed by considering the "mirror image" of the source as reflected across the plane of the wall. This is shown in Figure (2) for a source S, its image source S' and a receiver R. So the technique reflects sources across wall surfaces, a process that continues for higher order reflections by reflecting lower order sources across *new* wall boundaries. The signal received by the receiver is then the superposition of the sound signals originating from the mirror-sources plus the one of the direct sound.

For the calculations of the complex steady-state frequency response between the source and the receiver we used the following formula:

$$G = \sum_{i=0}^{l} \beta^{r_i}\frac{e^{-jkR_i}}{4\pi R_i}\tag{2}$$

where R_i is the distance between the receiver and the ith image source, β the wall reflection coefficient, r_i denotes the number of reflections that the sound ray undergoes

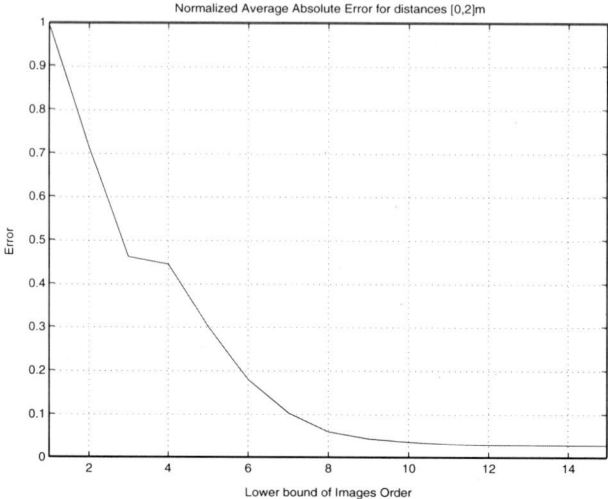

Fig. 3. Comparison of diffuse field and image models as the normalized average absolute difference of the values they predict for the correlation of of the $E\{G_r(\mathbf{y}_1, \mathbf{x}_n)G_r^*(\mathbf{y}_1, \mathbf{x}_m)\}$ term for increasing order of images. The random distances examined belong in $[0,2]$m.

along its path from the source to the receiver and l is the total number of considered images within a given radius. As expected, if the source is at the nominal source position, i.e., $\Delta = 0$, the MSE (1) reduces to zero only if $l \to \infty$. In practice, for exact equalization, it is enough to include images belonging to a circle of radius cT_{60} where c is the speed of sound and T_{60} the reverberation time of the room.

3 Results

Expression (2) attempts to calculate the reverberant contribution by using the image model. Experiments showed that the resulting values are not identical to the ones calculated by the diffuse field model, if we include the low-order image sources. Figure 3 presents the difference between the diffuse field and image models as the normalized absolute difference of the values they predict for the correlation of the $E\{G_r(\mathbf{y}_1, \mathbf{x}_n)G_r^*(\mathbf{y}_1, \mathbf{x}_m)\}$ term (i.e. the correlation of the reverberant terms between two receivers), as the number of contributing image sources is increased. The figure shows that we need to use images of 10th order or higher in order to approximate the values predicted by the respective diffuse field expression in [1]. This difference can be explained by remembering that the diffuse field assumptions aim in a more realistic simulation of real rooms that generalize the reverberant contribution to a *sinc* function dependent only on the distance between the two examined points (for which the reverberant transfer function is calculated).

Figure 4 shows the simulated error for an example setup as we increase the number of contributing images. The error is practically controlled to vary between a lower

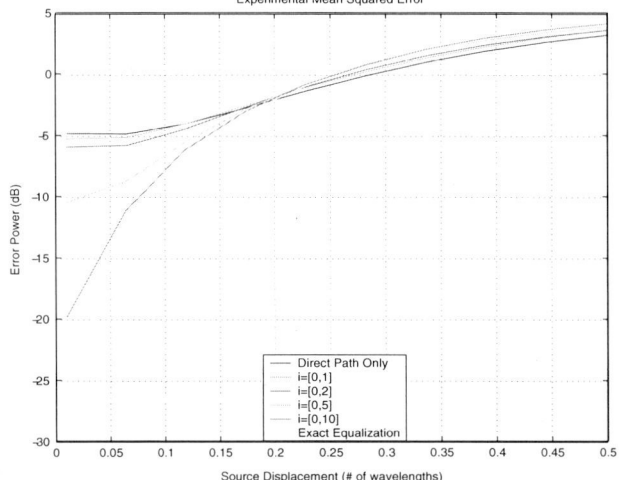

Fig. 4. Two-channel MSE of equalizers with uniform weights $w_n = 1/N$ for source displacements Δ up to 0.5λ. Results are shown for increasing number of contributing images. Total length of the array is 2m and the distance of the source from the mid-point of the array is 1m.

performance bound, derived when direct-path equalization is used, and a higher one produced when exact equalization is used. It is fair to say that to match the best case scenario (exact equalization) it is adequate to use an equalizer that equalizes the direct path and image sources belonging in the interval $i = [1, 10]$.

According to the image model simulations the addition of uniformly weighted sensors improves robustness. This is demonstrated in Fig. 5. The geometry of the setup also affects the robustness variation. Varying the values of the size of the linear array d and the distance R of the array from the source alters performance as well. The value of R is always proportional to the value of the error, for any type of equalization. On the other hand, d alters the value of the error according to the chosen equalization scheme. Increasing the value of d when only the 0th or the 0th plus a few of the first order images are equalized, makes the error slightly larger (Also odependent on the number of receivers and R). As we approach the exact equalization scheme d becomes proportional with the value of the error. The system starts benefiting from the increasing value of d for schemes that include images in the range $i = [0, 5]$ or higher. Finally, as in [1], the use of circular arrays improves performance even further (see Fig. 6).

4 Conclusions

We have examined the robustness performance of non-exact multi-channel equalization systems when used in reverberant environments. Specifically, using image model simulations, we investigated the expected mean square error when the source moves from the position for which the equalizer was designed.

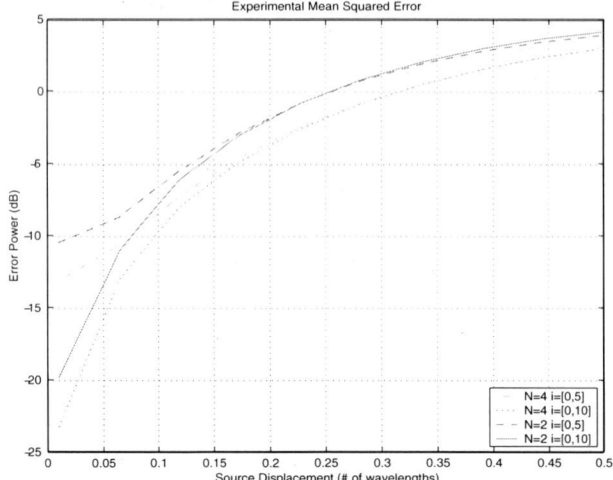

Fig. 5. Demonstration of robustness improvement for increasing number of receivers. Total length of the array is 2m and the distance of the source from the mid-point of the array is 1m.

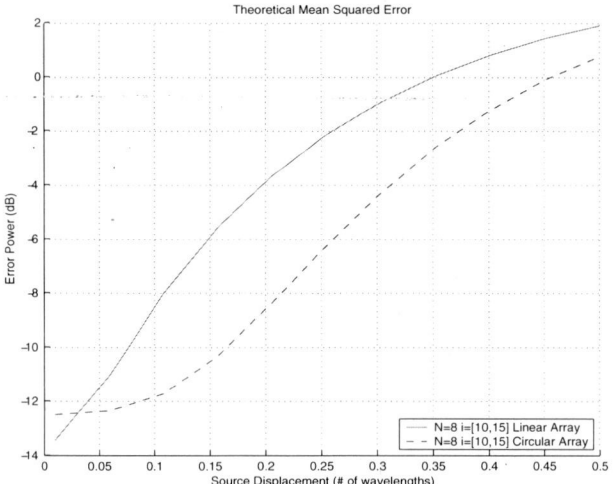

Fig. 6. Demonstration of robustness improvement for $N=4$ when circular geometry is used. Equalization of images belonging in $i = [0, 10]$. The radius of the array is 1m.

A series of different classes of equalizer were considered. In each case they were chosen to equalize a specific subset of order of images for a given set of geometrical and design parameters. Results are parameterized by the chosen equalizer type and physical quantities such as the room size, reverberation time, distance of the source from the array and array size. Our results show that there is a small difference between the results predicted by the diffuse field assumption presented in [1] and the image simulations of the present context. As expected the performance for a non-exact equalization system varied between the direct-path-only and exact equalization systems respective performances. It is fair to conclude that to much the performance of an exact equalization system for a given set of physical parameters we only need to equalize the direct path plus images of degree no higher than 10.

Again, although we have shown that the robustness of an acoustic equalizer can be improved by adding more receivers (depending on the geometry), the improvement is not significant, and the region in which the MSE is below 10dB is restricted to a fraction of a wavelength.

References

1. F. Talantzis, D. B. Ward, "Robustness Of Multi-Channel Equalization In Acoustical Reverberant Environments," *J. Acoust. Soc. Amer.*, vol.114, no.2, pp.833-841, 2003.
2. F. Talantzis and D.B. Ward, "Multi-Channel Equalization In An Acoustic Reverberant Environment: Establishment of Robustness Measures", *Proc. Institute of Acoustics Spring Conf.*, March 2002.
3. J.B. Allen and D.A. Berkley, "Image method for efficiently simulating small-room acoustics" *J. Acoust Soc. Amer.*, vol. 65, no. 4, pp. 943-950, 1979.
4. B.D. Radlovic, R.C. Williamson and R.A. Kennedy, "Equalization in an Acoustic Reverberant Environment: Robustness Results", *IEEE Trans. Speech Audio Processing*, vol. 8, no. 3, pp. 311-319, May. 2000.

Combining Finite State Machines and LDA for Voice Activity Detection

Elias Rentzeperis, Christos Boukis, Aristodemos Pnevmatikakis, and Lazaros C. Polymenakos

Athens Information Technology, 19.5 Km Markopoulo Ave., Peania/Athens 19002, Greece {eren,cbou,apne,lcp}@ait.edu.gr

Abstract. A robust speech activity detection system is presented in this paper. The proposed approach combines the well-known linear discriminant analysis with a finite state machine in order to successfully identify speech patterns within a recorded audio signal. The derived method is compared with existing ones to demonstrate its superiority, especially when performing on noisy audio signals, obtained with far field microphones.

1 Introduction

Voice activity detection (VAD) is a fundamental component of several modern speech processing systems like automatic speech recognition (ASR), voice commanding and teleconferencing. Providing such systems with accurate information about the existence of speech within an audio signal can result in reduction of the computational and energy requirements and improved performance of the overlying system.

Most VAD systems monitor a quantity and they compare it to a threshold in order to decide whether the observed signal is speech or not [1]. This quantity is usually the energy of the observed signal, which has presented remarkable performance with close talking (CT) microphones. The threshold can be chosen either with heuristic methods or adaptively [2], so as to be able to cope with non-stationary environments. Another approach is to use classification techniques, like the well-documented linear discriminant analysis [3], in order to distinguish speech from non-speech patterns. These techniques have noticeable results for both CT and far field (FF) microphones. The same holds for VAD systems that rely on the use of Hidden Markov Models (HMM).

The use of finite state machines (FSMs) in VAD was proposed as well [4]. These models pose some lower bounds on the duration of silence and speech intervals. Hence more accurate separation is performed since segments of very small duration characterised as speech within a silent interval are neglected and vice versa. In this paper we propose the use of a five state automaton, as was presented in [4, 5], which uses the LDA method applied to Mel Frequency Cepstral Coefficients (MFCC) as primary criterion for transition between states contrary to the approaches presented in [4, 5] which use the energy instead.

Please use the following format when citing this chapter:

Rentzeperis, E., Boukis, C., Pnevmatikakis, A., Polymenakos, L. C., 2007, in IFIP International Federation for Information Processing, Volume 247, Artificial Intelligence and Innovations 2007: From Theory to Applications, eds. Boukis, C., Pnevmatikakis, L., Polymenakos, L., (Boston: Springer), pp. 323-329.

Our approach was found to have improved performance. The energy was completely neglected, since it might vary depending on the relative position of the microphone and the speaker.

This paper is organised as follows: Section 2 provides the basic background and summarises the previous VAD methods that employ FSMs. In Section 3 the proposed system is presented. The results of the performance of the introduced approach are provided in Section 4 and are compared to those of other methods. Finally Section 5 concludes the paper.

2 Background

2.1 Mel Frequency Cepstral Coefficients

Mel Frequency Cepstral Coefficients (MFCC) are the dominant features used in speech applications. They are obtained by taking the inverse Fourier transform of the log spectrum after it is wrapped according to a nonlinear scale that is matching by properties of human hearing, the Mel scale. It was shown in our experiments that the addition of the first and second derivatives of the MFCC as well as of the energy of each preprocessed frame enhances the performance of the algorithm.

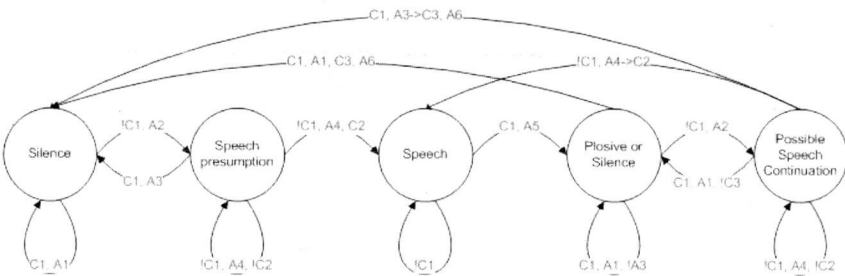

Fig. 1. Finite State Machine

2.2 Linear Discriminant Analysis

Linear discriminant analysis (LDA) is a method that efficiently separates data into classes [3]. In the case of VAD there are two classes to be discriminated, speech and non speech. The optimal discriminating line $\mathbf{w}$ is derived by maximising the following criterion function

$$J(\mathbf{w}) = \frac{\mathbf{w}^t S_B \mathbf{w}}{\mathbf{w}^t S_W \mathbf{w}} \tag{1}$$

where $\mathbf{S}_B$ is the *between-class scatter matrix* and $\mathbf{S}_W$ is the *within-class scatter matrix*. $\mathbf{S}_B$ is a measure of the separation of the means of the clusters, while $\mathbf{S}_W$ is a measure of the spread of the clusters. The maximization problem reduces to a general eigenvalue one, given by

$$\mathbf{S}_W^{-1}\mathbf{S}_B\mathbf{w} = \mathbf{w} \tag{2}$$

The eigenvector that corresponds to the greatest eigenvalue from the solutions is chosen as the projecting vector of the test vectors.

2.3 Finite State Model

In [4] the use of a five state automaton was proposed for VAD. Its five states were *silence, speech presumption, speech, plosive or silence and possible speech continuation*. The transitions between states were controlled by comparing the derived short and long term energy estimates with an energy threshold. From Fig. 1 and Tab. 1, where the introduced FSM and the associated conditions and actions are presented, it is observed that a segment is characterised as speech if its duration is longer than 64m sec AND its energy is above the employed threshold. Similarly, a silent interval smaller than 240m sec is classified as plosive, and thus speech.

Table 1. Conditions and Actions of the energy controlled five state automaton for VAD

Conditions	
C1	Energy<Energy_Threshold
C2	Speech_Duration (SD)>=64ms
C3	Silence_Duration (SiD)>=240ms

Actions	
A1	$SiD = SiD + l$
A2	$SD = l$
A3	$SiD = SiD + SD$
A4	$SD = SD + l$
A5	$SiD = l$
A6	$SiD = SD = 0$

In order to improve the performance of this system the introduction of an extra criterion was proposed in [5]. This system characterised as speech segments that satisfied not only the energy but the LDA criterion as well. It does not clarify though what happens when the results of the energy and the LDA criteria do not match. The LDA was trained by using two learning databases where the speech and non-speech intervals have been manually segmented. The LDA threshold was derived from these databases as well.

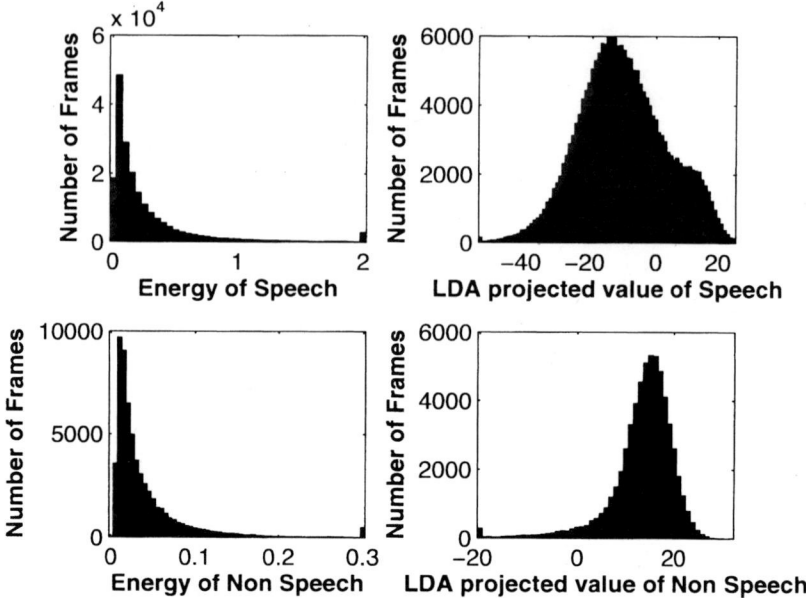

Fig. 2. Histograms of the energy and the LDA projected values of the speech/non-speech segments of the training data.

3 Proposed System

Embarking upon the observation that LDA provides more accurate discrimination between speech and non-speech classes than simply comparing the energy estimate with a threshold, and adopting the FSM of [4] a robust VAD system was developed. The choice to use LDA projection instead of energy is justified from Fig. 2 where is illustrated that the speech and silent segments have similar energy values but different LDA projections of their MFCC.

The proposed architecture used the five state automaton of Fig. 1, but the primary criterion that controlled the transition between states was derived by comparing the linear combination of the MFCC provided by the LDA, with a threshold. The LDA classifier was trained with manually segmented speech/non-speech signals. The threshold was obtained from the provided training data as well. Moreover, median filtering was applied to the results obtained from FSM in order to remove spiky decision regions and get improved error rates.

The audio signal was processed in frames. For each frame the corresponding MFCC were computed and subsequently their linear combination, which was derived by LDA, was compared to the *Threshold_LDA* to decide whether this is speech or not. Notice that the duration bounds and the time counters (SD ,S ̄D)

Table 2. Conditions and Actions of the proposed LDA controlled five state automaton for VAD

Conditions	
C1	Linear MFCC Combination<Threshold_LDA
C2	Speech_Duration (SD)>=5 frames
C3	Silence_Duration (SiD)>=16 frames
Actions	
A1	$SiD = SiD + 1$
A2	$SD = 1$
A3	$SiD = SiD + SD$
A4	$SD = SD + 1$
A5	$SiD = 1$
A6	$SiD = SD = 0$

are expressed in frames instead of msec. The proposed approach is summarised in Tab. 2.

4 Experiments

To evaluate its performance the introduced VAD system was compared to

- the approach of [4] that uses the same five state automaton, but the state transitions are controlled by the comparison of the energy estimates with an energy threshold
- the stand-alone LDA applied to MFFCs for the discrimination of the speech from the non-speech class
- the Energy Based Adaptive algorithm presented in [1] which relies on an estimation of the instantaneous SNR for the distinction of speech and non speech segments

The VAD systems were evaluated on a database collected by the University of Karlsruhe (ISL-UKA). The database is comprised of seven seminars. Each seminar contains four segments of audio data that are approximately five minutes long. The audio segments are sampled at a rate of 16.0 kHz. All the data were obtained from FF microphones resulting in comparable energy values of speech and non-speech segments (Fig. 2). Segments three and four were used for the training of the algorithm while one and two for testing. Manual human transcriptions were provided for the separation of the training segments and evaluation of the testing recordings.

The following metrics were used for the evaluation of the algorithms:

- Mismatch Rate (MR): the ratio of the incorrect decisions over the total time of the tested segment.

Table 3. Comparison of the proposed VAD with exiting approaches

Method	LDA Threshold	Energy Threshold	MR	SDER	NDER	ADER	Wpeps
LDA	4.9	-	10.09%	10.40%	8.62%	9.51%	0.09
Adaptive Energy Thresholding	-	-	18.10%	18.40%	15.60%	17.00%	0.08
FSM+LDA	4.9	-	**9.94%**	**10.19%**	**8.65%**	**9.42%**	**0.08**
FSM+Energy	-	0.043	17.28%	17.69%	14.63%	16.16%	0.08

- Speech Detection Error Rate (SDER): the ratio of incorrect decisions at speech segments over the total time of speech segments.
- Non Speech Detection Error Rate (NDER): the ratio of incorrect decisions at non speech segments over the total time of non speech segments.
- Average Detection Error Rate (ADER): the average of SDER and NDER.
- Working Point Epsilon (WPeps): an indicator of the balance between SDER and NDER. It is the absolute value of the difference between SDER and NDER over their sum.

Considering that SDER and NDER should be relatively balanced in order to draw any conclusions for the value of the algorithms, we required WPeps to be between 0 and 0.1 for the results to be valid. Under this constraint the parameter that we seek to optimize is the ADER.

Each frame consisted of 1024 samples. Furthermore the amount of overlapping between neighbouring frames was 75%. The LDA method was trained with manually segmented speech and nonspeech data. The SD threshold was 5 frames and the SiD one 16 frames, which correspond to 128 msec and 304 msec respectively, since the sampling rate was 16.0 kHz. The window size in the median filtering step was 29 frames long.

The performance of the compared VAD systems is presented in Tab. 3. From this table it is observed that the proposed method presents improved performance compared to the other approaches.

5 Conclusions

A robust voice activity detection system has been proposed in this paper, which combines a finite state machine along with the linear discriminant analysis in order to perform accurate segmentation of audio signals to speech/non-speech segments. This approach was found to outperform the stand-alone LDA and the existing approaches that combine FSMs with the energy criterion for VAD. Its performance was evaluated with noisy far field microphone recordings.

Acknowledgments: This work is sponsored by the European Union under the integrated project CHIL, contract number 506909.

References

1. D. A. Reynolds, R. C. Rose and M. J. T. Smith, PC-Based TMS320C30 Implementation of the Gaussian Mixture Model Text-Independent Speaker Recognition
   System, in International Conference on Signal Processing Applications and Technology, Hyatt Regency, Cambridge, Massachusetts, pp. 967–973, November 1992
2. S.Gökhun Tanyer and Hamza Özer, Voice Activity Detection in Nonstationary
   Noise, IEEE Trans. Sp. Au. Proc., vol. 8, no. 4, pp 479–482, Jul. 2000
3. R.O. Duda P.E. Hart and D.G. Stork, Pattern Classification, John Willey & Sons,
   2001
4. L. Mauuary and J. Monné, Speech/non-speech Detection for Voice Response Systems, in *Eurospeech'93*, Berlin, Germany, 1993, pp 1097–1100
5. A. Martin, D. Charlet and L. Mauuary, Robust Speech/Non-Speech Detection
   Using LDA Applied to MFCC, ICASSP, 2001

Performance Evaluation of TreeQ and LVQ Classifiers for Music Information Retrieval

Matina Charami, Rami Halloush, Sofia Tsekeridou
Athens Information Technology (AIT)
0.8 km Markopoulo Ave.
GR - 19002 Peania, Athens, Greece
{scha, raha, sots}@ait.edu.gr

Abstract. Classification algorithms are gaining more and more importance in many fields such as Artificial Intelligence, Information Retrieval, Data Mining and Machine Vision. Many classification algorithms have emerged, belonging to different families, among which the tree-based and the clustering-based ones. Such extensive availability of classifiers makes the selection of the optimal one per case a rather complex task. In this paper, we aim to address this issue by conducting extensive experiments in a music information retrieval application, specifically with respect to music genre queries, in order to compare the performance of two state-of-the-art classifiers belonging to the formerly mentioned two classes of classification algorithms, namely, TreeQ and LVQ, respectively, using a variety of music features for such a task. The deployed performance metrics are extensive: accuracy, precision, recall, F-measure, confidence. Conclusions on the best performance of either classifier to support music genre queries are finally drawn.

1 Introduction

With the explosive amount of music data available on the Internet in recent years, there has been much interest in developing new ways to search and retrieve such data effectively. Most on-line music databases today, such as Napster and mp3.com, rely on file names or text labels to do searching and indexing, using traditional text searching techniques. Although this approach has proven to be useful and widely accepted in the past, there are many reasons this is not enough nowadays. As the amount of musical content increases and the Web becomes an important mechanism for distributing music, we expect to see a rising demand for music search services. It would be nice to have more sophisticated search capabilities, namely, searching by content.

Music Information Retrieval Systems can be classified into two types: i) systems that depend on human generated annotations and decisions (textual-based), and ii)

Please use the following format when citing this chapter:

Charami, M., Halloush, R., Tsekeridou, S., 2007, in IFIP International Federation for Information Processing, Volume 247, Artificial Intelligence and Innovations 2007: From Theory to Applications, eds. Boukis, C., Pnevmatikakis, L., Polymenakos, L., (Boston: Springer), pp. 331-338.

systems that depend on extracting information from the audio signal (content-based). The first type is manual and hence demands a lot of effort, it is time consuming and susceptible to errors. We will concentrate on content-based music information retrieval in the rest of the paper.

Content-based music information retrieval involves processes such as representative music feature extraction, classification in apriori known classes, usually deploying training and testing (supervised classification) and similarity-based querying. Thus, the challenging aspects of setting up an efficient music information retrieval are: i) what features to select as most representative on the types of similarity-based queries (e.g. music genre queries), ii) which classifiers will perform optimally for the application and types of queries at hand.

In this paper, we aim to address the issue of selecting the optimal combination of representative features and classifiers to address queries on music genre, by conducting extensive experiments in a music information retrieval application. The aim is to compare the performance of two state-of-the-art classifiers, namely, TreeQ [1] and LVQ [2] (Learning Vector Quantization), described briefly in the sequel, using a variety of music features for such a task. The deployed performance metrics are extensive: accuracy, precision, recall, F-measure, confidence. Conclusions on the best performance of either classifier combined with specific music feature vectors are finally drawn.

2   LVQ Classifier: a short overview

In general, LVQ [6] is a supervised version of vector quantization, which is applicable to pattern recognition, multi-class classification and data compression. LVQ algorithms directly define class boundaries based on prototypes, a nearest-neighbour rule and a winner-takes-it-all paradigm. The main idea, as shown in Figure 1, is to cover the input space of samples with 'codebook vectors' (CVs), each representing a region labeled with a class. A CV is localized in the centre of a decision region, called 'Voronoi cell', in the input space.

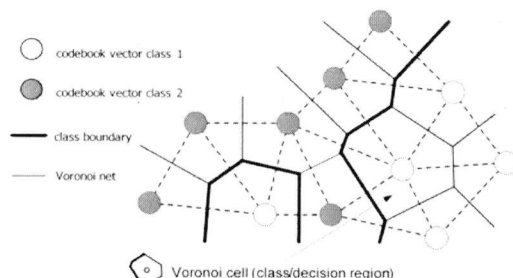

Fig. 1. LVQ space partitioning into decision regions by codebook vectors [2].

For the purpose of undertaken experiments, the LVQ software package of [7] has been used, which implements all algorithms necessary for statistical classification and pattern recognition. The performance of LVQ depends on the algorithm implementation, as well as the data used for training and testing, in terms of size and the degree of representative features extracted from such data. The basic three implementations of LVQ are LVQ1, LVQ2 and LVQ3. In our experiments, we have used the optimized OLVQ1 implementation [1], an enhanced version of LVQ1.

The basic idea behind this algorithm is that each class is represented in terms of a set of codevectors m_i, each of which is a point in the D-Dimensional feature space. This set is called codebook. Several codebook vectors are assigned to each class. A feature vector x is then assigned to the same class to which the nearest m_i belongs:

$$m_c = \arg\min_i \{\| x - m_i \|\}$$, where m_c is the nearest m_i to x

Values for m_i that approximately minimize the misclassification errors in the above nearest neighbour classification can be found as asymptotic values in the following learning process. Let $x(t)$ be a sample of input and let $m_i(t)$ represent sequences of m_i in the discrete time domain. Starting with properly defined initial values, the following equations define the basic LVQ1 process, where $0 < a(t) < 1$ and t is the iteration step:

- $m_c(t+1) = m_c(t) + a_c(t)[x(t) - m_c(t)]$, if x is classified correctly
- $m_c(t+1) = m_c(t) - a_c(t)[x(t) - m_c(t)]$, if x is classified incorrectly
- $m_i(t+1) = m_i(t)$, for $i \neq c$

OLVQ1 extends LVQ1 by modifying the latter so that an individual learning rate $a_i(t)$ is assigned to each m_i. Again, the discrete time learning process is given from above equations. For their fastest convergence, $a_i(t)$ is optimally determined by:

$$a_c(t) = \frac{a_c(t-1)}{1 + s(t)a_c(t-1)}$$

3   TreeQ Classifier: a short overview

For the purposes of the undertaken experiments, the TreeQ software package [3], [4], [5] has been considered, implementing the TreeQ machine learning algorithm. TreeQ is data-driven and therefore it can be used for any kind of data to find similarities by learning their differences. Especially for the case of audio data, the algorithm may be applied for speaker identification, speech and music classification, music and audio retrieval by similarity, audio segmentation.

Given labeled training data, the algorithm constructs templates that characterize these data, utilizing three main steps. First, it calculates spectral parameters for the audio data. Second, it grows a quantization tree from labeled parameterized data. This step learns those features that best characterize a class, i.e. given adequate training data, it learns the salient differences amongst classes and learns to ignore other insignificant differences. Third, the produced tree is used to construct the templates. As soon as the templates are constructed (class models), similarities can be measured by calculating distances between them and test data.

The basic operation of the system is illustrated in Figure 2. A suitable corpus of audio examples must be accumulated and parameterized into feature vectors. The corpus must contain examples of the classes of audio to be discriminated. Next, a tree-based quantizer is constructed. This is a "supervised" operation and requires the training data to be labeled with a class. The tree automatically partitions the feature space into regions, called 'cells', which have maximally different class populations.

To generate an audio template, represented by a histogram, for subsequent retrieval, parameterized data are quantized using the tree. An audio file can be characterized by finding into which cells the input data vectors are most likely to fall. A template is an estimate of the vector counts for each cell, which captures the salient characteristics of the input audio, since sounds from different classes will have very different counts in the various histogram bins, while similar audio data should have similar counts. To retrieve audio by similarity, a histogram is further constructed for the query audio. The query histogram is compared to the corpus histograms, a similarity measure is calculated for each audio file in the corpus, and finally the query template is associated with a corpus template.

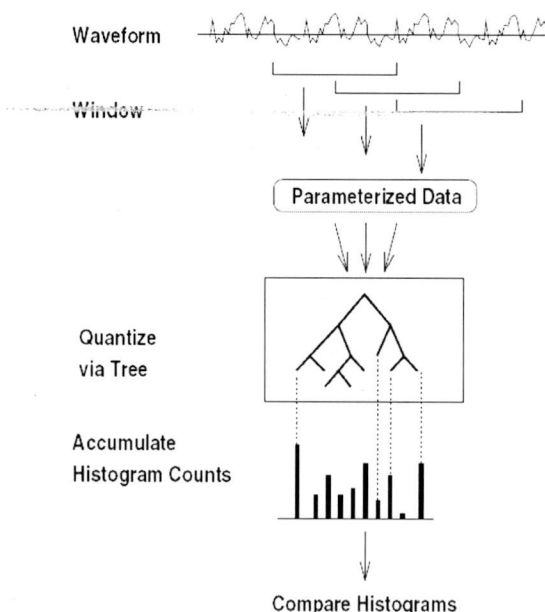

Fig. 2. An overview of the basic operations of the TreeQ algorithm [1].

4   Music Information Retrieval based on Genre Queries

It is a fact that the rapid development of technology continuously realizes scenarios that previously seemed science fiction. Web-based music stations like pandora.com give each user the opportunity to specify the kind of music he wants to listen to, and in the context of ambient intelligence, pervasive systems will dress the surroundings with music based on the human's mood. Given the above and a number of other emerging applications of music, classification and information retrieval based on music genres becomes not only important, but essential and fundamental.

Our work addresses this problem and aims to provide extended experiments in order to push TreeQ and LVQ to their limits and decide which gives the best results under what contexts of use. Before presenting our experimental results, we considered it necessary to briefly describe the music features used to parameterize the audio data, i.e. the input to the previously presented classifiers.

4.1   Music Feature Extraction

Few classifiers directly operate on raw data such as pixels of an image or samples of speech waveforms. Most pattern recognition tasks are preceded by a pre-processing transformation that extracts invariant features from raw data, such as spectral components of acoustical signals. Thus, in our case, decisions need to be made on the types of representative features to be used by classifiers to achieve optimal music classification based on genres. Such feature extraction task parameterizes the raw music data into sequences of representative feature vectors.

It is evident that the selection of the adequate pre-processing method is equally vital as to the selection of the proper classifier for optimal performance, thus, it requires careful consideration. For this task, we have used the HTK Toolkit [8], which supports Hidden Markov Models (HMMs) using both Fast Fourier Transformation (FFT) and Linear Predictive Coding (LPC). The feature extraction process is controlled by a customizable configuration file that specifies all the conversion parameters towards extracting the desirable feature vectors.

In the current investigation, we have considered widely known and used features, namely the mel-frequency cepstral coefficients (MFCCs) and the linear prediction coding coefficients (LPCs). Both are, in general, the parameterisation of choice for many speech recognition applications, since they attain good discrimination capabilities and are flexible towards a number of manipulations.

In linear prediction analysis [9], the following transfer function is considered:

$$H(z) = \frac{1}{\sum_{i=0}^{p} a_i z^{-i}}$$

where the filter coefficients $\{a_i\}$ are chosen so as to minimize the mean square filter prediction error summed over the analysis window.

On the other hand, cepstral parameters are calculated from the log filter-bank amplitudes $\{m_j\}$ using the Discrete Cosine Transform (DCT), where N is the number of filter-bank channels [9]:

$$c_i = \sqrt{\frac{2}{N}} \sum_{j=1}^{N} m_j \cos\left(\frac{\pi i}{N}(j - 0.5)\right)$$

5   Experimental Setup and Performance Evaluation

In order to evaluate the performance of the two classifiers, namely, TreeQ and LVQ, in music genre classification and retrieval, we performed a set of experiments that are described in the sequel.

Initially, the experimental corpus has been created carefully. Five music genres have been considered, namely, jazz, reggae, pop, post rock and electro techno. For each genre, the corpus contains twenty music pieces, summing up to a total of one hundred pieces for all genres. Each music clip is about ten seconds long and has been selected as the most representative part of the entire music file. We have used the holdout sampling method in order to split the corpus into training and test data. Thus, seventy five of the music clips were used for training (the first fifteen of each genre) while the remaining twenty five were used for testing. All music pieces were later parameterized using the HTK toolkit, in MFCC and LPC feature vectors.

Experimentation on the classifiers (TreeQ, OLVQ1) performance followed using the extracted feature vectors in different combinations of features-classifiers. For the TreeQ experiments, we first obtained the optimal window size and the target rate of the algorithm. This was achieved by measuring the performance with varying values and combinations for these two parameters. An iterative procedure was used during which a new parameter was added, tested and decided to be maintained only if the acquired performance was no worse than the best performance achieved that far. This was done for both MFCC and LPC features with or without using quantization into histograms. Due to lack of time, the OLVQ1 experiments were performed using only MFCCs, without histogram quantization. LVQ involved only two parameters, n (number of codebook vectors) and k (kNN parameter), whose optimal values were obtained in a similar manner as the optimal window size and target rate for TreeQ. In all the experiments, the classifier performance was measured using Precision, Recall, Accuracy, F1 on precision and recall, and Confidence measures. Results are summarized in Table 1. We observe that TreeQ outperforms OLVQ1, when LPC features are used, with histogram quantization, for all considered measures.

Table 1. Optimal performance achieved by TreeQ and OLVQ1.

Performance Metric	Classifier		
	TreeQ		LVQ
	MFCC	LPC - Histograms	MFCC
Overall Accuracy(%)	**68.00**	**68.00**	52.00
Average Accuracy (%)	86.00	**87.00**	79.00
Average Precision (%)	71.13	**75.00**	58.75
Average Recall (%)	65.00	**70.00**	55.00
Average F-1 (%)	66.10	**69.99**	52.36

Having obtained the optimal setup for each classifier, we created learning curves as shown in Figures 3, 4 and 5. From these curves, we cannot extract valid conclusions about the learning capability of the two algorithms. For instance, for TreeQ with MFCCs, the curve is still increasing at the final steps which might indicate that a larger training set could help us achieve better performance. On the other hand, at these final steps, the curve also seems to smoothen, so the improvement of the performance using more training data might be insignificant. Finally, comparing the two TreeQ curves with the OLVQ1 curve, we may say that TreeQ seems to better learn that OLVQ1. However, this is only an indication. More extensive experiments with a much larger dataset (and thus bigger test and training data sets) need to be undertaken to draw validated conclusions.

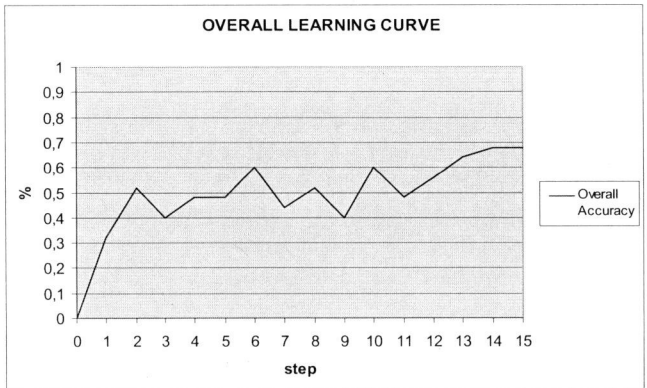

Fig. 3. Overall learning curve using MFCCs with TreeQ

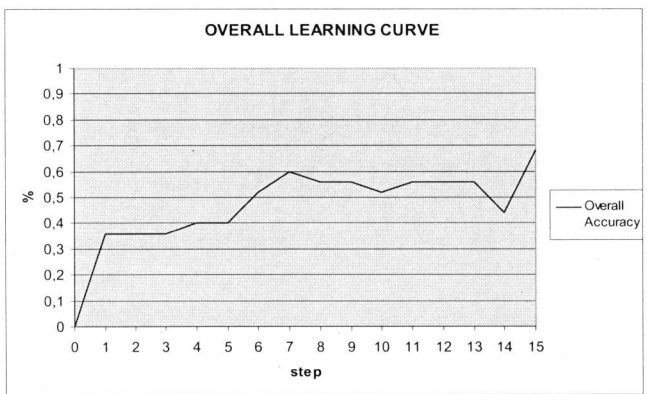

Fig. 4. Overall learning curve using LPCs with TreeQ

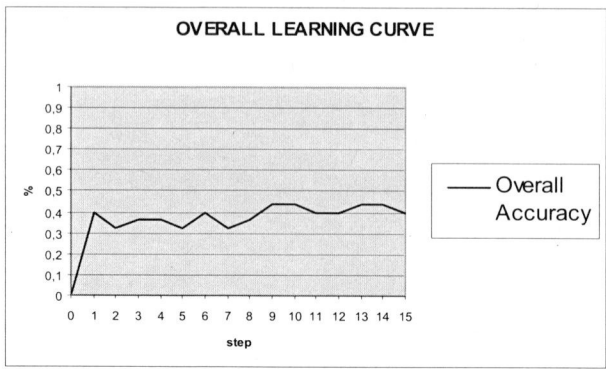

Fig. 5. Overall learning curve using MFCCs with LVQ

6   Conclusions and Future Work

In this paper, we have underlined the importance of content-based retrieval, which we addressed by conducting extensive experiments for music information retrieval, based on music genre queries, in order to compare the performance of two state-of-the-art classifiers, TreeQ and LVQ. From the performance evaluation, we could not reach valid conclusions, however, we have identified performance hints to extend the work further towards a certain direction. The learning capability of both algorithms needs to be further explored and hence we intend to undertake more experiments with a larger dataset as continuation of the currently reported work.

References

1.   Jonathan T. Foote, TreeQ Manual V0.8, September, 2003
2.   T. Kohonen, H. Hynninen, J. Kangas, H. Laaksonen, and K. Torkkola. LVQ-PAK: The learning vector quantization program package, Technical Report A30, Helsinki University of Technology, Laboratory of Computer and Information Science, FIN-02150 Espoo, Finland, 1996
3.   Jonathan T. Foote, Content-based retrieval of music and audio, Multimedia Storage and Archiving Systems II, Proceedings of SPIE, 1997
4.   Jonathan T. Foote, An overview of audio information retrieval, Multimedia Syst., Springer-Verlag New York, Inc., Secaucus, NJ, USA, 1999
5.   Music retrieval demo using open-source software package TreeQ by Jonathan T. Foote, http://www.rotorbrain.com/foote/musicr/doc16.html
6.   Forecasting with artificial neural networks, http://www.neural-forecasting.com
7.   Helsinki University of Technology – Neural Networks Research Centre, http://www.cis.hut.fi/research/som_lvq_pak.shtml
8.   The HTK Toolkit, http://htk.eng.cam.ac.uk/
9.   Steve Young et al., *The HTK Book* (1995-1999 Microsoft Corporation, 2001-2006 Cambridge University Engineering Department)

Image Compression with Competitive Networks and Pre-fixed Prototypes*

Enrique Mérida-Casermeiro[1], Domingo López-Rodríguez[1], and Juan M. Ortiz-de-Lazcano-Lobato[2]

[1] Department of Applied Mathematics, University of Málaga, Málaga, Spain; {merida,dlopez}@ctima.uma.es
[2] Department of Computer Science and Artificial Intelligence, University of Málaga, Málaga, Spain; jmortiz@lcc.uma.es

Abstract. Image compression techniques have required much attention from the neural networks community for the last years. In this work we intend to develop a new algorithm to perform image compression based on adding some pre-fixed prototypes to those obtained by a competitive neural network. Prototypes are selected to get a better representation of the compressed image, improving the computational time needed to encode the image and decreasing the code-book storage necessities of the standard approach. This new method has been tested with some well-known images and results proved that our proposal outperforms classical methods in terms of maximizing peak-signal-to-noise-ratio values.

1 Introduction

The storage or transmission of images are tasks demanding either large capacity and/or bandwidth. Thus, image compression is key in the development of various multimedia computer services and telecommunication applications, such as medical imaging [?], satellite transmission, teleconferencing, pattern recognition [?], etc. The goal of image coding is to reduce both the distortion introduced in the coding process and the bit rate (or, equivalently, the compression rate) to an acceptable level.

Recent publications show a substantial increase in the use of neural networks for image compression and coding. For a review in neural techniques for image compression, refer to [?].

Vector Quantization (VQ) is a lossy compression technique that can achieve high compression rates with good visual fidelity, see for example [?]. VQ is a coding method designed to represent a multidimensional space by means of a finite number of vectors, called representatives, prototypes or code-vectors. A vector quantizer statistically encodes data vectors in order to quantize and compress the data, by mapping each input vector in the p-dimensional Euclidean space $\mathbb{R}^p$ into one of the K prototypes.

* This work has been partially supported by Junta de Andalucía project number P06-TIC-01615.

Please use the following format when citing this chapter:

Mérida-Casermeiro, E., López-Rodríguez, D., Ortiz-de-Lazcano-Lobato, J. M., 2007, in IFIP International Federation for Information Processing, Volume 247, Artificial Intelligence and Innovations 2007: From Theory to Applications, eds. Boukis, C., Pnevmatikakis, L., Polymenakos, L., (Boston: Springer), pp. 339-346.

According to Shannon's rate distortion theory, VQ can always achieve better compression performance than any conventional coding technique based on the encoding of scalar quantities [?].

Linde, Buzo and Gray [?] proposed the well-known LBG algorithm for VQ which made no use of differentiation, and it is the standard approach to compute the codebook (the set of prototypes).

Competitive networks are designed to cluster the input data. Thus, by using VQ techniques in this type of networks, tasks such as data coding and compression can be performed.

The basic structure of a network of this type is as follows: given an input vector from a p-dimensional space, K neurons compute the VQ code-book in which each neuron relates to one code-vector via its coupling weights. The weight $\mathbf{w}_i = (w_{i,1}, \ldots, w_{i,p})$ associated with the i-th neuron is eventually trained to represent the code-vector $\mathbf{c}_i$ in the code-book. As the network is being trained, all the weights will be optimized to represent the best possible partition of all the input vectors.

The aim of this paper is to present a new technique for image compression based on competitive neural networks. This technique allows to reduce the number of code-vectors needed to achieve a high quality code-book. This method is based on the use of a combination of multiple prototypes to store one input vector, achieving a better representation of the input dataset.

2 The Standard Approach

Let us consider an image $I(i, j)$. In order to compress the image by means of VQ competitive networks, the image is subdivided into $N \times M$ square sub-images of size $k \times k$, called *windows*. These windows are our input patterns with $p = k^2$ components (these patterns are obtained by arranging the pixel values row by row from top to bottom).

The compression process consists in selecting a reduced set of K representative windows (corresponding to the solution prototypes) and replacing each window of the original image with the closest representative window among the prototypes. Thus, the compressed image I' is built.

In this work we have used the standard competitive learning (SCL) rule to build the code-book. Let $X = \{x_1, \ldots, x_n\}$ be the set of input patterns, and let $\{\mathbf{w}_1, \ldots, \mathbf{w}_K\}$ represent the code-book. The algorithm is as follows:

1. Choose an input pattern, x_i.
2. Compute the winning prototype (the closest to x_i), $\mathbf{w}_c$, verifying

$$\|x_i - \mathbf{w}_c\|^2 = \min_{j=1,\ldots,K} \|x_i - \mathbf{w}_j\|^2$$

3. Update the vector $\mathbf{w}_c$ according to

$$\mathbf{w}_c(t + 1) = \mathbf{w}_c(t) + \alpha(t) \cdot (x_i - \mathbf{w}_c(t))$$

where $\alpha(t)$ is the learning rate parameter, usually convergent to 0 as the number of iterations t tends to infinity. A typical value for $\alpha(t)$ is given by a linear decrease from 0.9 to 0 along the iterations.

4. Increase t, and repeat steps 1-4 until convergence is detected.

The bottleneck of this algorithm is the computation of the closest prototype, since it involves the calculation of K distances. Thus, the time spent by this algorithm to build the code-book when the whole set of input patterns is presented to the net is proportional to $n \cdot K$.

Though many other learning rules have been developed to obtain quasi-optimal code-books [?, ?, ?, ?, ?], we have used the SCL algorithm since its performance is very well-known and allows us to compare our technique to the standard approach.

3 Pre-fixed Prototypes

Our proposal differs from the standard approach in several points:

- Some of the prototypes used in the compression are *a priori* known by the encoder (transmitting the image) and decoder (receiving the image). Thus, with some prototypes pre-fixed in advance, the size of the code-book is reduced considerably.

  So, if, for example, we have $K = 32$ prototypes, and we fix $K' = 16$ of them, then the encoder only has to transmit $K - K' = 16$ prototypes after the encoding phase.
- In addition, since not all prototypes need to be computed, the encoding algorithm (the competitive neural network) will spend less time in computing the code-book.

Thus, with our proposal, we achieve a high quality compression by reducing computational time as well as the code-book storage space. Our technique maintains the same compression rate as the standard approach for the given number of prototypes.

This means that the transmission of the image from the encoder to the decoder (receiver) is improved, since the codebook storage space is halved.

The encoding algorithm is based in applying the standard competitive learning rule (SCL) mentioned above, but with the restriction of the pre-fixed prototypes:

1. Choose an input pattern, x_i.
2. Compute the winning prototype (the closest to x_i), $\mathbf{w}_c$, verifying

$$\|x_i - \mathbf{w}_c\|^2 = \min_{j=1,\dots,K} \|x_i - \mathbf{w}_j\|^2$$

3. If the winning unit $\mathbf{w}_c$ represents one of the fixed prototypes, it does not learn. Otherwise, update the vector $\mathbf{w}_c$ according to

$$\mathbf{w}_c(t+1) = \mathbf{w}_c(t) + \alpha(t) \cdot (x_i - \mathbf{w}_c(t))$$

where $\alpha(t)$ is the learning rate parameter.

4. Increase t, and repeat steps 1-4 until convergence is detected.

It seems reasonable to use $K' = \frac{K}{2}$, that is, to fix half the prototypes, since it allows an easy codification of each input pattern: if b bits $m_0, \ldots, m_{b-1}$ are used to encode a pattern, then m_0 will indicate whether the corresponding prototype is *a priori* known by both encoder and decoder ($m_0 = 0$) or not ($m_0 = 1$). The other $b - 1$ bits are used to encode the prototype number, from 0 to K'. So, the decoder, when a sequence of bits arrives, studies m_0 and looks for the prototype in the corresponding part of the code-book (the fixed or the transmitted, depending on m_0).

The intuitive idea behind the utilization of pre-fixed prototypes is that these prototypes are designed to fit in areas of the image in which there is little detail (sky, rivers, etc.), whilst the learnt prototypes focus on the areas of great detail.

4 Experimental Results

In this section we compare the efficiency of our proposal in image compression with respect to the standard approach.

We have considered a test set of images formed by 4 images (the well-known *Lenna* image plus 3 images from MatLab Image Processing Toolbox, see Fig. 1). Each image in our experiments has 256×256 pixels, and window size is 4×4. So, the number of input patterns for the standard algorithm is 4096. The number K of representative windows varies in the set $\mathcal{K} = \{32, 64\}$.

Two measures has been used in this work to compare the efficiency of our technique

- The *peak-signal-to-noise-ratio* (PSNR), defined as:

$$\text{PSNR} = 20 \log_{10} \left(\frac{255}{\text{RMSE}} \right)$$

and measured in decibels (dB), where the image has 256 gray levels and RMSE is the root mean square error between two images (the original and the compressed). Ideally, a value of PSNR $= \infty$ is the goal to attain, since it corresponds to a lossless compression. Thus, one tries to obtain the maximum value possible for PSNR.

- The 1-norm ($\| \cdot \|_1$) of the difference between the original image I and the compressed image I', defined as:

$$\| I - I' \|_1 = \max_j \sum_i |I(i, j) - I'(i, j)|$$

where $I(i, j)$ represents the value of the pixel (i,j) in the image I.
A lower value of this norm indicates a better approximation of the compressed image to the original one.

Some of the test images are shown in Fig. 1. The compressed images are shown in Figs. 2 and 3. In these figures, we can observe that our compressed images obtain higher visual fidelity than the standard approach.

Fig. 1. Sample images from the test set: lenna (top left), cameraman (top right), rice (bottom left) and kids (bottom right).

For our proposal, $\frac{K}{2}$ fixed prototypes were built by considering vectors of the form $\mathbf{w}_i = (c_i, \dots, c_i) \in \{0, \dots, 255\}^{k^2}$, that is, all components are equal, each prototype representing a window with a constant grey-level in all its pixels. c_i values $(i = 1, \dots, \frac{K}{2})$ were equally spaced in $\{0, \dots, 255\}$. The same pre-fixed prototypes were used for every test image.

In Table 1, there are represented the PSNR values of the compressed images using both the standard and our approach. It can be noted that if our method is used with $K' = K/2$ fixed prototypes, where K is the number of the standard approach, the PSNR value obtained is at least comparable, and better in some cases, to that of the standard approach.

This surprising fact may be explained as follows: since $K' = \frac{K}{2}$ prototypes are pre-fixed, the dimensionality of the problem is reduced to half. As the dimension is reduced, the number of possible local minima of the distortion function is also reduced. So, the learning phase can avoid certain bad local minima present when all K prototypes are considered.

This is also possible since prototypes with a constant gray-level in all its components are usually present in wide regions of most images (regions with little detail).

I can also be observed that the 1-norm of our proposal is lower in most cases than the corresponding of the standard approach.

Table 1. PSNR and $\|\cdot\|_1$ results for the considered compressed images. The quotient Δt is defined by $\Delta t = \dfrac{t_{\text{new}}}{t_{\text{old}}}$.

		Standard Approach			Prop.			
Image	K	PSNR	$\|\cdot\|_1$	t_{old}	PSNR	$\|\cdot\|_1$	t_{new}	Δt
cameraman	32	23.94	23.6	33.65	24.13	20.1	31.38	0.93
rice	32	28.00	11.8	33.31	28.47	10.5	32.01	0.96
lenna	32	25.41	16.9	33.46	25.39	16.0	31.12	0.93
kids	32	27.18	12.1	33.56	26.79	13.8	31.17	0.93
cameraman	64	25.32	19.3	53.40	25.16	18.9	45.64	0.85
rice	64	29.41	8.6	45.54	30.33	7.6	43.50	0.95
lenna	64	26.73	13.6	46.31	26.48	15.7	43.00	0.93
kids	64	27.92	11.8	53.73	27.87	11.24	42.18	0.78

The time spent by our algorithm to build the code-book is also lower than the standard, as shown in the last column of Table 1, where Δt indicates the quotient between the time spent by the standard approach and the time used by our proposal.

5 Conclusions

In this work we have presented a new algorithm to perform image compression based on combining fixed prototypes with the solution prototypes obtained by a competitive learning rule.

This new method is able to represent compressed images with higher visual fidelity than the standard approach, at the same time that achieves greater PSNR values in many cases. In addition, with this method, the computation of the code-book is less time-consuming, since fixed prototypes are never updated.

We have tested our approach using the standard competitive learning rule. Better results are expected if learning rules as [?, ?, ?] are used instead.

Our future work covers the study of new algorithms taking advantage of combining fixed and variable prototypes to form different windows in the compressed image. The development of a competitive learning rule to optimize the code-book is also an issue of research.

The application of this technique to specific scenarios or groups of images (biomedical images, satellite images, etc.) can improve their processing, segmentation, compression and transmission.

Fig. 2. Compressed images (from top to bottom): standard approach with 32 prototypes, our proposal with 32 prototypes, standard approach with 64 prototypes and our proposal with 64 prototypes.

Fig. 3. Compressed images (from top to bottom): standard approach with 32 prototypes, our proposal with 32 prototypes, standard approach with 64 prototypes and our proposal with 64 prototypes.

On the use of spatial relations between objects for image classification*

Nicolas Tsapatsoulis, Sergios Petridis, and Stavros J. Perantonis

Computational Intelligence Laboratory,
Institute of informatics and Telecommunications,
NCSR "Demokritos", Greece,
{petridis,ntsap}@iit.demokritos.gr.

Abstract. Image classification is addressed in this paper by utilizing spatial relation of detected objects in a rule-based fashion. Instances of particular object classes are detected combining bottom-up (learnable models based on simple features) and top-down information(object models consisting of primitive geometric shapes such as lines). The rule-based system acts as a model for the spatial configuration of objects, also providing a human interpretable justification of image classification. Experimental results in the athletic domain show that despite inefficiencies in object detection, spatial relations allow for efficient discrimination between visually similar images classes.

Key words: image classification, object detection, spatial realations

1 Introduction

Retrieving images based on their content is a challenging issue. Although the last decade research has being focusing on the query-by-example paradigm [1], an ambitious goal is to allow the user to formulate semantic queries through a natural language interface. Beside translating textual information into a semantically valid query, this goal also requires an association of semantic classes to their visual representations.

An approach to handle semantic queries has been to label images with coarse classes, such as indoor/outdoor and cities/landscapes, based on global characteristics of images. Such a labelling, though, tends to be inadequate in respect to realistic user-queries. At the same time, finer grain classification based directly on global image features, seems unfeasible. In more realistic scenarios, a user may wish to retrieve an image based on particular objects they appear in it. This brings up the question of detecting and classifying particular areas of images to one among a certain number of object classes. What's more, once

---

* This work was partially supported by the European Commission under the FP6-027538 contract.

Please use the following format when citing this chapter:

Tsapatsoulis, N., Petridis, S., Perantonis, S., J., 2007, in IFIP International Federation for Information Processing, Volume 247, Artificial Intelligence and Innovations 2007: From Theory to Applications, eds. Boukis, C., Pnevmatikakis, L., Polymenakos, L., (Boston: Springer), pp. 347-356.

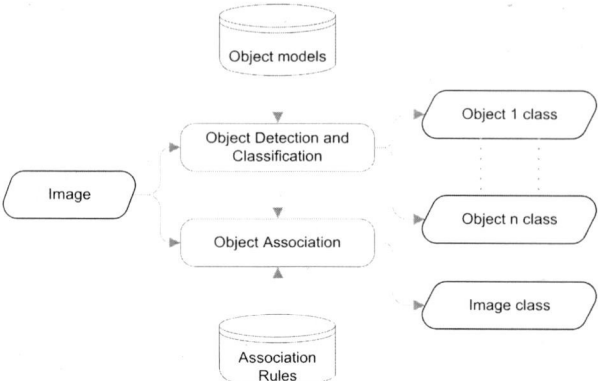

Fig. 1. Schematic diagram of the detection and classification process

this question is addressed, an overall image classification becomes conceivable, by resolving it to a particular spatial combination of objects it is made of.

In this study, we apply an object detection followed by image classification approach to detect objects and events in the athletics domain. Our object detection method results in finding image areas corresponding to a (possibly partially occluded) 2D-representation of an instance of a predefined set of object classes. To that end, we combine a top-down strategy, i.e. take into account modelling of specific object classes, with a bottom-up approach, i.e. determine region boundaries based on visual cues, as suggested in [2, 3, 4]. As a next step, we consider the image as a combination of distinct semantic objects corresponding to different area locations [5, 6, 7, 8]. We then verify the object spatial relations against a set of rules, to characterize the whole image.

In unconstrained images, there is a great variability of object classes in respect to lighting conditions and camera positions. Hence, most literature has been concentrating on very specific application domains, such as car plates recognition, horses, street scene analysis and face detection [9]. In this article, we present on-going work focused on the *athletic* domain, where (a) the objects to be identified are the humans and the athletic instruments and facilities and (b) the image is classified as a whole in respect to the athletic event it focuses on. Nevertheless, as it will be shown, our methodology allows to improve image classification results even when objects are missing or not properly detected.

2 System Overview

Semantics extraction from images has been frequently depicted as bridging the gap between concepts and their visual representations. Our approach consists of constructing this bridge with, as an intermediate abutment, the detection of particular image areas as instances of semantic classes. The overview of our method is depicted in Figure 1.

Our assumption is that in most circumstances, even when an image can be overall described by a single word, its semantics are too complex to be detected directly by visual cues. We refer to those semantics as high-level concepts. Instead, it may be easier to decompose the image semantics into a set of inter-related concepts corresponding to distinct visual areas of the image, which may be much more easily detectable. We will refer to these concepts as mid-level concepts [10], since they serve as intermediates between visual cues and the final image classification[2]. This has the advantage of being able to explicitly supplement the extraction system with known semantics regarding the relation between the mid-level concepts and the high-level ones, thus providing useful a-priories to the extraction procedure.

To illustrate our methodology, consider an example of the athletics domain, where an image shows an athlete holding a pole and jumping over an horizontal bar, whereas a pillar is also visible. Clearly, this may be interpreted as a photo taken from a pole-vault event, as long as the relative position of these objects does indicate this. Although a direct classification of an image as a pole-vault event is theoretically possible, detecting each object separately and then associate them seems a more robust and scalable solution, if a distinction between a very visually similar event, such as high jump, is desirable.

Our methodology results in semantic labelling of images as well as of objects within images, which makes it potentially suitable for image retrieval. An important issue that arises then is how the results are further used to allow for query answering. Although early approaches employed ad-hoc methods for querying specially crafted databases [11], the approach we suggest here is to populate an ontology, which can be then further queried using a standard reasoner (see [12]). This approach has the additional advantage of using further knowledge, implied by the T-box of the ontology, to answer complex semantic queries.

3 Object Detection

Our approach to object detection is a conjunction of bottom-up and top-down techniques to detect specific objects. Namely, following a domain-independent segmentation to find a first set of segments (bottom-up approach), particular algorithms [13] [14], taking into account information regarding the colour/texture of objects, are used to detect fragments of objects classes (top-down approach). Additional information regarding the expected shape of the object classes is also used either to merge adjacent fragments of the same object class or to directly

---

[2] Notice that although the concepts' qualifier "mid-level" refers to their role as intermediates in bridging the semantic gap, they can also be characterised as "atomic" in that they constitute the smallest *semantic* entities detected directly through image processing techniques.

locate them in the image (top-down). In the latter case, a further combination of the segments found with the general-purpose segmentation is used to optimally adjust the object boundaries. To further distinguish among object classes in a finer grain, we extract features of the detected objects and feed them to a learnable classifier, assigning the object class with the highest score.

In the remainder of this section, we describe in details the way detection is done for three object classes: human bodies, human faces and elongated objects. The choice of these object has been such that, as it will be shown at section 4, it will enable a final image classification based on their spatial relations.

Detection of human bodies To detect human bodies, the image I is first partitioned into segments $S = \{S_i\}$ using the JSEG [15] algorithm, such that

$$I = \bigcup_i S_i \tag{1}$$

To allow for more accurate object contour detection, over-segmentation is promoted, by choosing high values for the merging threshold of this algorithm. Subsequently, a small number among these segments is kept, based on whether these constitute foreground areas of the image. Foreground areas are modelled as the visually attended areas, computed with the aid of the algorithm described in [14]. The assumption here is that the human to be detected is always part of the foreground, since during photo capturing, the focus is on him. In particular, the set of segments S' kept as candidates for humans, comprises those having overlap precision ratio higher than a defined threshold T:

$$S' = \{S_i : \frac{|M_i \cap M_F|}{|M_i|} > T\} \tag{2}$$

where M_i denotes the mask of segment S_i, M_F denotes the mask of area detected as foreground, $\cap$ denotes the logical AND operation and $|\cdot|$ denotes the sum over pixel values. A typical value for the threshold T is 0.5.

To further reduce the elements of S', we make use of a classifier, which decodes wether a segment is part of a body, rather than some other object class. Since the same classifier is used to discriminate among object classes, it is described separately below. Finally, adjacent partitions of this set are, then, merged and the human body is considered as the largest (with respect to area measuring) candidates after merging.

Detection of human faces To detect human faces, we rely on two essential characteristics of a face: (a) faces are skin areas having significant intensity variability due to the presence of eyes, eyebrows, mouth and nostrils and (b) faces tend to have an oval-like shape. In particular, we first detect segments containing skins, based on the combination of the JSEG segmentation algorithm with a skin-detection algorithm described in [13]. Again, over-segmentation is pursuit in order to allow discrimination between the face and neighboring naked body parts (neck and arms)[3]. Having identified a number of potential face fragments, we proceed by selectively merging their corresponding segments. Segments are recursively merged under the condition that (a) they are adjacent and (b) the resulting segment jointly maximizes both the anticipated skin colour [13] and the *circularity* index, as compared to the largest of the component ones. The circularity index is computed as the ratio of the area of a circle having as radius the variance of the segment along its longest projection, to the actual area of the segment:

$$\frac{2\pi(\max_{|\mathbf{v}|=1} \mathrm{var}\{\mathbf{v}^{\top} S\})^2}{|S|} \tag{3}$$

The resulting candidate human faces segments are then given to the machine learning algorithm for a final scoring.

Detection of elongated objects Particular attention has been given to the detection of possibly occluded objects having an important elongated nature, since these are pertinent in respect to the athletics domain (horizontal bars, poles, pillars). Elongated objects have line segment characteristics and their detection involves the combination of the radon transform with hough transform. Namely, the image edges are first extracted, by using information from the gradient and the entropy of the pixels' images. Then, the matrix stemming from the radon transform, evaluated at angles with a small step (e.g. $3°$), is processed by a hough transform to find optimal angles, where the intensity of accumulation is important across a wide range of pixels. Subsequently, the image-mask corresponding to each of the angles found is dilated and combined with the original image with the AND operator. The detected objects are then fed to the classifier for a final decision. To allow for discrimination among several types of elongated object classes, features such as orientation and length are also extracted.

Finer Object Classes The above methods for human face, human body and elongated objects result in image segments that possibly correspond to one of these object classes. To further enhance the ability to discriminate among these classes, as well as to discriminate among sub-classes, we make use of a classifier. This requires generating a feature vector corresponding to each image segment. The features that have been used are area, colour, area entropy (texture), circularity index, angle, and position. The generated feature vectors are then fed to a multiclass 1-vs-all extension of an RBF-SVM classifier. The class with the maximum score is then used to finally characterize the segment.

4 Ruled-Based Image Classification

In the proposed methodology for image classification, the role of rules is to provide relations between semantic entities (objects) so as to allow for an overall

---

[3] Notice that this is not always feasible and is actually the main reason for achieving high area recall but low area precision values (see the evaluation section below).

image interpretation. The rules are derived automatically based on the manually annotated objects and refer to spatial relations between them. Justification of using rules referring to spatial relations was, first, identified during the manual image annotation process. The question there was: "Which are the discriminatory cues that allow (humans) for identifying the class of an image given a set of available classes?". In the athletics domain it turned out that these cues were: (a) Existence of particular athletic instruments (e.g., pole, hurdles, etc), (b) posture of athlete's body, and (c) recognition of an athlete and association with her/his athletic event of expertise. The existence of particular objects, in our approach, is verified through the object detection process. As already mentioned, however, object detection (even in the context of a particular domain like athletics) is neither easy nor reliable. Thus, rules of the form "if instrument X was found then input image belongs to class Y" are error pruned. On the other hand by using spatial rules between two objects we ensure that neither object detection false alarms nor object detection misses would be able to activate a rule because a spatial relation with another object needs also to be fulfilled. As far as the athlete's body posture cue is concerned, by defining human body and human face as different objects one can define rules describing a variety of postures. Finally, the third image classification cue implies face recognition abilities so as to recognize athletes from photos. Despite the lot of work done in this area, unconstrained face recognition from images is closed to impossible

In order to construct rules concerning the spatial relations between objects we have defined a set of spatial relations that can be easily identified in the 2D-projection of a physical scene through the use of image analysis techniques. In the first stage we have used the following spatial predicates: 'is above', 'is below','is left', 'is right', 'is adjacent', 'is near', 'is above left', 'is above right', 'is below left', 'is below right'. We are currently working towards reliable automatic extraction of the 'is behind' relation.

Rule extraction Rules are automatically extracted by using the manually annotated content. Spatial relations are then computed based on the object masks. Although formal rule extraction exist [16], in a preliminary study we have constructed spatial rules by exhaustive search in our training corpus. In particular we have tried to identify rules that frequently appear in the content of a particular image class and are able to separate this image class from the other classes. A sample of derived rules are shown in Table 1. For instance, the rule with id=10 can be expressed as 'a body is below an horizontal bar'; this rule holds in the 5% (see frequency field) of training images. The 75% (see confidence field) of these images belong to the pole vault class.

Image Classification In order to classify images w.r.t a set of available classes using the above mentioned rules we use a 'rule-voting' process. That is, given the object detection results for a particular image, every activated rule votes for its class with the rule's confidence value. The overall score for a particular class is the sum of votes for this class divided by the total number of activated rules. Imagine, for example, that the rules with ids 9,10,11 hold based on the image

rule id	relation	arg. a	arg. b	frequency	class	confidence
...						
9	is above right	body	pole	7	pole vault	1.00
10	is below	body	horizontal bar	5	pole vault	0.75
11	is left	face	horizontal bar	14	high jump	0.84
12	is right	face	horizontal bar	9	high jump	0.91
...						

Table 1. Example of spatial rules

analysis results. The 'voting' score for the pole vault class is $(1+.75)/3 = 0.5833$ while the corresponding score for the high Jump class is $0.8421/3 = 0.2807$. Given that the confidence score for each rule is bounded in the $[0, 1]$ interval it is obvious that the sum of voting scores for all classes is bounded by one. However, the upper bound is rarely reached in practice. On the other hand, there are cases (images) in which no rule is activated. In this case the image class is denoted as 'unknown'. In this way images, for which the evidence for their class estimation is poor, remain unlabelled.

We should note, here, that the aim is to transfer the knowledge captured through the rule extraction process, outlined earlier, into an ontology to allow for usage of description logics. This will allow rule combination and utilization of prior knowledge already available in the ontology. A further goal is then to use the ontology to guide the object extraction process, by also detecting object's configurations unlike to appear. To give an example, in the context of pole vault and high jump images, it is unlike that a body can be above a face and both of them below an horizontal, unless a pole is also present and touches the body.

5 Evaluation Results

The performance of the presented algorithms has been evaluated based on a set of manually annotated images spatial dimensions 480×600, taken from the IAAF web site [17]. In total 140 images illustrating pole vault (69) and high jump (71) events were manually annotated by two different annotators. In order to evaluate the consistency of the manually marked areas the inter-annotator agreement (IAG), which equals the ratio of the number of pixels belonging to both annotated areas to the number of pixels belonging to at least one annotated area, was used:

$$\mathrm{IAG}_i = \frac{|M_i^1 \cap M_i^2|}{|M_i^1 \cup M_i^2|} \tag{4}$$

The ground truth area for each object instance was set as the logical OR operation between the areas marked by the two annotators under the constrained that the IAG for these annotations is higher than 0.6. In this way a ground

object class	occurrences	recall	precision	MAR	MAP	MAM
horizontal bar	111	81.1	81.8	79.0	61.8	80.1
pole	61	73.8	81.8	62.3	65.1	85.6
human face	139	62.6	64.9	91.9	48.0	66.7
human body	140	67.2	72.9	93.1	84.7	88.3

Table 2. Evaluation Results for the detection of objects. The first three columns correspond to the number of occurrences of instances of each object class, the recall and precision of the object detection method. The following three columns are percentages in respect to the object correctly identified, conveying information about the area mathching: mean area Recall (MAR), mean area precision (MAP) and Mean Area Match between annotations (MAM).

truth set was built comprising of 140 human body instances, 139 human face instances (one face was fully occluded), 111 horizontal bars instances and 61 pole instances.

Table 2 presents the results of evaluation of the object classes at image level. We consider that a segment S_i detected automatically is correct when there exist a manually annotated segment S_i^m classified under the same object class with high overlap, in the sense of eq.(4). To be fair, we consider the threshold t as a function of the manually annotated segment size, so as to be more strict (respectively less strict) for large objects (respectively small objects). To this end, we used the sigmoid-shape function

$$t(S) = a(1 + \frac{b}{1 + exp(-c|S|/|I| + 1)}) \tag{5}$$

where $|S|$ and $|I|$ are the areas of the segment and image respectively, and a, b and c are parameters set to $a = 0.1$, $b = 3$ and $c = 10$. For the segments classified as correct, the area recall and recision have been evaluated as:

$$\frac{|M \cap M^a|}{|M^a|}, \quad \frac{|M \cap M^a|}{|M|} \tag{6}$$

where M and M^a denote the mask of a detected and its corresponding manually annotated segment respectively. Their mean values across all instances of the same class is shown in Table 2. An interesting point one can notice is the poor results in face detection. This can be assigned to the variability in pose (in very few images face appears in frontal position) and a frequent partial occlusion from human body and athletic objects. The authors believe that given the difficulty of face detection in such an unconstrained environment, results are more than satisfactory. Also notice that detection of horizonal bar is more accurate than pole's, though both are detected using the same principle (elongated objects). This is due to the higher variability in shape and orientation encountered in the visual appearance of poles.

In Table 3, the evaluation results for image classification are presented. To test the generalisation performance of the rules used, we tested them on a set

Sport	Performance		Confusion Matrix		
	Recall	Precision	HighJump	Pole Vault	Unknown
High Jump	86,7%	92.2%	13	2	1
Pole Vault	75.0%	85.7%	1	12	3

Table 3. Evaluation results for image classification – Confusion matrix

object class	occurrences	recall	precision
horizontal bar	24	79.2	79.2
pole	11	63.6	70.0
human face	30	66.7	69.0
human body	32	75.0	82.8

Table 4. Evaluation Results for the detection of objects in the test set.

of 32 pole vault and high jump images not used during the rule induction and object class learning process. Object detection results for the same set are shown in Table 4. Notice that the only object class which can be used for discriminating between pole vault and high jump images is pole, since all other object classes appear in both sports. However, as can be seen from Table 4, retrieving pole vault images only upon pole existence would result in poor performance (recall 63.6%, precision 70%). Rule-based classification achieves significantly higher rates (recall 75.0%, precision 85.7%), thus alleviating false alarms and misses during pole detection.

6 Conclusion and Future work

In this paper, we proposed a methodology that allows for fine-grain image classification. At a first step, a number of key-objects with specific semantics are detected. Subsequently, the spatial configuration of these objects has been taken into account by a set of rules, to ultimately characterize the entire image. The evaluation of our approach shows that spatial relations between objects have provided substantial information for image classification. The redundancy of cues induced by both detected objects and their spatial relations allows for tempering object misses and/or misclassifications, thus rendering the overall methodology robust.

Our future plans to improve upon our methodology involve two main directions. First, we investigating one-class learning models to measure the level confidence of the objects detection. The level of confidence can then be used as a weighting factor while applying the rules. A second research direction regards rules learning, which is currently done though through exhaustive search. We expect that elaborated machine learning methods for rule extraction that, in addition, allow for complex rule formation. can further improve the accuracy and robustness of image classification.

References

1. Smith, J., Chang, S.: Visually searching the Web for content. Multimedia, IEEE **4**(3) (1997) 12–20
2. Borenstein, E., Sharon, E., Ullman, S.: Combining Top-Down and Bottom-Up Segmentation. Computer Vision and Pattern Recognition Workshop, 2004 Conference on (2004) 46–46
3. Levin, A., Weiss, Y.: Learning to Combine Bottom-Up and Top-Down Segmentation. LECTURE NOTES IN COMPUTER SCIENCE **3954** (2006) 581
4. Kapoor, A., Winn, J.: Located Hidden Random Fields: Learning Discriminative Parts for Object Detection. European Conference on Computer Vision (2006)
5. Fan, X.: Contextual disambiguation for multi-class object detection. Image Processing, 2004. ICIP'04. 2004 International Conference on **5** (2004)
6. Wolf, L., Bileschi, S.: A Critical View of Context. International Journal of Computer Vision **69**(2) (2006) 251–261
7. Amit, Y., Geman, D., Fan, X.: A coarse-to-fine strategy for multiclass shape detection. Pattern Analysis and Machine Intelligence, IEEE Transactions on **26**(12) (2004) 1606–1621
8. Singhal, A., Luo, J., Zhu, W.: Probabilistic spatial context models for scene content understanding. Computer Vision and Pattern Recognition, 2003. Proceedings. 2003 IEEE Computer Society Conference on **1** (2003)
9. Fleuret, F., Geman, D.: Coarse-to-Fine Face Detection. International Journal of Computer Vision **41**(1) (2001) 85–107
10. Petridis, S., Tsapatsoulis, N., et al.: Methodology for Semantics Extraction from Multimedia Content. Deliverable, BOEMIE, FP6-027538 (2007) http://www.boemie.org/files/BOEMIE-d2_1-v2.pdf.
11. Li, W., Candan, K., Hirata, K., Hara, Y.: Hierarchical image modeling for object-based media retrieval. Data & Knowledge Engineering **27**(2) (1998) 139–176
12. Haarslev, V., Möller, R.: Racer: A Core Inference Engine for the Semantic Web. Proceedings of the 2nd International Workshop on Evaluation of Ontology-based Tools (2003) 27–36
13. Tsapatsoulis, N., Avrithis, Y., Kollias, S.: Facial Image Indexing in Multimedia Databases. Pattern Analysis & Applications **4**(2) (2001) 93–107
14. Tsapatsoulis, N., Pattichis, C., Kounoudes, A., Loizou, C., Constantinides, A., Taylor, J.: Visual Attention based Region of Interest Coding for Video-telephony Applications. In: Proc. CSNDSP, Patras, Greece. (2006)
15. Deng, Y., Manjunath, B.: Unsupervised segmentation of color-texture regions in images and video. IEEE Transactions on Pattern Analysis and Machine Intelligence **23**(8) (2001) 800–810
16. Bischog, W.: Learning Spatio-temporal relational structures. Applied Artificial Intelligence **15**(8) (2001) 707–722
17. IAAF: International association of athletics federations. http://www.iaaf.org (1996-2007)

A Knowledge Engineering Approach for Complex Violence Identification in Movies

Thanassis Perperis[1] and Sofia Tsekeridou[2]

[1] University of Athens, Greece a.perperis@di.uoa.gr
[2] Athens Information Technology, Greece sots@ait.edu.gr

Abstract. Along with the rapid increase of available multimedia data, comes the proliferation of objectionable content such as violence and pornography. We need efficient tools for automatically identifying, classifying and filtering out harmful or undesirable video content for the protection of sensitive user groups (e.g. children). In this paper we present a multimodal approach towards the identification and semantic analysis of violent content in video data. We propose a layered architecture and focus on ontological and knowledge engineering aspects of video analysis. We demonstrate the development of two ontologies defining violent hints hierarchy that low level analysis, in visual and audio modality, respectively should identify. Violence domain ontology, as a reality representation, defines higher-level semantics. Taking under consideration extracted violent hints, spatio-temporal relations and behavior patterns higher-level semantics automatic inference is possible.

1 Introduction

Psychological researches on media violence prove its negative effects on behavior, attitude and emotional state of vulnerable user groups (especially children). In the age of internet technologies and digital television, dissemination of dangerous content seems uncontrollable. Common users and industry demand intelligent, human-like methods, to automatically detect, annotate and filter out any violence hidden in video data, thus enabling high level parental control. The main obstacle towards this direction is the inability of machines to grasp high level semantic concepts from multimedia data (multimedia semantic gap). In order to tackle this problem we need efficient audio and visual medium level concept/event detectors, higher level domain knowledge represented in a formal way and tools to optimally handle their interoperation.

Previous research towards bridging multimedia semantic gap follow either a *unimodal* or a *multimodal* approach. The former case consists in classifying low level feature vectors, extracted from a *single* modality, in a set of predefined classes and the later in *fusing* each modalitys' low level analysis results. Multimodal fusion schemes either combine single modality features in a multimodal representation and feed those to machine learning algorithms to extract combined semantics (early fusion) or couple each modalitys' medium level se-

Please use the following format when citing this chapter:

Perperis, T., Tsekeridou, S., 2007, in IFIP International Federation for Information Processing, Volume 247, Artificial Intelligence and Innovations 2007: From Theory to Applications, eds. Boukis, C., Pnevmatikakis, L., Polymenakos, L., (Boston: Springer), pp. 357-364.

mantics (extracted using single modality analysis techniques) to achieve higher level of abstraction and improve semantics extraction accuracy (late fusion).

Ontologies and MPEG-7 tackle the problem of knowledge, content and semantics representation and annotation, which arise in either multimedia semantics analysis techniques. MPEG-7 [2] defines metadata descriptors for structural and low level aspects of multimedia documents, as well as, high level description schemes (Multimedia Description Schemes) encapsulating multimedia content semantics. Deploying Semantic Web trends and ontologies on multimedia data, which are complex in nature, multi-modal, of significant size, requiring extensive and efficient analysis to reduce the data space and extract representative features and descriptions, is a very challenging task. On the on hand multimedia ontologies, tackling the data characteristics, implement definition models for low- to medium-level descriptions, as the ones dictated by the Audio and Visual Parts of MPEG-7. On the other hand domain ontologies represent domain knowledge in the form of high-level concepts, hierarchies and relations. The interoperation of Multimedia and Domain Ontologies, along with the optimal definition of the latter, to support automated semantic annotation of multimedia data is a major research focus [5] in various application domains.

In this paper we propose a late fusion scheme for automatic identification and annotation of complex violent scenes in video data. We overlook medium level semantic extraction techniques (we use them as black boxes) and focus our attention on representing and inferring single and cross modality semantics using an ontological and knowledge engineering approach. Previous, mainly low level analysis based approaches tackle the problem at hand by detecting a limited and simple set of violence actions and semantics (i.e. kicking, fist fighting, explosions, gunshots), in order to ease the solution. Our approach by focusing on tackling an extensive range of complex violent acts in video data, based on violence domain knowledge representation, using ontologies and reasoning on or inferring from results obtained by multimodal analysis of both visual [10] and audio [8] modalities, attempts to proceed further.

The utmost goal is to automatically detect complex multimodal semantics around violence hidden in video data, annotate them accordingly and enable filtering of content for parental control. A crucial step in the overall methodology is the best possible definition of the underlying ontologies. To optimally combine multimedia descriptions with the violence domain ontology, the knowledge representation process has involved the definition of modality violence ontologies (audio, visual) that essentially map low-level analysis results to simple violence events and objects (medium-level semantics), as well as a violence domain ontology that defines the hierarchy of violence concepts and inherent relationships, irrespective of data, starting from abstract and complex ones to more simple and concrete ones (shared by all ontologies). The latter is used as input to the inference engine that undertakes the fusion of results from medium level semantics to lead to higher level ones and to infer knowledge about existing violence.

The paper is organized as follows. Section 2 briefly describes the overall architecture of the proposed solution and analyzes developed ontologies in detail. Section 3 discusses the creation of a violent movies corpus and the related ground truth. Finally, discussion for further work and conclusions are drawn in Section 4.

2 Knowledge Engineering Methodology for Violence Identification in Movies

Violence is a very abstract concept describing actions and situations, which may cause physical or mental harm to one or more persons, injury to animals, or damage to non-living objects. Violent content in video data refer to scenes that include such actions. Previous research towards violence identification in video data is limited and in most cases examines only low level features to extract simple semantics. In [7] the design of a simple feature space, for scene categorization based on the degree of action (i.e. degree of violence), is presented. In [3] detection of person on person violence, such as fist fighting, kicking, hitting with objects, in video data captured using a stationary camera, is accomplished using motion trajectory and orientation information of a person and its limbs. Audio data for violence detection is used as an additional feature in TV drama and movies in [6], where abrupt changes (i.e. explosions) in energy level of the audio signal are detected using the energy entropy criterion.

Combining violent objects, actions and events extracted from visual and audio modality respectively, towards composing and identifying higher level violent behaviors, seems a very promising approach for the problem at hand. A crucial step for this approach is to represent the violence domain knowledge as effectively as possible, in all its complexity, abstractness and hierarchy depth. A formal representation of the violence domain, to drive violent acts detection, has never been attempted before. We make a step forward towards this direction. Our overall goal is to devise a multimodal analysis, fusion and inferencing methodology towards automatic semantic violence extraction and annotation of video scenes, aiming further at content filtering and enabling parental control. The conceptual architecture of our overall methodology is shown in Fig. 1.

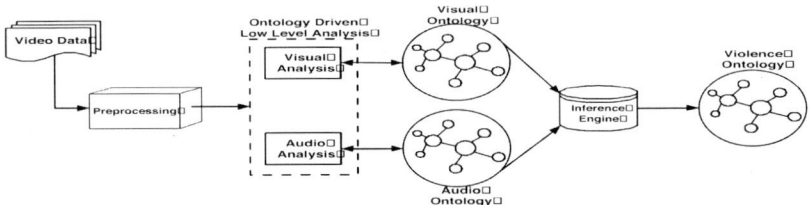

Fig. 1. Conceptual Architecture

A preprocessing step tackles the task of temporal video segmentation and feeds the low level audio and visual analysis algorithms with video shots and audio segments respectively. A visual and an audio ontology defining the hierarchy and relations of violent objects and primitive actions/events drive the corresponding segment based low level analysis procedures. Having recognized some audio and visual violent hints and instantiate the corresponding MPEG-7 descriptors, the inference engine using probabilistic reasoning, spatiotemporal relations and behavioral patterns maps sets and sequences of violent hints to higher level violent concepts represented in the domain ontology. In the following paragraphs we neglect the preprocessing and low level analysis steps (considered as black boxes) and we focus on the higher level of analysis, by presenting the corresponding ontologies and sketching the inference procedure.

2.1 Violence Domain Knowledge

As we pinpointed previously, effective violence domain representation, in all its complexity, abstractness and hierarchy depth is crucial towards tackling the problem at hand. Combining psychologists' view of violence and violent acts and extended investigation through observation of video data, we make the first attempt to conceptualize violence in an organized way. We define complex semantics of extensive violent acts, also found in movie data, along with crossmodal relations of medium level semantics, deploying Semantic Web languages, in violence domain ontology. The violence domain ontology as a knowledge representation can be further exploited by researchers and organizations investigating violence (i.e. psychologists, pedagogists, police).

Although our ontology comprises a generic representation of violence we will focus our analysis in the movie violence domain. In a movie scene containing violence (e.g. torture, fight, war) a spectator can quickly grasp the form of violence (e.g. fighting with weapons), recognize a sequence of violent (e.g. shooting, stabbing), of generic (e.g. running, walking) and of consequence (e.g. falling, crawling, scream) actions. The direct application of this process demonstrates how the hierarchy (taxonomy) of violent actions, along with their inter-relations (e.g. a stabbing is followed by a scream), is constructed, formulating the violence domain ontology. The presented movie violence ontology is implemented in OWL-DL [4] using Protégé. In Fig. 2 we present the higher level concepts of the violence ontology (left part) and an instantiation of the ontology (right part) for the violent action "stab" and the violent action "punch", demonstrating hierarchical and temporal concept's relations. The medium level classes (actions) of the ontology are strongly related with the inference engine, since they represent multimodal actions inferred using reasoning by relating to the visual and audio ontology and the single modality analysis and classification results. Additionally the simplest, more concrete, concepts (e.g. weapon, scream) are further represented, along with their low level feature descriptions, in the visual and audio ontologies, thus defining the association mechanisms of the three ontologies.

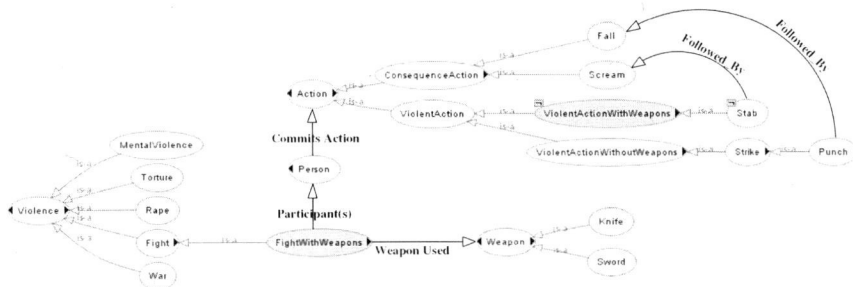

Fig. 2. Violence Ontology

2.2 Visual Semantics for Violence

Every violent behavior described in the domain ontology is usually composed of some primitive actions (performed from a person), or events (either visual or auditory) and include a set of objects (e.g. knifes, swords). The visual ontology (Fig. 3) for violence defines a taxonomy of moving objects (e.g. people, weapons, body parts, military vehicles), stationary (contextual) objects (e.g. walls, fences, furniture), abstract objects (e.g. explosions, fire, injuries) and primitive actions (e.g. crawling, running, falling). We note that the detection of some of the aforementioned concepts does not directly imply violence (e.g. bottle), but in the context of violence (e.g. hit on the head with bottle) its identification might be very important. The visual ontology further includes the MPEG-7 visual descriptors and MPEG-7 MDS (Multimedia Description Schemes), which describe visual features such as color, texture, shape and motion and semantic information of video respectively, associated with the above mentioned taxonomy entries. Furthermore it drives low level analysis algorithms towards extracting the specified objects and actions from the video data, along with their low level features. Thus the identified concepts and the corresponding features are instantiated based on the ontology. Following the previously reported examples of "punch" and "stab" recognition, in the marked area of Fig. 3 we demonstrate the description instantiation of the moving body part "arm", the visual object "knife" and the injury related concept "wound" (as a consequence of stab). This example further demonstrates the linking between the violence and the visual ontology through common terms, from a different viewpoint.

2.3 Audio Semantics for Violence

In violent scenes one can recognize a set of audio events indicative of violence like gunshots, screams, explosions, hit sounds. Moreover indication of violence can be drawn from the background music (e.g. action scenes with multiple persons fighting are accompanied with intense music) or the emotional speech of an actor

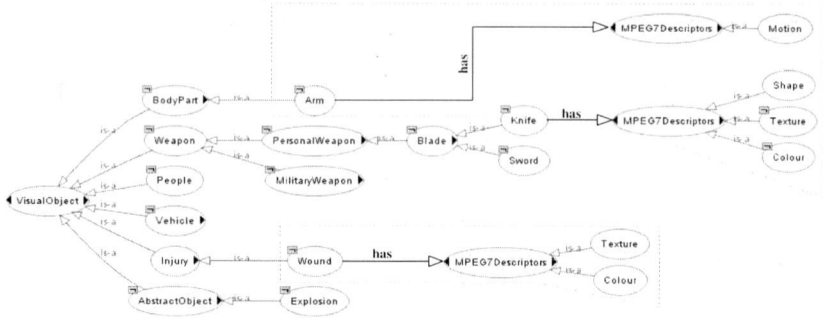

Fig. 3. Visual Ontology

(e.g. angry speech might be followed by some sort of fight). Thus, we have further implemented the aforementioned audio events (Fig. 4) in a taxonomic way, defining the audio ontology for violence. The ontology is extended with MPEG-7 audio descriptors and MPEG-7 MDS (Multimedia Description Schemes), to specify low level features and semantically describe the audio data respectively. As in the case of the visual ontology a set of classification algorithms [8] (e.g. Bayesian networks, SVMs) is responsible for instantiating audio descriptions in compliance with the ontology including the corresponding sound segments, their categorization and the values of their low level features (e.g. spectrum, timbre, energy, volume). In the marked area of Fig. 4 we demonstrate the instantiation potentials of "punch" and "scream" following the aforementioned example. We note that the high level actions (punch, scream) are also represented both in the violence domain and the audio ontology. Thus, as in the case of the visual ontology, the association between the two ontologies is evident.

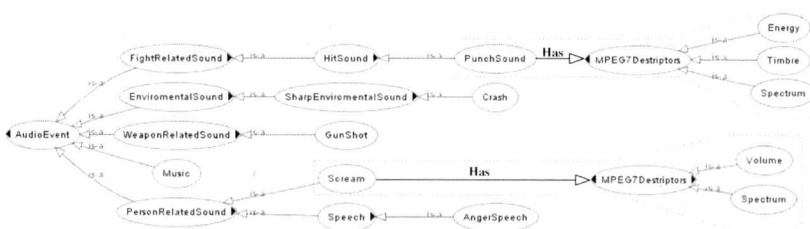

Fig. 4. Audio Ontology

2.4 Inference Engine Design

Having the adequate ontological descriptions for single modality medium level semantics and the corresponding low level extraction algorithms, we need efficient methods that taking under consideration spatio-temporal relations behavior patterns and uncertainty of extraction fuse and interchange medium level semantics from different modalities (audio and visual) to infer/reason about higher level violence behaviors (e.g. more complex, abstract and extensive violence cases). For example, the "punch" concept can be automatically extracted based on the initial analysis results and on the sequence or synchronicity of audio or visual detected events such as two person in visual data, the one moving towards the other, a hand is moving fast towards a face, while a punch sound and scream of pain is detected in the audio data.

To support reasoning mechanisms, it is required that apart from the ontological descriptions for each modality, there is a need for a cross-modality ontological description which interconnects all possible relations from each modality and constructs rules that are cross-modality specific and must tackle the following issues:

- Account for intra- and cross-modality spatial, temporal or spatio-temporal relationships.
- Represent the priorities/ordering among modalities for any multimodal concept.
- Take under consideration cross-modality synchronicity relationship (simultaneous semantic instances in different modalities).
- Handle the issue of importance of each modality for identifying a concept or semantic event.
- Capture uncertainty of extracted medium level semantics and support reasoning with partial, imprecise information.

Rule construction, either in some logic form (FOL, F-logic) or in the form of sequential if-then rules, seems an ideal solution for all sort of relationships' representation (spatio-temporal, ordering, synchronicity). Significance weights can represent the importance of each modality for identifying a concept or semantic event. Bayesian networks or fuzzy logic could handle the uncertainty imported in medium level semantics from low level analysis algorithms.

3 Experimental data setup

We have collected a corpus of 10 movies in MPEG-4 format, containing a variety of violent scenes, composed of both auditory and visual clues. We are in the process of producing manual annotations to form the essential ground truth, as MPEG-7 description instances, based on the violence terms and concepts existent in all defined ontologies. This ground truth data will be used by all processes involved, semantic audio analysis and violent events identification, semantic visual analysis and violent events identification, as well as late fusion methodology and inferencing for complex violent events identification, in order to assess their performance and identification accuracy.

4 Conclusions and Future Work

We have proposed an ontological and knowledge representation approach to define the underlying semantics for violence characterization in video data. This is the first step before providing the inferencing mechanisms in order to automatically identify violent scenes and their context in video data. Thus, this work has to further tackle the question: *how to fuse and interchange semantics from different modalities?*. We are in the process of exploring the usage of basic probabilistic inference methods (Bayesian/belief networks, HMMs), probabilistic reasoning (probabilistic logic, PR-OWL) and rule construction. Furthermore we intend to subsequently apply a similar approach by defining the corresponding ontologies to identify and filter out pornographic content.

References

1. Chandrasekaran B, Josephson J R, Benjamins R V: What Are Ontologies, and Why Do We Need Them? IEEE Intelligent Systems, 14, 1 (1999), 20-26.
2. Manjunath B S, Salembier P, Sikora T: Introduction to MPEG-7: Multimedia Content Description Interface. John Wiley and Sons / England (2002).
3. Datta A, Mubarak S, Lobo N: Person-on-Person Violence Detection in Video Data. Proc. of ICPR2002, Quebec City, Canada, Aug. (2002), 433-438.
4. Smith M K, Welty C, McGuinness D L: OWL Web Ontology Language Guide. W3C Recommendation 10 February 2004, www.w3.org/TR/owl-guide/.
5. Hunter J: Enhancing the Semantic Interoperability of Multimedia through a Core Ontology. IEEE Transactions on Circuits and Systems for Video Technology. Special Issue on Conceptual and Dynamical Aspects of Multimedia Content Description, 13, 1 (2003), 49-58.
6. Nam J, Tewfik A H: Event-driven video abstraction and visualisation. Multimedia Tools and Applications, 16(1-2), 55-77, 2002.
7. Vasconcelos N, Lippman A: Towards semantically meaningful feature spaces for the characterization of video content. Proc. of ICIP1997, Washington, DC, USA, Oct 1997, vol.1, 25-28.
8. Giannakopoulos T, Kosmopoulos D, Aristidou A, Theodoridis S: Violence Content Classification Using Audio Features. Proc. of 4th Hellenic Conference on Artificial Intelligence (SETN'06), Heraklion, Crete, Greece, May 18-20, 2006.
9. Pratikakis I, Tsekeridou S: Use Case : Semantic Media Analysis for Intelligent Retrieval. W3C Multimedia Semantics Incubator Group, www.w3.org/2005/Incubator/mmsem/wiki/Semantic_Media_Retrieval_Use_case.
10. Makris A, Kosmopoulos D, Perantonis S, Theodoridis S: Hierarchical feature fusion for visual tracking. Accepted to be published in Proceedings of IEEE International Conference on Image Processing 2007 (ICIP2007).

3D Tracking of Multiple People Using Their 2D Face Locations

Nikos Katsarakis , Aristodemos Pnevmatikakis and Michael Nechyba
Athens Information Technology, Autonomic and Grid Computing Group
0.8km Markopoulou Ave., PO Box 68, 19002 Peania, Greece
{nkat, apne}@ait.edu.gr
http://www.ait.edu.gr/research/RG1/overview.asp
Pittsburgh Pattern Recognition, 40 24th Street, Suite 240, Pittsburgh,
PA 15222, USA
michael@pittpatt.com
http://www. pittpatt.com

Abstract. In this paper, we address tracking of multiple people in complex 3D scenes, using multiple calibrated and synchronized far-field recordings. Our approach utilizes the faces detected in every camera view. Faces of the same person seen from the different cameras are associated by first finding all possible associations and then choosing the best option by means of a 3D stochastic tracker. The performance of the proposed system is evaluated by using the outputs of two grossly different 2D face detectors as input to our 3D algorithm. The multi-camera videos employed come from the CLEAR evaluation campaign. Even though the two 2D face detectors have very different performance, the 3D tracking performance of our system remains practically unchanged.

1   Introduction

Tracking and recognizing people is very important for applications such as surveillance, security and human-machine interfaces. In the visual modality, faces are the most commonly used cue for recognition. Finding the faces also helps resolve human bodies that are merged into one by the tracker. Hence face localization is of paramount importance in many applications.

Tracking in smart rooms can be very complicated due to the complex background and the crowded foreground. In smart room scenarios the cameras are placed a bit above body height, aiming to have their optical axes almost perpendicular to the faces and they are not panoramic, in order to have reasonable face sizes. This results to viewing conditions where a small group of four people can fill up a significant part of the frame. In such cases the targets no longer contain a

Please use the following format when citing this chapter:

Katsarakis, N., Pnevmatikakis, A., Nechyba, M., 2007, in IFIP International Federation for Information Processing, Volume 247, Artificial Intelligence and Innovations 2007: From Theory to Applications, eds. Boukis, C., Pnevmatikakis, L., Polymenakos, L., (Boston: Springer), pp. 365-373.

single person. As the bodies in the image plane touch each other, a formed target contains them all.

Resolving the problem using motion or color information is not generic enough; the bodies can have similar velocity vectors, and they can be dressed in similar colors, especially in military applications. What can help to resolve the problem is the existence of multiple cameras; information from all of them can be used to build a 3D understanding of the smart room, enabling 3D person tracking.

In this paper we address person tracking in 3D by utilizing the 2D face locations on multiple calibrated [1] and synchronized cameras. Effectively, we track the centroid of the head of every person in multi-view and multi-person recordings. Possible associations of the different views of a face are constructed by projecting a grid of 3D points onto the different image planes and collecting face evidence. A stochastic tracker then selects the best association.

The recordings of the CLEAR Evaluation (Classification of Events, Activities and Relationships) [2,3] are utilized to test the proposed system. These recordings comprise five cameras each (four at the room corners and one panoramic at the ceiling). They depict multiple people in cluttered backgrounds, recorded in five different sites. The situation recorded is of the business meeting with presentation type. Breaks where people move around the room a lot are also recorded. These recordings are quite challenging for tracking.

The paper is organized as follows: In section 2 the 2D face trackers employed are outlined. In section 3 the 3D tracking system is detailed. In section 4 the results are discussed, to be followed by the conclusions in Section 5.

2   Face tracking in 2D

Two different 2D face tracking algorithms are utilized to produce the location of the faces in every camera view. The one is from Athens Information Technology (AIT) and the other from Pittsburgh Pattern Recognition (PittPatt). Both algorithms participated in the 2D face tracking task of the CLEAR 2007 evaluation campaign, giving quite different results. They are summarized in the next two subsections. Their performance is also presented in a third subsection

2.1   AIT face tracker

The AIT face tracker is detailed in [4]. In summary, it operates as follows: The 2D face localization is constrained in the body areas provided by a body tracker. Three face detectors for frontal and left/right profile faces provide candidate face regions in the body areas. The face candidates are validated using the probability scores from a Gaussian Mixture Model. The surviving candidates are checked for possible merging, as both the profile detectors and the frontal one can detect different portions of the same face if the view is half-profile. The resulting face candidates are associated with faces existing in the previous frame and also with tracks that currently have no supporting evidence and are pending to either get an association, or be eliminated. Any faces of the previous frame that do not get associated with candidate faces at the current frame have a CAM-Shift tracker [5] initiated to attempt to track similarly colored regions in the current frame. If CAM-Shift also fails to track, then these past faces have their track in pending status for a predefined number of frames. Finally, all active face tracks are checked for duplicates, i.e. high spatial similarity. Typical results of the face tracker are shown in Fig. 1.

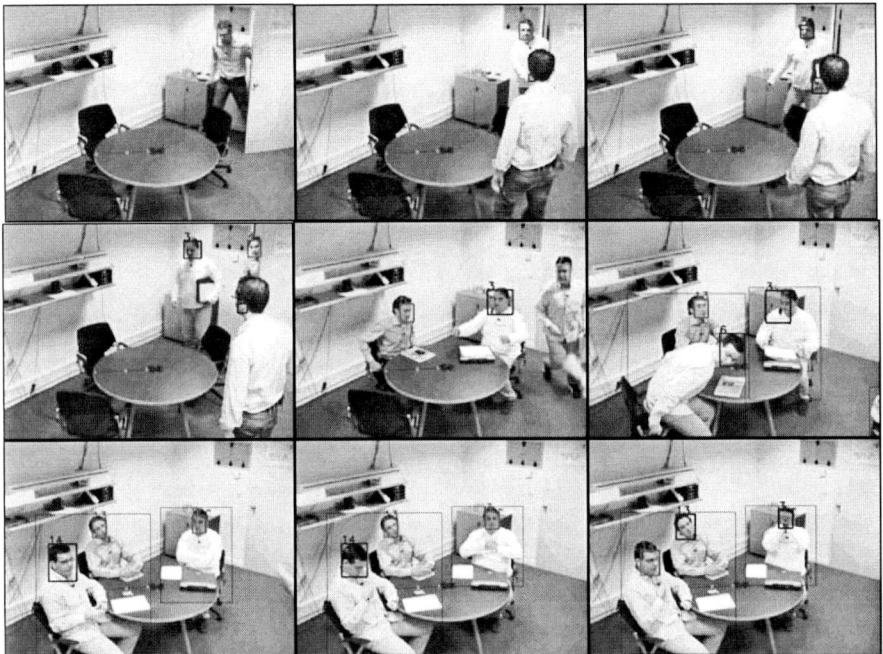

Fig. 1. Typical performance of the AIT face tracker. Detections of the three cascades of simple classifiers are marked in red, while faces being tracked by the CAM-Shift tracker are marked in blue. Notice that the latter are occluded or tilted faces

2.2   PittPatt face tracker

The PiiPatt face tracker is detailed in [6]. In summary, it proceeds in three stages: (1) frame-based face detection; (2) motion-based tracking; and (3) track filtering. At the heart of this system lies PittPatt's robust face detector, available for single-image testing through a web demo [7]. Conceptually, this version of the detection algorithm builds on the approach developed by Schneiderman [8]; however, a number of changes have been implemented recently that dramatically boost speed performance over previous versions. These changes include code-level as well as algorithmic optimizations, and have led to better than real-time processing of video on contemporary PC platforms. In motion-based tracking, single-frame observations are combined into face tracks -- each of which is ultimately associated with a unique subject ID -- by exploiting the spatiotemporal continuity of video through a second-order motion model. Finally, in track filtering, results are finalized by merging IDs for partial face tracks that meet certain spatial consistency criteria, and by eliminating face tracks likely to be false alarms. False alarm tracks are most often characterized by low classifier confidence throughout and/or exhibit very little movement throughout the lifetime of the track. It is these tracks that are eliminated in this last stage of processing.

2.3   Performance of the 2D face trackers

The quantitative evaluation of the both face trackers follows the CLEAR 2007 evaluation protocol [2,3]. According to it, the tracking system outputs (hypotheses) are mapped to annotated ground truths based on centroid distance and using the Hungarian algorithm [9]. The ground truths contain both the face bounding boxes and the number of fiducial points visible in the face. There such fiducial points are marked: the left and right eyes and the nose bridge. A marked face is considered of interest if at least two of the fiducial points are visible; faces with just one fiducial point are considered 'do not care' regions. The metrics for face tracking are five [2]. The Multiple Object Tracking Precision (MOTP) is the position error for all correctly tracked persons over all frames. It is a measure of how well the system performs when it actually finds the face. There are three kinds of errors for the tracker, false positives, misses and track identity mismatches. They are reported independently and also jointly in an accuracy metric, the Multiple Object Tracking Accuracy (MOTA). The MOTA is the residual of the sum of these three error rates from unity. There are 20 recordings, 4 from each recording site, employed in the evaluation. Each of them is 5 minutes long and comprises 4 corner cameras that are used for face tracking, and a fifth that is only optionally used in 3D tracking. The quantitative performance of the two systems is summarized in Tables 1 and 2.

Table 1. Per site and overall performance of the AIT face tracking system in the CLEAR 2007 multi-site and multi-camera recordings

Site	MOTP	MOTA	False positives	Misses	ID switches
AIT	0.67	46.52	13.1	33.99	6.39
IBM	0.66	16.46	42.66	34.93	5.96
ITC-IRST	0.68	-1.80	59.97	38.69	3.14
UKA	0.60	26.64	39.59	30.07	3.69
UPC	0.64	25.15	30.66	36.68	7.51
Overall	0.64	23.46	36.25	34.67	5.61

The two systems have a large difference in MOTA performance, mainly due to their difference in misses and false alarms. The difference in misses and part of the difference in false alarms is due to the superior performance of the Schneiderman face detector [8] employed in the PittPatt system, over the AdaBoost face detector [10] employed in the AIT system. A significant part though of the false positives is due to the color-based tracking using CAM-Shift [5] employed in the AIT system. This tracking allows the survival of targets that once have been faces, but then they have out-of-plane rotated, offering to the camera just some skin patch in the back of the neck/head or the cheeks. For examples, see the tracked skin patches in the third, fourth and ninth frames of Fig. 1.

Table 2. Per site and overall performance of the PittPatt face tracking system in the CLEAR 2007 multi-site and multi-camera recordings

Site	MOTP	MOTA	False positives	Misses	ID switches
AIT	0.68	77.39	11.21	10.06	1.34
IBM	0.70	58.04	5.19	36.20	0.57
ITC-IRST	0.65	65.92	12.16	21.14	0.78
UKA	0.70	65.38	18.49	15.23	0.91
UPC	0.67	77.94	7.20	13.38	1.48
Overall	0.68	68.81	10.31	19.85	1.03

While such patches contribute to false positives to the face tracking tasks, they are quite useful to the 3D head tracking task for which the 2D face tracks are to be used in the next section. In order to demonstrate this difference in the two face tracking systems, they are both evaluated including the faces with just one fiducial point marked on them. The overall results for both systems are shown in Table 3. Obviously the performance of the AIT system degrades more gracefully as these faces are included.

Table 3. Overall performance of both face tracking system in the CLEAR 2007 multi-site and multi-camera recordings when face patches with just one fiducial point are included in the evaluation

Site	MOTP	MOTA	False positives	Misses	ID switches
AIT	0.63	27.49	24.76	41.95	5.80
PittPatt	0.67	62.83	6.97	29.04	1.16

3   Head tracking in 3D

Our approach for 3D tracking utilizes the 2D face localization system presented in the previous section, applied on multiple calibrated [1] and synchronized cameras. To solve the problem of associating the views of the face of the same person from the different cameras, a 3D space to 2D image planes approach is utilized. The space is spanned by a 3D grid. Each point of the grid is projected onto the different image planes. Faces whose centers are close to the projected points are associated to the particular 3D point. 3D points that have more than one face associated to them are used to form possible associations of views of the face of the same person from the different cameras. If in each camera view c there are n_c faces then the k-th association (of the total K ones) that span the 3D space is of the form $a^{(k)} = \left\{ i_1^{(k)}, \ldots, i_C^{(k)} \right\}$, where C is the number of available cameras and $i_c^{(k)} \in \left\{ 0, 1, \ldots n_c \right\}$. A value $i_c^{(k)} = 0$ corresponds to no face from the c-th camera in the k-th association, while any other value corresponds to the membership of a face from those in the c-th camera in the k-th association. Obviously $\forall c \in \{1,...,C\}$, $i_c^{(k_1)} > 0$ and $k_1 \neq k_2$, it is $i_c^{(k_1)} \neq i_c^{(k_2)}$, i.e. the same face in a camera view cannot be a member of different valid associations This condition renders some of the associations mutually exclusive. After eliminating duplicate associations, the remaining ones are grouped into possible sets of mutually exclusive associations and sorted according to a weight that depends on the distance of each association from the face center and on the number of other associations that contradict it.

All the M mutually exclusive sets of possible associations $a^{(k)}$ are validated using a Kalman filter in the 3D space. For each new frame, all possible solutions are compared to the state established on the previous frame, penalizing solutions which fail to detect previously existing targets, or in which there are detections of new targets in the scene. While this strategy reduces the misses and false positives, it does not prevent new targets from appearing, as in the case of new people entering the room, all solution pairs will include that new target and thus will be equally penalized.

The recordings employed also offer a fifth camera, a panoramic one. Although this camera can not be used for face tracking, it is quite useful for 3D head tracking. The AIT body tracker [11] is employed to obtain body bounding boxes from the panoramic camera. Any head being tracked by the 3D system should be included in this bounding box. If it is not, then the 3D head track is actually the product of miss-association of actual 2D face tracks, or correct association of false positives 2D tracks. Therefore the panoramic camera is used to verify the associations and thus improve the accuracy of the 3D system.

4   Performance evaluation

3D person tracking is defined in the CLEAR evaluations as [2] tracking of the projection of the head centroid on the floor. Qualitatively, the performance of the 3D tracking system is shown in Fig. 2. For the quantitative performance analysis, the same metrics used in 2D face tracking are utilized here as well. The results are sown in Tables 4 to 7, where the 3D tracker operates on the 2D face tracking results of the AIT system without (Table 4) or with (Table 5) the use of the panoramic camera validation and on the 2D face tracking results of the PittPatt system without (Table 6) or with (Table 7) the use of the panoramic camera validation.

Table 4. Per site and overall performance of the proposed 3D tracking system operating on the 2D faces provided by the AIT face tracker, without the use of the panoramic camera validation

Site	MOTP (mm)	MOTA (%)	False positives	Misses	ID switches
AIT	84.10	59.91	3.06	34.90	2.12
IBM	94.40	61.19	6.81	30.72	1.28
ITC-IRST	102.1	59.22	7.15	31.53	2.10
UKA	96.50	46.97	5.15	45.77	2.11
UPC	91.20	65.19	7.16	25.61	2.04
Overall	94.08	58.37	6.06	33.66	1.90

Table 5. Per site and overall performance of the proposed 3D tracking system operating on the 2D faces provided by the AIT face tracker, with the use of the panoramic camera validation

Site	MOTP (mm)	MOTA (%)	False positives	Misses	ID switches
AIT	83.70	59.23	2.42	36.18	2.16
IBM	93.40	62.06	5.27	31.39	1.28
ITC-IRST	86.10	62.82	2.56	32.79	1.83
UKA	96.20	47.90	2.62	47.36	2.12
UPC	89.40	67.74	4.03	26.22	2.02
Overall	90.52	59.91	3.52	34.71	1.86

Table 6. Per site and overall performance of the proposed 3D tracking system operating on the 2D faces provided by the PittPatt face tracker, without the use of the panoramic camera validation

Site	MOTP (mm)	MOTA (%)	False positives	Misses	ID switches
AIT	79.10	66.99	2.59	28.43	2.00
IBM	92.60	36.12	3.45	58.47	1.97
ITC-IRST	85.40	62.98	2.85	32.18	1.99
UKA	100.2	47.31	4.40	46.25	2.05
UPC	76.00	77.81	2.02	18.67	1.50
Overall	87.39	57.21	3.11	37.80	1.89

Table 7. Per site and overall performance of the proposed 3D tracking system operating on the 2D faces provided by the PittPatt face tracker, with the use of the panoramic camera validation

Site	MOTP (mm)	MOTA (%)	False positives	Misses	ID switches
AIT	77.50	66.21	1.84	29.95	2.00
IBM	92.30	37.50	1.50	59.02	1.97
ITC-IRST	83.70	60.51	1.34	36.36	1.78
UKA	97.30	46.45	2.29	49.25	2.01
UPC	75.40	78.29	0.94	19.26	1.50
Overall	86.01	56.91	1.57	39.68	1.84

It is evident from the results that the averaged performance of the 3D tracker is similar, no matter which 2D face tracks are used, with the use of the AIT 2D tracker together with the panoramic camera validation scheme yielding somewhat better MOTA. Since the AIT and PittPatt 2D face trackers yield grossly different results, this seems a counterintuitive result. The reason for this is the way the two 2D face trackers function: The AIT system allows for skin-colored head patches to be tracked, while the PittPatt system does not. As a result, the AIT 2D face tracker has reduced performance for faces, but enhanced for heads, yielding more frequent head detections from more than one camera to be synthesized into 3D tracks by the 3D system. The stricter face tracks of the PittPatt 2D system result to less frequent head detections from more than one camera, hence to more difficult 3D associations. Examining the results per recording site, two of them have similar performance no matter the 2D tracker employed, two are somewhat better with the PittPatt 2D tracker, and another one is far better with the AIT 2D tracker. Not surprisingly, in the

IBM recordings in which the use of the PittPatt 2D tracker does not give good 3D tracking results, the PittPatt 2D tracker has increased misses, possibly due to the very small face sizes. In terms of precision, the use of the PittPatt 2D face tracker improves (reduces) MOTP.

Fig. 2. Operation of the individual 2D face trackers on the four corner cameras and association of the 2D evidence into 3D tracks. The detected faces are marked by bounding boxes. The IDs of the tracks are of the form AIT_XXX shown at the projection of the tracked head centroids on the floor. The tracks are also projected to a panoramic camera (not used by the system) for better visualization

A second observation has to do with the effectiveness of the panoramic camera validation. When the AIT 2D face tracks are utilized by the 3D tracker, this validation scheme yields some improvement of the overall MOTA. In particular, for the recordings suffering from high false positive rates, the validation scheme considerably reduces the false positives, at the expense of some increase of the misses. Overall, the MOTA is increased. On the other hand, regarding the utilization of the PittPatt 2D face tracks, the false positives are lower, leading to no room for drastic improvement with the application of the validation scheme. Since the misses are again increased, the overall MOTA decreases.

5   Conclusions

In this paper we have proposed a 3D head tracker for cluttered scenes and have evaluated its performance according to the CLEAR evaluation protocol. The tracker utilizes 2D face tracks obtained from synchronized and calibrated cameras. Two such 2D face tracking systems have been employed in the evaluation, demonstrating the robustness of the proposed 3D tracker. The 2D systems from AIT and PittPatt employed in the evaluation have grossly different face tracking performance, but their output combined in 3D head tracks by our system results to similar 3D performance.

Acknowledgements: This work is sponsored by the European Union under the integrated project CHIL, contract number 506909. The authors wish to thank the people involved in data collection, annotation and overall organization of the CLEAR 2007 evaluations for providing such a rich test-bed for the presented algorithms.

References

1.   Z. Zhang: A Flexible New Technique for Camera Calibration, Technical Report MSR-TR-98-71, Microsoft Research, (Aug. 2002).
2.   R. Stiefelhagen, K. Bernardin, R. Bowers, J. Garofolo, D. Mostefa and P. Soundararajan: The CLEAR 2006 Evaluation, in R. Stiefelhagen and J. Garofolo (eds.) *CLEAR 2006, Lecture Notes in Computer Science*, 4122 (2007), 1-44.
3.   www.clear-evaluation.org
4.   Stergiou, G. Karame, A. Pnevmatikakis and L. Polymenakos: The AIT 2D face detection and tracking system for CLEAR 2007, in R. Stiefelhagen, R. Bowers and J. Garofolo (eds.) *CLEAR 2007, Lecture Notes in Computer Science*, accepted.
5.   G. Bradski: Computer Vision Face Tracking for Use in a Perceptual User Interface, *Intel Technology Journal*, 2, (1998).
6.   M. Nechyba, L. Brandy and H. Schneiderman: PittPatt Face Detection and Tracking for the CLEAR 2007 Evaluation, in R. Stiefelhagen, R. Bowers and J. Garofolo (eds.) *CLEAR 2007, Lecture Notes in Computer Science*, accepted.
7.   http://demo.pittpaftt.com
8.   H. Schneiderman: Feature-Centric Evaluation for Efficient Cascaded Object Detection, in *Proceedings of IEEE Conference on Computer Vision and Pattern Recognition*, (June 2004).
9.   S. Blackman: Multiple-Target Tracking with Radar Applications, Artech House, Dedham, MA (1986), chapter 14.
10. G. Bradski, A. Kaehler and V. Pisarevsky: Learning-Based Computer Vision with Intel's Open Source Computer Vision Library, *Intel Technology Journal*, 9, (2005).
11. Pnevmatikakis and L. Polymenakos: Robust Estimation of Background for Fixed Cameras, in *International Conference on Computing (CIC2006)*, (2006).

Multimodal emotion recognition from expressive faces, body gestures and speech

George Caridakis , Ginevra Castellano , Loic Kessous , Amaryllis
Raouzaiou , Lori Malatesta , Stelios Asteriadis and Kostas Karpouzis
Image, Video and Multimedia Systems Laboratory,
National Technical University of Athens
9, Heroon Politechniou str., 15780, Athens, Greece
{gcari, araouz, lori, stiast, kkarpou}@image.ece.ntua.gr
InfoMus Lab, DIST - University of Genova
Viale Causa 13, I-16145, Genova, Italy
Ginevra.Castellano@unige.it
Department of Speech, Language and Hearing,
University of Tel Aviv
Sheba Center, 52621, Tel Aviv, Israel
kessous@post.tau.ac.il

Abstract. In this paper we present a multimodal approach for the recognition
of eight emotions that integrates information from facial expressions, body
movement and gestures and speech. We trained and tested a model with a
Bayesian classifier, using a multimodal corpus with eight emotions and ten
subjects. First individual classifiers were trained for each modality. Then data
were fused at the feature level and the decision level. Fusing multimodal data
increased very much the recognition rates in comparison with the unimodal
systems: the multimodal approach gave an improvement of more than 10%
with respect to the most successful unimodal system. Further, the fusion
performed at the feature level showed better results than the one performed at
the decision level.

Keywords: Affective body language, Affective speech, Emotion recognition,
Multimodal fusion

1 Introduction

In the last years, research in the human-computer interaction area increasingly
addressed the communication aspect related to the "implicit channel", that is the

Please use the following format when citing this chapter:

Caridakis, G., Castellano, G., Kessous, L., Raouzaiou, A., Malatesta, L., Asteriadis, S., Karpouzis, K., 2007, in IFIP
International Federation for Information Processing, Volume 247, Artificial Intelligence and Innovations 2007: From
Theory to Applications, eds. Boukis, C., Pnevmatikakis, L., Polymenakos, L., (Boston: Springer), pp. 375-388.

channel through which the emotional domain interacts with the verbal aspect of the communication [1]. One of the challenging issues is to endow a machine with an emotional intelligence. Emotionally intelligent systems must be able to create an affective interaction with users: they must be endowed with the ability to perceive, interpret, express and regulate emotions [2]. Recognising users' emotional state is then one of the main requirements for computers to successfully interact with humans. Most of the works in the affective computing field do not combine different modalities into a single system for the analysis of human emotional behaviour: different channels of information (mainly facial expressions and speech) are considered independently to each other. Further, there are only a few attempts to integrate information from body movement and gestures. Nevertheless, Sebe et al. [3] and Pantic et al. [4] highlight that an ideal system for automatic analysis and recognition of human affective information should be multimodal, as the human sensory system is. Moreover, studies from the psychology show the need to consider the integration of different non-verbal behaviour modalities in the human-human communication [5].

In this paper we present a multimodal approach for the recognition of eight acted emotional states (anger, despair, interest, pleasure, sadness, irritation, joy and pride) that integrates information from facial expressions, body movement and gestures and speech. In our work we trained and tested a model with a Bayesian classifier, using a multimodal corpus with ten subjects collected during the Third Summer School of the HUMAINE EU-IST project, held in Genova in September 2006. In the following sections we describe the systems based on the analysis of the single modalities and compare different strategies to perform the data fusion for the multimodal emotion recognition.

2   Related work

Emotion recognition has been investigated with three main types of databases: acted emotions, natural spontaneous emotions and elicited emotions. The best results are generally obtained with acted emotion databases because they contain strong emotional expressions. Literature on speech (see for example Banse and Scherer [6]) shows that most part of the studies were conducted with emotional acted speech. Feature sets for acted and spontaneous speech have recently been compared by [7]. Generally, few acted-emotion speech databases included speakers with several different native languages. In the last years, some attempts to collect multimodal data were done: some examples of multimodal databases can be found in [8] [9] [10].

In the area of unimodal emotion recognition, there have been many studies using different, but single, modalities. Facial expressions [11] [12], vocal features [13] [14], body movements and postures [15] [16], physiological signals [17] have been used as inputs during these attempts, while multimodal emotion recognition is currently gaining ground [18] [19] [20]. Nevertheless, most of the works consider the integration of information from facial expressions and speech and there are only a few attempts to combine information from body movement and gestures in a multimodal framework. Gunes and Piccardi [21] for example fused at different levels facial expressions and body gestures information for bimodal emotion recognition. Further, el Kaliouby and Robinson [22] proposed a vision-based computational model to infer acted mental states from head movements and facial expressions.

A wide variety of machine learning techniques have been used in emotion recognition approaches [11] [1]. Especially in the multimodal case [4], they all employ a large number of audio, visual or physiological features, a fact which usually impedes the training process; therefore, it is necessary to find a way to reduce the number of utilized features by picking out only those related to emotion. One possibility in this direction is to use neural networks, since they enable us to pinpoint the most relevant features with respect to the output, usually by observing their weights. An interesting work in this area is the sensitivity analysis approach by Engelbrecht et al. [23]. Sebe et al. [3] highlight that probabilistic graphical models, such as Hidden Markov Models, Bayesian networks and Dynamic Bayesian networks are very well suited for fusing different sources of information in multimodal emotion recognition and can also handle noisy features and missing values of features all by probabilistic inference.

In this work we combine a wrapper feature selection approach to reduce the number of features and a Bayesian classifier both for the unimodal and the multimodal emotion recognition.

3   Collection of multimodal data

The corpus used in this study was collected during Third Summer School of the HUMAINE EU-IST project, held in Genova in September 2006. The overall recording procedure was based on the GEMEP corpus [10], a multimodal collection of portrayed emotional expressions: we recorded data on facial expressions, body movement and gestures and speech.

3.1 Subjects

Ten participants of the summer school distributed as evenly as possible concerning their gender (Figure 1) participated to the recordings. Subjects represented five different nationalities: French, German, Greek, Hebrew, Italian.

Fig. 1. The participants who took part to the recordings.

3.2 Technical set up

Two DV cameras (25 fps) recorded the actors from a frontal view. One camera recorded the actor's body and the other one was focused on the actor's face. We have chosen such a setup because the resolution required for facial features extraction is much larger than the one for body movement detection or hand gestures tracking. This could only be achieved if one camera zoomed in the actor's face. Video streams were synchronised manually after the recording process. We adopted some restrictions concerning the actor's behaviour and clothing. Long sleeves and covered neck were preferred since the majority of the hand and head detection algorithms are based on colour tracking. Further, uniform background was used to make the background subtraction process easier. As for the facial features extraction process we considered some prerequisites such as the lack of eyeglasses, beards, moustaches.

For the voice recordings we used a direct-to-disk computer-based system. The speech samples were directly recorded on the hard disk of the computer using sound editing software. We used an external sound card connected to the computer by IEEE 1394 High Speed Serial Bus (also known as FireWire or i.Link). A microphone mounted on the actors' shirt was connected to an HF emitter (wireless system emitter) and the receiver was connected to the sound card using a XLR connector (balanced audio connector for high quality microphones and connections between equipments). The external sound card included a preamplifier (for two XLR inputs) that was used in order to adjust the input gain and to minimize the impact of signal-to-noise ratio of the recording system. The sampling rate of the recording was 44.1 kHz and the quantization was 16 bit, mono.

3.3 Procedure

Participants were asked to act eight emotional states: anger, despair, interest, pleasure, sadness, irritation, joy and pride, equally distributed in the space valence-arousal (see Table 1). During the recording process one of the authors had the role of the director guiding the actors through the process. Participants were asked to perform specific gestures that exemplify each emotion. Selected gestures are shown in Table 1.

Table 1. The acted emotions and the *emotion-specific gestures.*

Emotion	Valence	Arousal	Gesture
Anger	Negative	High	Violent descend of hands
Despair	Negative	High	Leave me alone
Interest	Positive	Low	Raise hands
Pleasure	Positive	Low	Open hands
Sadness	Negative	Low	Smooth falling hands
Irritation	Negative	Low	Smooth go away
Joy	Positive	High	Circular italianate movement
Pride	Positive	High	Close hands towards chest

As in the GEMEP corpus [10], a pseudo-linguistic sentence was pronounced by the actors during acting the emotional states. The sentence "Toko, damato ma gali sa" was designed in order to fulfil different needs. First, as the different speakers have different native languages, using a specific language was not so adequate to this study. Then we wanted the sentence to include phonemes that exist in all the languages of all the speakers. Also, the words in the sentence are composed of simple diphones ('ma' and 'sa'), two ('gali' 'toko') or three diphones ('damato'). Then, the vowels included ('o' , 'a' , 'i') are vowels that are relatively distant in a vowel space, for example the vowel triangle, and have a pronunciation mostly similar in all the languages of the group of speakers. We suggested the speakers a meaning for the sentence. 'Toko' is supposed to be the name of an 'agent', i.e., a real or artificial individual, who the speakers/users are interacting with. We chose for this word two stops consonants (also known as plosives or stop-plosives) /t/ and /k/ and two identical vowels /o/. This was done in order to allow the study of certain acoustic correlates. Then 'damato ma gali sa' is supposed to mean something like 'can you open it'. The word 'it' could correspond to a folder, a file, a box, a door or whatever.

Each emotion was acted three times by each actor, so that we collected 240 posed gestures, facial expressions and speech samples.

4 Feature extraction

4.1 Face feature extraction

An overview of the proposed methodology is illustrated in Figure 2. The face is first located, so that approximate facial feature locations can be estimated from the head position and rotation. Face roll rotation is estimated and corrected and the head is segmented focusing on the following facial areas: left eye/eyebrow, right eye/eyebrow, nose and mouth. Each of those areas, called feature-candidate areas, contains the features whose boundaries need to be extracted for our purposes. Inside the corresponding feature-candidate areas precise feature extraction is performed for each facial feature, i.e. eyes, eyebrows, mouth and nose, using a multi-cue approach, generating a small number of intermediate feature masks. Feature masks generated for each facial feature are fused together to produce the final mask for that feature. The mask fusion process uses anthropometric criteria [24] to perform validation and weight assignment on each intermediate mask; all the feature's weighted masks are then fused to produce a final mask along with confidence level estimation.

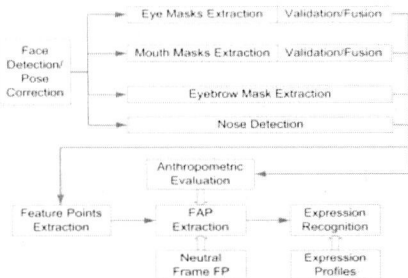

Fig. 2. High-level overview of the facial feature extraction process.

Since this procedure essentially locates and tracks points in the facial area, we chose to work with MPEG-4 FAPs (Facial Animation Parameters) and not Action

Units (AUs), since the former are explicitly defined to measure the deformation of these feature points. In addition to this, discrete points are easier to track in cases of extreme rotations and their position can be estimated based on anthropometry in cases of occlusion, whereas this is not usually the case with whole facial features. Another feature of FAPs which proved useful is their value (or magnitude), which is crucial in order to differentiate cases of varying activation of the same emotion (e.g. joy and exhilaration) [25] and exploit fuzziness in rule-based systems [12]. Measurement of FAPs requires the availability of a frame where the subject's expression is found to be neutral. This frame is called the *neutral frame* and is manually selected from video sequences to be analyzed or interactively provided to the system when initially brought into a specific user's ownership. The final feature masks are used to extract 19 Feature Points (FPs) [25]; Feature Points obtained from each frame are compared to FPs obtained from the neutral frame to estimate facial deformations and produce the FAPs. Confidence levels on FAP estimation are derived from the equivalent feature point confidence levels. The FAPs are used along with their confidence levels to provide the facial expression estimation.

In accordance with the other modalities, facial features need to be processed so as to have one vector of values per tune. FAPs originally correspond to every frame in the tune. Two approaches were reviewed. The first approach consisted of extracting the most prominent frame within a tune. During this process, a mean value is calculated for every FAP within the tune and next the frame with the highest variation is selected based on this set of values. On the other hand a way to imprint the temporal evolution of the FAP values is to calculate a set of statistical features over these values and their derivatives. The whole process was inspired by the equivalent process performed in the acoustic features. We have selected the latter since the recognition rate achieved was superior. More sophisticated techniques to extract the most prominent frame are included in our plans for future work.

4.2 Body feature extraction

Tracking of body and hands of the subjects was done using the EyesWeb platform [26]. Starting from the silhouette and the hands blobs of the actors, we extracted five main expressive motion cues, using the EyesWeb Expressive Gesture Processing Library [27]: quantity of motion and contraction index of the body, velocity, acceleration and fluidity of the hand's barycenter. The data were normalised according to the behaviour shown by each actor, considering the maximum and the minimum values of each motion cue in each actor, in order to compare data from all the subjects. Automatic extraction allows to obtain temporal series of the selected motion cues over time, depending on the video frame rate. For each profile of the motion cues we selected then a subset of features describing the dynamics of the cues over time. Based on the model proposed in [28] we extracted the following dynamic indicators of the motion cues temporal profile: initial and final slope, initial and final slope of the main peak, maximum value, ratio between the maximum value and the duration of the main peak, mean value, ratio between the mean and the maximum value, ratio between the absolute maximum and the biggest following relative maximum, centroid of energy, distance between maximum value and centroid of energy, symmetry index, shift index of the main peak, number of peaks, number of peaks preceding the main one, ratio between the main peak duration and the whole profile duration. This process was made for each motion cue of all the videos of the corpus, so that each gesture is characterised by a subset of 80 motion features.

4.3 Speech feature extraction

The set of features that we used contains features based on intensity, pitch, MFCC (Mel Frequency Cepstral Coefficient), Bark spectral bands, voiced segment characteristics and pause length. The full set contains 377 features. The features from the intensity contour and the pitch contour are extracted using a set of 32 statistical features. This set of features is applied both to the pitch and intensity contour and to their derivatives. Not any normalization has been applied before feature extraction. In particular, we didn't perform user or gender normalization for pitch contour as it is often done in order to remove difference between registers. We considered the following 32 features: maximum, mean and minimum values, sample mode (most frequently occurring value), interquartile range (difference between the 75th and 25th percentiles), kurtosis, the third central sample moment, first (slope) and second coefficients of linear regression, first, second and third coefficients of quadratic regression, percentiles at 2.5 %, 25 %, 50 %, 75 %, and 97.5 %, skewness, standard deviation, variance. Thus, we have 64 features based on the pitch contour and 64 features based on the intensity contour. This feature set was used originally for inspecting a contour such as a pitch contour or a loudness contour, but these features are also meaningful for inspecting evolution over time or spectral axis. Indeed, we also extracted similar features on the Bark spectral bands as done in [29]. We also extracted 13 MFCCs using time averaging on time windows. Features derived from pitch values and lengths of voiced segments were also extracted using a set of 35 features applied to both of them. We also extracted features based on pause (or silence) length and non-pauses lengths (35 each).

5   Uni-modal and multimodal emotion recognition

In order to compare the results of the unimodal and the multimodal systems, we used a common approach based on a Bayesian classifier (BayesNet) provided by the software Weka, a free toolbox containing a collection of machine learning algorithms for data mining tasks [30]. In Figure 3 we show an overview of the framework we propose:

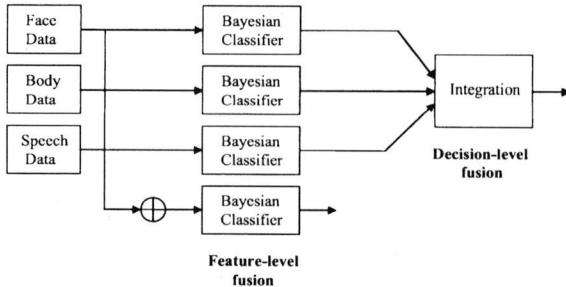

Fig.3. Overview of the framework.

As shown in the left part of the diagram, a separate Bayesian classifier was used for each modality (face, gestures, speech). All sets of data were normalized. Features discretisation based on Kononenko's MDL (minimum description length) criterion [31] was done to reduce the learning complexity. A wrapper approach to feature subset selection (which allows to evaluate the attribute sets by using a learning scheme) was used in order to reduce the number of inputs to the classifiers and find the features that maximize the performance of the classifier. A best-first search method in forward direction was used. Further, in all the systems, the corpus was trained and tested using the cross-validation method.

We evaluated two different models: (1) a model obtained training and testing all the 240 data samples, even when data from some modalities is missing in some samples; (2) a model obtained using only the data available for the three modalities. As shown in the results in the next section, the first model allows to manage also data with missing samples, but it is less precise; the second one is less flexible, but is more precise in the classification.

To fuse facial expressions, gestures and speech information, two different approaches were implemented (right of Figure 3): feature-level fusion, where a single classifier with features of the three modalities is used; and decision-level fusion, where a separate classifier is used for each modality and the outputs are combined a posteriori. In the second approach the output was computed combining the posterior probabilities of the unimodal systems. We made experiments using two different approaches for the decision-level fusion. The first approach consisted of selecting the emotion that received the best probability in the three modalities. The second approach consisted of selecting the emotion that corresponds to the majority of 'voting' from the three modalities; if a majority was not possible to define (for example when each unimodal system gives in output a different emotion), the emotion that received the best probability in the three modalities was selected.

6 Results

6.1 Emotion recognition from facial expressions

Table 2 shows the confusion matrix of the emotion recognition system based on facial expressions when all the samples are used (first model). The overall performance of this classifier was 48.3 % (it increases up to 59.6 % when only the samples available for all the modalities are used). The most recognised emotions were anger (56.67 %), irritation, joy and pleasure (53.33 %). Pride is misclassified with pleasure (20%), while sadness is misclassified with irritation (20 %), an emotion in the same valence-arousal quadrant.

George Caridakis , Ginevra Castellano, Loic Kessous, Amaryllis Raouzaiou, Lori Malatesta, Stelios Asteriadis and Kostas Karpouzis

Table 2: Confusion matrix of the emotion recognition system based on facial expressions.

a	b	c	d	e	f	g	h		
56.67	3.33	3.33	10	6.67	10	6.67	3.33	a	Anger
10	40	13.33	10	0	13.33	3.33	10	b	Despair
6.67	3.33	50	6.67	6.67	10	16.67	0	c	Interest
10	6.67	10	53.33	3.33	6.67	3.33	6.67	d	Irritation
3.33	0	13.33	16.67	53.33	10	0	3.33	e	Joy
6.67	13.33	6.67	0	6.67	53.33	13.33	0	f	Pleasure
6.67	3.33	16.67	6.67	13.33	20	33.33	0	g	Pride
3.33	6.67	3.33	20	0	13.33	6.67	46.67	h	Sadness

6.2 Emotion recognition from gestures

Table 3 shows the performance of the emotion recognition system based on gestures when all the samples are used (first model). The overall performance of this classifier was 67.1 % (it increases up to 83.2 % when only the samples available for all the modalities are used). Anger and pride are recognised with very high accuracy (80 and 96.67 % respectively). Sadness was partly misclassified with pride (36.67 %), as well as the majority of the emotions, except for anger.

Table 3: Confusion matrix of the emotion recognition system based on gestures.

a	b	c	d	e	f	g	h		
80	10	0	3.33	0	0	6.67	0	a	Anger
3.33	56.67	6.67	0	0	0	26.67	6.67	b	Despair
3.33	0	56.67	0	6.67	6.67	26.67	0	c	Interest
0	10	0	63.33	0	0	26.67	0	d	Irritation
0	10	0	6.67	60	0	23.33	0	e	Joy
0	6.67	3.33	0	0	66.67	23.33	0	f	Pleasure
0	0	0	3.33	0	0	96.67	0	g	Pride
0	3.33	0	3.33	0	0	36.67	56.67	h	Sadness

6.3 Emotion recognition from speech

Table 4 displays the confusion matrix of the emotion recognition system based on speech when all the samples are used (first model). The overall performance of this classifier was 57.1 (it increases up to 70.8 % when only the samples available for all the modalities are used). Anger and sadness are classified with high accuracy (93.33 and 76.67% respectively). Despair obtained a very low recognition rate and was mainly confused with pleasure (23.33%).

Table 4: Confusion matrix of the emotion recognition system based on speech.

a	b	c	d	e	f	g	h		
93.33	0	3.33	3.33	0	0	0	0	a	Anger
10	23.33	16.67	6.67	3.33	23.33	3.33	13.33	b	Despair
6.67	0	60	10	0	16.67	3.33	3.33	c	Interest
13.33	3.33	10	50	3.33	3.33	13.33	3.33	d	Irritation
20	0	10	13.33	43.33	10	3.33	0	e	Joy
3.33	6.67	6.67	6.67	0	53.33	6.67	16.67	f	Pleasure
3.33	10	3.33	13.33	0	13.33	56.67	0	g	Pride
0	6.67	3.33	10	0	3.33	0	76.67	h	Sadness

6.4 Feature-level fusion

Table 5 displays the confusion matrix of the multimodal emotion recognition system when all the samples are used (first model). The overall performance of this classifier was 78.3 % (it increases up to 89.4 % when only the samples available for all the modalities are used), which is much higher than the performance obtained by the most successful unimodal system, the one based on gestures. The diagonal components reveal that all the emotions, apart from despair, can be recognised with more than the 70 % of accuracy. Anger was the emotion recognised with highest accuracy, as in all the unimodal systems.

Table 5: Confusion matrix of the multimodal emotion recognition system.

a	b	c	d	e	f	g	h		
90	0	0	0	10	0	0	0	a	Anger
0	53.33	3.33	16.67	6.67	0	10	10	b	Despair
6.67	0	73.33	13.33	0	3.33	3.33	0	c	Interest
0	6.67	0	76.67	6.67	3.33	0	6.67	d	Irritation
0	0	0	0	93.33	0	6.67	0	e	Joy
0	3.33	3.33	13.33	3.33	70	6.67	0	f	Pleasure
3.33	3.33	0	3.33	0	0	86.67	3.33	g	Pride
0	0	0	16.67	0	0	0	83.33	h	Sadness

6.5 Decision level fusion

The approach based on decision-level fusion obtained lower recognition rates than that based on feature-level fusion. The performance of the classifier was 74.6 %, both using the best probability and the majority voting plus best probability approach.

The performance of the classifier increases up to 85.1 % for the first approach and 88.20 % for the second approach when only the samples available for all the modalities are used.

7 Discussion and conclusions

We presented a multimodal framework for analysis and recognition of emotion starting from expressive faces, gestures and speech. We trained and tested a model with a Bayesian classifier, using a multimodal corpus with eight acted emotions and ten subjects of five different nationalities.

We experimented our approach on a dataset of 240 samples for each modality (face, body, speech), considering also instances with missing values. We also evaluated a model built disregarding instances with missing values. The first model obtained lower recognition rates for the eight emotions than the second one, both in the unimodal systems and in the multimodal system, but it allows to manage also data with missing values, condition close to a real situation. Considering the performances of the unimodal emotion recognition systems, the one based on gestures appears to be the most successful, followed by the one based on speech and the one based on facial expressions. We note that in this study we used *emotion-specific gestures*: these are gestures that are selected so as to express each specific emotion. An alterative approach which may also be of interest would be to recognise emotions from different expressivity of the same gesture (one not necessarily associated with any specific emotion) performed under different emotional conditions. This would allow good comparison with contemporary systems based on facial expressions and speech and will be considered in our future work. Fusing multimodal data increased very much the recognition rates in comparison with the unimodal systems: the multimodal approach gave an improvement of more than 10 % compared to the performance of the system based on gestures, when all the 240 samples are used. Further, the fusion performed at the feature level showed better performances than the one performed at the decision-level, highlighting that processing input data in a joint feature space is more successful.

We can conclude that using three different modalities highly increases the recognition performance of an automatic emotion recognition system. That is helpful also when some values for features of some modalities are missing. On the other hand, humans use more than one modality to recognise emotions and process signals in a complementary manner, so it is expected that an automatic system shows a similar behaviour.

Acknowledgments: The research work has been realised in the framework of the EU-IST Project HUMAINE (Human-Machine Interaction Network on Emotion), a Network of Excellence (NoE) in the EU 6th Framework Programme (2004-2007).

References

1. Cowie, R., Douglas-Cowie, E., Tsapatsoulis, N., Votsis, G., Kollias, S., Fellenz, W., Taylor, J.G.: Emotion recognition in human-computer interaction, IEEE Signal Processing Magazine, January 2001.
2. Picard, R.: Affective computing, Boston, MA: MIT Press (1997).
3. Sebe, N., Cohen, I., Huang, T.S.: Multimodal Emotion Recognition, Handbook of Pattern Recognition and Computer Vision, World Scientific, ISBN 981-256-105-6, January 2005.
4. Pantic, M., Sebe, N., Cohn, J., Huang, T.S.: Affective Multimodal Human-Computer Interaction, ACM Multimedia, pp. 669 - 676, Singapore, November 2005.
5. Scherer, K. R., Wallbott, H. G.: Analysis of Nonverbal Behavior. HANDBOOK OF DISCOURSE: ANALYSIS, Vol. 2, Cap.11, Academic Press London (1985).
6. Banse, R., Scherer, K.R.: Acoustic Profiles in Vocal Emotion Expression. Journal of Personality and Social Psychology. 614-636 (1996).
7. Vogt, T., André, E.: Comparing feature sets for acted and spontaneous speech in view of automatic emotion recognition. IEEE International Conference on Multimedia & Expo (ICME 2005).
8. Gunes H., Piccardi M.: A Bimodal Face and Body Gesture Database for Automatic Analysis of Human Nonverbal Affective Behavior, Proc. of ICPR 2006 the 18th International Conference on Pattern Recognition, 20-24 Aug. 2006, Hong Kong, China.
9. Bänziger, T., Pirker, H., Scherer, K.: Gemep - geneva multimodal emotion portrayals: a corpus for the study of multimodal emotional expressions. In L. Deviller et al. (Ed.), Proceedings of LREC'06 Workshop on Corpora for Research on Emotion and Affect (pp. 15-019). Genoa. Italy (2006).
10. Douglas-Cowie, E., Campbell, N., Cowie, R., Roach, P.: Emotional speech: towards a new generation of databases. Speech Communication, 40, 33–60 (2003).

11. Pantic, M., Rothkrantz, L.J.M.: Automatic analysis of facial expressions: The state of the art. IEEE Trans. on Pattern Analysis and Machine Intelligence, 22(12):1424–1445 (2000).
12. Ioannou, S., Raouzaiou, A., Tzouvaras, V., Mailis, T., Karpouzis, K., Kollias, S. : Emotion recognition through facial expression analysis based on a neurofuzzy network, Neural Networks, Elsevier, Vol. 18, Issue 4, May 2005, pp. 423-435.
13. Cowie, R., Douglas-Cowie, E.: Automatic statistical analysis of the signal and prosodic signs of emotion in speech. In Proc. International Conf. on Spoken Language Processing, pp. 1989–1992 (1996).
14. K.R. Scherer: Adding the affective dimension: A new look in speech analysis and synthesis, In Proc. International Conf. on Spoken Language Processing, pp. 1808–1811, (1996).
15. Camurri, A., Lagerlöf, I, Volpe, G.: Recognizing Emotion from Dance Movement: Comparison of Spectator Recognition and Automated Techniques, International Journal of Human-Computer Studies, 59(1-2), pp. 213-225, Elsevier Science, July 2003.
16. Bianchi-Berthouze, N., Kleinsmith, A. A categorical approach to affective gesture recognition, Connection Science, V. 15, N. 4, pp. 259-269. (2003).
17. Picard, R.W., Vyzas, E., Healey, J.: Toward machine emotional intelligence: Analysis of affective physiological state, IEEE Trans. on Pattern Analysis and Machine Intelligence, 23(10):1175–1191 (2001).
18. Pantic M., Rothkrantz, L.J.M.: Towards an Affect-sensitive Multimodal Human-Computer Interaction, Proceedings of the IEEE, vol. 91, no. 9, pp. 1370-1390 (2003).
19. Busso, C., Deng, Z., Yildirim, S., Bulut, M., Lee, C.M., Kazemzaeh, A., Lee, S., Neumann, U., Narayanan, S.: "Analysis of Emotion Recognition using Facial Expressions, Speech and Multimodal information," Proc. of ACM 6th int'l Conf. on Multimodal Interfaces (ICMI 2004), State College, PA, Oct. 2004. pp205-211.
20. Kim, J., André, E., Rehm, M., Vogt, T., Wagner, J.: Integrating information from speech and physiological signals to achieve emotional sensitivity. Proc. of the 9th European Conference on Speech Communication and Technology (2005).
21. Gunes H, Piccardi M.: Bi-modal emotion recognition from expressive face and body gestures. Journal of Network and Computer Applications (2006), doi:10.1016/j.jnca.2006.09.007
22. el Kaliouby, R., Robinson, P.: Generalization of a Vision-Based Computational Model of Mind-Reading. In Proceedings of First International Conference on Affective Computing and Intelligent Interfaces, pp 582-589 (2005).
23. Engelbrecht, A.P., Fletcher, L., Cloete, I.: Variance analysis of sensitivity information for pruning multilayer feedforward neural networks, Neural Networks, 1999. IJCNN '99. International Joint Conference on, Vol.3, Iss., 1999, pp:1829-1833 vol.3.
24. Young, J. W.: Head and Face Anthropometry of Adult U.S. Civilians, FAA Civil Aeromedical Institute, 1963-1993 (final report 1993)
25. Raouzaiou, A., Tsapatsoulis, N., Karpouzis, K., Kollias, S.: Parameterized facial expression synthesis based on MPEG-4, EURASIP Journal on Applied Signal Processing, Vol. 2002, No 10, 2002, pp. 1021-1038.
26. Camurri, A., Coletta, P., Massari, A., Mazzarino, B., Peri, M., Ricchetti, M., Ricci, A. and Volpe, G.:Toward real-time multimodal processing: EyesWeb 4.0, in Proc. AISB 2004 Convention: Motion, Emotion and Cognition, Leeds, UK, March 2004.
27. Camurri, A., Mazzarino, B., and Volpe, G.: Analysis of Expressive Gesture: The Eyesweb Expressive Gesture Processing Library, in A. Camurri, G.Volpe (Eds.), Gesture-based Communication in Human-Computer Interaction, LNAI 2915, Springer Verlag (2004).
28. Castellano, G., Camurri, A., Mazzarino, B., Volpe, G.: A mathematical model to analyse the dynamics of gesture expressivity, in Proc. of AISB 2007 Convention: Artificial and Ambient Intelligence, Newcastle upon Tyne, UK, April 2007.

29. Kessous, L., Amir, N.: Comparison of feature extraction approaches based on the Bark time/frequency representation for classification of expressive speechpaper submitted to Interspeech 2007.
30. Witten, I.H., Frank, E.: Data Mining: Practical machine learning tools and techniques, 2nd Edition, Morgan Kaufmann, San Francisco (2005).
31. Kononenko, I.: On Biases in Estimating Multi-Valued Attributes. In: 14th International Joint Conference on Articial Intelligence, 1034-1040 (1995).

Semantic Multimedia Analysis based on Region Types and Visual Context

Evaggelos Spyrou, Phivos Mylonas and Yannis Avrithis

Image, Video and Multimedia Laboratory,
National Technical University of Athens
Zographou Campus, PC 15773, Athens, Greece
{espyrou, fmylonas, iavr}@image.ntua.gr

Abstract. In this paper previous work on the detection of high-level concepts within multimedia documents is extended by introducing a mid-level ontology as a means of exploiting the visual context of images in terms of the regions they consist of. More specifically, we construct a mid-level ontology, define its relations and integrate it in our knowledge modelling approach. In the past we have developed algorithms to address computationally efficient handling of visual context and extraction of mid-level characteristics and now we explain how these diverse algorithms and methodologies can be combined in order to approach a greater goal, that of semantic multimedia analysis. Early experimental results are presented using data derived from the *beach* domain.

1 Introduction

Although the well-known "semantic gap" [16] has been acknowledged for a long time, multimedia analysis approaches are still divided into two rather discrete categories; low-level multimedia analysis methods and tools, on the one hand (e.g. [13]) and high-level semantic annotation methods and tools, on the other (e.g. [20], [3]). It was only recently, that state-of-the-art multimedia analysis systems have started using semantic knowledge technologies, as the latter are defined by notions like ontologies [19] and whose advantages, when using them for the creation, manipulation and post-processing of multimedia metadata, are depicted in numerous research activities.

The main idea introduced herein relies on the integrated handling of concepts evident within multimedia content. Combining both low-level descriptors computed automatically from raw multimedia content and semantics in the form of detection of semantic features in video sequences has been the ultimate task in current and previous multimedia research efforts. For instance, a region-based approach using MPEG-7 visual features and ontological knowledge is presented in [21] and a lexicon-driven approach is introduced in [4]. Among others, a region-based approach in content retrieval that uses Latent Semantic Analysis is presented in [17], whereas a mean-shift algorithm is used in [14], in order to extract low-level concepts, after the image is clustered.

Please use the following format when citing this chapter:

Spyrou, E., Mylonas, P., Avrithis, Y., 2007, in IFIP International Federation for Information Processing, Volume 247, Artificial Intelligence and Innovations 2007: From Theory to Applications, eds. Boukis, C., Pnevmatikakis, L., Polymenakos, L., (Boston: Springer), pp. 389-398.

In this work, our effort focuses on an integrated approach, offering unified and unsupervised manipulation of multimedia content. It acts complementary to the current state-of-the-art as it tackles both aforementioned challenges. Focusing on semantic analysis of multimedia, it contributes towards bridging the gap between the semantic and raw nature of multimedia content and tackles one of the most interesting problems in multimedia content analysis, i.e. detection of high-level concepts within multimedia documents, based on the semantics of each object, in terms of its visual context information. It proves that the use of mid-level information improves the results of traditional knowledge-assisted image analysis, based on both *visual* and *contextual* information. In the process, initial image analysis results are enhanced by the utilization of domain-independent, semantic knowledge in terms of region types and relations between them. In principle, mid-level information takes the form of an in-between description, which can be described semantically, but does not express high-level concepts and thus is included in a corresponding mid-level concept ontology.

The structure of this paper is as follows: In Section 2, we present the utilized fuzzy context knowledge representation, including some basic notation used throughout the paper. Section 3 is dedicated to the mid-level instantiation of an image's region types, whereas subsection 3.2 describes a pre-processing contextualization step. Section 4 lists some preliminary experimental results and Section 5 briefly concludes our work.

2 Knowledge Representation

As can be found in the literature, the term *context* [9] may be interpreted and even defined in numerous ways, varying from the philosophical to the practical point of view [8]. However, since there is not a globally applicable aspect of context in the multimedia analysis chain, it is very important to establish a working representation for context, in order to benefit from and contribute to the proposed mid-level multimedia analysis. The problems to be addressed include how to represent and determine context, and how to use it to optimize the results of analysis. The latter are highly dependent on the domain an image belongs to and thus in many cases are not sufficient for the understanding of multimedia content. In general, the lack of contextual information significantly hinders optimal analysis performance [12] and along with similarities in low-level features of various object types, results in a significant number of misinterpretations.

In this work we introduce a method for improving the results of low-level based multimedia analysis by using the notion of mid-level region types. The latter build an ontology, described by the set of region types and the relations between them. In general, we may decompose such an ontology O into two parts, the set T of all region types and the set R_{t_i,t_j} of all relations amongst any two given region types t_i, t_j. More formally:

$$O = \{T, R_{t_i,t_j}\}, \quad R_{t_i,t_j} : T \times T \rightarrow \{0,1\}, \quad i,j = 1\ldots n \qquad (1)$$

Any kind of relation may be represented by an ontology, however, herein we restrict it to a "fuzzified" ad-hoc context ontology. The latter is introduced in order to express in an optimal way the real-world relationships that exist between the concepts of a scene. In order for this ontology type to be highly descriptive, it must contain a representative number of distinct and even diverse relations among region types, so as to exploit in an optimal manner the contextual information surrounding each one. Additionally, since modelling of real-life information is in most cases governed by uncertainty, it is our belief that these relations must incorporate fuzziness in their definition. Thus, we utilize a set of relations (Table 1), derived from the set of MPEG-7 relations suitable for image analysis [2] and re-define them in a way to incorporate fuzziness, i.e. a degree of confidence is associated to each relation, and assist in discriminating between objects exhibiting similar visual characteristics.

Table 1. Contextual relations between region types.

Name	Inverse	Symbol	Meaning
Similar	Similar	$Sim(a,b)$	region type similarity based on the i-th descriptor
Accompanier	AccompanierOf	$Acc(a,b)$	coexistence of two region types
Part	PartOf	$P(a,b)$	a region type is part of another region type
Component	ComponentOf	$Comp(a,b)$	combines two region types with each other
Combination	-	$Comb(a,b)$	combines more than two region types

As in [7], a fuzzy relation on T is a function $r_{t_i,t_j} : T \times T \rightarrow [0,1]$ and its inverse relation is defined as $r_{t_i,t_j}^{-1} = r_{t_j,t_i}$. Based on the above relations, a domain-specific, "fuzzified" version of a region type ontology may be described by O_F:

$$O_F = \{T, r_{t_i,t_j}\}, \quad i,j = 1\ldots n, \quad i \neq j \tag{2}$$

where T represents again the set of all possible region types,

$$F(R_{t_i,t_j}) = r_{t_i,t_j} : T \times T \rightarrow [0,1] \tag{3}$$

denotes a fuzzy ontological relation amongst two region types t_i, t_j and

$$R_{t_i,t_j} = \{Sim, Acc, P, Comp, Comb, A, B, R, L\} \tag{4}$$

denotes any possible non-fuzzy relation amongst two region types. The final, meaningful combination of relations

$$CR = (\bigcup_i r_{t_i,t_j}^{p_i}), \quad p_i \in \{-1, 0, 1\}, \quad i = 1\ldots n \tag{5}$$

forms an RDF [22] graph and constitutes the abstract contextual knowledge model to be used during the analysis phase (Fig. 2). The value of p_i is determined by the semantics of each relation R_{t_i,t_j} used in the construction of CR. More specifically:

- $p_i = 1$, if the semantics of R_{t_i,t_j} imply it should be considered as is

- $p_i = -1$, if the semantics of R_{t_i,t_j} imply its inverse should be considered
- $p_i = 0$, if the semantics of R_{t_i,t_j} do not allow its participation in the construction of the combined relation CR.

The graph of the proposed model contains nodes (i.e. region types) and edges (i.e. contextual fuzzy relations between region types). The degree of confidence of each edge represents fuzziness in the model. Non-existing edges imply non-existing relations (i.e. relations with zero confidence values are omitted). As each region type has a different probability to appear in the scene, a flat context model would not have been sufficient in this case.

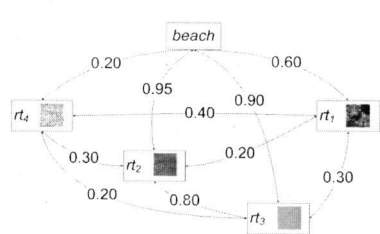

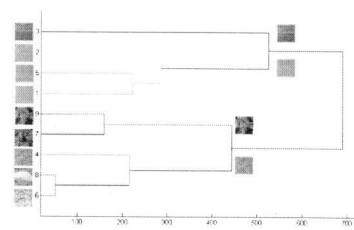

(a) A fragment of the *beach* region type ontology.

(b) Region type selection using hierarchical clustering.

```
<rdf:Description rdf:about="#Relation1">
    <rdf:subject rdf:resource="&dom;rt1"/>
    <rdf:predicate rdf:resource="&dom;Part"/>
    <rdf:object>rdf:resource="&dom;rt2"</rdf:object>
    <rdf:type rdf:resource="http://www.w3.org/1999/02/22-rdf-syntax-ns#Statement"/>
    <context:Part rdf:datatype="http://www.w3.org/2001/XMLSchema#float">0.85</context:Part>
</rdf:Description>
```

(c) RDF ontology fragment.

Fig. 1. From region thesaurus to mid-level ontology.

Describing the accompanying degree of confidence is carried out using RDF reification [23]. Reification is used in knowledge representation to represent facts that must then be manipulated in some way; for instance, to compare logical assertions from different witnesses to determine their credibility. The message "Ben is the leader of the group" is an assertion of truth that commits the sender to the fact, whereas the reified statement, "Juliet reports that Ben is the leader of the group" defers this commitment to Juliet. In this way, statements may include fuzzy information (i.e. "Ben is the leader of the group with a degree of confidence equal to 0.85"), without creating contradictions in reasoning, since a statement is being made about the original statement, which contains the degree information. Of course, the reified statement should not be asserted automatically, a fact that proves the use of the above technique to be acceptable. For instance, having an RDF triple such as: "*blue partOf green*" and a degree of confidence of "*0.85*" for this statement, does obviously not entail, that a *blue* region type will always be part of a *green* region type in the scene.

3 Semantic Multimedia Analysis

3.1 Region Type Analysis

The first step towards the construction of the mid-level ontology is the selection of the region types it will include. Thus, an arbitrary large number of candidate region types is initially needed. To gather it a color segmentation algorithm is first applied on all images of the available training set, as a pre-processing step. The algorithm is a multiresolution implementation of the well-known RSST method [1], tuned to produce a coarse segmentation. We choose to tune the segmentation algorithm this way, since we want the produced segmentation to intuitively provide a qualitative description of the image. Then the segmentation results are used to define the candidate region types from each image.

These regions are then represented by a combination of their low-level visual features. Thereby, visual descriptors from the ISO/IEC MPEG-7 standard [5] are selected to capture a standardized description of their visual content. For representing the color features of the image regions, three MPEG-7 color descriptors are used: The *Color Layout Descriptor*, the *Scalable Color Descriptor* and the *Color Structure Descriptor* and for representing the texture features, the *Homogeneous Texture Descriptor* is selected. For the extraction of the aforementioned descriptors, the MPEG-7 eXperimentation Model (XM)[11] is used.

Given the entire set of regions, derived from the aforementioned segmentation process and their extracted low-level features, one can easily observe that those that belong to similar semantic concepts, also have similar low-level descriptions and also those images that contain the same high-level concepts are consisted of similar regions. As a natural sequence of this observation we apply a *hierarchical clustering* [6] algorithm on the regions of the given training set. We should note that each cluster may or may not represent a high-level feature and each high-level feature may be represented by one or more clusters; i.e. the concept *sand* can have many instances differing e.g. in the color of the sand. Moreover, in a cluster that may contain instances from a semantic entity (e.g. *sea*), these instances could be mixed up with parts from another visually similar concept (e.g. *sky*). A dendrogram describing the hierarchical clustering and the selection of the region types is depicted in figure 2(b). In this simplistic example an initial set of 9 candidate region types derived from 4 images is clustered and we choose to keep 4 region types to represent their visual content in terms of mid-level concepts.

Then we form a region *thesaurus*, in order to combine and manipulate effectively a list of every region type in a given domain of knowledge (e.g. *beach*) and a set of related regions (synonyms) for each region type. These region types can be characterized as "mid-level" concepts, incorporating both low- and high-level information. Then, we use the thesaurus to facilitate the association of the low-level features of the image with the corresponding high-level concepts in the following way: A *model vector* is formed for each image. Its dimensionality is equal to the number of concepts constituting the thesaurus. The distance of a region to a region type is calculated as a linear combination of the average descriptor distances, as in [18]. Having calculated the distance of each region of the image to all the region types of the constructed thesaurus, the model vector D_m that semantically describes the visual content of the image is formed by keeping the bigger confidence value for each mid-level concept and is depicted in equation 6.

$$D_m = [min\{d_i^1\}, min\{d_i^2\}, ..., min\{d_i^{N_C}\}], i = 1, 2, ..., numOfRegions \quad (6)$$

Where d_i^j is the confidence value that the i-th region of the image corresponds to the j-th region type, $numOfRegions$ is the number of the segmented image regions and N_C the size of the region thesaurus.

3.2 Visual Context Optimization

Once a model vector for an image is calculated, a modified version of the context-based confidence value readjustment algorithm [12] is applied, so as to satisfy the needs of the problem at hand. The latter forms the last pre-processing step of the analysis process and provides an optimized re-estimation of the initial regions' degrees of confidence to the selected region types. Consequently, it updates the values of each model vector, allowing an optimized training process of the classifier, thus achieving significantly optimized evaluation results.

In a more formal manner, the problem that this work attempts to address is summarized in the following statement: the visual context analysis algorithm readjusts in a meaningful way the initial region type confidence values produced by the previous step of region type analysis. In this section, the remaining problems to be addressed include how to meaningfully readjust the initial membership degrees and how to use visual context to influence the overall results of knowledge-assisted image analysis towards higher performance.

An estimation of the degree of membership of each mid-level region type is derived from direct and indirect relationships of the latter with other region types in the graph, using a meaningful compatibility indicator or distance metric. Depending on the nature of the domains provided in the domain ontology, the best indicator could be selected using the max or the min operator, respectively. Of course the ideal distance metric for two region types is again one that quantifies their semantic correlation. For the problem at hand, the max value is a meaningful measure of correlation for both of them.

The general structure of the modified degree of membership re-evaluation algorithm is now as follows:

1. the considered domain imposes the use of a domain similarity (or dissimilarity) measure: $dnp \in [0, 1]$.
2. for each region type t we may describe the fuzzy set L_t using the widely applied [10] sum notation $L_t = \sum_{i=1}^{|T|} t_i/w_i = \{t_1/w_1, t_2/w_2, \ldots, t_n/w_n\}$, where w_i describes the membership function: $w_i = \mu_{L_t}(t_i)$.

3. for each region type t_i in the fuzzy set L_t with a degree of membership w_i, obtain the particular contextual information in the form of its relations to the set of any other region types: $\{r_{t_i,t_j} : t_i, t_j \in T, \quad i \neq j\}$.

4. Calculate the new degree of membership w_i, taking into account each domain's similarity measure. In the case of multiple mid-level region type relations, relating region type t_i to more than the *root* concept, an intermediate aggregation step should be applied for the estimation of w_i by considering the *context relevance* notion cr_{t_i}, introduced in [12].

We express the calculation of w_i with the recursive formula:

$$w_i^n = w_i^{n-1} - dnp(w_i^{n-1} - cr_{t_i}) \tag{7}$$

where n denotes the iteration used. Equivalently, for an arbitrary iteration n:

$$w_i^n = (1 - dnp)^n \cdot w_i^0 + (1 - (1 - dnp)^n) \cdot cr_{t_i} \tag{8}$$

where w_i^0 represents the initial degree of membership for region type t_i. Typical values for n reside between 3 and 5.

4 Experimental Results

In this section we provide some early experimental results facilitating the proposed approach. We carried out experiments utilizing 287 images and 25 region types derived from the *beach* domain, acquired from personal collections and the Internet. A ground truth was manually constructed, consisting of a number of region types associated to a unique concept. We utilized 57 images (merely 20% of the dataset) as our clustering training set and after an extensive try-and-error process selected $dnp = 0.12$ as the optimal normalization parameter for the given domain. For the sake of space we present an indicative *beach* image use case example (Fig. 2): (a) the original input image and (b) the segmentation output of the image, where we consider a simpler region thesaurus, consisting of only 4 region types. The original model vector deriving from the comparison of the image regions to the region types of the region thesaurus is:

$$\mathbf{MV}_{before} = \begin{bmatrix} 0.723 \ 0.220 \ 0.753 \ 0.364 \end{bmatrix} \tag{9}$$

Since we can observe that the given image consists of *sky* and *sea*, we should expect that region types that correspond to these semantic concepts should have larger values. The case here is that sea has a quite different color than the region type of the thesaurus that has occurred from a *sea* region. This color appears even similar to *rock* regions. We would like to increase this confidence to the region type and also decrease the confidence that corresponds to a *rock* region (2nd and 4th constituent of the model vector). After we apply the algorithm described in section 3.2, the model vector becomes:

$$\mathbf{MV}_{before} = \begin{bmatrix} 0.778 \ 0.452 \ 0.800 \ 0.338 \end{bmatrix} \tag{10}$$

(a) Input image   (b) Segmentation

Fig. 2. Indicative *beach* image example.

In order to provide a first measure of overall evaluation for the proposed technique, we further present precision scores from its application to the entire dataset on a per high-level concept basis (i.e., after the final classification step is applied on the optimized model vector). Evaluation results for 6 high-level *beach* concepts are presented in Table 2. Each concept's row displays the precision value before and after the use of context.

Table 2. Overall precision scores per high-level *beach* concept

Concepts	before	after	%
sea	0.72	0.77	6.85%
water	0.36	0.38	5.56%
sky	0.85	0.97	11.69%
sand	0.70	0.74	6.06%
rock	0.68	0.73	6.15%
vegetation	0.43	0.48	10.87%
Overall	**0,62**	**0,68**	7.86%

5 Conclusions

Our current research efforts indicate clearly that high-level concepts can be efficiently detected when an image is represented by a model vector with the aid of a visual thesaurus and context. Amongst the core contribution of this work has been the implementation of a novel, mid-level visual context interpretation utilizing a fuzzy, ontology-based representation of knowledge. Early research results were presented, indicating a significant high-level concept detection optimization (i.e. 5.56%-11.69% per concept - 7.86% overall) over the entire dataset utilized. Although the improvement is not impressive, we believe that minor enhancements on the implemented model should boost further its performance.

References

1. Avrithis, Y., Doulamis, A., Doulamis, N., Kollias, S.: A stochastic framework for optimal key frame extraction from mpeg video databases. (1999)
2. Benitez, A. B., Zhong, D., Chang, S.-F., Smith, J. R., *MPEG-7 MDS Content Description Tools and Applications*, Lecture Notes in Computer Science, 2001.
3. Benitez, A. B., and Chang, S.-F., *Image Classification Using Multimedia Knowledge Networks*, Proceedings of the IEEE Int. Conf. on Image Processing (ICIP'03), Barcelona, Spain, 2003.
4. Cees, D. C. K., Snoek, G.M., Worring, M., and Smeulders, A. W., *Learned lexicon-driven interactive video retrieval*, 2006.
5. Chang, S.F., Sikora, T., Puri, A.: Overview of the mpeg-7 standard. IEEE trans. on Circuits and Systems for Video Technology 11(6) (2001) 688–695
6. Duda, R.O., Hart, P.E., Stork, D.G.: Pattern Classification. 2 edn. Wiley Interscience (2000)
7. Klir, G., and Yuan, B., *Fuzzy Sets and Fuzzy Logic, Theory and Applications*, New Jersey, Prentice Hall, 1995.
8. Lewis, D., *Index, Context, and Content*, in Kanger, S. and Ohman, S. (Eds.), Philosophy and Grammar, Reidel Publishing, 1980.
9. McCarthy, J., *Notes on Formalizing Context*, in Proc. of the 13th International Joint Conference on Artificial Intelligence (IJCAI 1993), Chambéry, France, August-September 1993, pp. 81-98.
10. Miyamoto, S., *Fuzzy Sets in Information Retrieval and Cluster Analysis*, Kluwer Academic Publishers, Dordrecht / Boston / London, 1990.
11. MPEG-7: Visual experimentation model (xm) version 10.0. ISO/IEC/ JTC1/SC29/WG11, Doc. N4062 (2001)
12. Mylonas, P., Athanasiadis, T., & Avrithis, Y. *Improving image analysis using a contextual approach*, In Proc. of 7th International Workshop on Image Analysis for Multimedia Interactive Services (WIAMIS), Seoul, Korea.
13. Rapantzikos, K., Avrithis, Y., Kollias, S., *On the use of spatiotemporal visual attention for video classification*, Proceedings of International Workshop on Very Low Bitrate Video Coding (VLBV '05), Sardinia, Italy, September 2005.
14. Saux, B., and Amato, G., *Image classifiers for scene analysis*, In Proc. of International Conference on Computer Vision and Graphics, 2004.
15. Skiadopoulos, S., Giannoukos, C., Sarkas, N., Vassiliadis, P., Sellis,T., Koubarakis, M., *2D topological and direction relations in the world of minimum bounding circles*, IEEE trans. on Knowledge and Data Engineering, Vol. 17(12), pp. 16101623, 2005.
16. Smeulders, A. W. M., Worring, M., Santini, S., Gupta, A. and Jain, R., *Content-Based Image Retrieval at the End of the Early Years*, IEEE Transactions on Pattern Analysis and Machine Intelligence, vol. 22, pp. 1349-1380, 2000.
17. Souvannavong, F., Merialdo, B., and Huet, B., *Region-based video content indexing and retrieval*, In Proc. of 4th International Workshop on Content-Based Multimedia Indexing, Riga, Latvia, 2005.
18. Spyrou, E., LeBorgne, H., Mailis, T., Cooke, E., Avrithis, Y., O'Connor, N., *Fusing mpeg-7 visual descriptors for image classification*, In: International Conference on Artificial Neural Networks (ICANN), 2005.
19. Staab, S., and Studer, R., *Handbook on Ontologies*, International Handbooks on Information Systems, Springer-Verlag, Heidelberg, 2004.

20. Tsechpenakis, G., Akrivas, G., Andreou, G., Stamou, G., and Kollias, S., *Knowledge-Assisted Video Analysis and Object Detection*, Proceedings of European Symposium on Intelligent Technologies, Hybrid Systems and their Implementation on Smart Adaptive Systems (Eunite02), Albufeira, Portugal, September 2002.
21. Voisine, N., Dasiopoulou, S., Mezaris, V., Spyrou, E., Athanasiadis, T., Kompatsiaris, I., Avrithis, Y., and Strintzis, M. G., *Knowledge-assisted video analysis using a genetic algorithm*, In Proc. of 6th International Workshop on Image Analysis for Multimedia Interactive Services (WIAMIS 2005), April 13-15, 2005.
22. W3C, RDF, http://www.w3.org/RDF/
23. W3C,   *RDF   Reification*,   http://www.w3.org/TR/rdf-schema/#ch_reificationvocab

Mimicking adaptation processes in the human brain with neural network retraining

Lori Malatesta, Amaryllis Raouzaiou, George Caridakis, Kostas Karpouzis
Image, Video and Multimedia Systems Laboratory, National Technical
University of Athens,
9, Heroon Politechniou str., Zografou 15780, Greece
{lori, araouz, gcari, kkarpou}@image.ece.ntua.gr

Abstract. Human brain processes undergo cycles of adaptation in order to meet the requirements of novel conditions. In affective state recognition, brain processes tend to adapt to new subjects as well as environmental changes. By using adaptive neural network architectures and by collecting and analysing data from specific environments we present an effective approach in mimicking these processes and modelling the way the need for adaptation is detected as well as the actual adaptation. Video sequences of subjects displaying emotions are used as data for our classifier. Facial expressions and body gestures are used as system input and system output quality is monitored in order to identify when retraining is required. This architecture can be used as an automatic analyzer of human affective feedback in human computer interaction applications.

1 Introduction

The ability to detect and understand affective states and other social signals of someone with whom we are communicating is the core of social and emotional intelligence and relies upon finely tuned neural mechanisms in the brain. This kind of intelligence is a facet of human intelligence that has been argued to be indispensable and even the most important for a successful social life 2. Neuropsychological (8) and neuroimaging data (9) with humans have suggested that recognition of some distinct facial expressions engages specific neural circuits. Although various brain regions have therefore been correlated with facial expression recognition, the nature of their contributions remains unresolved. The act of seeing is so effortless that it is difficult to appreciate the sophisticated mechanisms underlying it. However, current computing technology does not account for the fact that human-human communication is always socially situated and that discussions are not just facts but part of a larger social interplay. Not all computers will need social and

Please use the following format when citing this chapter:

Malatesta, L., Raouzaiou, A., Caridakis, G., Karpouzis, K., 2007, in IFIP International Federation for Information Processing, Volume 247, Artificial Intelligence and Innovations 2007: From Theory to Applications, eds. Boukis, C., Pnevmatikakis, L., Polymenakos, L., (Boston: Springer), pp. 399-408.

emotional intelligence and none will need all of the related skills humans have. Yet, human-machine interactive systems capable of sensing stress, inattention, confusion, and heedfulness, and capable of adapting and responding to these affective states of users are likely to be perceived as more natural, efficacious, and trustworthy (see 6).

Regarding personalized expressivity, it is well known (see, for example, recent results, on emotional signs from signals, of the Humaine network of Excellence 4) that in human computer interaction, the emotional characteristics and signs of signals captured from a specific user, although adhering to some general descriptive theories and psychological models, differ, sometimes significantly, between different persons. Thus, emotion recognition is a research problem, the solution of which highly depends on individual human characteristics and way of behaviour. Emotion recognition systems are generally based on a rule base system, or on a system that has learnt to solve the problem through extensive training. In either case, if such a system is to be used in a real life experiment, it further needs to take into account, i.e., to adapt its knowledge to the specific user characteristics as well as behavioural and environmental conditions, i.e., the context of interaction.

In all cases, it is essential that systems are derived which are able to adapt their performance to environmental changes, by detecting deterioration of their performance, and refining it with data obtained by the specific environment and respective cues provided by the user or by cross-correlating different modalities. Neural networks fit well with this requirement, since adaptation is their main advantage when compared with knowledge-based systems, where updating of knowledge is a complex, generally off-line procedure. Both supervised, such as multilayered feed-forward networks, and unsupervised networks, such as SOM or k-NN based approaches can be used for this purpose. In the rest of the paper an adaptive supervised feed-forward network is described and used for human computer interaction enriched with emotion analysis capabilities, showing that it can provide an effective approach to handling of the above described problems. The basic methodology can be extended to unsupervised, clustering techniques.

Section 0 describes the adaptive network architecture, while its use in different contexts is presented in section 0. An experimental study, with emotion datasets showing, not only extreme emotions, but also intermediate real-life ones, generated in the framework of the EC IST Humaine Network of Excellence, is given in section 0, while conclusions and further work are discussed in section 0.

1.1 Neural Architectures for Emotion Recognition

Taylor and Fragopanagos describe a neural network architecture in 7 in which features, from various modalities, that correlate with the user's emotional state are fed to a hidden layer, representing the emotional content of the input message. The output is a label of this state. Attention acts as a feedback modulation onto the feature inputs, so as to amplify or inhibit the various feature inputs, as they are or are not useful for the emotional state detection. The basic architecture is thus based on a feed-forward neural network, but with the addition of a feedback layer (IMC in **Error! Reference source not found.**), modulating the activity in the inputs to the hidden layer.

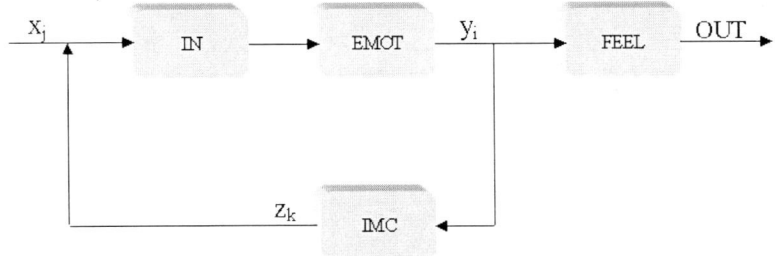

Fig. 1. Information flow in the system. IMC= inverse model controller; EMOT = hidden layer emotional state; FEEL = output state emotion classifier

Results have been presented for the success levels of the trained neural system based on a multimodal database, including time series streams of text (from an emotional dictionary), prosodic features (as determined by a prosodic speech feature extraction) and facial features (facial animation parameters). The obtained results are different for different viewers who helped to annotate the datasets. These results show high success levels on certain viewers, while lower (but still good) levels on other ones. In particular very high success was obtained using only prediction of activation values for one user who seemed to use mainly facial cues, whilst a similar, but slightly lower success level, was obtained on an annotator, who used predominantly prosodic cues. Other two annotators appeared to use cues from all modalities, and for them, the success levels were still good but not so outstanding.

This leads to the need for a further study to follow up the spread of such cue-extraction across the populace, since if this is an important component then it would be important to know how broad is this spread, as well as to develop ways to handle such a spread (such as having a battery of networks, each trained on the appropriate subset of cues). It is, thus evident that adaptation to specific users and contexts is a crucial aspect in this type of fusion. Decision-level fusion caters for integrating asynchronous but temporally correlated modalities. Here, each modality is first classified independently and the final classification is based on fusion of the outputs of the different modalities. Designing optimal strategies for decision level fusion is still an open research issue. Various approaches have been proposed, e.g. sum rule, product rule, using weights, max/min/median rule, majority vote etc. As a general rule, semantic fusion builds on individual recognizers, followed by an integration process; individual recognisers can be trained using unimodal data, which are easier to collect.

In the rest of this paper, we examine the confidence produced by each classifier, such as a feed-forward multilayer neural network, handling a single modality - focusing on facial expressions - and we derive an efficient methodology for adapting the classifier's performance, when detecting such a need, by collecting data from its specific environment. Thus, in the framework presented here, facial expression is considered as the dominant modality; this means that most of the time classification is performed using the facial features as input. In cases where the network trained with the facial data does not perform well (hence, the need to adapt arises), speech prosody or gestures can be utilized as "fall-back" solutions, possibly providing the expected output for the adaptation process.

2 The Adaptive neural network architecture

Let us assume that we seek to classify, to one of, say, p available emotion classes ω, each input vector $\underline{x}_i$ containing the features extracted from the input signal. A neural network produces a p-dimensional output vector $\underline{y}(\underline{x}_i)$

$$\underline{y}(\underline{x}_i) = \left[p_{\omega_1}^i \, p_{\omega_2}^i \cdots p_{\omega_p}^i \right]^T$$

(1)

where $p_{\omega_j}^i$ denotes the probability that the ith input belongs to the jth class.

Let us first consider that the neural network has been initially trained to perform the classification task using a specific training set, say, $S_b = \left\{ \left(\underline{x}'_1, \underline{d}'_1 \right), \cdots, \left(\underline{x}'_{m_b}, \underline{d}'_{m_b} \right) \right\}$, where vectors $\underline{x}'_i$ and $\underline{d}'_i$ with $i = 1, 2, \cdots, m_b$ denote the ith input training vector and the corresponding desired output vector consisting of p elements.

Then, let $\underline{y}(\underline{x}_i)$ denote the network output when applied to a new set of inputs, and let us consider the ith input outside the training set, possibly corresponding to a new user, or to a change of the environmental conditions. Based on the above described discussion, slightly different network weights should probably be estimated in such cases, through a network adaptation procedure.

Let $\underline{w}_b$ include all weights of the network before adaptation, and $\underline{w}_a$ the new weight vector which is obtained after adaptation is performed. To perform the adaptation, a training set S_C has to be extracted from the current operational situation composed of, (one or more), say, m_C inputs; $S_c = \left\{ \left(\underline{x}_1, \underline{d}_1 \right), \cdots, \left(\underline{x}_{m_c}, \underline{d}_{m_c} \right) \right\}$ where $\underline{x}_i$ and $\underline{d}_i$ with $i = 1, 2, \cdots, m_c$ similarly correspond to the i-th input and desired output data used for adaptation. The adaptation algorithm that is activated, whenever such a need is detected, computes the new network weights $\underline{w}_a$, minimizing the following error criteria with respect to weights,

$$E_a = E_{c,a} + \eta E_{f,a}$$

$$E_{c,a} = \frac{1}{2} \sum_{i=1}^{m_c} \left\| \underline{z}_a(\underline{x}_i) - \underline{d}_i \right\|_2$$

$$E_{f,a} = \frac{1}{2} \sum_{i=1}^{m_b} \left\| \underline{z}_a(\underline{x}'_i) - \underline{d}'_i \right\|_2$$

(2)

where $E_{c,a}$ is the error performed over training set S_c ("current" knowledge), $E_{f,a}$ the corresponding error over training set S_b ("former" knowledge); $\underline{z}_a(\underline{x}_i)$ and $\underline{z}_a(\underline{x}'_i)$ are the outputs of the adapted network, corresponding to input vectors $\underline{x}_i$ and $\underline{x}'_i$ respectively, of the network consisting of weights $\underline{w}_a$. Similarly $\underline{z}_b(\underline{x}_i)$ would represent the output of the network, consisting of weights $\underline{w}_b$, when accepting vector $\underline{x}_i$ at its input; when adapting the network for the first time $\underline{z}_b(\underline{x}_i)$ is identical to $\underline{y}(\underline{x}_i)$. Parameter η is a weighting factor accounting for the significance of the current training set compared to the former one and $\|\cdot\|_2$ denotes the L_2-norm.

The goal of the training procedure is to minimize (2) and estimate the new network weights $\underline{w}_a$. The adopted algorithm has been proposed by the authors in 1. Let us first assume that a small perturbation of the network weights (before adaptation) $\underline{w}_b$ is enough to achieve good classification performance. Then,

$$\underline{w}_a = \underline{w}_b + \Delta\underline{w}$$

where $\Delta\underline{w}$ are small increments. This assumption leads to an analytical and tractable solution for estimating $\underline{w}_a$, since it permits linearization of the non-linear activation function of the neuron, using a first order Taylor series expansion.

Equation (2) indicates that the new network weights are estimated taking into account both the current and the previous network knowledge. To stress, however, the importance of current training data in (2), one can replace the first term by the constraint that the actual network outputs are equal to the desired ones, that is

$$z_a(\underline{x}_i) = d_i \quad i = 1,...,m_c, \quad \text{for all data in } S_c \tag{3}$$

Through linearization, solution of (3) with respect to the weight increments is equivalent to a set of linear equations

$$\underline{c} = \mathbf{A} \cdot \Delta\underline{w} \tag{4}$$

where vector $\underline{c}$ and matrix $\mathbf{A}$ are appropriately expressed in terms of the previous network weights. In particular,

$$\underline{c} = \left[d_1 \cdots d_{m_c}\right]^T - \left[z_b(\underline{x}_1) \cdots z_b(\underline{x}_{m_c})\right]^T \tag{5}$$

Moreover, minimization of the second term of (2), which expresses the effect of the new network weights over data set S_b, can be considered as minimization of the absolute difference of the error over data in S_b with respect to the previous and the current network weights. This means that the weight increments are minimally modified, with respect to the following error criterion

$$E_S = \|E_{f,a} - E_{f,b}\|_2 \tag{6}$$

with $E_{f,b}$ defined similarly to $E_{f,a}$, with $\underline{z}_a$ replaced by $\underline{z}_b$ in (2).

It can be shown 5 that (6) takes the form of

$$E_S = \frac{1}{2}(\Delta\underline{w})^T \cdot \mathbf{K}^T \cdot \mathbf{K} \cdot \Delta\underline{w} \tag{7}$$

where the elements of matrix $\mathbf{K}$ are expressed in terms of the previous network weights $\underline{w}_b$ and the training data in S_b. The error function defined by (7) is convex since it is of squared form. Thus, the weight increments can be estimated through solution of (7). The gradient projection method has been used in [6] to estimate the weight increments.

Each time the decision mechanism ascertains that adaptation is required, a new training set S_c is created, which represents the current condition. Then, new network weights are estimated taking into account both the current information (data in S_c) and the former knowledge (data in S_b). Since the set S_c has been optimized only for the current condition, it cannot be considered suitable for following or future states of the environment. This is due to the fact that data obtained from future states of the environment may be in conflict with data obtained from the current one. On the contrary, it is assumed that the training set S_b, which is in general based on extensive experimentation, is able to roughly approximate the desired network performance at any state of the environment. Consequently, in every network adaptation phase, a new training set S_c is created and the previous one is discarded, while new weights are estimated based on the current set S_c and the old one S_b, which remains constant throughout network operation.

3 Detecting the need for adaptation

The purpose of this mechanism is to detect when the output of the neural network classifier is not appropriate and consequently to activate the adaptation algorithm at those time instances when a change of the environment occurs.

Let us first assume that a network adaptation has taken place and let us focus visual inputs. Let $x(k)$ denote the feature vector of the k-th image or image frame, following the time at which adaptation occurred. Index k is therefore reset each time adaptation takes place, with $x(0)$ corresponding to the feature vector of the image where the adaptation of the network was accomplished. At this input, the network performance had deteriorated, i.e., the network output deviated from the desired one. Let us recall that vector c in eq. (5) expresses the difference between the desired and the actual network outputs based on weights w_b and applied to the current data set. As a result, if the norm of vector c increases, network performance deviates from the desired one and adaptation should be applied. On the contrary, if vector c takes small values, then no adaptation is required. In the following we use the difference between the output of the adapted network and of that produced by the initially trained classifier to approximate the value of c. Moreover, we assume that the difference computed when processing input $x(0)$ constitutes a good estimate of the level of improvement that can be achieved by the adaptation procedure. Let us denote by $e(0)$ this difference and let $e(k)$ denote the difference between the corresponding classifiers' outputs, when the two networks are applied to $x(k)$. It is anticipated that the level of improvement expressed by $e(k)$ will be close to that of $e(0)$ as long as the classification results are good. This will occur when input images are similar to the ones used during the adaptation phase. An error $e(k)$, which is quite different from $e(0)$, is generally due to a change of the environment. Thus, the quantity $a(k) = |e(k) - e(0)|$ can be used for detecting the change of the environment or equivalently the time instances where adaptation should occur. Thus, no adaptation is needed if:

$$a(k) < T$$

(8)

where T is a threshold which expresses the max tolerance, beyond which adaptation is required for improving the network performance.

Such an approach detects with high accuracy the adaptation time instances both in cases of abrupt and gradual changes of the operational environment since the comparison is performed between the current error difference $e(k)$ and the one obtained right after adaptation, i.e., $e(0)$. In an abrupt operational change, error $e(k)$ will not be close to $e(0)$; consequently, $a(k)$ exceeds threshold T and adaptation is activated. In case of a gradual change, error $e(k)$ will gradually deviate from $e(0)$ so that the quantity $a(k)$ gradually increases and adaptation is activated at the frame where $a(k) > T$.

Network adaptation can be instantaneously executed each time the system is put in operation by the user. Thus, the quantity $a(0)$ initially exceeds threshold T and adaptation is forced to take place.

4 Experimental Study

Our experiments aimed at investigating the practical stand of the proposed adaptation procedure. The main idea of the experimental study was to explore the performance of the adapted networks over inputs belonging to the same tune, but not used for adaptation, as well as to tunes of the same emotional quadrant as the one used for adaptation purposes.

Out of approximately 35.000 frames, belonging to 477 tunes of the SAL database 3, we selected a merely 500 frames – from all four subjects - for training a feed-forward back-propagation network referred from now as NetProm. The architecture details for NetProm are three layers consisting of 10 and 5 neurons on the first and second hidden layers respectively and 5 neurons of the output layer. The targets were formatted as a 5x1 vector for every frame so as to only one, of the 5 candidate classes, was equal to 1. So for example if the frame used for training belonged to the first quadrant the output vector would be [1 0 0 0 0]. The fifth class of the classification problem corresponds to the neutral emotional state and the other four to the four quadrants of the Whissel's wheel.

The selection of the 500 frames used for training the NetProm network was made following a prominence criterion. More specifically, for every frame, a metric was assigned denoting the distance of the values of the FAPs for that specific frame with reference to the mean values of the FAPs of the other frames belonging to the same class. This metric of FAP variance was the sorting parameter for the frames. Under the constraint that each class should be represented as equally as possible we selected the 500 most prominent frames and used it as input for training the NetProm network.

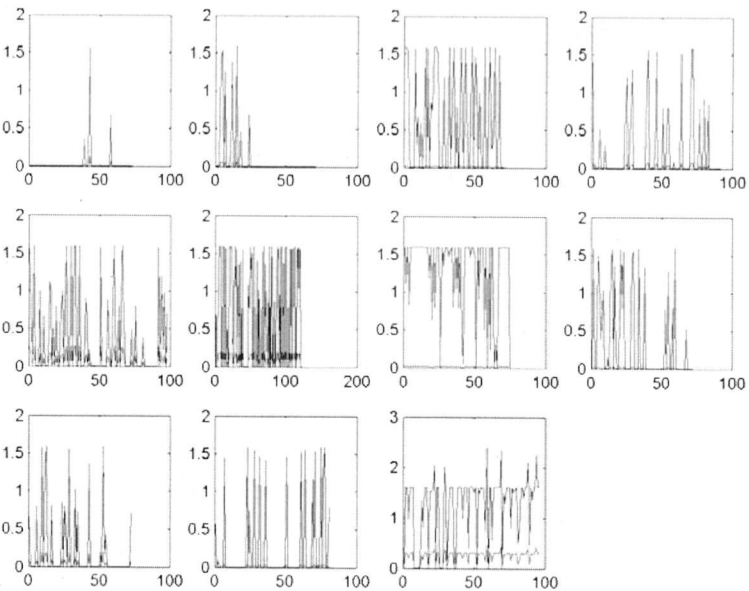

Fig. 2. MSE of NetProm (blue) and Neti (red)

With regard to the adaptation phase we selected eleven tunes - from a single subject - consisting of the largest number of frames. This selection was based on the idea that it would not make much sense selecting very short tunes, because the adaptation data would be very sparse as will be explained later. Also we made sure that no frame belonging to these eleven tunes was used for training NetProm. Each of the eleven tunes was divided into two groups of frames, the adaptation group and the testing group containing 30% and 70% of the total frames of the original tune, sorted by the prominence criterion, respectively.

NetProm was adapted using the adaptation group of the eleven tunes and produced eleven new networks Net_i, $i=1..11$. Each Net_i was then tested on the testing group of the respective tune and the results can be seen in **Error! Reference source not found.**. It is clear that the adaptation procedure has been beneficial and greatly reduced the MSE for every tune it was applied.

Furthermore, we tested the procedure proposed in section 4 for detecting when adaptation is necessary. In particular, we used the above derived Net_i and compared their performance with that of NetProm through criterion (8) in 11 synthetic experiments, shown in Figure 3. In the first 6 experiments and in the 9th, there was no change of the subject showing the expression. It can be verified that the value of $e(k)$, for all values of k shown in the horizontal axis, are close to the $e(0)$ value, so no need for adaptation was detected. On the contrary, the 7th, 8th, 10th and 11th experiments contained one or more frames where a different subject (the first) showed a similar expression. In most of these cases the $a(k)$ value was raised due to the inappropriateness of the adapted (to the fourth subject) network to cope well with the specific characteristics of the first subject. Consequently the need for (new) adaptation was detected through usage of criterion (8).

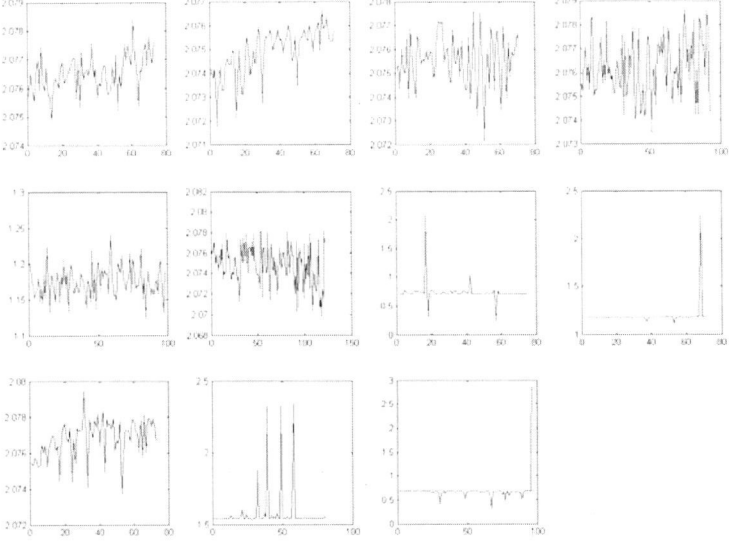

Fig. 3. Detecting the need for network adaptation using the criterion of eq.(8)

These results are very promising indicating that the proposed process can form an effective adaptation tool in expression/emotion recognition.

5   Conclusions – Future work

Recognition of facial expressions is an important part of human-computer interaction, especially since psychological research has shown that the face is a vital ingredient of human expressivity. However, in everyday HCI, emotions are usually subtle, hence difficult to pick out using a small set of universal labels; to tackle this, one needs to consider multiple modalities as a "fall-back" or reinforcement solution. In addition to this, personalized expressivity and context-dependence make generalization of learning techniques a daunting task.

In this paper we proposed an extension of a neural network adaptation procedure which caters for training from different modalities. After training and testing on a particular subject, the best-performing network is adapted using prominent samples from discourse with another subject, so as to adapt and improve its ability to generalize. Results shown here indicate that the performance of the network is improved using this approach, without the need to train a specific network for each subject, which would wipe out the nice generalization attribute of the network. Future work includes the extension of this work to include speech-related modalities, deployment on different naturalistic contexts and introduction of mechanisms to handle uncertainty in the various modalities and decide which of them would be the more robust to depend upon for co-training.

Acknowledgments: This research is partly supported by the European Commission as part of the FEELIX GROWING project (http://www.feelix-growing.org) under contract FP6 IST-045169. The views expressed in this paper are those of the authors, and not necessarily those of the consortium.

References

1. N. Doulamis, A. Doulamis and S. Kollias, On-Line Retrainable Neural Networks: Improving Performance of Neural Networks in Image Analysis Problems, IEEE Transactions on Neural Networks, vol. 11, no.1, pp.1-20, January 2000.
2. D. Goleman, Emotional Intelligence. Bantam Books, New York, NY, USA, 1995.
3. S. Ioannou, A. Raouzaiou, V. Tzouvaras, T. Mailis, K. Karpouzis, S. Kollias, Emotion recognition through facial expression analysis based on a neurofuzzy network, Neural Networks, Elsevier, Volume 18, Issue 4, May 2005, Pages 423-435
4. Humaine Network of Excellence on Emotions, http://emotion-research.net
5. D. Park, M. A. EL-Sharkawi, and R. J. Marks II, An adaptively trained neural network, IEEE Trans. Neural Networks, vol. 2, pp. 334–345, 1991.
6. R. Picard, Affective Computing, The MIT Press, Cambridge, MA, USA, 1997.
7. J. Taylor, N. Fragopanagos, The interaction of attention and emotion, Neural Networks , Volume 18, Issue 4, May 2005, pp. 353 – 369.
8. R. Adolphs, D. Tranel, H. Damasio and A. Damasio, Impaired recognition of emotion in facial expressions following bilateral damage to the human amygdale, Nature, 372, 669-672, 1994.
9. M.L Phillips, A. W. Young, C. Senior, M. Brammer, C. Andrew, A.J. Calder, E.T. Bullmore, D.I. Perrett, D. Rowland, S.C.R. Williams, J.A. Gray & A.S. David, A specific neural substrate for perceiving facial expressions of disgust, Nature 389, 495-498, 1997.